FRONTIERS OF INPUT–OUTPUT ANALYSIS

Frontiers
of Input–Output
Analysis

Edited by

RONALD E. MILLER

KAREN R. POLENSKE

ADAM Z. ROSE

New York   Oxford
OXFORD UNIVERSITY PRESS
1989

Oxford University Press

OXFORD NEW YORK TORONTO
DELHI BOMBAY CALCUTTA MADRAS KARACHI
PETALING JAYA SINGAPORE HONG KONG TOYKO
NAIROBI DAR ES SALAAM CAPE TOWN
MELBOURNE AUCKLAND

AND ASSOCIATED COMPANIES IN
BERLIN IBADAN

Published by Oxford University Press, Inc.,
200 Madison Avenue, New York, New York 10016

Oxford is a registered trademark of Oxford University Press

Library of Congress Cataloging-in-Publication Data
Frontiers of input-output analysis
edited by Ronald E. Miller, Karen R. Polenske, and Adam Z. Rose.
p. cm. Bibliography: p. Includes index.
ISBN 0-19-505758-9
1. Input-output analysis.   I. Miller, Ronald E.
II. Polenske, Karen R.   III. Rose, Adam Zachary.
HB142.F76 1989   339.2'3—dc 19   89–3040 CIP

987654321
Printed in the United States of America
on acid-free paper

Foreword

This volume includes selected papers from three conferences held in 1986 to celebrate two important events in the evolution of economics. The first two conferences commemorated the 50th anniversary of the paper by Wassily Leontief that launched input–output analysis as a new field of economics. The sessions were held at the annual meeting of the American Economic Association, in New Orleans, and the Eighth International Conference on Input–Output Techniques, in Sapporo, Japan. The third set of sessions marked the 35th anniversary of Walter Isard's seminal paper on regional input–output models. They were held at the annual North American Meetings of the Regional Science Association in Columbus, Ohio.

Input–output analysis attracted a number of followers during its embryonic period because it represented a break with conventional microeconomics, and because many found it an attractive alternative to the highly-aggregated macroeconomics that emerged during the early days of the "Keynesian revolution." The theoretical antecedents of input–output analysis are to be found in the early work of Quesnay and, more particularly, in Walrasian general equilibrium theory.

Conventional econometrics, pioneered by Frisch and Klein, was built on macroeconomic theory, which quickly became part of mainstream economics. For a considerable time, after World War II, these two strands of quantitative economics went their separate ways. But the papers in Part I show that more recently there has been a merger of these two methods. One of the more interesting spinoffs from Leontief's basic model has been the appearance of alternative social accounting frameworks. A selection of these is included in Part II.

Recent research has extended the basic input–output model beyond its original focus on production. Some of those extensions are discussed in Part III, while Part IV is concerned with a number of regional, interregional, and international issues.

Problems associated with measurement error, and the paucity of data suitable for input–output models, are as old as input–output analysis itself. Every advance seems to uncover new problems, so there is always room for fresh insights. Several are discussed in this section. The final section, Part V, discusses the use of input–output models in the analysis of technological change.

This is an impressive volume. The editors had to choose 22 papers from about 200 candidates. The papers presented here provide a cross section of the current status of input–output research. They show the most important branches that have sprouted from the seed planted by Wassily Leontief over a half-century ago. They also show that input–output analysis remains as vigorous as ever, and that the strength of the input–output model is its versatility and adaptability. The world has changed greatly since Leontief published the first paper outlining the basic input–output model, but input–output analysis has kept up with this change, and the present volume brings us up-to-date.

The world will continue to change, of course, and the scholars represented in this book, as well as their successors, will continue to adapt input–output models to new circumstances. Some economic theories, and models, are time- or place-specific. They eventually become obsolete, and are relegated to the history of economic thought. The input–output model, however, is not limited to any given era, nor is it tied to any political or economic system. Thus, the future of input–output research, and its use in policy analysis, are without temporal or spatial limits. The present volume will be indispensable to future generations of input–output scholars as they, in turn, further extend, modify, and find new applications for this powerful and versatile tool of analysis.

William H. Miernyk

Preface

The year 1986 marked the 50th anniversary of Professor Wassily Leontief's completion of the first input–output table and of its publication. This and subsequent work, for which Professor Leontief was awarded a Nobel prize, inspired an entirely new field of inquiry that has contributed significantly to economic analysis and policy making. The same year also marked the 35th anniversary of Professor Walter Isard's publication of the first regional input–output framework. Subsequently, the input–output model has become one of the major tools of analysis in regional science.

Most papers in this volume were selected by us from sessions at three conferences held in 1986 to commemorate one or both of these two anniversaries. A session at the annual meeting of the American Economic Association in New Orleans, Louisiana, honored Professor Leontief, and his contributions were also highlighted at the Eighth International Conference on Input–Output Techniques in Sapporo, Japan. Both anniversaries were celebrated by three special sessions at the North American Meetings of the Regional Science Association in Columbus, Ohio. Clearly, 1986 was a year of intensive interaction and exchange among input–output scholars and practitioners from around the world.

Our intention is to make available the valuable work inspired by these important input–output anniversaries and to establish a lasting tribute to the pioneers in this field. Many of these papers represent work at the frontiers; others show the broad range of theoretical and empirical input–output research being conducted today. Several of the papers also identify modeling and data collection needs, thus providing a rich research agenda for those interested in the input–output model and its applications.

The variety of subjects covered by the papers in this volume illustrates the extraordinary versatility of the input–output framework, the extensions and refinements currently under development, and the kinds of important questions that are analyzed using input–output data. At the same time, a single volume cannot contain the entire breadth of past and potential applications.

The papers in this book could not have been written without the efforts of the pioneers in the field of input–output analysis and the many throughout the world who have carried on and expanded the input–output tradition. These researchers are too many to name here, and we can only acknowledge their efforts through the hundreds of references in this volume.

We are thankful to the many people involved in the organization of the conferences and special sessions at which these papers were presented, and to the several formal discussants and audience participants who provided valuable feedback on an earlier stage of the research. Also, we wish to thank the following people who assisted the editors by typing or providing clerical support for the manuscript: Angela Durham, Todie Fleming, Yuhung Hong, Mary Lou Myer, and Nancy Warner.

Finally, we acknowledge the help of the professionals at Oxford University Press, who helped transform this research to a form that would enable it to be accessible to a broad readership. We single out Herbert Addison, Executive Editor at Oxford, for his help and encouragement.

June, 1988   R. E. M.
                                                                                                K. R. P.
                                                                                                A. Z. R.

Contents

Contributors

YUTAKA AKIYAMA
Department of Economics
Keio University
Tokyo, Japan

CLOPPER ALMON
Department of Economics
University of Maryland
College Park, Maryland, U.S.A.

PETER W. J. BATEY
Department of Civic Design
University of Liverpool
Liverpool, U.K.

PAUL M. BEAUMONT
Department of Economics
Florida State University
Tallahassee, Florida, U.S.A.

WILLIAM B. BEYERS
Department of Geography
University of Washington
Seattle, Washington, U.S.A.

PETER D. BLAIR
Office of Technology Assessment
U.S. Congress
Washington, D.C., U.S.A.

RANKO BON
Department of Architecture
Massachusetts Institute of Technology
Cambridge, Massachusetts, U.S.A.

SOLOMON I. COHEN
Economics Faculty
Erasmus University
Rotterdam, The Netherlands

FAYE DUCHIN
Institute for Economic Analysis
New York University
New York, New York, U.S.A.

GEOFFREY J. D. HEWINGS
Department of Geography
University of Illinois
Urbana, Illinois, U.S.A.

DAVID R. HOWELL
Department of Economics
New York University
New York, New York, U.S.A.

RANDALL W. JACKSON
Department of Geography
Ohio State University
Columbus, Ohio, U.S.A.

HIDEO KANEMITSU
Department of Economics
Sophia University
Tokyo, Japan

LAWRENCE R. KLEIN
Department of Economics
University of Pennsylvania
Philadelphia, Pennsylvania, U.S.A.

MICHAEL L. LAHR
Regional Science Department
University of Pennsylvania
Philadelphia, Pennsylvania, U.S.A.

PETER NIJKAMP
Department of Economics
Free University
Amsterdam, The Netherlands

HIROSHI OHNISHI
Department of Economics
Sophia University
Tokyo, Japan

WILLIAM PETERSON
Faculty of Economics and Politics
University of Cambridge
Cambridge, U.K.

KAREN R. POLENSKE
Department of Urban Studies and Planning
Massachusetts Institute of Technology
Cambridge, Massachusetts, U.S.A.

NORBERT RAINER
Austrian Central Statistical Bureau
Vienna, Austria

AURA REGGIANI
Department of Mathematics
University of Bergamo
Bergamo, Italy

ADAM ROSE
Department of Mineral Economics
Pennsylvania State University
University Park, Pennsylvania, U.S.A.

JEFFERY I. ROUND
Department of Economics
University of Warwick
Coventry, U.K.

SEUNG-JIN SHIM
Department of Economics
Keio University
Tokyo, Japan

MICHAEL SONIS
Department of Geography
Bar Ilan University
Ramat Gan, Israel

REINER STÄGLIN
German Institute for Economic Research
Berlin, Federal Republic of Germany

BENJAMIN H. STEVENS
Regional Science Research Institute
Peace Dale, Rhode Island, U.S.A.

JANUSZ SZYRMER
Regional Science Department
University of Pennsylvania
Philadelphia, Pennsylvania, U.S.A.

YASUHIKO TORII
Department of Economics
Keio University
Tokyo, Japan

GEORGE I. TREYZ
Department of Economics
University of Massachusetts
Amherst, Massachusetts, U.S.A.

MELVYN J. WEEKS
Regional Science Department
University of Pennsylvania
Philadelphia, Pennsylvania, U.S.A.

GUY R. WEST
Department of Economics
University of Queensland
St. Lucia, Australia

EDWARD H. WOLFF
Department of Economics
New York University
New York, New York, U.S.A.

ANDREW W. WYCKOFF
Office of Technology Assessment
U.S. Congress
Washington, D.C., U.S.A.

Introduction

The first section of the book deals with the relationship between "Input–Output and Econometric Models." The two approaches nicely complement each other in that econometric forecasts are often used to "drive" input–output models, and in other cases the input–output model provides a sectorally disaggregated component in many econometric models. Nobel laureate Lawrence Klein traces some of the history of the input–output/econometric linkage and identifies current issues in this area. This is followed by a paper by Almon that summarizes recent policy applications of one of the most advanced and widely used input–output econometric forecasting models. Capping off the section, the paper by Peterson represents an example of a more recent trend toward econometric estimation of production in multisectoral forecasting models.

The second section of papers, on "Alternative Accounting Frameworks," takes as a point of departure the Social Accounting Matrix (SAM) developed by Nobel laureate Richard Stone, which explicitly includes institutions and their interactions into a generalized accounting framework. Polenske traces the historical development and recent progress of input–output, SAM, and other accounting approaches in developed countries and developing countries alike, including very new ventures into this area by countries such as China. The newer "rectangular" input–output table format, which distinguishes industries and commodities, is now being implemented by an increasing number of countries so as to achieve some consistency with the System of National Accounts and to facilitate cross-country comparisons. Rainer describes the application of this framework to the Austrian experience. Stäglin illustrates how the vastly expanding "information sector" can be incorporated into an input–output model. In the final paper in this section, Cohen presents a comprehensive SAM model framework, and he compares results from ten developing countries: Colombia, Egypt, Kenya, Korea, India, Indonesia, Iran, Pakistan, Sri Lanka, and Surinam.

The next section of the book focuses on the related topics of "Extended Models and Multiplier Decompositions." The extended input–output model refers to a version that disaggregates the final demand and payments components according to socioeconomic variables. These disaggregations enable the calculation of numerous types of multipliers, and the process of matrix decomposition facilitates this calculation and a comparison of the unique contribution of each of the newly included variables to the multiplier values. In the first paper in this section, Round presents decomposition methods that are appropriate to both extended input–output models and social accounting matrices. The paper by Batey and Weeks shows how the

payments and consumption components in input–output models can be disaggregated to account for the presence of unemployed workers, the entrance of immigrants,
and alterations in unemployment benefits necessary to make accurate economic
impact assessments of new projects. Next, Rose and Beaumont present the first set of
empirical "interrelational multipliers" for the U.S. which measure how direct changes
in the income of each income bracket result in total income changes in all other
brackets. Finally, Wolff and Howell show how a further disaggregation of the labor
input component of an input–output model among occupational lines can be used to
provide insight into productivity growth.

   The section "Regional, Interregional and International Issues" deals with
interconnectedness between input–output tables and the economies they represent.
Torii, Shim, and Akiyama use the ASEAN International Input–Output Table to
investigate the effects of tariff reduction alternatives on Gross Domestic Product,
trade flows and trade balances for Japan, Korea, the United States, and the ASEAN
countries. Their approach embeds international input–output relationships within a
linear programming optimization model. Beyers is concerned with the problem of
measuring structural change in interregional input–output systems and, in particular,
with changes in interdependence among regions over time. Nijkamp and Reggiani
develop a framework for relating spatial aspects of input–output models to dynamic,
stochastic, and multi-objective considerations.

   The section on "Measurement Error and Data Scarcity" focuses on the recent
heightened emphasis on evaluating the accuracy of input–output models in a formal
manner. This stems from the realization that input–output data are becoming
increasingly expensive to collect, especially at the regional level, or that such data may
not be easy to collect, as in the case of many developing countries. Jackson and West
provide an overview of the literature in which they interpret the input–output model
as a stochastic system, with particular emphasis on analysis of probabilistic error
structure. Next, Bon examines the kinds of conclusions that can be reached in an
input–output framework that records only qualitative information, with the intention
of exploring ways by which to circumvent problems of data scarcity. Sonis and
Hewings focus their attention on ways to assess the importance of change in input
coefficients on the elements of the Leontief inverse matrix, and, hence, on the results of
input–output analyses that must be carried out without a fully up-to-date set of
technical coefficients. Next, Stevens, Treyz, and Lahr analyze the problem of
estimating a set of regional data—namely, the proportion of regional demand for a
good or service that is met by local production as opposed to imports into the region
(regional purchase coefficients). Finally, Szyrmer examines how the amount of "error"
in an RAS-estimated table is influenced by the total amount of true data, or
"information," that is introduced into the RAS procedure.

   The final section of the book deals with the topic of technological change, which
is one of the most important phenomena of our era, and also represents one of the
major reasons for complex problems with the accuracy of input–output tables.
Duchin summarizes how input–output analysis has been and can be utilized to
evaluate the important trend toward automation in the U.S. economy. Blair and
Wykoff employ the formal method of structural decomposition analysis, which
involves the comparative static adjustment of groups of input–output coefficients or
aspects of final demand, to analyze the changing pattern of the U.S. economy between
1972 and 1984. Finally, Kanemitsu and Ohnishi provide a similar analysis, but with a

relatively greater emphasis on international trade, for the Japanese economy between 1970 and 1980. The juxtaposition of these two papers provides an interesting way of evaluating changes in the relative competitiveness of the economies of the two nations.

In summary, the papers in this volume deal with exciting new areas or with new ideas in established areas—new accounting frameworks, modeling of economic interconnections across space, assessments of structural change and its implications for an economy, new approaches to problems of scarce data and error estimation, extended models used for analysis of income and occupational distribution issues, and interactions between input–output and econometric modeling approaches. Of course, the book has to be limited to contributions from a subset of analysts who presented papers at three anniversary conferences, and not all important topics are represented here. Still, the book draws on a highly qualified and diverse set of experts in the input–output field and includes many topics that are likely to be of great interest to researchers and policy makers for years to come.

I

INPUT–OUTPUT AND ECONOMETRIC MODELS

1

Econometric Aspects of Input–Output Analysis

LAWRENCE R. KLEIN

The literal interpretation of the meaning of "econometrics" would be economic measurement or perhaps measurement in economics. Input–output analysis is clearly a case of economic measurement and therefore solidly in the mainstream of econometrics.

When I first joined the staff of the Cowles Commission, more than 40 years ago, to work on macroeconometric model building, I had just arrived from Cambridge, Massachusetts, and was duly impressed with the importance of input–output analysis for the problem at hand but was put off by my colleagues, one of whom said that it was simply an accounting subject. Input–output analysis is more than an accounting subject, but from my perspective, social accounting systems are integral parts of macroeconometric models, and input–output analysis should have received more sympathetic and welcome treatment at the Cowles Commission in the mid-1940s.

Almost 20 years later, when areas of investigation were being determined for the Social Science Research Council–Brookings Model of the United States, I insisted that a separate, but integral, role be accorded to input–output analysis. It was studied from the viewpoint of explaining part of the production technology of the model, and was used for the treatment of intermediate factor inputs on the supply side of the model. The traditional production functions involving labor and capital, as original factor inputs, then completed the description of the production process. From that period forward, the role of input–output relationships in macroeconometric models became clearer to me and turned out to be very fruitful in a whole succession of econometric models that paid attention to the conditions of supply. A permanent role for input–output analysis in econometric modeling was established.

ECONOMETRICS AND MEASUREMENT

First, let me discuss the pure measurement problem. My own approach to macroeconometric model specification is to lay out initially the underlying social–accounting structure of the system being investigated and to design the model's specifications to explain (or generate) the entries in the accounting system.

Three accounts typically describe a social entity. They are

national income and product accounts (NIPA)

input–output accounts

flow-of-funds accounts

The first set (NIPA) explains the income and expenditure accounts, in the same way that an income (profit and loss) statement explains the accounts of an enterprise. In a social system, however, NIPA entities represent final flows from either the expenditure or income side of the accounts.

The input–output accounts are different from the NIPA system because intermediate flows are, by design, excluded or eliminated from the income and product accounts. This is done to avoid multiple counting. Input–output accounts include both final and intermediate flows. Such counting can, in many processes, be very revealing in showing how the economic system functions. The multiple stages of goods and services can be traced as long as the accounting is correct and large aggregates that count the same transactions more than once are not constructed. Input–output systems are properly constructed with intermediate flows, final demand deliveries, and value-added inputs. Important accounting identities can be constructed to show the precise relationship between input–output and NIPA systems.

The flow-of-funds accounts are essentially first-differences (flows) of wealth statements for the branches of the economy as a whole. Just as income statements and balance sheets provide a complete accounting picture of an establishment, so NIPA and flow-of-fund statements provide a complete accounting picture of a social aggregate. In both cases, subsidiary statements on intermediate operations show the inside working of the entity being studied, that is, what input–output systems do for the national economy.

In macro model building for econometric analysis, input–output systems play an important accounting role that is necessary for displaying many identities and is part of the system of measurement. It is not only the accounting structure that requires appropriate use of input–output analysis, but also the study of price determination and inventory behavior by stage of fabrication. These processes are extremely important in analyzing inflation and business-cycle fluctuations. The natural way to study these phenomena is through input–output analysis.

PRODUCTION FUNCTIONS

Input–output analysis is much more than a pure accounting system. As an accounting system it is needed in system design, but it is also needed to explain the production structure of a macroeconometric model. It is possible to reduce the system and substitute out the appropriate intermediate flows, but the information loss is significant, and the heart of many macro problems is obscured.

It is traditional to write macro production functions as

$$VA = f(L, K, t)$$

where

VA = real value added
L = labor input
K = capital input
t = time, as a surrogate for technical progress.

But *VA* is not produced in an identifiable form; it is an economist's synthetic construct—to avoid multiple counting.

Early analysis of production functions in agriculture displayed seed, feed, fertilizer, irrigation, and insecticide as separate inputs, together with land, labor, and physical capital, the traditional inputs. Output was measured as crop tonnage, fluid production, bales, bushels, or other meaningful gross figures. This is seen in production and is not an economist's construct, as in the case of value added.

Investigating the output of any sector, such as agriculture, reveals the need for using intermediate inputs and gross output as explicit variables. Another case in which intermediate inputs become a key factor in the production process was the period of the oil embargo, in 1973. The energy crisis and changes in terms of trade between energy exporting and importing countries showed the need for energy modeling, either as a stand-alone sector or within the context of a complete system. For the United States energy is not only an intermediate input that gets used up in the production process, but it is simultaneously imported, exported, and consumed out of domestic production. Econometric energy modeling quite naturally followed the lead of input–output analysis, but while it was being worked out and quick responses were needed, it was essential to look at the one place in which energy already played an explicit role in the model of the production process—input–output models.

There are many ways that input–output models could be, and indeed were, used to estimate the consequence of the embargo and changes in the terms of trade, but the method that was finally worked out for the Wharton model has some unique characteristics. There were two production sectors that dealt with oil production: mining, a primary sector in which extractions of crude, together with imports, were part of production, and refining, a secondary sector that generated oil products. Because domestic production was at full capacity utilization and imports were limited by the embargo, imperfect as it was, we could make approximations to ceiling values for the output of the two crucial sectors.

We created inputs for the total model, including informed (by the industry) adjustments to imports, consumer spending on energy, and energy prices. We then solved the Wharton model,[1] with its input–output models, and examined two key equations relating gross outputs of oil extraction and oil refining, X_i and X_j, respectively, to find demands of individual sectors, F_k, thus:

$$X_i = \sum_{k=1}^{n} \alpha_{ik} F_k + \delta_i$$

$$X_j = \sum_{k=1}^{n} \alpha_{jk} F_k + \delta_j$$

We used search methods to find δ_i and δ_j, values such that X_i and X_j hit their ceiling values. With these two extra values δ_i, δ_j we had a system that could be used for simulation analysis and that provided realistic baseline forecasts of the embargoed economy.

Actually, using these forecasts, we were able to spot a recession as a result of the crisis, within 2 weeks of the imposition of the embargo, and I have notes from a meeting at the U.S. Treasury, during which such recessionary forecasts were disputed by people who did not have a model equipped with an input–output system. In this

---

1. The Wharton Model has gone through various generations, but the version used at the time of the oil embargo is described in Preston (1976).

model, technology was estimated to be in place and unchanged; only exogenous inputs were changed. This was, however, only an approximation to deal with urgent questions of the time.

Input–output model building and energy modeling have significant long-run aspects, and further econometric studies were called for to establish a better base, with input–output foundations, for dealing with energy and related issues. This brings up a basic problem involved in input–output analysis. In the fundamental matrix equation of an input–output model

$$(I - A)X_t = F_t$$

where

I = identity matrix
A = interindustry matrix (square) of direct input coefficients
X_t = column vector of gross output
F_t = column vector of final demand,

we cannot legitimately assume that A is a matrix of parametric constants.

In particular, we noted that the energy–Gross National Product (GNP) ratio has steadily declined in the United States since 1973.[2] This was not the result of exogenous technical changes or an ongoing process that was already taking place. This tendency toward medium-term conservation occurred as a result of responses to changes in relative prices, as well as to legal–institutional changes (energy tax credits, 55 mile-per-hour speed limits, exhortations to lower thermostat settings, mandates for fuel-efficient cars, etc.).

In the fundamental equation, the elements of A are

$$\frac{X_{ij}}{X_j} = a_{ij}$$

where

X_{ij} = intermediate input delivered from i to j
X_j = gross output of j.

By assuming the direct input coefficients, a_{ij}, or similar magnitudes to be fixed for long periods of time, many engineers and scientists calculated that the world economy would break down and that major oil producers would control both the physical and financial magnitudes that govern the operation of the economic system. A recession was predicted by the Wharton (U.S.) and LINK (world) systems, using the input–output approximations indicated, but for the longer run we developed an alternative model, which was simply an extension of the input–output system.[3] Our system had the equation

$$\frac{X_{ik}}{X_{jk}} = f_k\left(\frac{P_i}{P_j}\right) e_{ijk}$$

2. In 1973, the U.S. economy consumed 59.2 thousand British Thermal Units (BTUs) per unit of GNP (1972$). This ratio fell steadily and a decade later was 46.0 thousand BTUs per unit of GNP (1972$) (Wharton Econometrics).

3. For a description of the LINK system as it was specified during the 1970s, see Hickman and Klein (1979).

where

P_i = price of good i
P_j = price of good j
e_{ijk} = random error.

The parameters of f were to replace the a_{ij} parameters. In effect, we argued that input–output matrices consist of variable elements and that they can be projected on the basis of relative price movements. This is how changes in relative energy prices were viewed as contributing to substitution of inputs in the production process and giving rise to the improved energy efficiency that later came to be recognized.

There are many approaches to the estimation of f_k. In 1952, I interpreted the input–output coefficients as being generated by an extended Cobb–Douglas technology (Klein, 1952–1953)[4]

$$X_k = A_k \prod_i^n X_{ik}^{\alpha_{ik}} L_k^{\alpha_k} K_k^{\beta_k} e_k$$

This gives rise to the simple result that current value input–output tables produce stable coefficients instead of physical or constant-priced tables. Such systems were estimated on a large scale for both Japan and the United States by Saito (1972).

After 1973, Preston (1976) estimated f_k from a constant elasticity of substitution (CES) technology for intermediate inputs, combined with a familiar Cobb–Douglas technology for original factor inputs, with an implicit value-added specification of part of the production process. Sheinin (1980) has proposed a nested CES technology, and Jorgenson a translog technology (Hudson and Jorgenson, 1974). All these technologies are simply generalizations of Leontief's original specification with constant coefficients, and they all have a common thread; they vary technical coefficients as relative prices vary (see, for example, Hudson and Jorgenson, 1974).

The original specification is econometric but nonstochastic because the coefficients are estimated from one-element samples, as the ratio of two variables, namely

$$\frac{X_{ijt_0}}{X_{jt_0}} = a_{ij}$$

where

t_0 = single observation period for determination of the input–output accounting flows.

We say that there are no degrees of freedom in this estimation because there is one observation for each ratio, and one parameter to be estimated. Stochastic variation plays no role.

In the extended model, estimation with degrees of freedom occurs because X_{ik}/X_{jk} varies over i,j pairs, within sector k, and it may also vary over time if there are multiple observations for X_{ikt}/X_{jkt}, X_{kt}, P_{it}/P_{jt}, L_{kt}, and K_{kt}. These samples pool variation in cross sections over i,j pairs and through time, over t.

Competitive market behavior is generally assumed to prevail. This, in itself, is a significant assumption, but even if it is valid, on average, the noise factor incurred by

---

4. The α_{ik} are parameters of the Cobb–Douglas technology and are not the same as in the linear expressions used above to relate elements of X to those of F.

relying on price signals to adjust input values for both intermediate and original factors may be substantial. For input–output analysis in the market economies of the Organization for Economic Cooperation and Development area, this appears to be a good approach. For socialist and developing countries, the response to relative price signals may be too small or erratic. What can be done?

ADJUSTMENT PROCEDURES

When relative price responses are too small or erratic, the most straightforward and probably the best approach is to use technological information from engineers, scientists, and production supervisors. Changes in production coefficients are not made, in that case, by methods of statistical inference from the usual kinds of samples but are made by direct measurement. In many cases the use of direct measurement from nonsample data may lead to superior econometric results. The only problem is that technological data are not complete and have not been systematically studied within the context of input–output analysis over a medium-range time period.

The model is

$$a_{ijt} = a_{ij} + \delta_{ijt}$$

where δ_{ijt} = technologists' assessment of modification of requirements of i to produce one unit of j in time period t. The δ_{ijt} is a modification of the basic set of a_{ij} and is determined from direct technological information. Of course, mixed systems of information can be used, some from price signals and some from technologists' information. Some such method would be recommended for centrally planned and developing economies in which price signals play a small role or are not observed frequently.

The problem with lack of constancy of the A matrix is that we generally do not have large data samples for alternative observed values, hence the use of technological information instead of a sample, in the conventional sense. In some countries, however, there are frequent readings on the A matrix. In the United States, there are a few such readings.

$$A_{t_1}, A_{t_2}, A_{t_3}, \cdots$$

A linear interpolation, element-by-element, can be made, after adjustment for uniformity of sector definitions and classifications for different time periods. In general, after such an interpolation, there is no guarantee that crucial accounting identities hold; in particular

$$\sum_{j=1}^{n} X_{ijt} + F_{it} = X_{it}$$

$$\sum_{j=1}^{n} X_{jit} + (VA)_{it} = X_{it}$$

may not hold for interpolated periods between direct observation points.

An automatic technique, which amounts to least-squares data adjustment, common in numerical analysis, is to use the RAS method. Linear interpolation plus RAS provides an historical method of analysis with a changing A matrix, but does not show how to make projections.

In a dynamic system, last period's A matrix can be used for preliminary estimates

$$X_t = (I - A_{t-1})F_t$$

where X_t and F_t are jointly estimated in a complete econometric model that uses the input–output module in the production function. Given the preliminary estimates of X_t and F_t [and $(VA)_t$], the RAS method can be applied to the data for period t, providing an estimate of A_t. With this updated estimate of the technology, the solution can be iterated with another RAS adjustment. This is needed because market values for prices, interest rates, wage rates, and other variables are in a feedback relation with the input–output module and as the latter changes from A_{t-1} to A_t, they will change, X_t will change, F_t will change, and $(VA)_t$ will change. Iterations should be repeated until convergence is obtained.

The RAS procedure can be used with or without linear interpolation of data between successive direct measurements of A. Also, RAS techniques can be used in conjunction with direct technological information.

Because time series of X_{it}, F_{it}, and $(VA)_{it}$ are generally available, another econometric approach, using indirect inference rather than direct observation, is to estimate coefficients in

$$X_{it} = \sum_{j=1}^{n} a_{ij} X_{jt} + F_{it} + u_{it}$$

These coefficients are constant and not variable over time; this is a drawback. Also, collinearity and sampling errors probably produce estimates of a_{ij} from the above linear equations that are inefficient and subject to considerable error.

Yet another approach has been to model the sample residuals in

$$X_{it} - \sum_{j=1}^{n} a_{ij} X_{jt} - F_{it} = r_{it}$$

as time-series processes

$$r_{it} = \sum_{k=1}^{m} \rho_k r_{i,t-k} + v_{it}$$

where

r_{it} = historical residuals using a constant matrix
v_{it} = random error.

This approach leaves the input–output matrix intact (or lagging), with adjustments made only to the values of residuals. The residuals can also be modeled as functions of relative prices, in an expenditure system guaranteeing adding-up properties.

THE CAPITAL MATRIX

The flow matrix associated with intermediate deliveries of goods from one sector to another formed the original focus of input–output analysis, but the capital matrix opens up other analytical possibilities. In many respects, the reasoning behind the capital matrix represents a large-scale sectoral generalization of the acceleration principle of investment, which is derived from a stable capital–output ratio. In macroeconometric work, we have generally found the strict acceleration principle to be too restrictive and also inconsistent with a general view of a production function that permits substitution between capital and other inputs.

If investment and, correspondingly, fixed capital stock are determined by movements in capital costs (interest rates, tax rates, prices, depreciation rates, and other variables), then the hypothesis of stable ratios of capital to output is implausible. The stability through time of capital coefficients seems to be questionable whether the coefficient is defined as K_j/X_j or K_{ij}/X_j. Either measure will be strongly influenced by fluctuations in market variables.

When an input—output flow matrix is imbedded in a complete macro-econometric model with production functions that include both intermediate inputs and original factors, together with factor demand equations, then as much scope is given to the role of capital in the economic process as is obtained from a capital matrix, and the linkage to market conditions is also taken into account.

For these reasons, I prefer to work with the input—output flow matrix in econometric model analysis but not with the capital matrix. Types of capital, such as equipment, machinery, tools, and plant, can readily be given separate econometric treatment in the kind of system I prefer; therefore, I believe that there is no significant loss of information from the factor supply side and that there is a gain of information on the factor demand side.

RELATED APPLICATIONS

The influence of the methods and applications of input—output analysis extends far beyond their interpretation and use as the intermediate parts of the production system within large complete models of the economy as a whole. Transition matrices of the way that people move among income classes, with restrictions, lead in the limit to equilibrium distributions that are well known. They take the form

$$N_t = P'N_{t-1}$$

where

N_t = a column vector of numbers of units in each income class
P' = matrix of transition probabilities (unit column sums).

The resemblance to the setup of an input—output table is obvious, but there is no vector corresponding to final demands in this system; in other words, the system is linear and homogeneous of degree one. Not only income but other social distributions, such as processes of occupational choice, education, and social mobility, are studied in this framework.

The shipment of goods from one area to another can also be treated the same way. The world trade matrix with exporting countries listed in rows and importing countries in columns has been studied by drawing analogies with input—output systems. Armington's (1969) analysis of trading systems with consumer expenditures survey (CES) indexes generated the idea of moving the technical coefficients of the trade matrix system

$$E = SM$$

where

E = export column vector
M = import column vector
S = matrix of import share coefficients,

according to movements in relative trade prices. The adaptation of variable input–output matrices in an extended CES production system followed, completely by analogy, the results worked out for the Armington trade system. When viewed in this way, we see that the input–output specification is only one case of general linear systems (with variable coefficients) explaining a modular part of a larger system—the trade module, the production module, the income-distribution module, and so on. It is a very natural specification, lends itself well to enhancement, and displays the interrelatedness of economic systems. It is an important branch of economic measurement and accordingly a branch of econometrics.

CONCLUSION

In a variety of ways, input–output analysis as originally conceived by Leontief plays an important role in quantitative economics and is an integral part of econometrics, whether coupled with methods of statistical inference in the usual way that the subject is used in econometrics, or more directly in the form of nonstochastic measurement. In both ways, I depend heavily on input–output techniques in econometric model building and operation. New developments in the study of technical change appear to be particularly promising when approached within the framework of input–output analysis.

The use of the ideas of input–output analysis in econometrics extends far beyond conventional macro model building. By analogy it affects many branches of econometric work, and I have found it most useful in analyzing the generation of income distributions and in modeling international trade flows.

REFERENCES

Armington, Paul S. 1969. "A Theory of Demand for Products Distinguished by Place of Production." *International Monetary Fund Papers.* Vol. 16 (March), pp. 159–176.

Hickman, Bert G., and Lawrence R. Klein. 1979. "A Decade of Research by Project LINK." *Items.* Vol. 33 (December), pp. 49–56.

Hudson, E. A., and Dale Jorgenson. 1974. "U.S. Energy Policy and Economic Growth." *Bell Journal of Economics and Management.* Vol. 5, pp. 461–514.

Klein, Lawrence R. 1952–1953. "On the Interpretation of Professor Leontief's System." *Review of Economic Studies.* Vol. 20, pp. 131–136.

Preston, Ross S. 1976. "The Wharton Long-Term Model: Input–Output within the Context of a Macro Forecasting Model." In *Econometric Model Performance*, edited by L. R. Klein and E. Burmeister. Philadelphia, PA: University of Pennsylvania Press, pp. 271–287.

Saito, Mitsuo. 1972. "A General Equilibrium Analysis of Prices and Outputs in Japan, 1953–1965." In *The Working of Econometric Models*, edited by M. Morishima et al. Cambridge, England: Cambridge University Press, pp. 147–240.

Sheinen, Yacov. 1980. "The Demand for Factor Inputs under a Three-Level CES Four-Factor Production Function." Ph.D. Dissertation. Philadelphia, PA: Department of Economics, University of Pennsylvania.

2

Industrial Impacts of Macroeconomic Policies in the INFORUM Model

CLOPPER ALMON

What effect will the Gramm–Rudman automatic deficit reduction plan have on the airline industry or the copper industry? What would 6 percent growth in the money supply mean for the lumber industry? How will the U.S. Chemical industry be affected by the recent decline in the dollar? What impact will the sweeping changes contemplated in the U.S. income tax laws have on employment in various industries?

These questions are all examples of concern about the industrial impacts of macroeconomic developments. Most economists would agree that it is appropriate to use input–output analysis in some form and at some stage in answering such questions. There is, however, a difference of opinion about the right stage. One approach is to use an aggregate macroeconomic model to ascertain the macro-economic effects and then to use input–output analysis to indicate the industrial consequences. A second approach is to build an integrated model that puts the input–output information and certain macroeconomic relations into one model, so that the industry effects are incorporated directly into the macro results. Later in this chapter I will use such an integrated model to deal with several examples. First, however, I want to discuss the differences between the two approaches and the pros and cons of the integrated model versus the two-model system. I have used both approaches and can see important advantages and disadvantages of each (Almon, 1986; Nyhus, 1988; see also Polak and Rogers, 1982; Barker, 1986).

COMPARISON OF TWO APPROACHES
TO INDUSTRY EFFECTS
OF MACRO DEVELOPMENTS

To make the comparison clear, each approach must first be described in slightly more detail. The description of the integrated model will be based on Long-term Interindustry Forecasting Tool (LIFT), the 78-industry model built by Interindustry Forecasting at the University of Maryland (INFORUM) that I shall use later in this chapter. In LIFT there are some key macroeconomic equations that work at the aggregate level only. For example, personal saving is determined by a single aggregate equation. Similarly, the short- and long-term interest rates are each determined by a single aggregate equation; average nominal wages are determined by one equation, though there are relative wage equations for each industry. All of the equations for converting national income by factors to personal disposable income work without industry detail; however, they do involve the size distribution of income. On the other hand, whereas the typical aggregate model of the U.S. economy has four investment equations (residences, other construction, equipment, and inventories), LIFT has 31 equations for different types of construction, 54 for equipment investment by industries, and a separate inventory equation for each product carried in inventory. There are equations for labor productivity and employment at the level of the same 54 industries used for investment, and productivity improvement is, in some versions of the model, connected with investment. There are equations for changes in input–output coefficients. For each industry, there are equations for the wages, profits, interest, depreciation, and indirect taxes, and these components of value added are converted to prices of products by input–output calculations. Because LIFT determines all of the magnitudes with which macroeconomics is concerned but with the interindustry relations imbedded in the heart of the model, it seems reasonable to call it an "interindustry macro model."

The two-model approach has usually been used by groups that already had an aggregate model and wanted to make its implications for industries explicit without calling into question its macro results. The transition to the input–output model is made by taking components of final demand from the aggregate model, applying them to constant vectors to distribute them to industries, summing across components of demand to get a final demand vector, multiplying this vector by a constant inverse matrix, and then introducing a correction factor for each industry to account for the errors the method produced over recent history.

The two methods will be compared on three points: ease of implementation, accuracy of predictions, and internal consistency of results.

Ease of Implementation

Here the two-model approach has the undisputed advantage. Often an aggregate model is already available. Even if it is not, the cost of constructing one is trivial in comparison to the work involved in making an integrated model. I do not make that statement as an outsider to the building of aggregate models, having built one with some 200 equations of which about 30 are statistically estimated. INFORUM operates and publishes the forecasts of this model each month. It does about as well at forecasting as do other aggregate models, and has, I believe, better simulation properties than other aggregate models I know well. Although I have worked hard on this model myself, and have had some part-time assistance, the labor involved is a tiny fraction of what has gone into the creation of LIFT.

Why is the building of an integrated model so much more labor intensive than using the two-model approach? The first factor involves the data. With aggregate models, data are readily available. Most of them are national-accounts and the flow-of-funds data. By contrast, the builder of a unified model for the U.S. economy and many (but not all) other countries must contend with the fact that there are no officially published series on industry outputs that are consistent with the national accounts. A precondition for building an integrated model is a long and laborious struggle to develop a consistent time series of at least the margins of the input–output tables, that is, of final demands by industry, industry output, and value added by industry. This struggle can be and usually is omitted by the user of the two-model approach, who does not even pretend that the industry results can be reconciled through the discipline of the input–output table with the macroeconomic totals. The correction factors for the individual industries, necessary to make the results look plausible, eliminate the possibility of a consistency check. (Indeed, a major part of the genius of aggregate model building is dealing with inconsistent data without being troubled by those inconsistencies. In the United States, many models use, in addition to the national accounts—which are their cornerstone—both flow-of-funds data and industrial production indexes. Yet these two bodies of data are widely inconsistent with the national accounts. The modeler may reasonably say, "If the government statisticians can live with those inconsistencies, so can I." But that sentiment cannot be accepted by one who delights in the coherence of an input–output table.)

A second factor making the integrated model more labor intensive is simply the care and attention that go into the estimation of individual equations. It is easy to spend more time developing an investment equation for just the automobile industry—to select a thorny example—than developing the one equipment invest-ment equation needed for an aggregate model. The same is true for each industry and for each element of the model. The richness and idiosyncracies of individual industries, in fact, disappear in the aggregate; the aggregate equation is sometimes too easy to develop, whereas each industry equation may pose problems that are never really solved.

A final time-consuming element in making the integrated model is checking, tuning, and adjusting. The aggregate model runs in about 2 seconds per quarter on a micro computer; LIFT requires an hour or more on a minicomputer that is about four times as fast. If something looks peculiar, there are many more places that may be the source of the trouble. Identifying the problem and correcting it are much more complex tasks.

Accuracy of Forecasts

On this question, there is not much difference in the models. It is always possible for an aggregate model to be exactly right in its forecast, whereas a much more carefully built sectoral model does poorly. On the other hand, our experience indicates that the integrated model does about as well as the aggregate models in forecasting totals 1 year ahead. Usually, there is not, as might be hoped, a substantial gain in aggregate forecasting from doing it at a detailed industry level. There have been, however, important exceptions to that generalization. One concerned the forecasting of labor productivity in the 1970s. By analyzing trends at the industry level and correctly aggregating them to the national total, INFORUM correctly forecast the decline in the growth rate of aggregate productivity in the later part of the 1970s and the early 1980s. The aggregate forecasters did less well, because shifting product composition of GNP masked the slowdown, which was evident in the trends for individual industries.

A related question is the currency of data. Because the two-model approach works with inconsistent data, it is possible to be up-to-the-minute. The principal data lag in the case of the LIFT model is in the series that depend on the Annual Survey of Manufactures, the fundamental data source for manufacturing industries. The always-up-to-date alternative, for industry outputs, is the index of industrial production. Although these series deviate significantly from output measures obtained from the

Annual Survey, it is possible to use them in regression equations to extend the Annual Survey series. These series will, however, almost always be inconsistent with data available from the national accounts; consequently, they cannot be introduced directly into the integrated model. Instead, we rely on the outputs generated by the model, given all of the final demands found in the national accounts. The choice between good data and current data remains a thorny question to which no satisfactory solution exists except, of course, to get the government's statistical staff to work faster.

Internal Consistency of Results

This is, of course, the strength of the integrated model. Let us note some of the consistency built into it that is missing in the two-model approach. Suppose, for example, that we ask about the industry effects of the recent 25 percent fall in the dollar. The LIFT model calculates the direct impact on the exports and imports of each of the 78 products. It calculates the change in the cost of production and, consequently, of the price of each domestic product. These changes in prices then enter the consumption functions, in which they suppress purchases more in some industries than in others. These changes in consumption, exports, and imports then affect industry outputs, which, in turn, affect employment by industry, which affects income by industry, which determines total income, which affects consumption and imports, and so on, in circular interdependence involving industry detail at almost every step. Furthermore, the changes in output by each industry influence investment by the corresponding industry, thus affecting output, employment, and profits in each industry involved directly or indirectly in providing those investment goods. Note that the investment goods needed for expansion of the textile industry are very different from those needed for expansion of the airline industry. Just as in the economy itself, the integrated model builds in all these industry-specific effects in the process of working out the macroeconomic effects. When we look at the macro effects of the decline in the dollar and its industry effects, there is no doubt that those industry effects imply exactly the macro effects shown.

The two-model approach leaves this last question entirely open. Because there is no feedback from the industry model to the aggregate model, there is no particular reason to believe that the macro effects would be implied by the industry effects.

Note that in the integrated model the causation runs from industry detail to macro totals by accounting identity, by the indisputable process of addition. In the two-model system, the causation runs from macro totals to industry detail by questionable assumptions and fallible regression equations.

Although in some particular case a two-model system may happen to produce the right answer, while an integrated model goes astray, this is an extremely unlikely event.

INDUSTRY EFFECTS
OF MACROECONOMIC CHANGES

As a macro model, LIFT has some noteworthy features not common in macro models, one of which is the inclusion of unemployment in the equation for the savings rate. It requires no particular insight to recognize that unemployed people are not likely to save, and statistically unemployment proves to be a reliable variable in explaining savings. This dependence works as an important stabilizer in the LIFT model. A second significant stabilizer is the dependence of profits on unemployment. Low levels of unemployment imply high capacity utilization and consequent high profits. The high profits, through the input—output relations, become high prices. The high profits do little to stimulate spending by either business or persons, whereas the high prices reduce the real purchasing power of income and dampen the boom that produced the low levels of unemployment. By recognizing the action of these two stabilizers, LIFT shows an economy that gravitates toward its potential output. For example, choosing either to follow a balanced budget or run a large deficit has little long-term effect on the level of unemployment, though its initial impact may be substantial.

Let us look at three specific results.

Case 1: Effects of the Gramm—Rudman—Hollings Automatic Deficit Reduction Law

Late in 1985, the U.S. Congress passed an extraordinary law, known as the Gramm—Rudman—Hollings act (GRH), to provide for automatic spending cuts aimed at balancing the budget by 1991. If the budget enacted by Congress fails to meet certain deficit targets, cuts automatically occur to bring the deficit within those targets. Half of the cuts are to be made in the defense part of the budget and half in the nondefense part. Furthermore, some of the largest nondefense programs—particularly the transfer programs—are protected against the cuts.

It is not possible to model the effects of the law exactly, for they depend on the budgets enacted by Congress before the automatic cuts are effected. If the enacted law produces an expected deficit within the GRH limits, then the law, strictly speaking, has no effect. To discuss the effects of the law, it will be assumed that without it, government spending continues as projected in last year's budget and that with it, spending is cut to bring the deficit within the bounds of GRH. Those assumptions imply cutting 1991 defense spending by 32 percent of its base-year value and pruning nondefense purchases of goods and services by 57 percent. (The percentage for nondefense is higher because GRH calls for reductions of equal amounts, not equal percentages, between defense and nondefense; and the nondefense base is smaller.) In the base projection, there is substantial real growth in defense but almost none in nondefense purchases of goods and services. Consequently, the 32 percent "cut" in 1991 defense spending is a cut of only about 12 percent below the 1986 level in real terms. In stark contrast, the 57 percent cut in nondefense purchases of goods and services is about a 50 percent cut below the 1986 level in real terms.

These cuts do meet the GRH targets and yield a balanced budget by 1991. They reduce the deficit by $53 billion between 1986 and 1988 and then by another $125 billion between 1988 and 1991. Although at first it might be supposed that the worst macro economic impacts would occur during these last 3 years when the rate of drop of the deficit is steepest, LIFT, in two projections, shows that the spread between real GNP will widen most rapidly between 1986 and 1988, when it reaches 3.1 percent. By 1991, it is actually down slightly to 2.9 percent. The spread in the unemployment rate is 2.2 percentage points in 1988, and it gradually rises to 2.5 points in 1991. In neither projection does real GNP ever decline from 1 year to the next.

The GRH reductions do not put the economy into a tailspin because the stabilizers in the economy offset them. Imports drop. The rise in the unemployment rate reduces savings. The difference in personal consumption expenditures is actually greater in 1988 (1.0 percent) than in 1991 (0.8 percent). The decline in the deficit makes interest rates lower in the GRH run; the lower rates stimulate residential construction, which is actually 3.6 percent higher in 1991 under GRH than in the base. Nonresidential investment, which is 5.0 percent below the base in 1988, is only 1.2 percent below by 1991. The increased unemployment results in slightly lower prices under GRH.

What do the industry effects look like? Given the fact that nondefense spending has been cut much more sharply than defense spending, it might be supposed that the defense industries would not be severely jolted. However, the reverse is the case. In comparison to the base, the GRH projection was, by 1991, 28 percent lower for Aerospace, 19 percent lower for Ships and Boats, 13 percent lower for Communications Equipment, 8 percent lower for Copper, and 6 percent lower for Engines and Turbines, which are all defense dependent. Air Transport is down 5 percent and Railroads 3 percent. By contrast, the deviation in Service Industry Machinery, Restaurants, Food, Household Appliances, and Motor Vehicles is each about 1 percent. Output of Shoes and Leather Products is actually larger under GRH. Why were the adverse effects so concentrated on defense industries? Simply because those industries did not benefit from any of the compensating effects in the economy. The laid-off government workers who found jobs in the private sector did not use their pay checks to buy airplanes, rockets, ships, or radar systems. Thus, although GRH would cut defense spending proportionally much less than nondefense spending, the defense industries are hit hardest by the changes. As previously emphasized, we know that the aggregate effects are consistent with these industry effects because aggregate investment, income, and employment are simply the sum of investment, income, and employment by industry.

Case 2: Industrial Effects of the Fall of the Dollar

The long-expected fall of the dollar finally began at the end of 1985. By early May 1986, it had declined approximately 25 percent relative to other currencies. What will be the macroeconomic and industrial effects of this drop? Is this 25 percent fall sufficient, excessive, or inadequate? The LIFT model is well-suited to answer these questions. One of the exogenous inputs into the model is the exchange rate relative to each of six other major currencies. Through international trade the model is linked to similar models of Japan, Canada, Belgium, France, Italy, and West Germany. U.S. exports of each product in LIFT to these countries depend upon domestic demand in these countries for that product and on relative prices. The same is true for exports for each of the other countries. The entire system has been run under two alternative assumptions about exchange rates: (1) those prevailing just before the decline in the dollar began—the High$ scenario, and (2) those of early May 1986—the Low$ scenario. Thus, the effects described arise from individual product equations for the U.S. model and also take into account both the industrial and the macroeconomic impacts of the change in other countries.

Some of the industrial impacts are shown graphically in Figure 2-1. For each of the nine industries shown, the left bar gives the difference between 1987 industry

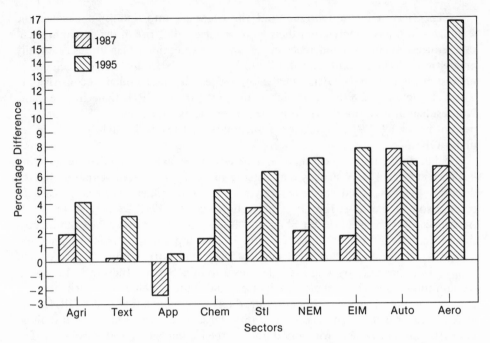

FIGURE 2-1   Effects of 25 percent fall of dollar. Low$ output relative to High$ output.

output under Low$ and under High$, expressed as a percentage of the High$ output. The right bar gives the same comparison for 1995. Some of the results are immediately comprehensible. In the Aerospace industry (Aero), output is higher under Low$ by 6.6 percent in 1987 and by 16.7 percent in 1995, when the price differential has had time to make itself fully felt on exports and imports. Similar, though smaller, effects are seen in Agriculture (Agri), Textiles (Text), Chemicals (Chem), Steel (Stl), Nonelectrical Machinery (NEM), and Electrical Machinery (EIM). It may seem surprising that Apparel (App) output is lower in 1987 under the Low$ than under the High$ scenario. That effect comes about through the macroeconomic part of LIFT. Because prices of imports are higher under the Low$ assumption, real personal income is lower under this assumption, and consumer expenditures on Apparel are lower than under the High$ assumption. The distributed lag on apparel imports and exports shows a delay in the effects of the price changes on exports and imports, so that in 1987 the strongest effect on output is the income effect, which is negative. It is also noteworthy that for Automobiles (Auto), a greater percentage change is obtained for 1987 than for 1995. Closer examination of this sector shows that the initial impacts of prices on imports are larger than the long-run impact.

Is the 25 percent decline in the dollar sufficient to eliminate the deficit in the U.S. balance of payments on goods and services? According to these LIFT calculations, it is not. In fact, even by 1995, it will have reduced the deficit by only about a little more than one-third relative to the High$ scenario. Because LIFT is not at its best in handling the nonmerchandise parts of trade, it should be mentioned that approximately the same result holds for just the merchandise trade. Thus, it appears that a substantial further decline in the dollar will be necessary to return the United States to the approximate balance in goods and services it had for several decades prior to 1983.

Before leaving this example, it is worth stressing the interaction between industry-level equations and aggregate equations. The initial impact of the change in exchange rates comes at the industry level, in the equations for prices of products (which consider the cost of imported materials) and in the equations for exports and imports. The changes in exports and imports change outputs by industry, and these changes alter employment, wages, and profits by industry. So far, all of the action has come from industry-level equations. Income by industry is summed, and adjustments are made to get aggregate personal income and its size distribution. This aggregate income is then deflated by a price index, based on the individual product prices, and the deflated income then enters the aggregate savings function. Total consumption expenditure is then allocated to products, using consumption functions that have relative prices of products as well as income and its size distribution. New outputs, new exports, new imports, new levels of investment, employment, income, and prices must be calculated, and all of the calculations repeated until convergence is reached. Essentially all of the calculations are made at the industry level except (1) the calculation of personal taxes and transfers and (2) the division of personal income among savings, interest payments, and the various categories of personal consumption expenditure. Consequently, there can be no doubt that the aggregate results are implied by the industry results.

Case 3: Industrial Effects of Money Supply Growth

Rapid creation of money is sometimes thought to be an "industrially neutral" way to stimulate the economy. However, the LIFT model shows that, under fixed exchange rates, although it may help some industries and hurt others, it has almost no stimulative effect on the overall economy. The main exogenous monetary policy variable in LIFT is M2, a broad definition of the money supply. We ran LIFT to 1995 once with 7 percent per year growth in M2 (scenario 7M2) and once with 9 percent per year (scenario 9M2). The same exchange rates were assumed for both runs. Because domestic prices will rise faster with the high rate of growth of money, this exchange rate assumption will make fast money supply growth suppress exports and stimulate imports. In 7M2, inflation between 1986 and 1995 averaged 4.6 percent per year; in 9M2, it was 5.7. In spite of the higher inflation rate, interest rates were lower under 9M2. In 1995, 9M2 shows a commercial paper rate of only 6.0 percent versus 8.8 percent under 7M2. The faster rate of growth of the money supply is slowly turning into inflation, and the inflation will eventually affect interest rates. Availability of money, however, also directly affects interest rates; even after 10 years, the easier money policy still has the lower rates. These lower interest rates stimulate residential construction, which is 7.4 percent higher in 1995 under 9M2 than under 7M2, and producer durable equipment investment, which is 5 percent higher under 9M2. These stimulative effects, however, were more than offset by the drop in exports and the rise in imports. The unemployment rate is 0.10 percent higher in 1995 under 9M2, and real GNP is 0.10 percent lower. Thus, the faster monetary growth has not stimulated the economy in the aggregate. Figure 2-2, however, shows that the industrial effects of the policy difference are anything but neutral. Construction (Cns) is up 0.9 percent under 9M2, because of low interest rates under this assumption. Likewise, Nonelectrical Machinery (NEM) is up 0.8 percent. Sectors strongly affected by foreign trade,

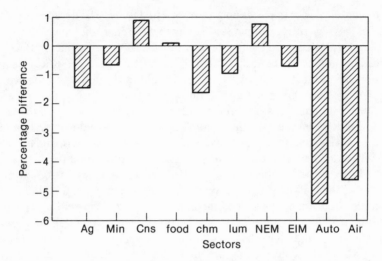

FIGURE 2-2   Easy money and 1995 outputs. Percentage difference: 9 percent M2 relative to 7 percent M2.

however, were adversely affected by 9M2. In 1995, under 9M2, Agriculture was 1.4 percent lower, Aerospace (Air) was 4.6 percent lower, and Automobiles were 5.4 percent lower. Even Lumber, in spite of its use in residential construction, was down 0.9 percent.

We could have made these calculations by changing exchange rates to eliminate any difference in the balance of payments on goods and services between the two runs. History, however, lends little support to the notion of automatic, instant, and inevitable compensation of domestic price movements by exchange rate changes. Our scenario shows what pressures develop in the absence of exchange rate adjustment. Even if we did adjust rates, it is unlikely that a single exchange rate change could even out industry effects as diverse as those found.

CONCLUSION

Some analysts still believe that "input–output" models and "econometric" models are two different and separate species. There is no demarcation line in the model we have been using. Input–output tables and regression equations interact at all points. The view that there is a dichotomy hopefully will fade from its failure to fit the developments on the frontiers of model building.

I hope that these examples illustrate that all the usual macroeconomic information can be obtained from a model that builds in industry detail from the ground up. The industry details can be given with complete confidence that they will not contradict the macro results, because the macro results are based on them. Although it is more work to build an integrated model than a two-model system, the integrated model rewards the user with the knowledge that, just as in the real economy, aggregate totals are the passive sum of what happens at the industry level, which is where the action is.

REFERENCES

Almon, Clopper, 1986. "Principles and Practice of the Inforum Approach to Input–Output Modeling." *Vierteljahrshefte* of the Deutsches Institut fuer Wirtlchaftsforschung, Heft 3, pp. 156–166.

Barker, Terry. 1986. "Analysing Economic Policy with a Large-Scale Multisectoral Dynamic Model: The Cambridge Model of the UK Economy." *Vierteljahrshefte* of the Deutsches Institut fuer Wirtshaftsforschung, Heft 3, pp. 156–166.

Nyhus, Douglas. 1988. "The INFORUM-ERI International System of Macroeconomic Input-Output Models." In *Input-Output Models: Current Developments*, edited by M. Ciaschini. London: Chapman and Hall.

Polak, Ruth, and Gina Rogers. 1982. "DRI's Second Generation Interindustry Model." *DRI Interindustry Review*. pp. 1.21–1.35.

3

Supply Functions in an Input–Output Framework

WILLIAM PETERSON

The purpose of this chapter is to consider how "supply-side effects" can be integrated into the multisectoral dynamic forecasting model of the economy of the United Kingdom, which has been developed by the Cambridge Growth Project. This Multisectoral Dynamic Model (MDM) has been fully described elsewhere (Barker and Peterson, 1987); therefore, in this chapter we consider only those features of the model that are relevant to the willingness of domestic producers to supply commodities to domestic intermediate and final users. Although the focus of this chapter and the empirical estimates presented arise out of the process of designing a particular model, the questions about supply-side modeling that the chapter attempts to raise are of more general significance.

In the first versions of the open input–output model (Leontief, 1953), industrial output was entirely determined by the level and structure of final demand. The dual price equations provided information about relative prices, but the assumption that in any period there was a single technology available, which was characterized by constant returns to scale, was sufficient to ensure that these prices were invariant with respect to the level and composition of output the firms were required to produce. The nonsubstitution theorem of Samuelson, Arrow, and others (Koopmans, 1951) meant that under constant returns the assumption of a single technique could be dropped, because even if many techniques were available, the fact that labor was ultimately the only scarce resource was sufficient to ensure that only one technique would be observed in practice. Thus, the only relevant supply constraint for the economy was the maximum sustainable aggregate level of employment.

This specification of technology has provided a convenient starting-point for two distinct applications of the input–output framework. Models developed for planning, principally in the less developed and the socialist countries, have elaborated the constraints on industrial activity by recognizing that labor is not homogeneous, that foreign exchange is typically an important scarce resource, and that the indivisibility and specific nature of industrial plant impose significant limits on the ability of the economy to supply whatever intermediate and final consumers demand. Thus, the problem becomes one of finding an efficient way to allocate the planned volume of industrial output between competing demands, while at the same time ensuring through government control over investment and production that the structure of output reflects as far as possible the socially optimal pattern of demand.

In contrast the industrial forecasting models that have been developed in a number of market economies (Almon et al., 1974; Eckstein and Warbur, 1983; McCracken, 1973) have integrated an input–output table and disaggregated approach to the analysis of production with a macroeconomic model of final demand, which is basically Keynesian in character. This macroeconomic model determines the overall level of activity in the economy. Although the composition of demand, particularly from domestic consumers, may respond to relative prices, there is little explicit attempt to model supply-side factors. Such an approach was appropriate under the policy regime in effect until the late 1970s, because it was realistic to regard governments as committed to intervening through discretionary fiscal and monetary policy to achieve the full-employment target. It is true that the importance to the United Kingdom during this period of the external trade constraint, and the attempt from 1967 onward to relax this through exchange rate policy, meant that it was essential to include a comprehensive analysis of foreign trade flows, and the impact on them of relative price changes. However, exchange rate policy was still essentially seen as a method of shifting the composition of demand from domestic output to net exports, so that the appropriate supply constraint for the economy remained the aggregate level of employment.

The decline of Keynesian macroeconomics and the growing influence of the new classical school pose a problem for the designer of a multisectoral forecasting model. It is clear that the compromise outlined, in which the aggregate level of economic activity is constrained by government policy intervention whereas its composition is determined by the structure of demand (which may, in turn, be responsive to relative prices), is no longer tenable. On the other hand, it does not appear either feasible or sensible to introduce aggregate concepts such as the "surprise" supply function or the "natural" level of unemployment into a model in which industrial disaggregation is an important feature. Rather, it seems appropriate to consider how far existing practice in multisectoral models already embodies an implicit treatment of the industrial supply function, and whether by adopting a specification that makes such a concept explicit, it is possible to derive and estimate supply functions for an individual industry that will yield a consistent treatment of the influence of factors such as profitability and capacity utilization.

The model of industrial supply set out and estimated in this chapter is one that is appropriate only for those industries producing commodities that are both tradeable and storeable. For industries in which this is not the case (electricity, construction, and services), imbalances between demand and supply are typically prevented either by the provision of substantial excess capacity, combined possibly with time-of-day pricing schemes to smooth short-run peaks in demand, or by informal rationing schemes that involve the involuntary postponement of completion dates. For most manufactured products, however, it seems more realistic to regard trade flows and stock changes as implying that (except perhaps in the very short run) demand and supply are equal, and domestic consumers are not rationed in any way.

This assumption that there is no physical rationing of domestic final or intermediate consumers is critical, in that it allows supply-side effects to be treated in a consistent way without being forced to consider the indirect effects on other industries of physical shortages. Rationing of intermediate demand would clearly imply that the supply of the rationed industry ought to be adversely affected, and would therefore require us to move in the direction of constructing a model designed for physical planning rather than for forecasting. Rationing of domestic consumers is difficult to handle for technical reasons, in that our model of consumer demand is based on a different "functional" classification from our disaggregation of commodities, so that we would have to make arbitrary assumptions about the impact of commodity shortages on the individual categories of consumption.

If domestic final and intermediate consumers are not rationed, the commodity balance identity for a typical industry can be written as

$$q_i + m_i = h_i + \Delta s_i + x_i \qquad (3\text{-}1)$$

where

$\quad q_i$ = domestic output of commodity i

$\quad m_i$ = imports of commodity i, inclusive of base year tariffs

$\quad h_i$ = domestic intermediate and final demand for commodity i, exclusive of changes in stocks

$\quad \Delta s_i$ = change in stocks for commodity i

$\quad x_i$ = exports of commodity i.

The assumption that domestic final and intermediate consumers are never rationed implies that, for a given level of domestic activity and structure of relative prices, h_i can be regarded by the producer as an exogenously given level of demand. Thus, Equation (3-1) can be rearranged to yield

$$q_i + m_i - \Delta s_i - x_i = h_i \qquad (3\text{-}2)$$

The determinants of the four terms on the left-hand side of this equation can be defined as the "supply-side" of the economy. It should be noted that some of the components of h_i, such as individual categories of consumption or certain cells of the input–output flow matrix of intermediate transactions, may well be functions of relative prices. If this is the case, and if relative prices are themselves affected by the level or composition of activity, then there will be an additional indirect feedback by which supply factors can affect the equilibrium solution of the model.

CONCEPT OF AN IMPLICIT SUPPLY FUNCTION

The approach that has generally been adopted in multisectoral models, including the current version of MDM, has been to estimate independently behavioral equations for trade flows and stock changes, and then to use the commodity-balance identity to derive the level of commodity output, q_i, as a residual. Such models therefore contain an implicit supply function for each industry, because any variable entering the trade or stock change equations, such as capacity utilization, interest rates, or profitability, must also enter into the determination of supply: if the variable concerned comes in through the import equation, the sign attached to its effect is reversed in the supply function.

This concept of an implicit supply function can be illustrated by looking at the relevant equations for the mechanical engineering industry in the latest version of MDM. The export quantity equations (Barker, 1987) in this version are clearly to be construed as demand equations for the rest of the world, because export prices enter measured in terms of foreign currency, there are no terms representing domestic capacity utilization or profitability, and the equations used for forecasting are constrained to ensure that the effects of domestic and world price changes are symmetric and "correctly" signed. If price and quantity effects relating to the exogenous foreign variables are subsumed into the constant, the equation for mechanical engineering takes the form

$$\ln x = \alpha_0 - (0.25494 + 0.29566L)\ln(px/EX) \tag{3-3}$$

where L denotes the lag operator [i.e., $Lx(t) = x(t-1)$]. Because this equation is derived as a demand function, the response, ceteris paribus, of exports to any change in sterling export prices is perverse from the supply-oriented perspective that we are adopting: when export prices fall, with a constant world price level and exchange rate, exports increase even though exporting is now less profitable relative to selling to the domestic market. This problem does not arise in the case of the import functions (Barker, 1987), because in this case the increase in import volumes resulting from a fall in the relative price can be interpreted as either a demand response on the part of domestic consumers or a supply response on the part of the agents importing into the United Kingdom. If we subsume all foreign price effects into the constant, the import equation for mechanical engineering has the form

$$\ln m = \alpha_0 + \ln(q - x) + (0.42520 + 1.37154L)\ln pq + 0.0\ln cu \tag{3-4}$$

where

cu = capacity-utilization index, defined below
pq = producer-price index for domestic output.

The remaining variable in the implicit supply side of MDM is inventory accumulation. In the full model, we distinguish three types of inventory; however, it is more convenient to regard stocks of raw materials held by other industries as a component of demand the firm must produce, thus limiting any supply effects to stocks of work in progress and finished goods. The current treatment of these variables is documented by Landesmann (1987). Inventory accumulation is a function of current and lagged output volumes, lagged stocks, and terms that represent the impact of interest rates and liquidity constraints on the willingness of firms to hold stocks. The relevant equations for mechanical engineering can be written as

$$\Delta s_1 = -343 + (0.04083 + 0.12262L - 0.06939L^2)y - 0.25852Ls + 0.0ps + 0.0lr \tag{3-5}$$

$$\Delta s_2 = 44 + (0.01854 + 0.01867L - 0.04362L^2)y - 0.00598Ls + 0.0ps + 0.0lr \tag{3-6}$$

where

y = industry (rather than commodity) output
Ls = lagged level of stocks
ps = a measure of the cost of holding stocks
lr = a measure of "real" liquid assets held by the industry.

The system of equations represented by the commodity-balance Equation (3-2) and the behavioral Equations (3-3)–(3-6) is clearly nonlinear, so that to derive the implicit supply equation we must approximate the actual values for a specific date. We also simplify by ignoring the distinction between commodity output q, which enters the import and commodity balance equations, and industry output y, which enters the inventory equations. For mechanical engineering, this distinction amounts to approximately 1 percent of gross output. We can then write a differential approximation to the implicit supply system in the neighborhood of the actual 1981 values as

$$\begin{bmatrix} 1 & 1 & -1 & -1 \\ -\theta_1 & 1 & \theta_1 & 0 \\ 0 & 0 & 1 & 0 \\ 0 & -\theta_4 & 0 & 1 \end{bmatrix} \begin{bmatrix} dq \\ dm \\ dx \\ d\Delta s \end{bmatrix} = \begin{bmatrix} dhs \\ \theta_2 dpq \\ \theta_3 dpx \\ 0 \end{bmatrix} \qquad (3\text{-}7)$$

where

$$\begin{aligned} \theta_1 &= m/(q - x) && = 0.6288 \\ \theta_2 &= 0.42520m/pq && = 392 \\ \theta_3 &= -0.25494x/px && = -387 \\ \theta_4 &= 0.04083 + 0.01854 = 0.05937. \end{aligned}$$

Inverting the matrix of coefficients in this system gives the implicit supply function, as well as a set of quasi-reduced form equations for imports, exports, and stockbuilding. These equations can be written as

$$dq = 0.62835dhs - 232dpq - 387dpx$$

$$dm = 0.39511dhs + 246dpq + 0.0dpx \qquad (3\text{-}8)$$

$$dx = 0.0dhs + 0.0dpq - 387\,dpx$$

$$d\Delta s = 0.02346dhs + 15dpq + 0.0dpx$$

Although the coefficients in this system of equations appear plausible, given that exports are regarded as being determined from the demand side, it is clearly difficult to interpret the equation determining output as incorporating any of the supply-side factors, such as industrial profitability, which economists have claimed may be important. Obviously, such variables can be added to the individual equations, on the basis of single-equation significance tests, but such an approach can rapidly become rather arbitrary. Furthermore, the commodity-balance constraint (3-2) clearly implies that any variable included in one of the four equations should also play an explanatory role in at least one of the others. Thus, an ad hoc approach to the modeling of supply-side effects can lead to an implicit supply function with unknown and undesirable properties.

AN INTERDEPENDENT SYSTEM OF
SUPPLY EQUATIONS

Instead of following the above approach, we model the supply behavior of the industry as an interdependent system by analyzing the decision problem facing a fictitious agent, the "middleman." The middleman can purchase output from current domestic production or from imports; alternatively, he can induce a rundown of existing stocks (or a reduction in the volume of current production allocated to stock increases) or a withdrawal of goods from the export market. The middleman is assumed to choose between these alternatives in accordance with an objective of minimizing the costs of supply, so that under perfect competition his problem can be expressed as

$$\text{Min } C = uc_i q_i + pm_i m_i - px_i x_i - ps_i \Delta s_i \tag{3-9}$$

where

uc_i = current unit production cost of domestic output
pm_i = import price inclusive of tariffs
px_i = export price
ps_i = shadow value of changes to stock.

Minimization of the objective function given by Equation (3-9), which is linear in the vector of decision variables $\{q_i, m_i, -x_i, -\Delta s_i\}$, subject to the linear commodity balance constraint given by Equation (3-2), will yield an unbounded solution unless there is no price variation across sources of supply and markets. Thus, for example, the middleman may attempt to purchase an infinite volume of imports either to reexport them or to add them to stock. This reflects the fact that the assumption of perfect competition under which this objective function is appropriate is also sufficient to ensure that arbitrage across sources and markets will continue until all components of the price vector $\{uc_i, pm_i, px_i, ps_i\}$ are the same. The problem is thus precisely analogous to that encountered in econometric studies of energy demand: if the agent's objective is taken to be the purchase of a specified volume of energy, measured in terms of either original or useful thermal content using fixed conversion ratios based on physical data, the efficient solution will require that the cost per unit of thermal content should be the same for all fuels purchased.

The fact that price variations across source of supply and markets are observed in practice, as are differences in the cost per unit of thermal content of different fuels, suggests that at the level of disaggregation considered in multisectoral models, such as MDM, perfect competition and product homogeneity are inappropriate assumptions. If instead it is assumed that the middleman faces imperfectly competitive markets, so that the price vector $\{uc_i, pm_i, px_i, ps_i\}$ can be written as a function of the vector of supply decisions $\{v_i\} = \{q_i, m_i, -x_i, -\Delta s_i\}$, then the objective function becomes

$$\text{Min } C' = uc_i\{v_i\}q_i + pm_i\{v_i\}m_i - px_i\{v_i\}x_i - ps_i\{v_i\}\Delta s_i \tag{3-10}$$

subject to the commodity-balance constraint (3-2). Expressing the solution to this problem as a function of the level of supply h_i and the prices $\{uc_i, pm_i, px_i, ps_i\}$ yields a "pseudo-cost" function [analogous to the pseudo-profit function discussed by Diewert (1982)] for the middleman

$$C^*(h_i, \{uc_i, pm_i, px_i, ps_i\}) = \text{Min } C' \tag{3-11}$$

We can now use standard duality results and argue that, by choosing a suitable functional form for C^* and differentiating with respect to each component of the price vector, we will obtain a set of interrelated equations for the optimal supply vector $\{q_i, m_i, -x_i, -\Delta s_i\}$.

For empirical purposes, it is convenient to work with a pseudo-cost function that is based on the translog cost function introduced into econometric use by Christensen et al. (1973). This takes the form

$$\ln C^*(h_i, \{p_i\}) = \beta_0 + \sum \alpha_j \ln p_j + \sum\sum \gamma_{jk} \ln p_j \ln p_{k_2} + \delta_0 \ln h_i + \sum \delta_j \ln p_j \ln h_i + \varepsilon(\ln h_i)^2 \tag{3-12}$$

Then, because

$$\partial \ln C(h_i, \{p_i\})/\partial \ln p_j = p_j v_j/C = \alpha_j \tag{3-13}$$

we obtain estimating equations for the ratio (valued at current prices) of each component of supply to the value (excluding profits) of home sales. For exports, this ratio will be negative, whereas for stockbuilding it may be either negative (implying a desired increase in stocks) or positive (implying a rundown).

So far we have analyzed the problem facing the middleman in purely static terms. In practice, of course, the existence of inventories reflects an intertemporal aspect of the supply decision, and we have implicitly recognized this by defining ps_i as the shadow value of changes to stocks, which is derived from the solution to the full dynamic optimization problem. If storage were costless, production instantaneously variable, and consumers indifferent between goods purchased from stock and from current production, producers would wish to hold finite stocks only if they anticipated that the unit cost of production, uc_i, would rise through time at a rate equal to the market rate of interest. If it were rising faster, they would wish to expand production now to produce nothing in future periods, whereas if it were rising more slowly, they would not wish to hold stocks at all.

This argument shows how in dynamic equilibrium, with producers holding stocks, the shadow value of changes in stock should be equal to the present value of the expected production cost in the next period. In addition, we should allow for the fact that by holding stocks the middleman incurs positive storage costs, which are assumed to rise in line with other production costs, and that he risks being unable to dispose of the stored commodity at the same price as its currently produced equivalent. Thus, even if we assume, for example, that price and quantity indices for automobiles correct appropriately for quality changes, consumers are likely to demand additional discounts if they are to be persuaded to clear the surviving stocks of last year's model. The shadow value of changes in stock can therefore be written as

$$ps_i(t) = \theta_i(t)uc_i(t + 1)/[1 + r(t)] \tag{3-14}$$

where

θ_i = "storage cost" function
r = suitable short-term interest rate.

The storage cost function θ_i is likely to take a higher value if stocks are currently high relative to output, both because warehouse space will be in short supply and because a high level of stocks makes it more likely that the middleman will find himself with obsolete goods. We proxy these effects by including the lagged ratio of stocks to output in our regressions. To the extent that other excluded effects are proportional to uc_i our choice of a logarithmic specification ensures that they will be absorbed in the constant of the regression. Similarly, our definition of the interest rate can include any constant risk premia, provided that these are proportional to the discount factor $[1 + r(t)]$.

The remaining problem in specifying the shadow value of changes in stock is that, as Equation (3-14) makes clear, this variable depends on the *anticipated* level of unit costs next year. Rather than specify a forecasting mechanism to model these anticipations, we have used the *actual* value of next year's unit costs as a proxy for the *expected* value. It should be noted that although this strategy is compatible with the assumption that agents' cost expectations are formed rationally, it is not equivalent to use of the "substitution" method (McCallum, 1976) for estimation of rational expectations models. This is because the substitution method requires the resulting equations to be estimated using instrumental variables, because the expectational variable is measured with error. However, since in this case the expectational variable is a "lead" variable, the expectational error should not be correlated with any of the other explanatory variables in the model.

The derivation of the system of supply equations given by (3-13) from the minimization of a pseudo-cost function by a fictitious middleman leads to a number of restrictions on the parameters β_j, γ_{jk} of the system. These fall into two distinct groups. In the first place, if the system is expressed in share form, it is well known (Barten, 1969) that one equation is redundant, in the sense that its parameters and their standard errors can be derived using the estimates of the remaining equations and the adding-up constraints

$$\Sigma_j \beta_j = 1$$

$$\Sigma_j \gamma_{jk} = 0 \qquad k = 1, \ldots, n. \qquad (3\text{-}15)$$

A similar adding-up constraint applies whenever an additional explanatory variable is included in the set of regression equations. These constraints have no economic significance, and they cannot be subjected to statistical tests. However, the empirical estimates presented below were in fact calculated not by dropping a redundant equation, but by an alternative technique in which the full set of equations is estimated, allowing for the singularity of the variance–covariance matrix, and the restrictions (3-15) are used to identify the model parameters. The two procedures have been shown by Barten to be equivalent for the class of static allocation model under consideration.

The derivation of Equation (3-13) also implies a number of economically significant, and statistically testable, constraints on the parameters of the share equations. First, each of the equations should be homogeneous of degree zero in prices, implying that

$$\Sigma_k \gamma_{jk} = 0 \qquad j = 1, \ldots, n \qquad (3\text{-}16)$$

Second, the price responses should be symmetric, which implies that

$$\gamma_{jk} = \gamma_{kj} \qquad j, k = 1, \ldots, n \qquad (3\text{-}17)$$

Because these constraints can be expressed as linear parametric restrictions on the estimated coefficients it is straightforward to test their validity, and such a procedure can help assess whether the integrated approach to supply modeling suggested in this chapter is likely to be valuable. Derivation of the supply functions from an optimisation problem also implies a further set of constraints, that the matrix of second derivatives $[\partial^2\{v\}/\partial\{p\}\partial\{p\}]$ should be negative semidefinite. However, since this requirement can be expressed only in terms of a set of observation-dependent inequality restrictions, we do not consider testing it in this chapter.

EMPIRICAL RESULTS

The model of supply determination given by Equation (3-13) has been applied to four of the larger manufacturing industries distinguished in the current version of MDM: food processing, chemicals, mechanical engineering, and textiles. These industries all satisfy the condition mentioned for the application of our integrated approach, in that the output they produce is both tradeable and storeable. Data for these four industries covering the estimation period 1957–1980 were taken from the disaggregated databank maintained by the Cambridge Growth Project. In addition to the price variables suggested by the theory, we included a time trend and an index of capacity utilization (defined as the ratio of output to its 9-year moving average) in all the regressions.

Because we aim to test the validity of the economically significant restrictions that can be derived from our model of supply behavior, we estimated a number of alternative models for each industry. The first, unrestricted, model imposes only the adding-up constraints given as (3-15) above; therefore, this model is that which would be estimated using unrestricted ordinary least squares (OLS) on the output, import, export, and inventory equations independently, but including the full range of explanatory variables. We next imposed the homogeneity restrictions (3-16) on each equation, producing a model in which the four equations are independently consistent with economic theory, but in which the interrelation between them is neglected. Finally, we estimated a model with both homogeneity and symmetry imposed. These three models were estimated both with and without the additional explanatory variable ln h_i, the level of home sales measured at constant prices. If the coefficients on this variable are not jointly significant, it would imply that the pattern of supply responses is not affected by the size of the domestic market. Because one obvious defect of our approach is the omission of adjustment costs, we also considered a generalization of this model in which lagged as well as current prices are included, with the various restrictions on the price effects assumed to apply to the sum of the current and lagged coefficients. In view of the limited number of degrees of freedom available, this model was only estimated only without the home sales variable ln h_i.

Table 3-1 gives the values of the maximized log-likelihood function for each of the three models that include this last variable. The choice between models is based on the Likelihood-Ratio principle, that twice the difference in the log-likelihood between the unrestricted and restricted models is asymptotically distributed as $\chi^2(r)$, where r is the number of additional overidentifying restrictions in the restricted model. Thus,

TABLE 3-1. Log-Likelihood Values for Rival Models

Industry	Unrestricted	Homogeneity	Symmetry
Food processing	347.69	334.81	328.98
Chemicals	271.77	265.98	262.63
Mechanical engineering	227.65	226.90	218.30
Textiles	259.46	241.76	240.84
Parameters	36	36	36
Restrictions	9	12	15
Overidentifying restrictions	0	3	6

	Degrees of Freedom	Correction Factor	χ^2	F statistic
H against U	3	4.08	7.81	10.80
S against H	3	3.92	7.81	10.35

since homogeneity implies three additional restrictions, with adding-up ensuring that the restriction is automatically satisfied for the fourth equation, twice the difference between columns 1 and 2 of Table 3-1 should be distributed as $\chi^2(3)$. The relevant 5 percent critical values of the χ^2 statistic are given at the foot of the table. In addition, because there is substantial evidence that the use of an asymptotic test leads to overrejection in small samples, we give the degrees-of-freedom adjustment and alternative critical values (based on the F statistic) that have been advocated by Pudney (1981).

It is clear from Table 3-1 that even if we correct for the small sample size, the homogeneity restriction on the system of equations taken together is rejected for food processing and textiles. This is not a surprising result, given the frequency with which the analog of this restriction is rejected in demand and production studies (Laitinen, 1978). The linearity of the share system that we estimated makes it possible to explore the cause of this rejection. Because the unrestricted estimates are identical to those that would be generated by applying single-equation OLS, whereas homogeneity is a within-equation restriction, we can examine the ratios of the single-equation root mean square errors (RMSE) to see whether rejection is associated with a particular equation. The information needed for this comparison is given in Table 3-2.

The results given in Table 3-2 show that the major problems with the homogeneity restriction arise in the case of the import equations. This result is in line with earlier findings (Barker, 1987) that this restriction is violated in a substantial number of the unrestricted import equations estimated for the current version of MDM. It is not clear why this should be the case, although it is possible that there is a sufficiently close correlation between general inflation and the increased penetration of the U.K. market by imports to mean that absolute price changes can help explain changes in the relevant shares, in apparent contradiction to the propositions of economic theory. This tentative explanation gains additional support from the fact that the rejection of the homogeneity restriction is more significant for the models that exclude the explanatory variable ln h_i, which measures the size of the domestic market. Although the coefficients of this variable were not jointly significant in the case of the unrestricted models for chemicals and textiles, in comparing the restricted models, we found that they were always jointly significant at the 5 percent level. We can therefore conclude that the exclusion of this variable represents a misspecification, and is likely to lead to an unjustified rejection of the model under investigation.

Conditional on homogeneity, the symmetry restrictions are accepted for two of the four industries (after making the appropriate small-sample corrections), with rejection for the other two industries being marginal. Although there is no computationally simple method of testing for dynamic misspecification in a system of interrelated equations, an examination of the single-equation Durbin–Watson

TABLE 3-2. Ratio of Restricted to Unrestricted RMSE by Equation

Industry	Output	Imports	Exports	Stocks
Food processing	1.409	1.423	1.052	1.000
Chemicals	1.000	1.235	1.067	1.103
Mechanical engineering	1.014	1.016	1.000	1.010
Textiles	1.000	1.583	1.020	1.750

statistics provides weak evidence that the imposition of cross-equation restrictions is inducing mild positive autocorrelation. Although one interpretation of this is that the restrictions are invalid, it is also possible that the true dynamic structure is more complex than our simple static model will allow. The effects of such a misspecification are likely to be more obvious in the restricted model. However, a simple extension of the model (without the $\ln h_i$ variable) by including lagged price terms leads to no major improvement. The additional parameters are jointly significant asymptotically at the 5 percent level only for textiles, and if small-sample corrections are made they cease to be so.

Full results for the preferred model, which includes the market-size variable and imposes the homogeneity and symmetry constraints, are available from the author on request. Examination of these results indicates that the trend variables are clearly significant and show a tendency in three of the four equations (the exception being food processing) for an increased import share of the home market to be accompanied by a negative trend in the export equation, implying (since exports are measured with the sign reversed) a movement toward greater international specialization. For food and textiles, there is also evidence that the proportion of output going into stocks is increasing. Our hypothesis that decisions about the components of supply are related gains some support from the effects of lagged stock levels and capacity utilization. A high level of stocks is associated with a reduction in imports and an increase in supply from stocks to the domestic market. Stock levels affect exports significantly only for textiles, and here the effect is negative, suggesting that this relationship may not be correctly specified. High levels of utilization are associated with higher imports for three of the four industries. However, they are also associated with higher exports and output, and with increases in stockbuilding, so that it is clear that there are problems in identifying the direction of causation correctly.

In order to discuss the main features of the estimated price responses, it is convenient to derive the own- and cross-price elasticities. These measure the response of a component of supply to a change in the prices facing the middleman, and can be computed using the relationship

$$\varepsilon_{jk} = \partial \ln v_j / \partial \ln p_k = \gamma_{jk}/\alpha_j + \alpha_k - \delta_{jk} \qquad (3\text{-}18)$$

where $\delta_{jk} = 1$ for $j = k$ and 0 otherwise. These elasticities depend on the observed supply shares and are therefore not constant over time. Table 3-3 presents computed values for each of the four industries for 1980, the last year of the data sample.

The formula (3-18) for the computation of price elasticities implies that where the relevant share concerned is small the elasticities will be poorly determined, and for this reason it is not possible to attach much importance to the computed elasticities with respect to changes in the shadow value of stocks, given in the last row of each table. The diagonal terms give the own-price responses, which for output are small and ambiguously signed (the prior expectation is that they should be negative), implying that changes in domestic unit costs have comparatively little effect on output. The own-price response of imports is negative as expected for all industries except food processing. The own-price response of exports is consistently negative, implying, since exports are measured as a negative component of supply, that an increase in export prices relative to other domestic costs and prices leads to an increase in the volume of

TABLE 3-3. Computed Price Elasticities

	Output	*Imports*	*Exports*	*Stocks*
		Food Processing		
Output	−0.1259	0.0495	−0.0320	0.1084
Imports	0.2313	0.1424	−0.1484	−0.2253
Exports	0.3847	0.3820	−0.9610	0.1943
Stocks	15.850	−7.0502	−2.3625	−6.4370
		Chemicals		
Output	−0.0958	0.1723	−0.1344	0.0580
Imports	0.6857	−0.2382	−0.3985	−0.0490
Exports	0.3712	0.2765	−0.6391	−0.0087
Stocks	4.0717	−0.8653	0.2209	−3.4273
		Mechanical Engineering		
Output	0.1849	0.2948	−0.3293	−0.1504
Imports	1.2516	−0.5571	−0.7633	0.0688
Exports	0.7282	0.3976	−1.4544	0.3287
Stocks	109.44	−11.794	108.16	—
		Textiles		
Output	0.0842	0.5615	−0.4897	−0.1560
Imports	1.7476	−1.1203	−0.7225	0.0952
Exports	1.7128	0.8119	−2.4456	−0.0790
Stocks	−8.5774	1.6815	1.2425	5.6534

exports. This does not of course rule out a negatively signed response when export prices change relative to prices abroad. It is harder to find a consistent pattern in the cross-price effects, but it should be noted that, as would be expected, imports and domestic production are substitutes for all the industries considered.

CONCLUSION

In this chapter we have set out a framework for the analysis of supply decisions in the context of a disaggregated forecasting model, and we have shown how this framework can be applied using theoretical results and estimation techniques drawn from the literature of production and demand analysis. Although this is a preliminary exercise, the results are moderately encouraging. The homogeneity restriction is accepted for two out of four industries, and symmetry is also acceptable in two cases. In no case are these economically significant restrictions overwhelmingly rejected. Clearly, the model suggested here is capable of significant further extension: one obvious direction is the explicit treatment of the dynamic aspects of the supply decision, which enter both through inventory behavior and through the costs of adjusting supply to particular markets. Another is the integration of the supply model presented here with a production model for the firm, thus allowing unit production cost to be endogenously determined as a result of decisions about employment, energy, and raw material use. We hope to be able to explore some of these extensions in further research.

ACKNOWLEDGMENTS

This work was partly financed by a grant from the U.K. Economic and Social Research Council (ESRC) to the Cambridge Growth Project. I am grateful to members of the Cambridge Growth Project, in particular to Terry Barker, Michael Landesmann, and Martin Weale, for the use of industrial data they compiled. All responsibility for errors remains mine.

REFERENCES

Almon, C., et al. 1974. *1985: Interindustry Forecasts of the American Economy.* Lexington, MA: D.C. Heath.

Barker, T. S. 1987. "Exports and Imports." In *The Cambridge Multisectoral Dynamic Model of the British Economy,* edited by T. S. Barker and A. W. A. Peterson. Cambridge: Cambridge University Press, pp. 201–245.

Barker, T. S., and A. W. A. Peterson. 1987. *The Cambridge Multisectoral Dynamic Model of the British Economy.* Cambridge: Cambridge University Press.

Barten, A. P. 1969. "Maximum Likelihood Estimation of a Complete System of Demand Equations." *European Economic Review.* Vol. 1, pp. 7–73.

Christensen, L. R., D. W. Jorgenson, and L. J. Lau, 1973. "Transcendental Logarithmic Production Frontiers." *Review of Economics and Statistics.* Vol. 55, pp. 28–45.

Diewert, W. E. 1982. "Duality Approaches to Microeconomic Theory." In *Handbook of Mathematical Economics II,* edited by K. J. Arrow and M. D. Intriligator. Amsterdam: North-Holland.

Eckstein, O., and P. M. Warbur. 1983. *The DRI Model of the US Economy.* New York: McGraw-Hill.

Koopmans, T.C. 1951. *Activity Analysis of Production and Allocation.* New York: John Wiley.

Laitinen, K. 1978. "Why Is Demand Homogeneity So Often Rejected?" *Economics Letters.* Vol. 1, pp. 187–191.

Landesmann, M. 1987. "Stockbuilding." In *The Cambridge Multisectoral Dynamic Model of the British Economy,* edited by T. S. Barker and A. W. A. Peterson. Cambridge: Cambridge University Press, pp. 185–200.

Leontief, W. W. 1953. *Studies in the Structure of the American Economy.* New York: Oxford University Press.

McCallum, B. T. 1976. "Rational Expectations and the Natural Rate Hypothesis." *Econometrica.* Vol. 44, pp. 43–52.

McCracken, M.S. 1973. *An Overview of CANDIDE Model 1.0.* Ottawa, Canada: Economic Council of Canada.

Pudney, S. E. 1981. "An "Empirical Method of Approximating the Separable Structure of Consumer Preferences." *Review of Economic Studies.* Vol. 48, pp. 561–577.

II

ALTERNATIVE ACCOUNTING FRAMEWORKS

4

Historical and New International Perspectives on Input–Output Accounts

KAREN R. POLENSKE

Input–output analysis covers a broad range of topics, including accounting, modeling, planning, and forecasting. Commemoration of the fiftieth anniversary of input–output analysis seems an appropriate occasion to draw attention to one important, but somewhat neglected, aspect—the input–output accounting structure. Three economists—Simon Kuznets, Wassily Leontief, and Richard Stone—received Nobel Prizes, in part, at least, for the work they did to advance our knowledge and use of national economic accounts. Knowledge of accounts, of how they are structured, of the different forms they take, and of how different types of accounts can be linked contributes to the outstanding work of these three economists. We will review some of the key pioneering efforts and new developments in the construction of accounting systems and input–output accounts, alternative levels (from the firm to the world) for which accounts are structured, and main features of different types of input–output accounts.

DIFFERENT ACCOUNTING SYSTEMS

Accounting systems have traditionally been structured in two different forms: the material product system and the system of national accounts. Because input–output accounts are incorporated into each system, we will discuss the primary purpose of each and provide a brief history.

The Material Product System

The Material Product System (MPS), sometimes referred to as the System of Balances of the National Economy, is the earliest of the two accounting systems and records production only of material goods and services. It is used primarily in socialist countries. Using the MPS, analysts develop input–output tables to assist with planning in these countries. Three important milestones in the development of the MPS are (1) Quesnay's work, (2) input–output accounts in the Union of Soviet Socialist Republics, and (3) input–output accounts in the People's Republic of China.

Quesnay's Tableau Économique

The earliest accounting structure was Quesnay's *Tableau Économique*, its structure being prescribed by theories and policies of eighteenth-century France. His simple table is separated into three kinds of expenditures: productive (relating to agriculture), revenue after tax deductions, and sterile (relating to industry), reflecting the Physiocrats' view that only agriculture producers were "productive," and generated wealth; all other producers were "nonproductive" (Kuczynski and Meed, 1972).

Adam Smith and other classical economists extended the Physiocrats' definition of productive labor to include producers of any physical output, such as manufactured goods. The distinction between productive and nonproductive was then adopted by Marx, and the MPS reflects the theoretical differentiation between the two types of labor.

Union of Soviet Socialist Republics

Work on input–output accounts in the Union of Soviet Socialist Republics (USSR) started with construction of balance sheets. In the early 1920s, the State Planning Commission, GOSPLAN, asked the Central Statistical Administration—of which Popov was the director—to construct a balance sheet for the 1923/1924 national economy. Popov published a book on these balance sheets in 1926, stating that "the balance-sheet data provide all the elements needed to envisage the process of reproduction of the Soviet economy" (Popov, 1964, p. 79). Because the balance sheet is based upon the principle of material accounting, only production of physical goods is measured.

Leontief, who wrote a short comment on the national balances in 1925, was dissatisfied, particularly with the method of calculating the total income of the economy (1964, pp. 88–94). He later combined his knowledge of Quesnay's Tableau Économique, USSR national balances, and the theoretical structure of Walras' general equilibrium system to create a new and simple, but elegant, accounting and theoretical system.

Although the first USSR balance sheets were constructed in the 1920s, Stalin stopped further work, saying that they were "not a balance but a game with figures" (quoted in Spulber and Dadkhah, 1975, p. 27). After Stalin died, the first USSR input–output table was constructed in value, physical, and labor units for 1959 by the Central Statistical Administration (TsSu), published in 1971 (Ellman, 1972, pp. 2–3). The staff at TsSu also assembled a 1966 capital–stock matrix. National and regional accounting and planning input–output tables are now constructed by staff at various agencies: staff at the Chief Computing Center of GOSPLAN assembled the first planning input–output tables in physical terms for 1962, 1963–1965, and 1970; staff at its Research Institute constructed the first tables in value terms for 1962, 1970, 1975, and 1980; and staff at the Central Economic Mathematical Institute, USSR Academy of Sciences (TSEMI), constructed the first regional table (Ellman, 1972, pp. 2–3, 75). In the USSR, an input–output table "forms a link between planning the national economic indices and the plans for separate industries and regions" (Ellman, 1972, p. 81).

The centralization of regional planning in the USSR led to the assembly of regional accounts. The first regional input–output table was constructed for Mordovia for 1959, followed by many regional tables and an interregional 239-sector 1961 table for the Baltic region. During the 1970s, tables were constructed for all republics for 1966 and 1972, most data being collected by special surveys. Interregional trade data were considered to be so important that a special conference was held in 1971 to establish the methodology for handling trade data (Bond, 1974, p. 13).

At the Science Centre of Novosibirsk, most research is focused on regional issues. In 1967, an optimization intersectoral interregional model (OIIM) was developed to calculate the development and allocation of productive forces to 1990. Bandman has published many books and articles on territorial industrial complexes (TIC), which "while having industry as its basis, also includes settlements, and that means their infrastructure and, of course, their population" (Bandman, 1980, p. 22). Although details on the accounting structure and data used for the OIIM and TIC models are not available, Granberg (1976) indicates that the accounts include regional input–output tables (separated into mobile and nonmobile production), transportation linkages, and consumption and employment data. Thus, in the USSR, input–output tables are constructed both for national and regional economies, using the material product system.

People's Republic of China

There has been (and is) an astonishing amount of research on input–output accounts in Eastern European and many other socialist countries, one of these being the People's Republic of China. Prior to 1988, the Chinese primarily used the MPS rather than the System of National Accounts (SNA) to construct their accounts; however, the 1987 national and a number of regional tables were constructed using the SNA system. Accounts have been constructed in China at the national, provincial, urban, and enterprise levels (Polenske, 1988). Prior to the Cultural Revolution (1966–1976), the first empirical input–output research was conducted for enterprises (Tianjin Chemical Plant and the Anshan Iron and Steel Company) and a region (Shanxi Province). The empirical work was started at these levels because it was easier to obtain permission for the collection of data from a plant manager or a provincial official than from a state official.

Only limited input–output research was conducted prior to the late 1970s. During most of the Cultural Revolution, all official input–output work in China was discontinued because the input–output technique was considered to be a tool of capitalism as discussed in Polenske (1988). The first official Chinese national input–output table was constructed for 1973. In late 1986, the 1981 national input–output table was published in Chinese, and in 1987 it was published in English. Until now, the only tables easily available for the People's Republic of China were constructed by western analysts.

In China, many enterprise staff assemble and use input–output accounts to help them plan both for the current period and for the future. The enterprise input–output account usually shows all sales and purchases by the firm, both those occurring within a firm and those the firm makes with others in the economy.[1] Such an accounting system can be extremely useful to an enterprise as it plans its production.

1. In Yugoslavia, these accounts are sometimes linked into regional and national MPS accounts and used to help plan and project enterprise outputs in conjunction with state plan targets (Filipic, 1986). In the West, national and regional input–output accounts have been used by corporations for analysis, but the transactions among different divisions within a firm have usually not been assembled.

So far, almost all regional input–output accounts are constructed in China by conducting sample surveys in the province, county, city, or enterprise, usually combined with data from secondary data sources, such as censuses (Polenske, 1988). Even today, published literature on national, regional, and enterprise accounts is relatively scarce in China, although many unpublished papers exist.

System of National Accounts

The SNA is a system of accounts, one component of which is the input–output account. As evident from recent attempts to reconcile SNA and MPS accounting systems and to determine their conceptual similarities and differences, the SNA is a more comprehensive system than the MPS (Stone, 1970; Ivanov, 1987). The focus here is on SNA concepts and definitions of the input–output portion of the system. At present, the main documentation of the SNA is available in a publication referred to as "the blue book," which, in addition to other information, provides guidelines for constructing input–output accounts (United Nations, 1968). Even when the accounts are supposedly constructed with these guidelines, they may differ from country to country.

The SNA is a way to portray "clearly and concisely a framework within which the statistical information needed to analyze the economic process in all its many aspects could be organized and related" (Stone, 1970, p. 163). Stone was the chief architect of this accounting system. High priority has not been given to extending the accounts to regions, partly because to do so would require handling new conceptual and measurement problems (United Nations, 1968, p. 15). The SNA is separated into four accounts: production, consumption, accumulation, and rest of the world. In the 1968 revision, input–output accounts were included as an integral part of the SNA to represent the structural characteristics of the economy.

The first SNA was published by the United Nations in 1953, followed by revisions, the third being published in 1968 (United Nations, 1968). For the 1968 revision, four major changes in input–output accounts were suggested: (1) full integration with national income and product accounts, (2) construction of an absorption or use table (commodity-by-industry) and a make table (industry-by-commodity), (3) assembly of input–output data initially at basic (producer values minus commodity taxes) or purchaser values (producer value plus trade and transport margins), and (4) inclusion of output of goods and services sold to government or to private nonprofit agencies on current account as part of the intermediate, rather than the final demand, sector (United Nations Statistical Office, 1986).

In the current (late 1980s) SNA revisions, no major restructuring will supposedly occur, but at least five changes may slightly affect the input–output tables (United Nations Statistical Office, 1986): (1) revisions to classification codes, attempting to create a greater correspondence than exists at present between the various classification systems, (2) revisions to the valuation of flows, particularly to those of public enterprises, (3) improvements to the specification of certain intermediate demand items, such as banks and financial intermediaries, (4) changes in the classification of final demands, affecting the values for consumption, capital stocks and flows, and foreign exports and imports, and (5) expansions of the input–output framework to include socioeconomic breakdowns in a social accounting matrix (SAM) framework.

An expert panel met in Vienna in March 1988 to review the suggested changes, and the new revisions are expected to be completed by 1990.

The inclusion of input–output accounts as part of the SNA contributed to the spread of input–output work throughout the world. In 1966, 32 countries, including capitalist and socialist, were listed as having compiled input–output tables. By that year, in fact, the Netherlands had 20 tables, Norway 16, and Denmark 14, and the number of sectors ranged from a low of 10 for the United Arab Republic to 450 for Japan and the United States (United Nations, 1966, pp. 132–138). Now, tables are available for more than 80 countries, and several European countries construct annual input–output accounts, thus providing a time series of tables (UNIDO, 1986).

Documentation of international standards of constructing input–output tables is currently available only in very cryptic form in two publications by the United Nations (1968, pp. 36–53; 1973) and one by UNIDO (1985, pp. 1–13). According to *The Review of Income and Wealth* (1986, p. 110), an extensive documentation is being prepared by the United Nations, entitled *Input–Output Statistics*. Additional documentation of procedures for compiling SNA accounts is required if reliable comparisons are to be made of accounts from different years for the same country and of accounts from different countries. The superb documentation of Norwegian input–output accounts, which since 1952 have been fully integrated with national income and product accounts, could well serve as a role model for other countries (Fløttum, 1981).

U.S. Input–Output Accounts

Input–output accounts present a comprehensive portrayal of sales and purchases by each industry in the economy. Because transactions are arranged in matrix form, each cell represents simultaneously a sale and a purchase. Along each row, the sale by an industry to each intermediate and final user is shown. Final users include private consumers, public consumers (government), private and public investors, and foreign traders. It is the total of these sales to final users that represents the gross domestic product (GDP). Total output in the economy is comprised of the GDP plus all sales to intermediate users (such as agriculture, mining, manufacturing, and services). In each column of an input–output table, purchases from intermediate producers and primary factors of production (labor, capital, and land) are recorded. National income and product accounts, which since 1958 form one part of U.S. input–output accounts, record only all incomes received by primary factors of production and expenditures made by final users. The complete specification of all interindustry transactions distinguishes input–output accounts from national income and product accounts and helps to bridge the macro and sectoral components of an economy. The double-counting in input–output accounts provides detailed information for analysis and planning purposes.

Many important accounting balances must be maintained in constructing an input–output account. The first major accounting balance is that total outlays by an industry (the total of elements in a column) must equal total output of the industry — total sales of output of the industry to all intermediate and final users (the total of elements in the row for the respective industry). Differences between these two totals help input–output accountants identify problems with the basic data collected by surveys, censuses, and other means. The second major accounting balance is that the sum of all income earned by the factors of production (gross income received) must be equal to the sum of all expenditures made by final users (gross domestic product). This accounting balance ensures that all income recorded as received is also shown as being spent. As researchers assemble tables, each of the many accounting balances must be checked to ensure complete consistency in all components of the accounts.

Input–output accounts are more comprehensive than MPS accounts in that the former include production of all goods and services in the economy rather than being restricted only to the production of material goods. In the System of National Accounts, input–output accounts are included as part of the total accounting system.

Brief history

Leontief's original 1936 article contained a table for 1919. He then constructed a table for 1929, which was included in the 1941 version of his book *The Structure of American Economy*. The 1939 table was constructed at Harvard University under the direction of Leontief by a team of analysts from the Bureau of Labor Statistics (BLS). The importance Leontief gave to collection of data and structuring of accounts is shown by the many pages of his 1951 book devoted to these issues.

The 1947 U.S. input–output table is probably the most extensively documented set of accounts anywhere. Details on the subcomponents of final demand and value added and on each of the 450 sectors were published in mimeographed BLS worksheets (U.S. Department of Labor, n.d.). General information on each major account component was consolidated into a Technical Supplement (National Bureau of Economic Research, 1954). Not until 1980 was a revised, but rather limited, version of the input–output documentation published by the U.S. Department of Commerce. The need for continual review of existing accounts means that excellent documentation is required. Many details on the history of U.S. input–output accounts are presented by Duncan and Shelton (1978).

During the 1950s and 1960s, economic analysts from U.S. universities, business, and the government met periodically to discuss input–output and other national accounts concepts and to propose changes in them, some of which are documented in National Bureau of Economic Research publications (1955, 1958). Under the Eisenhower administration, official U.S. input–output work was terminated from 1954 to 1959. It is ironical that the input–output technique was considered to be a tool of socialism in the United States and a tool of capitalism in the People's Republic of China (Duncan and Shelton, 1978, p. 111; Polenske, 1988, p. 3). One of the major recommendations of a National Accounts Review Committee was for input–output work to be resumed as part of a coordinated national economic accounting program (National Bureau of Economic Research, 1955) and to be fully integrated with the national income and product accounts.

Leontief foresaw the potential for using input–output at the regional level. He included a chapter on interregional theory in his 1953 volume (Leontief, 1953, pp. 93–115). Usually with the assistance of others, he developed the intranational (Leontief, 1953, pp. 93–115), gravity-trade (Leontief and Strout, 1963, pp. 119–150), and world (Leontief et al. 1977) models, all of which are different ways of modeling "regional" economies. He was also the first analyst to propose the theoretical structure for a partially closed model. Input–output accounts have been expanded within this consistent framework for numerous studies, including income distribution, pollution, government expenditures, and foreign trade.

Extensions of national input–output accounts

Weisskoff (1970) and Cline (1972) were two of the earliest analysts to extend national input–output accounts to "explore the linkages from the distribution of income to the structure of demand to the structure of production and hence back to employment and income distribution" (Robinson, 1988, p. 27). In the United States, a national industry-by-occupation matrix, fully consistent with input–output sectors, was first constructed by the BLS staff for 1950 and used to determine occupational requirements of defense-related industries for any major mobilization (U.S. Department of Labor, 1955). Rose and Beaumont in Chapter 10 and Wolff and Howell in Chapter 11 of this book illustrate two of the many ways in which the accounts are now expanded for analyses of incomes and occupations. Additional examples of income distribution, employment, and other extensions exist at the regional level.

In 1951, Isard published his first article on regional input–output. It was probably the 1960 book, *Methods of Regional Analysis*, he and others wrote, however, that encouraged many colleagues to construct regional input–output accounts. Bourque, Emerson, Hirsch, Isard, Miernyk, Tiebout, and Udis pioneered in constructing regional input–output accounts from surveys in cities such as Boulder, Philadelphia, and St. Louis, in states such as West Virginia, Washington, and Kansas, and in the Colorado River Basin. The Boulder accounts, constructed by Miernyk et al. (1967), are particularly interesting in that they represent one of the earliest extensions of input–output to reflect consumption expenditures by different types of consumers. Many nonsurvey regional input–output accounts were also constructed, often using either national input coefficients or creating regional flows by adjusting national coefficients.

Another major breakthrough was the construction of interregional and multiregional input–output accounts. In the 1950s, multiregional input–output (MRIO) models were used to analyze regions in Italy by Chenery (1953) and in the United States by Moses (1955). Although MRIO accounts were used in both cases, regional data were used only for some of the account components because of their scarcity, and the emphasis of the research was on the analysis rather than the structuring of the accounts. Venezuela is another country that has relatively large MRIO accounts. Palacios and his staff at the Central University in Venezuela constructed a set of accounts for 1978 for 9 regions and 10 industries (Palacios et al., 1982). In the 1960s, the Japanese constructed interregional input–output (IRIO) accounts, using Isard's accounting structure (Isard, 1951). These Japanese IRIO accounts are now available for 9 regions and about 40 industries for 1960, 1965, 1970, 1975, and 1980 (Abe, 1986).

During the late 1960s, Polenske (1970, 1980) and her staff at the Harvard Economic Research Project (HERP), along with the staff at Jack Faucett Associates, Inc. (JFA), constructed the first U.S. multiregional input–output (MRIO) accounts (Polenske et al., 1972, 1974; Rodgers, 1972, 1973; Scheppach, 1972). Regional 1963 data were assembled for 51 regions (50 states plus Washington, D.C.) and 79 industries. The 1977 MRIO accounts were constructed by JFA staff (1983) for 51 regions and 122 industries. These input–output accounts, from which direct input coefficients can be calculated, are supplemented by interregional trade accounts, from which column-trade coefficients can be calculated. This is the only accounting system that provides gross, rather than just net, trade flows. As far as possible, all data were assembled using regional statistics from secondary sources, such as censuses, published surveys, and special studies (Polenske, 1980).

Golladay and Haveman (1977) constructed one of the most extensive expansions of the 1963 MRIO accounts, using data for 114 occupations and 177 socioeconomic consumer units to examine regional effects of tax and transfer policies. Detailed occupational, employment, and personal consumption expenditures data were also used in expanding the 1963 and 1977 MRIO accounts for the Multiregional Policy Impact Simulation (MRPIS) research, conducted under the direction of Bluestone (Social Welfare Research Institute et al., 1980). Shalizi (1979) adapted Miyazawa's (1976) extensions of the Japanese input–output and the IRIO accounts for the MRIO accounts for the study of U.S. regional and income distribution issues. The U.S. 1963 MRIO accounts were extended by Pai (1979) to include pollution data for particulates, sulfur oxides, nitrogen oxides, hydrocarbons, and carbon monoxides to examine the regional economic effects of the 1974 Clean Air Act.

For the MRIO accounts, two more major accounting balances must be maintained than for national accounts (Polenske, 1980, pp. 51–80). First, output consumed in the region, shown in the input–output accounts, must equal the total shipments (including intraregional) into the region, shown in the interregional trade accounts. Second, all output produced in a region must be used in the region or shipped from it. The incorporation of interregional shipments allows analysts to study regional outputs and transportation flows within a consistent input–output accounting framework, in which accounting balances must be maintained among all components of the accounts.

Social Accounting Matrices

Expansion of input–output accounts to include socioeconomic breakdowns of final demand and value added components is critical for the study of structural change. As noted earlier, many expansions have been made both at the national and regional level. Frequently, analysts now refer to accounts that contain expansions of the factor and final product markets as a social accounting matrix (SAM). Input–output and SAM accounts provide two similar views of an economy. Analysts using SAMs usually provide less detail than those using input–output accounts for the interindustry portion of the accounting system and more detail for the factor and final product markets. Exceptions exist for both accounts however. In most countries, input–output accounts have been assembled first, then final demand and value added components are expanded and rearranged to fit the SAM classification.

For SAM accounts, extensions are usually made specifically to study links among growth, income distribution, employment, and poverty alleviation. "The approach serves to emphasize the fact that the distribution of employment opportunities and living standards is inextricably interwoven with the structure of production and the distribution of resources" (Pyatt and Round, 1985, p. 2). The focus of most early studies using SAMs was on the impact of policies to raise living levels of the people, thus on the elimination of poverty in developing countries (Pyatt, Roe, and associates, 1977, p. 2).

Early research on SAMs was conducted at the Cambridge Growth Project, under the direction of Stone. In 1970, he published a table, called "An Illustration of the Complete System," to show how the production, consumption, accumulation, and rest-of-the-world accounts could be integrated into a single accounting system, and he discussed social accounting matrices (Stone, 1970). Descriptions of SAMs are now available in many publications, including Pyatt and Thorbecke (1976), Taylor (1979), and King (1981).

Pyatt's 1970 SAM for Iran (Pyatt et al., 1972) is the first SAM for a developing country. For interindustry transactions, a single set of flows (not separated into use and make components) was provided; for final demand, the components were first divided into current and capital (investment) accounts, and each of these was subdivided into household, government, and rest-of-the-world components; for value added, subdivisions were also made.

The 1971–1972 SAM for Swaziland (Pyatt and Round, 1977; Webster, 1985) was the first in which commodity and activity accounts were distinguished. In addition, special attention was given to the organization of the supply of agricultural factor services because of the several forms of public and private ownership in the country. Finally, in the Swaziland SAM, factors and institutions are distinguished more clearly than in previous SAMs (Pyatt and Round, 1985, pp. 63–65).

For the 1970 SAM for Sri Lanka, 1965 input–output data were used to represent the 1970 production structure (Pyatt et al., 1977). They differed in three ways from the Iran SAM: (1) details were provided for the first time in a SAM on factors of production, (2) the accounts were rearranged, with the factor accounts, rather than the interindustry accounts, being placed in the upper left-hand corner, and (3) the accounts were compiled through the assembly of a set of commodity balances.

The second difference is the one that is stressed the most by Pyatt and Round:

> The arrangement of the accounts is a conscious attempt to capture the circular flow of income . . . and it is also an attempt to give prominence within the SAM to things that matter most . . . thus our accounts start with factor incomes and move to the incomes of households and other institutions in the economy. These, not structure of production, are our primary concerns. (1985, p. 60)

Interindustry transactions were transferred from the upper left-hand corner to the center of the overall accounting matrix. The way rows and columns are rearranged, however, does not matter. If position of an accounting component indicates importance, almost all input–output research would center on agriculture, the first row(s) in most tables. Yet, these input–output accounts are rarely used to study agriculture; rather, manufacturing sectors, which are in the center of the accounts, have been the focus of most studies. Pyatt and his associates have effectively emphasized distribution issues not by rearranging the rows and columns in the account, but by their own persistence and effectiveness in writing about these critical issues, stressing also the coherence and consistency of the accounting system within which the expansions are made. The change in position of the interindustry flows makes the current SAM framework look superficially different from the input–output framework. When expanded forms of the two accounting structures are compared, however, all but minor differences disappear.

Many SAM accounts are constructed to include details on the household sector (Stone, 1985), tax and subsidy sectors (Pleskovic, 1982), and differentiated accounts for public and private sectors (Pleskovic and Treviño, 1985; Pyatt, 1987). One of the most innovative extensions—to incorporate financial flow-of-funds accounts—was applied by Benjamin to the Cameroons in a study for the World Bank. Only unpublished studies of such financial linkages exist in the input–output literature. Other uses for SAMS include multiplier analyses, distributional studies across socioeconomic groups, and as inputs to computable general equilibrium models that are used to study trade, growth, economic structure, and income distribution (Dervis et al. 1982; Robinson, 1988). Now, SAMs have been constructed for many countries, including Cyprus, Egypt, Indonesia, Malaysia, the Philippines, Republic of Korea, Saudi Arabia, Thailand, and Turkey (Pyatt and Round, 1985; Cohen, Chapter 7, this volume). The incorporation of all accounts into a single consistent framework is one of the current SNA revision proposals.

In the current SNA review, four suggestions are made for revisions to the SAM framework (United Nations Statistical Office, 1986): (1) separating products with different pricing or marketing systems and different cost structures, (2) distinguishing in the value added and final demand sectors different socioeconomic groups of people, (3) separating market from nonmarket activities, and (4) separating the four types of public-sector units, three that generally produce goods and a fourth that produces services. Overall, the aim is to design a flexible set of accounts that can be expanded in different dimensions, depending upon specific policies being analyzed.

Throughout the SAM literature, emphasis is given to the formulation of an appropriate accounting structure, internal consistency of the accounts, development of relevant estimates for missing data, and documentation of the account structure, estimation procedures, and data sources. Tables are provided with all the detailed data for each country. Most important, Pyatt and his colleagues show how critical well-designed accounts are for economic analysis of distributional issues for developing countries.

CONCLUSION

Our purpose in this chapter has been to provide a review of pioneering efforts and new developments in the construction of accounting systems and input–output accounts. For many studies being made today, entirely new accounting systems may be needed. The world is changing. When accounts were first constructed, economies were basically agricultural; therefore, Quesnay included only agriculture as a productive sector of the economy. Input–output accounts were formulated at a time when manufacturing activities dominated in industrialized countries; consequently, the focus on technologies of manufacturing industries helped to define the initial work on those accounts. New developments in modeling, such as the linkage of input–output and econometric models, input–output and microsimulation models, supply-side and demand-side input–output models, and computable general equilibrium models have underlying implications for new designs of the accounting structure.

Accounting structures should reflect economic, political, social, and cultural institutions, such as the family, military, educational, and financial, existing in a country (Polenske, 1982). None of the present accounts, however, provides an adequate link with prevailing institutional theories, partly because current economic categories are not necessarily useful for a study of quantitative and qualitative relations between institutions. Although SAM accounts have sectors referred to as institutions, an entirely different account design is probably required to clarify the structure and interrelations of the institutions previously mentioned and their changes over time. The type and structure of institutions in each country affect the distributions existing between different socioeconomic groups, regions, and the relationship of the country to the global community. The field of institutional theory is evolving. A simultaneous reformulation of the theory and the construction of a relevant accounting structure to study institutions and their effect on people may prove extremely productive.

A second important new development may be the increased use of computer information–management systems for the collection and assembly of accounting data. With the use of computers, it is now possible to have accounting data no more than a year old. Automation also makes it feasible to construct accounts detailing the internal structure of establishments and to link those data into a comprehensive accounting system for the region and nation in which the firm is located and then to a global account. In this way, the increasing economic interdependencies in the world can be studied at the micro and macro levels simultaneously.

Many other exciting new ideas should help to revitalize interest in accounts, their conceptual framework, the measurement of data, and links between accounts, institutions, theories, and policies.

ACKNOWLEDGMENTS

Many colleagues provided me with comments on earlier drafts of this chapter. I especially thank Ranko Bon, Ronald E. Miller, Boris Pleskovic, Graham Pyatt, and Adam Rose. Needless to say, I accept responsibility for any errors and for the viewpoints expressed.

REFERENCES

Abe, K. 1986. "Input–Output Tables in Japan and Application for Interregional Analysis." Paper presented at the Eighth International Conference on Input–Output Techniques, Sapporo, Japan, July 28–August 2.

Bandman, M. K., ed. 1980. *Territorial Industrial Complexes: Optimisation Models and General Aspects*, translated by H. Campbell Creighton. Moscow: Progress Publishers.

Bond, Daniel L. 1974. "A Comparison of the Soviet and U.S. Multiregional Interindustry Accounts." Paper presented at the Inaugural Convention of the Eastern Economic Association, Albany, NY, October 27.

Chenery, Hollis. 1953. "Regional Analysis." In *The Structure and Growth of the Italian Economy*, edited by H. Chenery and P. Clark. Rome: Mutual Security Agency, pp. 96–115.

Cline, William R. 1972. *Potential Effects of Income Redistribution on Economic Growth: Latin American Cases*. New York: Praeger.

Dervis, Kemal, Jaime DeMelo, and Sherman Robinson. 1982. *General Equilibrium Models for Development Policy*. Cambridge, England: Cambridge University Press.

Duncan, Joseph W., and William C. Shelton. 1978. *Revolution in United States Government Statistics: 1926–1976*. Washington, D.C.: Office of Federal Statistical Policy and Standards, U.S. Department of Commerce.

Ellman, Michael. 1972. *Soviet Planning Today: Proposals for an Optimally Functioning Economic System*. Cambridge, England: Cambridge University Press.

[Jack] Faucett Associates, Inc. 1983. "The Multiregional Input–Output Accounts, 1977: Introduction and Summary. Vol. I (Final Report). Prepared for the U.S. Department of

Health and Human Services, Washington, D.C. Chevy Chase, MD: Jack Faucett Associates, Inc.

Filipic, Petar. 1986. "Input–Output Model as the (Quantitative) Basis of a Self-Management Planning System." Paper presented at the Eighth International Conference on Input–Output Techniques, Sapporo, Japan.

Fløttum, Erling J. 1981. *National Accounts of Norway: System and Methods of Estimation*. Oslo, Norway: Central Bureau of Statistics.

Golladay, Fredrick L., and Robert H. Haveman. 1977. *The Economic Impacts of Tax-Transfer Policy: Regional and Distributional Effects*. New York: Academic Press.

Granberg, A. G. 1976. *Spatial National Economic Models*. Novosibirsk, Union of Soviet Socialist Republics: The USSR Academy of Sciences, Siberian Branch, Institute of Economics and Industrial Engineering.

Isard, Walter. 1951. "Interregional and Regional Input–Output Analysis: A Model of a Space Economy." *The Review of Economics and Statistics*. Vol. 33, pp. 318–328.

Isard, Walter, et al. 1960. *Methods of Regional Analysis: An Introduction to Regional Science*. Cambridge, MA: The M.I.T. Press.

Ivanov, Youri. 1987. "Possibilities and Problems of Reconciliation of the SNA and MPS." *The Review of Income and Wealth*. Series 33, pp. 1–18.

King, Benjamin B. 1981. *What Is a SAM? A Layman's Guide to Social Accounting Matrices*. World Bank Staff Working Paper No. 463. Washington, D.C.: The World Bank (June).

Kuczynski, Marguerite, and Ronald L. Meed, eds. 1972. *Quesnay's Tableau Économique*. New York: Augustus M. Kelly Publishers.

Leontief, Wassily. 1936. "Quantitative Input and Output Relations in the Economic System of the United States." *The Review of Economic Statistics*. Vol. 18, pp. 105–125.

Leontief, Wassily W. 1941. *The Structure of American Economy, 1919–1929*: An Empirical Application of Equilibrium Analysis. Cambridge, MA: Harvard University Press.

Leontief, Wassily W. 1951. *The Structure of American Economy, 1919–1939*: An Empirical Application of Equilibrium Analysis. New York: Oxford University Press.

Leontief, Wassily. 1953. "Interregional Theory." In *Studies in the Structure of the American Economy*, edited by Wassily Leontief et al. New York: Oxford University Press, pp. 93–115.

Leontief, Wassily. 1964. "The Balance of the Economy of the USSR." In *Foundations of Soviet Strategy for Economic Growth*, edited by Nicolas Spulber. Bloomington, Indiana: Indiana University Press.

Leontief, Wassily, Anne P. Carter, and Peter Petri. 1977. *The Future of the World Economy*. New York: Oxford University Press.

Leontief, Wassily, and Alan Strout. 1963. "Multiregional Input–Output Analysis." In *Structural Interdependence and Economic Development*, edited by Tibor Barna. New York: St. Martin's Press, pp. 119–150.

Miernyk, William H., Ernest R. Bonner, John H. Chapman, Jr., and Kenneth Shellhammer. 1967. *Impact of the Space Economy on a Local Economy: An Input–Output Analysis*. Morgantown, WV: West Virginia University Library.

Miyazawa, Kenichi. 1976. *Input–Output Analysis and the Structure of Income Distribution*. New York: Springer-Verlag.

Moses, Leon N. 1955. "The Stability of Interregional Trading Patterns and Input–Output Analysis." *American Economic Review*. Vol. 45, pp. 803–832.

National Bureau of Economic Research. 1954. *Input–Output Analysis: Technical Supplement*. Conference on Income and Wealth. Princeton, NJ: Princeton University Press.

National Bureau of Economic Research. 1955. *Input–Output Analysis: An Appraisal*. Vol. 18. Princeton, NJ: Princeton University Press.

National Bureau of Economic Research. 1958. *The National Economic Accounts of the United States: Review, Appraisal, and Recommendations*. (A Report by the National Accounts Review Committee.) New York: Arno Press.

Pai, Gregory G. Y. 1979. "Environmental Pollution Control Policy: An Assessment of Regional Economic Impacts." Ph.D. Dissertation. Cambridge, MA: Department of Urban Studies and Planning, Massachusetts Institute of Technology.

Palacios, Luis Carlos, Ricardo Infante, and Irene Niculescu. 1982. "Venezuela: Matriz Nacional de Insumo-Producto: 1978." Caracas, Venezuela: Facultad de Arquitectura y Urbanismo, Universidad Central de Venezuela.

Pleskovic, Boris. 1982. "A Methodology of Fiscal Incidence Using Social Accounting Matrix Framework and the Harberger Model." Ph.D. Dissertation. Cambridge, MA: Department of Urban Studies and Planning, Massachusetts Institute of Technology.

Pleskovic, Boris, and Gustavo Treviño. 1985. *The Use of a Social Accounting Matrix Framework for Public-Sector Analysis: The Case Study of Mexico.* Ljubljana, Yugoslavia: International Center for Public Enterprises in Developing Countries.

Polenske, Karen R. 1970. "A Multiregional Input–Output Model for the United States." EDA Report No. 21. Prepared for the Economic Development Administration, U.S. Department of Commerce, Washington, D.C. Cambridge, MA: Harvard Economic Research Project.

Polenske, Karen R. 1980. *The U.S. Multiregional Input–Output Accounts and Model.* Lexington, MA: Lexington Books, D.C. Heath.

Polenske, Karen R. 1982. "Constructing and Implementing Multiregional Models for the Study of Distributional Impacts." In *International Use of Input–Output Analysis*, edited by Reiner Stäglin. Göttingen, Germany: Vandenhoeck & Ruprecht, pp. 131–173.

Polenske, Karen R. 1988. "Chinese Input–Output Research in Western Perspective." Revised version of paper presented at the Eighth International Conference on Input–Output Techniques, Sapporo, Japan, July 28–August 2.

Polenske, Karen R., Carolyn W. Anderson, Richard Berner, William R. Buechner, Bo Carlsson, Orani Dixon, Peter Dixon, W. Norton Grubb, Frans Kok, Mary M. Shirley, and John V. Wells. 1972. *State Estimates of the Gross National Product, 1947, 1958, 1963.* Lexington, MA: Lexington Books, D.C. Heath.

Polenske, Karen R., Carolyn W. Anderson, Orani Dixon, Roger M. Kubarych, Mary M. Shirley, and John V. Wells. 1974. *State Estimates of Technology, 1963.* Lexington, MA: Lexington Books, D.C. Heath.

Popov, P. I. 1964. "Balance Sheet of the National Economy as a Whole." In *Foundations of Soviet Strategy for Economic Growth*, edited by Nicolas Spulber. Bloomington, IN: Indiana University Press.

Pyatt, Graham. 1987. "Public Enterprises: A SAM Perspective." Paper prepared for the International Centre for Public Enterprises in Developing Countries, Ljubljana, Yugoslavia. Coventry, England: Department of Economics, University of Warwick (March).

Pyatt, Graham, and Jeffery I. Round. 1977. "Social Accounting Matrices for Development Planning." *Review of Income and Wealth.* Series 23, pp. 339–364.

Pyatt, Graham, and Jeffery I. Round. 1985. *Social Accounting Matrices: A Basis for Planning.* Washington, D.C.: The World Bank.

Pyatt, Graham, and Eric Thorbecke. 1976. *Planning Techniques for a Better Future.* Geneva: International Labour Office.

Pyatt, Graham, Alan R. Roe, and associates. 1977. *Social Accounting for Development Planning: With Special Reference to Sri Lanka.* Cambridge, England: Cambridge University Press.

Pyatt, Graham, Julian Bharier, Robert Lindley, Robert Mabro, and Yves Sabolo. 1972. "A Methodology for Development Planning Applied to Iran." Report prepared for Comprehensive Employment Mission to Iran, World Employment Programme, International Labour Office. Warwick, England (February).

The Review of Income and Wealth. 1986. Series 33, No. 1 (March).

Robinson, Sherman. 1988. "Multisectoral Models of Developing Countries: A Survey." In *Handbook of Development Economics*, edited by H. B. Chenery and T. N. Srinivasan. Amsterdam: North-Holland.

Rodgers, John M. 1972. *State Estimates of Outputs, Employment, and Payrolls,* 1947, 1958, 1963. Lexington, MA: Lexington Books, D.C. Heath.

Rodgers, John M. 1973. *State Estimates of Interregional Commodity Trade,* 1963. Lexington, MA: Lexington Books, D.C. Heath.

Scheppach, Raymond C., Jr. 1972. *State Projections of the Gross National Product,* 1970, 1980. Lexington, MA: Lexington Books, D.C. Heath.

Shalizi, Zmarak M. 1979. "Multiregional Input–Output Multipliers and the Partitioned Matrix Solution of the Augmented MRIO Model." Ph.D. Dissertation. Cambridge, MA: Department of Urban Studies and Planning, Massachusetts Institute of Technology.

Social Welfare Research Institute, Boston College; Multiregional Planning Staff, Massachusetts Institute of Technology; and Sistemas, Inc. 1980. "MRPIS: A Research Strategy: A Policy Impact Study for Developing a Multiregional Policy Impact Simulation (MRPIS) Model." Prepared for the Assistant Secretary for Planning and Evaluation, U.S. Department of Health and Human Services (March).

Spulber, Nicolas, and Kamran Moayed Dadkhah. 1975. "The Pioneering Stage in Input–Output Economics: The Soviet National Economic Balance 1923–24, After Fifty Years." *The Review of Economics and Statistics.* Vol. 57, pp. 27–34.

Stone, Richard. 1970. *Mathematical Models of the Economy and Other Essays.* London: Chapman and Hall Ltd.

Stone, Sir Richard. 1985. "The Disaggregation of the Household Sector in the National Accounts." In *Social Accounting Matrices: A Basis for Planning,* edited by Graham Pyatt and Jeffery I. Round. Washington, D.C.: The World Bank, pp. 145–185.

Taylor, Lance. 1979. *Macro Models for Developing Countries.* New York: McGraw-Hill.

United Nations. 1966. *Problems of Input–Output Tables and Analysis.* Studies in Methods, Series F, No. 14. New York: United Nations.

United Nations. 1968. *A System of National Accounts.* Studies in Methods, Series F, No. 2, Rev. 3. New York: United Nations.

United Nations. 1973. *Input–Output Tables and Analysis.* Studies in Methods, Series F, No. 14, Rev. 1. New York: United Nations.

United Nations Industrial Development Organization (UNIDO). 1985. *Input–Output Tables for Developing Countries.* Vienna, Austria: UNIDO.

United Nations Industrial Development Organization (UNIDO). 1986. "Inventory Lists of Input–Output Tables." Vienna, Austria: UNIDO.

United Nations Statistical Office. 1986. "Input–Output Standards in the SNA Framework." In *Problems of Compilation of Input–Output Tables,* edited by Alfred Franz and Norbert Rainer. Vienna, Austria: Verlag Orac.

U.S. Department of Commerce. 1980. *Definitions and Conventions of the 1972 Input–Output Study.* Bureau of Economic Analysis Staff Paper BEA-SP 80-034 (July). Washington, D.C.: Bureau of Economic Analysis.

U.S. Department of Labor, Bureau of Labor Statistics. n.d. "The 1947 Interindustry Relations Study: Industry Reports." Washington, D.C.: U.S. Department of Labor, Bureau of Labor Statistics.

U.S. Department of Labor, Bureau of Labor Statistics. 1955. *Factbook for Estimating the Manpower Needs of Federal Programs.* BLS Bulletin No. 1832. Washington, D.C.: U.S. Government Printing Office.

Webster, S. S. 1985. "A Social Accounting Matrix for Swaziland, 1971–1972." In *Social Accounting Matrices: A Basis for Planning,* edited by Graham Pyatt and Jeffery I. Round. Washington, D.C.: The World Bank, pp. 108–125.

Weisskoff, Richard. 1970. "Income Distribution and Economic Growth in Puerto Rico, Argentina, and Mexico." *Review of Income and Wealth.* Vol. 16 (December), pp. 303–332.

5

Descriptive versus Analytical Make-Use Systems: Some Austrian Experiences

NORBERT RAINER

According to a recent survey made by the United Nations Statistical Office (UNSO) on country practices in the compilation of input–output tables (UNSO, 1986a), only 24 of 53 countries have fully adopted the System of National Accounts (SNA) recommendations (United Nations, 1968a) to distinguish explicitly between make and absorption matrices. Another UNSO document (UNSO, 1986b) shows that most of the countries using the make-use concept apply the industry technology assumption for the derivation of "pure" input–output tables.

In establishing a make-use system in Austria, we found the SNA concept of separate matrices for outputs and inputs to be very flexible and well suited to accommodate the basic statistical data. By distinguishing a greater number of commodities than industries, we can provide a detailed description of supply and use of the commodity flows of an economy. The separate description of secondary production is perhaps the most important advantage. Furthermore, the make-use system opens additional possibilities for input–output analyses. In addition to the "pure" industry and commodity technology, different kinds of "mixed" technologies can be applied, which are themselves based on a sophisticated simultaneous application of both the industry and commodity technology.

These statistical and analytical advantages do not always seem to be fully recognized: analysts in most countries still rely on traditional methods, and those applying the SNA concept derive technology matrices solely on the basis of industry technology. However, industry technology alone does not seem suitable to represent the input–output relationships of the whole economy. Application of commodity technology is considered to be more in accordance with the basic input–output philosophy, but it leads to the well-known problem of negative coefficients, a complicated phenomenon that cannot easily be treated. The question is whether the negative figures are the result of a failure in the data or the result of the technology hypotheses? In fact, the answer may be that both are involved. In addition, we can ask whether the make-use data in their original statistical form are at all suitable for any of the technology assumptions.

These considerations lead to the fundamental question regarding the principal character of a make-use system: should the make-use matrices be established according to the statistical data base, or should they be adapted and aligned for analytical purposes? The closer the make-use matrices are to the statistical data base, the less those data will be suited directly for applying technology assumptions, and the more negative coefficients will result when a commodity technology is assumed. In our view, a make-use system is in the first instance an excellent means of accommodating basic data of economic statistics in a consistent way and with minimum adjustments. When using the make and absorption matrices as a basis for technology analysis, we often need various adaptations and data rearrangements. Two kinds of make-use systems should therefore be developed: a descriptive make-use system and an analytical make-use system.

Deriving technology matrices can be done only when some additional assumptions are applied. Technology matrices are not the result of statistics, but the result of a model. This statement might seem a bit strange, because in countries that prepare input–output tables in the conventional way, the compilation work cannot be separated from questions of implicit technology assumptions and analysis. In this sense, conventional input–output tables can also be viewed as a type of model and not only as a statistical data system.

It is our aim to evaluate cautiously such arguments in favor of contrasting, simultaneous concepts of input–output statistics. First, we summarize Austrian experience in implementing a make-use system, with particular attention to the Austrian statistical concepts that have been applied in view of the above-mentioned distinction between a descriptive and an analytical version of the make-use concept.[1] Second, we discuss the problems and options of deriving merged tables. Third, we introduce that analytical version of the Austrian make-use system that formed the basis of a published technology version, i.e., industry technology. We then analyze the system on the assumption of commodity technology and discuss the problem of negatives. We argue that adequate data rearrangements better deal with negative coefficients than applying formal methods that cancel out negatives. The basic problems are nonhomogeneities and the nondecomposability of statistical units.

AUSTRIAN 1976 MAKE-USE SYSTEM: DESCRIPTIVE VERSION

With our 1976 input–output project, SNA concepts have been fully applied in Austria for the first time. In the published version, 239 activities (industries) and 204 commodities are distinguished (Österreichisches Statistisches Zentralamt, 1985). The number of activities exceeds the number of commodities because it was not always possible to establish the commodity accounts on the same level of detail used for the respective production accounts. To achieve symmetry between activities and commodities, we aggregated such activities. This results in 189 activities. The 15 extra commodities are primarily commodities that either have no or more than one characteristic producer (e.g., coke, repair services, scrap and waste).

---

1. The Austrian view of a distinction between a descriptive and an analytical system seems to be in some respect analogous to the concept of the core and the building block approach developed by the Dutch national accounts experts for the revision of the SNA (van Bochove and van Tuinen, 1985).

The activity classification of the make-use data is based on the activity code (three-digit level) of the 1968 Standard Industrial Classification (SIC) officially used in Austrian economic statistics. In some instances, we modified the official taxonomy by combining, reclassifying, or breaking down the codes.

The final demand matrix distinguishes thirteen categories: one for the private household final consumption expenditures, two for government expenditures, one for private nonprofit bodies, seven for gross fixed capital formation, one for changes in stocks (at book values), and one for exports.

Value added is shown by ten components, three of which belong to the compensation of employees (wages and salaries, employers' contributions to social security schemes for their employees, and unfunded imputed employee welfare contributions). The indirect taxes and subsidies are each subdivided into three categories: attributable to commodities, not attributable to commodities, and on wages and salaries. The last component of value added comprises the operating surplus combined with consumption of fixed capital.

The commodity flows are valued at producers' prices, net of deductible and nondeductible value-added tax (VAT) and net of import duties. The amounts of VAT and import duties are shown in separate "dummy" sectors, so that value added is equal to Gross Domestic Product (GDP) at market prices. To achieve the uniform valuation at producers' prices, we compiled a full set of distributive margins matrices. Nine types of margins were distinguished: wholesale trade, retail sale, transport by mode of transport (road, railway, water, air, and pipeline), transport forwarding, and transport insurance (Rainer, 1986). On the use side, the Austrian make-use system distinguishes domestic and imported commodities; in other words, separate import matrices are compiled (version B).

The make-use data refer to 1976, because there is a nonagricultural general census covering almost all market production for this year. In this census, data were gathered on the basis of the accounts (cost accounting) of the statistical units. With only a few exceptions, the statistical unit in Austrian economic statistics is the establishment, or an establishment-type unit. In the make-use system not only the market, but also the nonmarket producers have been broken down by activities. Analogous to the establishment unit, the office was chosen as the appropriate statistical unit (Österreichisches Statistisches Zentralamt, 1983).

Specific Concepts

Some specific concepts of the descriptive Austrian make-use system will be summarized. The concepts treated here are those that best show the differences between a descriptive and an analytical system (see also Fleischmann and Rainer, 1986).

Treatment of transactors of the system

In the SNA, three types of transactors are distinguished: market producers (industries), producers of government services, and producers of private nonprofit services. As noted, the nonmarket producers are also broken down by activities. For this the concept of "coincident categories" was introduced (Franz et al., 1982, 1983). Accordingly, the taxonomy of economic activities can be subdivided into three categories:

- Activities in which only market producers can be found [in International Standard Industrial Classification (ISIC) terms, this would be major ISIC groups 1–8];
- Activities solely reserved for nonmarket producers (these are the activities of ISIC group 91);
- "Coincident categories," Activities in which market producers as well as nonmarket producers are engaged (ISIC groups 92–94).

In the resulting make-use system, the make and the absorption matrices are split not only by activities and commodities, but also by transactors and type of commodities (market and nonmarket commodities).

Transformation versus specification

Any production process can be viewed as a transformation process, in which inputs are transformed into new outputs. In the case of government services, the SNA presently adheres to the principle of specification rather than transformation: the purchases of goods and services paid by government but distributed to the households without transformation should be added to the intermediate consumption of government. Such purchases automatically appear as outputs of government, without any distinction from other transformed output. As recently shown (Petre, 1981), this solution is unsatisfactory for several reasons. Therefore, in Austrian input–output statistics, nontransformed production is presented in separate accounts. This separation leads to the distinction between transformed and nontransformed public consumption.

Head offices and other ancillary units

When applying establishments as statistical units, there is always the question of how to deal with overhead costs that are not directly attributable to the establishments. Two possibilities exist: (1) to distribute overhead costs in proportion to gross outputs or value added of the establishments, and (2) to identify head offices and other ancillary units as separate statistical units. The second approach is to some extent applied in the Austrian economic statistics: in large-scale manufacturing, such units are statistically treated as separate establishments. This is done first by determining a gross output of the head offices and other ancillary units and then by attributing this gross output as an input to the other establishments. Gross output of the head offices is measured by their costs, which is a way of determining gross output analogously to nonmarket producers.

These conventions of the basic statistics have been adopted in the descriptive make-use system. Contrary to the basic statistics, the head offices are shown as a separate newly defined group of activities, not included in the basic SIC.

Treatment of repair services and production contracts

In the Austrian SIC, some activities are devoted to repair services and production on a contract basis, such as repair of motor vehicles and textile finishing. The observed input structure differs between production of a certain commodity and its repair and also between production of a commodity on own account and on a contract basis.

In order to differentiate between these kinds of commodities, we attempted to identify the statistical units primarily engaged in production on a contract basis and repair services and to reclassify them with some newly defined activities, so that the SIC was augmented and some new characteristic commodities defined. The procedure of reclassifying did not solve the entire problem, because the greater part of such services was noncharacteristic output of statistical units not primarily engaged in repairing or producing on a contract basis. It seemed best to show such outputs in a descriptive system as specific commodities, even if these commodities do not exactly correspond with the activity classification.

Own-account fixed capital formation

In the case of own-account fixed capital formation, the practice of commercial accounting suggests two alternative treatments:

- Gross treatment: all the costs connected with the production of such fixed assets are entered as inputs (materials and wages) and are accordingly included in the gross output;
- Net treatment: in the production accounts, only the payment of wages appear as production costs; the costs for the materials are directly assigned to fixed capital formation.

Both ways of treating own-account fixed capital formation can be found in the statistical data. For input–output purposes, the gross treatment is clearly the better way; however, in the descriptive make-use system, the net data have not been converted to a gross basis.

In summary, the Austrian descriptive make-use system can be characterized as a system of commodity and production accounts that comes close to the concepts and peculiarities of the statistical data basis and comprises all the specific SNA concepts of the production, consumption, and capital formation accounts. All the necessary imputations are included (e.g., VAT, import duties, imputed bank services charges) and shown in separate accounts.

Choices and Problems of Deriving "Pure" Input–Output Tables

Input–output analysts confront several important problems when deriving pure tables.

Problem of secondary output

The main advantage of the SNA concept is that secondary production is statistically exhibited separately. Thus, different kinds of treatment become possible under an analytical view. Obviously, the problems are more important the higher the share of secondary production. This will be particularly true if the underlying statistical units are enterprises rather than establishments and if the system is rather disaggregated.

There is extensive literature about the typology of the noncharacteristic production and its "best" treatment for input–output analysis (see, for example, United Nations, 1968a, 1973; Stone, 1961; Bulmer-Thomas, 1982). A minimum list of different kinds of noncharacteristic production comprises subsidiary products, by-products, and joint products. The methods of merging are conventionally divided into two groups: transfers of outputs alone and transfers of inputs and outputs.

Transfers of outputs alone   At least two methods—particularly for treating by-products—can be found in the literature (see, for example, United Nations, 1973; UNSO, 1986b):

- Treatment of secondary products as a positive input into the industry for which this kind of secondary product is principal, and
- Treatment as a negative input in the industry in which it is produced.

Both of these treatments result in unsatisfactory shortcomings in input–output analyses.

Transfers of inputs and outputs   A distinction can be made between methods that rely solely on one technology assumption (either industry or commodity technology) and methods based on hybrid assumptions, two of which are treated in the SNA. Other forms of hybrid assumptions are those by Gigantes (1970), Armstrong (1975), and recently ten Raa et al. (1984). These methods of merging the output and the input table are, of course, much more satisfactory than the methods of transfer of outputs alone; the same applies to the hybrid technologies compared with the industry or commodity technology alone. Because the hybrid methods are a combination of both the industry and commodity technology, we can assume that in the end all these methods are combinations of more or less mechanical procedures. Therefore, we argue that such methods should always be scrutinized and supplemented by "manual" methods of data rearrangements and redefinitions, as suitable. Such methods may be employed before applying any technology assumptions or during the technology-based merging procedure, or afterward (e.g., to eliminate negative coefficients). We prefer applying redefinitions before using mechanical methods.

Four questions and options

Four major questions or options have to be considered before a given make-use system is recast as an input–output table.

Industry technology versus commodity technology assumptions   Only the extreme assumptions are discussed. The *industry technology assumption* raises no problems of negative coefficients and the mechanical method of reweighting the input structures of the absorption matrix is easy to understand. The industry technology assumption has been criticized because it presumes fixed market shares. The main point of criticism should be the inadequacy of the assumption as compared with "reality." Being aware of this fact, analysts in some countries redefine the data before applying the assumption. In the United States, for instance, these redefinitions relate to secondary construction output, secondary output of wholesale and retail services, and secondary rental output (Young, 1986). In this way, extreme and unrealistic reweighting of the input structures can be avoided, but the question is how many and for what kinds of secondary output such "manual" redefinitions should be applied?

From a theoretical point of view, the *commodity technology assumption* seems to be more appropriate for most secondary outputs. The problem with this assumption is the possible negative elements. Three techniques have been applied for the removal of negative coefficients:

1. Set the negatives to zero;
2. Estimate the input coefficients by an iterative process and set any emerging negatives to zero at each stage of the iteration (Almon, 1972);
3. Set the majority of the negatives to zero, but, in some cases, replace the negatives by a positive value; make compensating adjustments in other entries to maintain the totals unchanged (Armstrong, 1975).

There are many different reasons for negative values to emerge, and it is these reasons that should determine the treatment of the negatives. In that sense, a negative value is only one, although a particularly conspicuous, indicator of a problem. Stahmer (1985) proposes a modified transformation procedure based on the commodity technology assumption using special transformation matrices for certain rows and columns, thus influencing the procedure and making use of additional data.

Commodity-by-commodity versus industry-by-industry tables   In the SNA and in the input–output literature, commodity-by-commodity and industry-by-industry matrices are treated as two equivalent possibilities. The question raised is whether these two possibilities are equivalent alternatives? In the case of a commodity-by-commodity table, the entries show the input of commodity *i* necessary for the production of commodity *j* and in the case of an industry-by-industry table, the input of industry *i* necessary for the production of the output of industry *j*. As each industry may have noncharacteristic output, the flows in the industry-by-industry table are necessarily nonhomogeneous, which conflicts with one of the main assumptions of input–output analysis. When applying the commodity technology in the industry-by-industry variant, we find that the number of negative coefficients is greater than with the commodity-by-commodity version.

Rectangular versus square tables   Some countries distinguish many more commodities than industries in their make-use data (see, for example, Lal, 1982, for Canada, and Thage, 1982, for Denmark). The advantage of rectangular make and absorption matrices is that the commodity flows of an economy can be shown in much more detail. However, when these tables form the basis of derivation of pure input–output tables, there is one important limitation: the commodity technology assumption (and the mixed technologies assumption) cannot be applied. On the basis of a rectangular system with, for instance, 100 industries and 1500 commodities, it is possible to derive merged tables on the industry technology assumption of the industry-by-industry type (100×100) as well as the commodity-by-commodity type (1500×1500). The input structures for the 1500 commodities, however, would be the results of reweighting of the given input structures of the 100 industries only. Thus, an industry-by-industry table would be the only possibility (Thage, 1986). When applying the commodity technology assumption, the 1500 commodities have to be aggregated to 100 commodities; therefore, the question arises of how a possible trade-off between disaggregation and technology assumption is viewed (Olsen, 1985).

Descriptive versus analytical basic data   Our discussion of the use of descriptive versus analytical data concentrates on the data structure itself, rather than on analytical choices. Therefore, to what extent should the basic data be adapted so as best to fit the technology assumption applied? This can be illustrated by the distinction between a descriptive and an analytical version of the make-use system. For the integration of detailed production and commodity accounts within the conventional national accounts framework, a data structure close to the statistical data basis is advantageous.

It is clear that starting from such a descriptive system, some data rearrangements will be unavoidable to yield an analytical data base. The question that should always be raised is whether the data structure is adequate with a view to the technology assumption. In that sense, more than one analytical version will result. For one technology assumption, certain data rearrangements might be appropriate, whereas for another, additional or other types of reallocations might seem useful. Later, we illustrate this issue by means of the Austrian data system.

DERIVING AN ANALYTICAL MAKE-USE SYSTEM

Austrian experiences in deriving pure input–output tables on the basis of a make-use system are summarized here. Particular reference is made to the redefinition part of the derivation process, which transforms the descriptive make-use system into an analytical one. By a series of aggregations and certain redefinitions, the descriptive system illustrated earlier was transformed into a square system (Österreichisches Statistisches Zentralamt, 1986a). In the following, this analytical version is referred to as the basis for further discussion of needed data rearrangements and redefinitions. For simplicity, we concentrate on the commodity technology assumption only, leaving aside the mixed technologies assumption.

Derivation of the 175×175 Basic Data

Between the 1976 descriptive make-use system and the 175×175 analytical variant, the following redefinitions and aggregations have been applied.

Removal of certain "dummy" sectors

As in the national accounts, the VAT and import duties are shown as separate sectors; therefore, in the descriptive make-use system, these two indirect taxes are treated as dummy industries and dummy commodities, respectively. Another sector removed was the imputation of own-account residential building construction. Because of lack of data, this imputation was estimated on a net basis (i.e., gross output = value added).

Treatment of imputed bank services charges

In the descriptive version, bank service charges are treated as delivered to a dummy sector with zero gross output. For analytical purposes, some data rearrangements are necessary. Three ways of distributing the service charges are possible[2]:

1. Transfer to final demand as a whole;
2. Distribute over intermediate and final demand sectors;
3. Distribute over intermediate sectors only, where again two different methods are possible: allocating to the banking sector as a whole and allocating over diverse intermediate sectors.

In Austria, we used a variation of the last method: the imputed bank services charges were distributed over the activities of the market producers according to their gross output.

Derivation of a square table

Four steps led from the nonsquare descriptive system to a system of square matrices:

Step 1. In the case in which either the commodity breakdown or the activity breakdown was more detailed than the respective activity or commodity breakdown, simple aggregation was applied.

Step 2. As shown earlier, the descriptive variant differentiates on the activity side three types of transactors (market producers, producers of government services, and producers of private nonprofit services) and on the commodity side two types of commodities (market and nonmarket commodities, distinguishing between nonmarket sales and own-account consumption). For input–output purposes, all these differentiations were omitted by simple aggregation.

Step 3. By-products, such as scrap, and two other commodities (coke and alcohol) that are produced characteristically by more than one industry are shown in the descriptive version separately. They were redefined as principal products of those industries that have each produced them as part of their secondary output.

Step 4. In addition to scrap, several commodities on the activity level in the descriptive version lack exact correspondence: four commodities for repair and six commodities for production on a contract basis. In order to yield a square table, a simple approach was used, namely, to redefine these commodities with principal products, being aware that this is not the optimum solution.

In addition to these procedures, some minor aggregations were applied, so that the final make-use system consisted of 175 industries and 175 commodities. As a result of these procedures (redefinitions and aggregations), the average percentage of noncharacteristic output diminished to 9.4 percent, compared with 10.3 percent in the descriptive version.

Results of the Commodity Technology Assumption

Commodity technology was applied to the (primary) analytical make-use system in version A. The overall results, particularly for negative values, are summarized as follows.

2. For different country practices, see UNSO (1986b).

In the resulting flow tables, the total is of course equal to the total of the absorption matrix, namely, the sum of domestic and imported commodities used in the production process. In the 1976 Austrian table, this sum amounts to 594,622 million Austrian Schillings (AS), that is, 40.1 percent of total supply. The total of negative values when the commodity technology is applied amounts to

8,441 million AS (1.4 percent of total intermediate use), in the case of commodity-by-commodity, and

29,735 million AS (5.0 percent of total intermediate use), in the case of industry-by-industry.

Thus, the negative values in the industry-by-industry table are 3.5 times higher than in the commodity-by-commodity table. This holds true not only for the total, but also for most of the 175 commodities and industries individually. Table 5-1 shows the structure of the negative values for both the commodity-by-commodity and industry-by-industry variant. Although in the commodity-by-commodity table, the inputs of 32 commodities do not show any negative values, there are only 5 industries for which this holds true in the industry-by-industry table. For about one-half of the commodities, the input structure shows either no negative values or values that amount to less than 1 percent of the respective total inputs, which may not seem worthy of any more sophisticated treatment. In the case of the industry-by-industry table, only 9 percent of the industries have either no negative values or values that are less than 1 percent.

As noted above, the problem of negative values is to some extent not a widespread phenomenon. This is also the case using absolute values: the negative values in the input of just 24 commodities comprise 60.1 percent of the total negatives; for the 46 commodities with the highest negatives, this share reaches 79.7 percent. In the following we refer to the commodity-by-commodity table only.

Data Rearrangements Suggested by Negative Values

We assumed that negative figures in the merged tables indicate problems yet to be solved, either in the data or in the adequacy of the technology assumption. In fact, the assumption of a commodity technology seems to be unsuitable for some secondary products. The output of chemical products of the mineral oil industry, for example, would be better represented by the assumption of an industry technology.[3] We do not, however, intend to discuss this question further. Nor do we intend to discuss those peculiarities of the 175×175 analytical variant, in which the data rearrangements shown above are clearly insufficient for the commodity technology.

The commodity technology is rather stringent since it is assumed that for each commodity there is only one specific technology, but the data on which the commodity technology is applied are not for single commodities but for aggregates. If the basic assumption of specific inputs for each (single) commodity holds true, the negative figures are a consequence of nonhomogeneity. Furthermore, the industries are aggregates of statistical units, like establishments. As a rule, they are not singular

---

3. A problem, of course, is how to determine those outputs that should better be subject to the industry technology assumption. In this context, Franz (1986) proposes that the activity classifications themselves should give support in that they incorporate the distinction between "input" and "process" as different criteria of a classification structure.

TABLE 5-1. Comparison of Negative Inputs in the Commodity-by-Commodity and Industry-by-Industry Flow Table: Commodity Technology, Austria 1976

| | Number of | |
| | Commodities | Industries |
Negative Inputs as a Percentage of Total Intermediate Input (Percent)	Commodity-by-Commodity Input–Output Matrix	Industry-by-Industry Input–Output Matrix
0	32	5
0–1	60	11
1–2	27	18
2–3	9	19
3–5	15	48
5–10	18	49
More than 10	14	25
Total	175	175

output units. The production accounts show only the commodities that are flowing into the statistical units and that come out. They do not show what happens within the statistical units.

In the following, these considerations are illustrated by the analysis of negative figures:

- As shown earlier, head offices are partly identified separately in the basic statistics and are aggregated as separate sectors in the descriptive version. Applying the commodity technology, we obtain negative figures for 650 million AS (7.6 percent of all negatives). The reason is that head offices are identified separately only for large-scale manufacturing. Accordingly, for an analytical version of the commodity technology assumption there must be some data rearrangements.
- In the descriptive version, there is one industry characteristically producing and distributing electricity within this branch as well as to the users outside. That internal distribution is shown on a gross basis, so that a rather high input coefficient of electricity results. This yields negative inputs of electricity in some of the activities that are also delivering electricity to other users. The noncharacteristic output of electricity usually comprises production only, but no distribution. The negatives amount to about 200 million AS (2.3 percent of all negatives). In the case of an industry technology, the treatment of the descriptive version seems to be better suited; otherwise, the technology assumption "reweights" all the inputs needed by noncharacteristic producers of electricity accordingly. Using the commodity technology, we should treat the distribution better as a "margin." The ideal solution, however, would be to disaggregate the data into a production and distribution sector.
- It is frequently the case that a noncharacteristic output comprises only a part of the commodity bundle defined as characteristic output. This leads to negative figures if the effective technologies within this bundle are different. An instructive example is the output of services of confectioners and cafeterias of the bakery industry. As

there is only one industry and commodity for hotels and all kinds of restaurants (including cafeterias) combined, the commodity technology results in negative inputs of meat for bakery products. The only way to solve the problem is to disaggregate (or to aggregate bakeries with hotels and restaurants).

- In the above example, the commodity bundle can be disaggregated into different commodities, all belonging to the same stage in the production chain. Yet, there are some commodities in which more than one stage of the production chain is incorporated, thus leading to large flows along the main diagonal of the input matrix. If there is a noncharacteristic output at the first step in the production chain, this must clearly result in negatives.
- A similar problem arises when there are different commodities for each of the stages in the production chain, but with vertical concentration in the statistical units, for example, mining and manufacturing of mining products. Such a data constellation yields negative inputs of mining products in the mining industry when this industry also manufactures mining products. One possible data rearrangement could be to convert the outputs and inputs of mining products in the mining industry to a gross basis.

These examples should show that there are very different reasons for the existence of negatives and that these are not necessarily caused by failure in the data. However, it seems to be more useful to try to adapt the data than to apply some mechanical methods for cancelling negatives: if there are some negatives, there are also some positives that are too high. All problems cannot be solved by data rearrangements, for example, service inputs (in which 8.2 percent of the total negative values can be observed): there the commodity technology must be considered too stringent, and hybrid methods do not help either. The problems encountered in the case of negatives can be viewed as the problem of approximation of a model (that is commodity technology) to reality (measured by the statistical data).

CONCLUSION

A statistical system—such as the make and absorption system—is, in the first instance, a set of consistent data compiled under certain concepts and rules. The most important feature of the make-use system is that the concept of the production and commodity accounts fully coincides with the surveyability of the micro information. A descriptive make-use system will show the actual flows of statistical units. This provides insight into the real structure of the way units organize their production activities. An analytical system has to meet some additional requirements based on the input–output model. The descriptive system may serve as the basis for the derivation of an analytical system.

The discrepancies between statistical possibilities and the requirements of the input–output model also exist when the data base is a make-use system, whereas in a conventional input–output model these problems are somehow "solved" in the implementation phase by the statisticians. These discrepancies are exhibited on the basis of a make-use system explicitly. The negative coefficients in the case of the commodity technology assumption are nothing more than the numerical expression of these problems. A possible way of treating these problems seems to be to apply various kinds of data rearrangements and to some extent to cancel negatives. Such rearrangements will themselves be a kind of a model, however, and should be kept separate from the compilation of the basic data system.

ACKNOWLEDGMENTS

The author is indebted to A. Franz and J. Richter for valuable comments on an earlier draft and to M. Biczo who did the electronic data processing work.

REFERENCES

Almon, Clopper. 1972. "Investment in Input–Output Models and the Treatment of Secondary Products." In *Applications of Input–Output Analysis*, edited by Anne P. Carter and Andrew Bródy. Amsterdam-London: North-Holland, pp. 103–116.

Armstrong, A. G. 1975. "Technology Assumptions in the Construction of U.K. Input–Output Tables." In *Estimating and Projecting Input–Output Coefficients*, edited by R.I.G. Allen and W. F. Gossling. London: Input–Output Publishing Co., pp. 68–93.

Bulmer-Thomas, Victor. 1982. *Input–Output Analysis in Developing Countries*. New York: John Wiley.

Fleischmann, Eduard, and Norbert Rainer. 1986. "How to Define Gross Output? A Review of Borderline Cases." In *Problems of Compilation of Input–Output Tables*, edited by Alfred Franz and Norbert Rainer. Proceedings of an International Meeting organized by the Austrian Statistical Society, Baden, Austria, May 1985. Vienna: Verlag Orac, pp. 447–459.

Franz, Alfred. 1986. "Supplementary Breakdown of Activity and Commodity Classifications for Input–Output Purposes." In *Problems of Compilation of Input–Output Tables*, edited by Alfred Franz and Norbert Rainer. Proceedings of an International Meeting organized by the Austrian Statistical Society, Baden, Austria, May 1985. Vienna: Verlag Orac, pp. 461–469.

Franz, Alfred, Eduard Fleischmann, and Norbert Rainer. 1982. "Some Reflections on the Integration of Government Services." In *Input–Output Techniques*, Proceedings of the Third Hungarian Conference on Input–Output Techniques. Budapest, Hungary, pp. 64–74.

Franz, Alfred, Eduard Fleischmann, and Norbert Rainer. 1983. "Activity-by-Function Approach for Government in IO-Statistics." Contributed paper to the 18th General Conference of the International Association for Research in Income and Wealth, August 1983, Luxemburg.

Gigantes, T. 1970. "The Representation of Technology in Input–Output Systems." In *Contributions to Input–Output Analysis*, edited by Anne P. Carter and Andrew Bródy. Amsterdam-London: North-Holland, pp. 270–290.

Lal, Kishori. 1982. "Compilation of Input–Output Tables: Canada." In *Compilation of Input–Output Tables*, edited by Jiri Skolka. New York: Springer, pp. 8–36.

Olsen, J. Asger. 1985. "Adaptation of Detailed Input–Output Information: Restructuring and Aggregation." *The Review of Income and Wealth*. Series 31, No. 4 (December), pp. 397–411.

Österreichisches Statistisches Zentralamt (Austrian Central Statistical Office). 1983. "Produktionskonten für die öffentlichen Dienste, Make- und Absorptionsmatrizen (Production Accounts for Producers of Government Services, Make and Absorption Matrices)." Input-Output-Statistik, Vorberichte, Vol. 4. Vienna, Austria.

Österreichisches Statistisches Zentralamt (Austrian Central Statistical Office). 1985. "Input–Output-Tabelle, 1976." Band 1, *Güter- und Produktionskonten* ("Input–Output Table, 1976." Vol. 1, *Commodity and Production Accounts*).

64   *Alternative Accounting Frameworks*

Österreichisches Statistisches Zentralamt (Austrian Central Statistical Office). 1986a. "Input–Output-Tabelle 1976." Band 2, *Technologiematrizen* ("Input–Output Table, 1976." Vol. 2, *Technology Matrices*). Vienna, Austria.

Österreichisches Statistisches Zentralamt (Austrian Central Statistical Office). 1986b. "Input–Output-Tabelle, 1976." Band 3, *Bewertungsvarianten, Investitionsmatrix, Beschäftigte* ("Input–Output Table, 1976." Vol. 3, *Variants of Valuation, Investment Matrix, Employment*). Vienna, Austria.

Petre, Jean. 1981. "The Treatment in the National Accounts of Goods and Services for Individual Consumption Produced, Distributed, or Paid for by Government." Paper presented at the 17th General Conference of the International Association for Research in Income and Wealth, Gouvieux, France, August 1981.

Rainer, Norbert. 1986. "The Set of Trade and Transport Margin Matrices in the Austrian IO-System." In *Problems of Compilation of Input–Output Tables*, edited by Alfred Franz and Norbert Rainer. Proceedings of an International Meeting organized by the Austrian Statistical Society, Baden, Austria, May 1985. Vienna: Verlag Orac, pp. 47–68.

Stahmer, Carsten. 1985. "Transformation Matrices in Input–Output Compilation." In *Input–Output Modeling*, edited by Anatoli Smyshlyaev. New York: Springer, pp. 225–236.

Stone, Richard. 1961. *Input–Output and National Accounts*. Paris: OECD.

ten Raa, Thijs, Debesh Chakraborty, and J. Anthony Small. 1984. "An Alternative Treatment of Secondary Products in Input–Output Analysis." *Review of Economics and Statistics*. Vol. 66, pp. 88–97.

Thage, Bent. 1982. "Techniques in the Compilation of Danish Input–Output Tables: A New Approach in the Treatment of Imports." In *Compilation of Input–Output Tables*, edited by Jiri Skolka. New York: Springer, pp. 138–162.

Thage, Bent. 1986. "Balancing Procedures in the Detailed Commodity Flow System Used as a Basis for Annual Input–Output Tables in Denmark." In *Problems of Compilation of Input–Output Tables*, edited by Alfred Franz and Norbert Rainer. Proceedings of an International Meeting organized by the Austrian Statistical Society, Baden, Austria, May 1985. Vienna: Verlag Orac, pp. 233–262.

United Nations. 1968a. *A System of National Accounts*. Series F, No. 2, Rev. 3, New York: United Nations.

United Nations. 1968b. *International Standard Industrial Classification*. Series F, No. 14, Rev. 1, New York: United Nations.

United Nations. 1973. *Input–Output Tables and Analysis*. Series F, No. 14, Rev. 1, New York: United Nations.

United Nations Statistical Office. 1986a. "Input–Output Standards in the SNA Framework." In *Problems of Compilation of Input–Output Tables*, edited by Alfred Franz and Norbert Rainer. Proceedings of an International Meeting organized by the Austrian Statistical Society, Baden, Austria, May 1985. Vienna: Verlag Orac, pp. 525–566.

United Nations Statistical Office. 1986b. "Study of the Country Practices in Implementing the SNA Input–Output Framework in the 70's." Report to the Working Party on National Accounts and Balances, 3–7 March 1986, CES/WP.22/82/Add.1.

van Bochove, C. A., and H. K. van Tuinen. 1985. "Revision of the System of National Accounts: The Case for Flexibility." Paper presented at the 19th General Conference of the International Association for Research in Income and Wealth, Noordwijkerhout, The Netherlands, August 1985.

Young, Paula C. 1986. "The U.S. Input–Output Experience—Present Status and Future Prospects." In *Problems of Compilation of Input–Output Tables*, Compilation of Input–Output Tables, edited by Alfred Franz and Norbert Rainer. Proceedings of an International Meeting organized by the Austrian Statistical Society, Baden, Austria, May 1985. Vienna: Verlag Orac, pp. 121–145.

6

Toward an Input–Output Subsystem for the Information Sector

REINER STÄGLIN

Over the last decade increasing attention has been given to the information sector or the information economy, particularly with regard to the "information revolution" as an argument for structural changes in advanced economies. Two different research lines have been followed. Analysts have concentrated, on the one hand, on the impact of new information technology on employment and economic development, and on the other hand, on the relevance of information activities and information occupations and their collection in the so-called fourth sector or information sector.

Numerous publications and research papers were produced in the debate on the consequences of microelectronic technology (Bundesministerium für Wissenschaft und Forschung, 1981; Ernst, 1982; Kaplinsky, 1985; Rathenau, 1980), new generations of computers (OTA, 1984; Peitchinis, 1984), robotics and word processors (Hunt and Hunt, 1983; OECD 1982), computer-controlled machine tools (Leontief and Duchin, 1986; Roessner, 1984), and revolutionary advances in communications technology (Eliasson, 1982; Soete, 1985; Zeman, 1979). An excellent synopsis of many of these works is given by Freeman and Soete (1985) in their assessment on information technology and employment.

There are not many publications that emphasize information activities. The origins of this research can be traced to the pioneering books by Machlup (1962) on *Production and Distribution of Knowledge in The United States* and by Bell (1973) on *The Coming of Post-Industrial Society.* Over the past 10 years, some sociologists and economists, such as Masuda (1980), Stornier (1984), and Wallace (1986), took this information route and emphasized the trend toward the information society by stressing the growth of information-related occupations in every industry. Many analysts refer to this approach to the information sector. Some of them describe the economies of information (Arrow, 1980), the computerization of society (Nora and Minc, 1980), and the fourth economic sector (DIW, 1986, Ch. 4; Gassmann, 1981); others deal with the new service economy (Gershuny and Miles, 1983), the postindustrial economy (Stornier, 1984), or the information economy itself (Karunaratne, 1984; Porat and Rubin, 1977). Studies are also available that depict the information market (DIW and IFO, 1986), and the production of knowledge (Machlup, 1980), but in all information studies, the methodology for measuring the volume of information activities is not dealt with in detail.

To understand the methodology, we refer to the efforts of the Organisation for Economic Co-operation and Development (OECD) in the field of Information, Computer, and Communications Policy (ICCP), particularly to the questionnaire for updating the information-related data base (OECD, 1981, 1982, 1986), and to the connected DIW Information Report (1984). Additionally, the contributions of Karunaratne (1986) and Lamberton (1982) have to be taken into account.

The OECD staff have proposed standardized concepts and catalogues of "informational" and "noninformational" activities (goods, services, and occupations) to ensure intercountry comparisons with regard to the size of the information sector as a percentage of gross domestic product (GDP) at factor cost. The correspondingly collected data for the Federal Republic of Germany by the German Institute for Economic Research (DIW Information Report, 1984) have shown that a classification of goods and services as "informational" and "noninformational" according to the guidelines of the OECD causes some confusion. This can be overcome by using the input–output framework. An input–output table reveals the interdependencies between intermediate and final outputs and allows for the distinction between informational and noninformational activities if an input–output subsystem for the information sector can be developed (see also Karunaratne, 1986). Such an informational subsystem corresponds to the extension of the traditional input–output framework to account for interindustry energy flows and for environmental issues (Miller and Blair, 1985, Chs. 6 and 7).

DEFINITION OF THE INFORMATION SECTOR

The OECD (1981) analysis in the field of Information, Computer, and Communications distinguishes three separate, yet related, types of information activities:

- the primary information sector,
- the secondary information sector, and
- the information occupations.

The primary information sector includes "goods and services which intrinsically convey information (such as books) or which are directly useful in its production, processing, or distribution (such as computers). Further, these goods and services must be transacted on established markets" (OECD, 1981, p. 21). The secondary information sector records the value added by information activities used in producing noninformation goods and services, which mainly include employee compensation of information workers and depreciation on information capital. The information occupations, measured as a proportion of the total labor force employed, include those employees who produce information (scientific and technical, consultative services, etc.), process information (administrative and managerial, clerical and related, etc.), and distribute information (educators, communication workers, etc.) as well as persons employed in the information infrastructure (information machine workers, postal and telecommunications workers, etc.).

We will concentrate on the primary information sector for which the OECD staff have proposed a rather voluminous inventory of goods and services that are assumed to be informational, comprising final products as well as intermediate goods. This inventory is based on the International Standard Industrial Classification (ISIC) of all economic activities (United Nations, 1971).

Although this OECD catalogue of primary information sector components offers a base for estimating the value-added contribution of the production of information goods and services, methodological problems arise with regard to intermediate products: The glass curved for clocks and watches is included in the inventory, but the parts of iron and steel for clockworks, for instance, are not. The same is true for chips produced in electrical engineering. They are classified as noninformational, although automatic switching devices, which include various kinds of chips, are listed with the ISIC category. These problems and some corresponding classification difficulties with respect to double-counting and omissions can be shown only on the basis of an input–output table, which divides total production into intermediate and final output and allows an analyst to assess the indirect production needs of the information sector. Though the input–output idea has not yet been adopted by the OECD, the DIW (1984) has made a first attempt following these lines when updating and improving the data base on information activities for the Federal Republic of Germany as presented in the ICCP Report No. 6. This first step has to be followed by other investigations to provide an improved approach, probably that of an informational input–output subsystem as presented in this chapter.

AN INPUT–OUTPUT SUBSYSTEM FOR THE PRIMARY INFORMATION SECTOR

The use of an input–output framework is helpful in collecting and arranging data on information goods and services according to the categories of gross production and intermediate and final demand, because it ensures consistency with macroeconomic variables. In addition, the possibility of disaggregating intermediate demand according to production sectors enables the evaluation of interdependencies between the primary information sector and other parts of the economy. In an informational input–output subsystem, therefore, the definitions and classifications should correspond to those of an available input–output table.

Framework of an Informational Input–Output Subsystem

The idea of an input–output subsystem for the primary information sector is given in Figure 6-1, in which the different matrices of this system are defined.[1] Matrix A reflects the starting point. It shows the traditional input–output table extended by breaking down each of the n production sectors into an informational part, I, and a noninformational part, NI. The theoretical (hypothetical) framework of matrix A includes three separate tables on information activities: an informational output table, a corresponding input table, and an informational input and output table. In these tables, three issues of the primary information sector are represented: the output pattern of information goods and services to noninformational parts of the various sectors and to final demand components (matrix B), the input pattern of information goods and services from noninformational suppliers and from primary inputs (matrix C), and the output and input pattern within the informational parts of the different sectors 1 to n (matrix D).

1. A first definition of these informational matrices was presented at the Sixth Starnberger Kolloquium zur Weiterentwicklung der Volkswirtschaftlichen Gesamtrechnungen (Sixth Colloquium in Starnberg on further development on national accounts) (Stäglin, 1988).

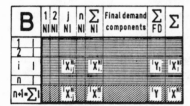

FIGURE 6-1   Matrices of an informational input–output subsystem. (A) Input–output table with an informational (I) and noninformational (NI) breakdown. (B) Informational output table. (C) Informational input table. (D) Informational input and output table.

The three informational matrices form the input–output subsystem for the primary information sector. This can also be seen from Figure 6-2 with the final input–output table (matrix E), in which the information sector is shown as sector $n + 1$. The different hatching of rows and columns shows the coincidence among the three informational matrices B, C, and D, the theoretical basis of matrix A, and the final input–output matrix E. If the detailed listing of the primary information sector components in matrix E (Figure 6-2) is disregarded, the output pattern and the input pattern of the information sector $n + 1$ as a whole ($\sum I$) can be taken from the matrices B, C, and D (Figure 6-1). The column totals of the informational output table yield the row distribution of the primary information sector in the final input–output matrix E, the row totals of the input table result in the column distribution, and the overall total of the intrasectoral informational input and output table adds the intrasectoral cell $^{I}x^{I}$. These interconnections can be confirmed by the specified elements in the different matrices.

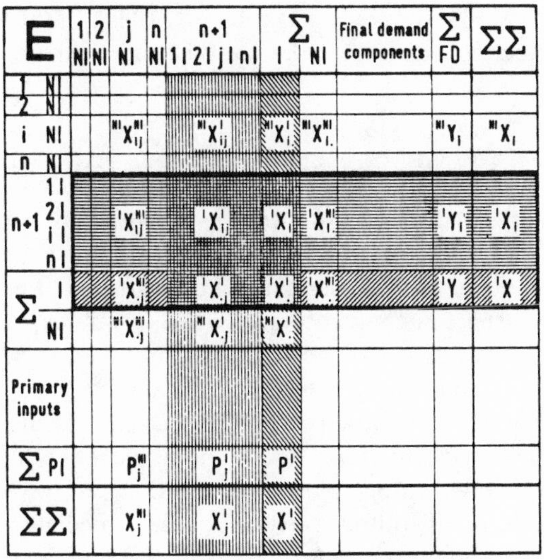

FIGURE 6-2 Input–output table with a separate primary information sector.

It should be emphasized that the informational input–output system developed so far is limited to the primary information sector, that is, it excludes the secondary information sector.[2] Additionally, the primary information sector is not completely recorded: imported information goods and services are not yet taken into account explicitly. They also can be divided into intermediate inputs and final goods. The intermediate imports are used for producing information goods and services, but also for noninformation outputs.

Partial Implementation of an Informational Input–Output Subsystem

Although the input–output subsystem for the primary information sector is still incomplete, it has been partially implemented by the DIW in the process of data collection on information activities for the Federal Republic of Germany. Figures 6-1 and 6-2 indicate the kind of data collected on information goods and services and their arrangement according to the input–output subsystem. This can be seen as well from parts of the matrices B, D, and E. It concerns all rows of the informational output table and all elements of the informational input and output table. Thus, the output distribution of the separate primary information sector can be shown (matrix E). By eliminating the informational parts I from matrix A, we can also derive the noninformational parts NI, summarized in matrix E.

The procedure of compiling the output pattern of the primary information sector

2. The secondary information sector is included in the input–output approach followed by Karunaratne (1986, pp. 18–21). He does not start with the empirical disaggregation of an input–output table, but he makes use of the input–output method by introducing "information intensity coefficients." These coefficients are also used to generate the primary information economy on the basis of the industry technology assumption. This implies that information intensity of intermediate inputs is proportional to the informational intensity prevailing in the total sectoral output, which is not the case in the DIW input–output approach.

is described in detail in the DIW Information Report (1984). In the following sections we present a summary, concentrating on the needs of an informational input–output subsystem.

Output data for the primary information sector in 1980

The starting point of the data collection was given with the institutionally based input–output table for 1980 compiled by the DIW. This table contains 60 sectors of production, 6 components of final demand, and 7 components of primary inputs and was published as a wall-chart in cooperation with Spektrum der Wissenschaft (1985). For our purpose the table was aggregated into 12 production sectors. A detailed description of the classification is available from the author.

The input–output table was used twice: first, as a classification scheme for allocating the ISIC items of informational goods and services to branches and, second, as a basis for estimating the output pattern of the different information products according to the detailed input–output categories of intermediate and final demand. The figures on 1980 production of information goods and services were mainly collected from statistics of the Federal Statistical Office on manufacturing, on taxable turnover, on foreign trade, and from national accounts. Compilation problems arise because of scarce statistical data and missing counterparts of ISIC items in the official German nomenclature.

Table 6-1 shows the aggregated information for the 1980 production value of informational ISIC items listed in the OECD inventory and the distribution of these items to total intermediate and final demand. Furthermore, the noninformation goods and services belonging to the 12 sectors of origin are shown. The addition of the data for informational and noninformational activities results in the totals. Hence, it is possible to calculate the informational goods and services as a percentage of the total (informational and noninformational) deliveries.

Informational output table and informational input and output table for 1980

The implementation of the informational output table (matrix B) and of the informational input and output table (matrix D) enables us to calculate all output elements of the primary information sector in matrix E. The informational output table in Table 6-2 shows the deliveries of the information goods and services according to their sectors of origin and destination. The purchasing sectors are divided into noninformational sectors and final demand components. It can be seen from Table 6-2 that the noninformational part of the service sector (11) purchases most information goods and services, followed by the trade and transport sector (10). Within the final demand components, private and government consumption covers most of the informational output. The intersectoral flows between the informational part and the noninformational part of the 12 production sectors reflect the different importance of information activities.

The same is true for the transaction values in Table 6-3 although they reflect informational flows only. In this informational input and output table, the rows and columns represent the informational part of the production sectors, that is, Table 6-3 shows the intrasectoral transactions within the primary information sector expressed by $n + 1$ in matrix E of Figure 6-2. Analyzing the results, we see that the service sector

TABLE 6-1 Intermediate Demand, Final Demand, and Gross Production for Informational and Noninformational Goods and Services in the Federal Republic of Germany, 1980[a] (Million DM[b] and Percent)

Sector		(1–12) Intermediate Demand	(13–17) Final Demand	(1–17) Gross Production
1. Agriculture	Informational	5	—	5
	Noninformational	48,709	15,926	64,635
	Inform. (% of total)	0.01	—	0.01
2. Energy, Mining	Informational	530	240	770
	Noninformational	98,347	36,923	135,270
	Inform. (% of total)	0.54	0.65	0.57
3. Chemical	Informational	1,927	3,136	5,063
	Noninformational	195,210	138,611	333,821
	Inform. (% of total)	0.98	2.21	1.49
4. Metals	Informational	—	—	—
	Noninformational	77,617	39,710	117,327
	Inform. (% of total)	—	—	—
5. Mach, Veh	Informational	5,395	19,139	24,534
	Noninformational	74,371	225,564	299,935
	Inform. (% of total)	6.76	7.82	7.56
6. Electric	Informational	9.975	36,614	46,589
	Noninformational	59,827	85,122	144,949
	Inform. (% of total)	14.29	30.08	24.32
7. Timb, Tex	Informational	21,166	10,071	31,237
	Noninformational	52,102	82,945	135,047
	Inform. (% of total)	28.89	10.83	18.79
8. Food, Bev	Informational	—	—	—
	Noninformational	67,455	119,293	186,748
	Inform. (% of total)	—	—	—
9. Construc	Informational	—	13,504	13,504
	Noninformational	23,446	158,724	182,170
	Inform. (% of total)	—	7.84	6.90
10. Trade, Tr	Informational	27,471	30,458	57,929
	Noninformational	157,553	177,547	335,100
	Inform. (% of total)	14.85	14.64	14.74
11. Services	Informational	155,524	85,452	240,976
	Noninformational	75,749	182,538	258,287
	Inform. (% of total)	67.25	31.89	48.27
12. Pub, Priv	Informational	6,616	76,469	83,085
	Noninformational	7,070	120,425	127,495
	Inform. (% of total)	48.34	38.84	39.46
(1–12)	Informational	228,609	275,083	503,692
	Noninformational	937,456	1,383,328	2,320,784
	Inform. (% of total)	19.61	16.59	17.83

Source: New calculations on the basis of the DIN information report (1984) and input–output accounting.
[a]Sector definitions are available from the authors. Inform., Informational.
[b]DM, Deutsche Mark.

TABLE 6–2 Informational Output Table for the Federal Republic of Germany, 1980[a] (Million DM[b] at Current Prices)

Sector	1 Agricult	2 Energy, M	3 Chemical	4 Metals	5 Mach, Veh	6 Electric	7 Timb, Tex	8 Food, Bev	9 Construc
1. Agricult	5	—	—	—	—	—	—	—	—
2. Energy, M	—	530	—	—	—	—	—	—	—
3. Chemical	4	6	47	13	58	36	21	27	27
4. Metals	—	—	—	—	—	—	—	—	—
5. Mach, Veh	12	77	518	223	644	488	281	226	307
6. Electric	3	16	116	50	2,705	2,581	68	36	74
7. Timb, Tex	11	369	1,239	371	982	811	1,699	1,053	703
8. Food, Bev	—	—	—	—	—	—	—	—	—
9. Construc	—	—	—	—	—	—	—	—	—
10. Trade, Tr	202	403	2,030	433	2,135	2,108	1,138	979	861
11. Services	6,227	2,577	6,991	3,873	9,088	4,435	4,436	5,237	6,082
12. Pub, Priv	176	148	541	212	647	338	280	440	338
(1–12)	6,640	4,126	11,482	5,175	16,259	10,797	7,923	7,998	8,392

Sector	10 Trade, Tr	11 Services	12 Pub, Priv	(1–12) Intern Demand	13+14 Pr + Gov Consump	15+16 Cap. Form + Stocks	17 Exports	(13–17) Final Demand	(1–17) Gross Product
1. Agricult	—	—	—	5	—	—	—	—	5
2. Energy, M	—	—	—	530	—	—	240	240	770
3. Chemical	209	119	40	607	462	56	2,618	3,136	3,743
4. Metals	—	—	—	—	—	—	—	—	—
5. Mach, Veh	466	497	58	3,797	962	7,128	11,049	19,139	22,936
6. Electric	152	186	13	6,000	7,685	6,599	22,330	36,614	42,614
7. Timb, Tex	1,352	1,482	120	10,192	4,664	1,376	4,031	10,071	20,263
8. Food, Bev	—	—	—	—	—	—	—	—	—
9. Construc	—	—	—	—	—	13,504	—	13,504	13,504
10. Trade, Tr	6,059	3,551	490	20,389	26,132	2,867	1,459	30,458	50,847
11. Services	20,675	25,906	2,624	98,151	76,249	4,295	4,908	85,452	183,603
12. Pub, Priv	843	2,132	164	6,259	76,254	63	152	76,469	82,728
(1–12)	29,756	33,873	3,509	145,930	192,408	35,888	46,787	275,083	421,013

Source: New calculations on the basis of the DIN information report (1984) and input–output accounting.
[a]Sector definitions are available from the author.
[b]DM, Deutsche Mark.

TABLE 6–3 Informational Input and Output Table for the Federal Republic of Germany, 1980[a] (Million DM[b] at Current Prices)

Sector	1 Agricult	2 Energy, N	3 Chemical	4 Metals	5 Mach, Veh	6 Electric	7 Timb, Tex
1. Agricult	—	—	—	—	—	—	—
2. Energy, M	—	—	—	—	—	—	—
3. Chemical	—	—	—	—	2	322	809
4. Metals	—	—	—	—	—	—	—
5. Mach, Veh	—	—	10	—	83	104	89
6. Electric	—	1	14	—	385	2,901	46
7. Timb, Tex	—	1	62	—	149	464	2,482
8. Food, Bev	—	—	—	—	—	—	—
9. Construc	—	—	—	—	—	—	—
10. Trade, Tr	—	—	26	—	268	282	490
11. Services	—	3	54	—	371	402	1,278
12. Pub, Priv	—	—	—	—	16	—	36
(1–12)	—	5	166	—	1,274	4,475	5,230

Sector	8 Food, Bev	9 Construc	10 Trade, TR	11 Services	12 Pub, Priv	(1–12)
1. Agricult	—	—	—	—	—	—
2. Energy, M	—	—	—	—	—	—
3. Chemical	—	—	17	170	—	1,320
4. Metals	—	—	—	—	—	—
5. Mach, Veh	—	5	48	1,253	6	1,598
6. Electric	—	1	395	229	3	3,975
7. Timb, Tex	—	221	342	7,239	14	10,974
8. Food, Bev	—	—	—	—	—	—
9. Construc	—	—	—	—	—	—
10. Trade, Tr	—	35	457	5,484	40	7,082
11. Services	—	168	1,776	53,245	76	57,373
12. Pub, Priv	—	—	9	296	—	357
(1–12)	—	430	3,044	67,916	139	82,679

Source: New calculations on the basis of the DIM information report (1984) and input–output accounting.
*Sector definitions are available from the author.
*DM. Deutsche Mark.

(11) appears as the most important branch on the output side as well as on the input side. Only 52 of the 144 cells of the estimated informational input and output table contain figures.

USE AND FURTHER DEVELOPMENT

The definition of an input–output subsystem for the information sector as well as the compilation of the two informational matrices have shown that it is beneficial to express the primary information sector as a subsystem of an input–output table. The matrices of this informational input–output subsystem can be used for empirically oriented structural analysis as they depict the composition of the fourth sector. They reflect the importance of information activities in the different sectors of production. An intertemporal analysis of these matrices for several years would show the internal versus the external development of information goods and services.

The input–output subsystem for the information sector (matrix E in Figure 6-2) can also be used for measuring the direct and indirect information content of final demand. This approach includes the Leontief inverse, multipliers, and linkages (Karunaratne, 1986). In addition, many of the evaluations that are feasible for energy and environmental input–output analysis (Miller and Blair, 1985, Chs. 6 and 7) can be performed for the primary information sector, too. By integrating the occupation-by-sector matrices, that is, one component of the secondary information sector, we also can compute the information-induced employment effects. Further development of the informational input–output subsystem can contribute to an extension of the statistics on services, one of the important issues for structural analysis of the "services society."

One aspect has priority for future explorations: the estimation of input patterns of the primary information sector including a disaggregation in accordance with the informational parts of the different production sectors (matrix C). Independent from this proceeding, the OECD inventory on information goods and services should be improved by covering the conceptional understanding of the input–output framework. Finally, the secondary information sector has to be included in the input–output subsystem to estimate the size of all information activities in the Federal Republic of Germany.

ACKNOWLEDGMENT

I would like to express thanks to my colleague Mrs. Ingrid Ludwig for contributing to this chapter.

REFERENCES

Arrow, K. J. 1980. "The Economies of Information." In *The Computer Age: A Twenty-Year View*, edited by M. L. Dertonzos and J. Moses. Cambridge, MA: MIT Press.

Bell, D. 1973. *The Coming of Post-Industrial Society: A Venture in Social Forecasting.* New York: Basic Books.

Bundesministerium für Wissenschaft und Forschung. 1981. *Mikroelektronik, Anwendungen, Verbreitung und Auswirkungen am Beispiel Österreichs* (Micro-electronics: Use, Diffusion, and Repercussions Shown for Austria as Example). Vienna.

DIW/Deutsches Institut für Wirtschaftsforschung. 1984. "Information Activities: Updating and Improving the Data Base for the Federal Republic of Germany," ICCP (Information, Computer, and Communications Policy) Report No. 6, By R. Filip-Köhn, G. Neckermann, and R. Stäglin (DIW) in cooperation with W. Dostal (IAB) and J. Seetzen (Heinrich-Hertz Institute). Forschungsprojekt im Auftrag des Bundesministers für Forschung und Technologie. (Research project for the Federal Ministry of Research and Technology) (December). Berlin.

DIW/Deutsches Institut für Wirtschaftsforschung. 1986. "Die Nutzung von grenzüberschreitendem Datenfluss (GDF) in der Bundesrepublik Deutschland und ihre gesamtwirtschaftliche Bedeutung." Gutachten im Auftrag des Bundesministers für Wirtschaft. (The Use of Intercountry Data Flows in the Federal Republic of Germany and Their Economic Importance). (Report for the Federal Ministry of Economic Affairs) (January). Berlin.

DIW and IFO/Deutsches Institut für Wirtschaftsforschung und IFO-Institut für Wirtschaftsforschung. 1986. "Wirtschaftsinformation in der Bundesrepublik Deutschland—Schwachstellen und Verbesserungsmöglichkeiten." Teil I: "Zusammenfassung und Schlussfolgerungen." Gutachten im Auftrag des Bundesministers für Wirtschaft. (Economic Information in the Federal Republic of Germany—Weak Points and Possibilities to Improve. Part I: Summary and Conclusions). (Report for the Federal Ministry of Economic Affairs) (August). München.

Eliasson, G. 1982. "Electronics, Economic Growth and Employment—Revolution or Evolution." IVI. Booklet No. 131. Stockholm.

Ernst, D. 1982. *The Global Race in Micro-Electronics: Innovation and Corporate Strategies in a Period of Crisis.* Frankfurt: Campus.

Freeman, C., and L. Soete. 1985. "Information Technology and Employment: An Assessment." Science Policy Research Unit (April). Brighton, England: University of Sussex.

Gassmann, H. P. 1981. "Is There a Fourth Economic Sector?" *OECD Observer* (November), Paris.

Gershuny, I., and I. Miles. 1983. *The New Service Economy—the Transformation of Employment in Industrial Society.* New York: Praeger.

Hunt, H. A., and T. L. Hunt. 1983. *The Human Resource Implications of Robotics.* Kalamazoo, Michigan: Upjohn Institute for Employment Research.

Kaplinsky, R. 1985. *Micro-electronics and Employment.* Geneva: International Labour Organization.

Karunaratne, N. D. 1984. "Planning for the Australian Information Economy." *Information Economics and Policy.* Vol. 1, pp. 365–367.

Karunaratne, N. D. 1986. "Empirics of the Information Economy." Paper presented at the Eighth International Conference on Input–Output Techniques, 28 July–2 August, Sapporo, Japan.

Lamberton, D. 1982. "The Theoretical Implications of Measuring the Communication Sector." In *Communication Economics and Development*, edited by M. Jussawalla and D. Lamberton. New York: Pergamon Press.

Leontief, W. and F. Duchin. 1986. *The Future Impact of Automation on Workers.* New York: Oxford University Press.

Machlup, F. 1962. *The Production and Distribution of Knowledge in the United States.* Princeton, NJ: Princeton University Press.

Machlup, F. 1980. *Knowledge and Knowledge Production.* Princeton, NJ: Princeton University Press.

Masuda, Y. 1980. *The Information Society.* Tokyo: Institute for the Information Society.

Miller, R. E., and P. D. Blair. 1985. *Input–Output Analysis: Foundations and Extensions.* Englewood Cliffs, NJ: Prentice-Hall, pp. 200–265.

Nora, S., and A. Minc. 1980. *The Computerization Society: A Report to the President of France.* Cambridge, MA: MIT Press.

OECD [Organisation for Economic Co-operation and Development]. 1981. "Information Activities, Electronics and Telecommunications Technologies. Impact on Employment, Growth and Trade." ICCP Report No. 6. Vol. 1. Paris: OECD, pp. 34–38.

OECD. 1982. "Micro-electronics, Robotics, and Jobs." Paris: OECD, Committee for Information, Computer and Communications Policy.

OECD. 1986. "Trends in the Information Economy." ICCP. Paris: OECD.

OTA. 1984. "Computerized Manufacturing Automation: Employment, Education and the Workplace." Washington, D.C.: Office of Technology Assessment. Congress of the United States. OTA-CIT 235 (April).

Peitchinis, S. 1984. *Computer Technology and Employment: Retrospect and Prospect*. London: St. Martin's Press.

Porat, M. U., and M. R. Rubin, 1977. *The Information Economy*. OTC. Washington D.C.: Government Printing Office.

Rathenau, W. 1980. "The Social Impact of Microelectronics" (The Rathenau Report). The Hague: Government Publishing Office.

Roessner, D. S. 1984. "Impact of Office Automation on Office Workers." Vol. 2. Atlanta, GA: Georgia Institute of Technology (April).

Soete, L. 1985. *Technological Trends and Employment: 3, Electronics and Communications*. London: Gower Press.

Spektrum der Wissenschaft in Zusammenarbeit mit dem DIW. 1985. Input/Output-Struktur für die Wirtschaft der Bundesrepublik Deutschland. Input/Output-Wandtafel. (Input–Output Structure for the Economy of the Federal Republic of Germany. Input–Output Wall-Chart). Heidelberg and Berlin.

Stäglin, R. 1988. "Der Informationssektor als Satellitensystem der Input–Output-Rechnung". (The Information Sector as Satellite System of Input–Output Accounting). In Schriftenreihe Forum der Bundesstatistik. Band 5. Edited by Statistisches Bundesamt. Stuttgart and Mainz.

Stornier, T. 1984. *The Wealth of Information. A Profile of the Post-Industrial Economy*. London: Thomas Methuen.

United Nations. 1971. *ISIC*. Series M. No. 4. Revision 2. Add. 1. New York: United Nations.

Wallace, D. 1986. "Introduction to Information Society. Text/Workbook with "Hands-On" Microcomputer Exercises." Philadelphia, PA: Institute for Information Studies (July).

Zeman, P. 1979. "The Impact of Computer/Communications on Employment in Canada: Overview of Current OECD Debates." Montreal: Institute for Research on Public Policy.

7

Multiplier Analyses in Social Accounting and Input–Output Frameworks: Evidence for Several Countries

SOLOMON I. COHEN

In the past decade, there has been a noticeable shift of interest from the basic input–output table to the social accounting matrix (SAM) as evident from the increased momentum in the design, construction, and use of social accounting matrices in developing countries (Pyatt and Roe, 1977; Cohen et al., 1984; Pyatt and Round, 1985). The argument in favor of working with the SAM or extended input–output models is the increasingly prevalent requirement by policy-makers and the larger public in developing and developed countries alike to appraise, in addition to production objectives, those development objectives pertaining to income policy and the allotment of basic provisions and obligations among population groups.

The purpose of this chapter is to examine the use of SAM multipliers as a solid framework for gaining insight into development policy on issues of growth and distribution and for conducting international comparisons on the structure of socioeconomic systems of different countries. The increased availability of SAMs provides a good opportunity for this type of analysis.

For purposes of exposition, we start with Colombia and extend the analysis at a later stage to a comparison of 10 countries: Colombia, Suriname, Egypt, Kenya, India, Indonesia, Iran, Korea, Pakistan, and Sri Lanka. First, the SAM for Colombia is introduced. Second, the matrix is used as an aid, though limited, in predicting the course of the economy. Third, multipliers and their decomposition into transfer, open-, and closed-loop effects are analyzed. Fourth, results of the multiplier analysis for the 10 countries are compared.

CHARACTERISTICS

Social accounting matrices are compiled according to the same accounting principles used for input–output tables; each transaction is recorded twice so that any inflow to one account must be balanced by an outflow of another account. SAMs contain a complete list of accounts describing income, expenditure, transfers, and production flows:

(1.0) Wants account;
(2.0) Factors-of-production account;
(3.0) Institutions account, which can be further disaggregated by type of institution as far as current transactions are concerned:
    (3.1) Households account,
    (3.2) Firms account,
    (3.3) Government account, and
    (3.4) Institutions capital account;
(4.0) Activities account; and
(5.0) Rest of the world account.

These accounts have been disaggregated to give a 33 dimension 1970 SAM for Colombia in Table (7-1). The first set of accounts in Table 7-1 is the wants accounts. Rows 1 through 6 contain one large block of entries on the intersections with columns 10 through 19, giving the breakdown of final consumer demand over the six wants categories and over the ten household groups. The outflows of the wants account, columns 1 through 6, are entered as inflows to the activities account, rows 23 through 30. This block of entries converts the broad categories of consumer demand, such as food, into the more well-known sectoral classification. The next set of accounts is the factor account, showing, for instance, that the largest part of urban labor income originates in the services sectors, while the largest source of rural labor income is agriculture. Next are the institutional current accounts. The receipts of the different institutions are directly readable from their respective rows, while the expenditures are found in their respective columns, and so on.

ESTIMATION

In order to obtain consistency within the SAM, we made the account aggregates in Table 7-1 consistent with the Colombia national accounts statistics, as published by the Banco de la Republica (BR). The next step was to use other data sources to break down these aggregates into the detailed categories indicated in Table 7-1. In particular, there are two main types of other data sources.

The first type of data used is the input–output table, based upon the manufacturing survey and published by Departamento Administrativo Nacional de Estadistica (DANE). This gives slightly higher final demand and factor cost, about 2 percent more than the BR national accounts, although BR and DANE show differences in certain categories of final demand of between plus and minus 6 percent (Cohen and Jellema, 1986).

The second type of data used is the 1971 Household Income and Expenditure Survey of DANE. This source overestimates total household income and expenditure by margins of 6 and 14 percent, respectively. The survey estimates have been downscaled accordingly (for details, see Cohen and Jellema, 1986).

Finally, the submatrix that converts private consumption categories in the wants account to final demand categories in the activities account has been made consistent by applying the RAS method to a converter matrix obtained from DANE and the predetermined column and row totals of private consumption and final demand categories, respectively.

TABLE 7-1   Disaggregated SAM, Colombia, 1970[a]

	Want Account					
	1	*2*	*3*	*4*	*5*	*6*
Want account						
1 Food	—	—	—	—	—	—
2 Nonfood	—	—	—	—	—	—
3 Housing	—	—	—	—	—.	—
4 Health	—	—	—	—	—˙	—
5 Education	—	—	—	—	—	—
6 Other social services	—	—	—	—	—	—
Factor account						
7 Urban labor rem.	—	—	—	—	—	—
8 Rural labor rem.	—	—	—	—	—	—
9 Gross profits	—	—	—	—	—	—
Institutional current account						
10 Urban employed	—	—	—	—	—	—
11 Urban worker	—	—	—	—	—	—
12 Urban capitalist	—	—	—	—	—	—
13 Urban self-employed	—	—	—	—	—	—
14 Urban inactive	—	—	—	—	—	—
15 Rural employed	—	—	—	—	—	—
16 Rural worker	—	—	—	—	—	—
17 Rural capitalist	—	—	—	—	—	—
18 Rural self-employed	—	—	—	—	—	—
19 Rural inactive	—	—	—	—	—	—
20 Firms	—	—	—	—	—	—
21 Government	—	—	—	—	—	—
Capital Account						
22 Aggr. Capital account	—	—	—	—	—	—
Activities account						
23 Agriculture	13661.6	23.5	425.3	—	—	148.5
24 Mining	—	3.7	67.9	—	—	54.4
25 Processed coffee	853.7	—	—	—	—	—
26 Industry	29885.2	12034.2	43.0	1064.2	—	1628.1
27 Elect., gas, and water	—	—	—	—	—	934.1
28 Modern services	—	751.6	13626.8	—	—	3378.5
29 Personal services	—	7739.5	—	1944.3	3632.0	1207.6
30 Govt. services	33.8	394.5	68.4	69.0	99.3	90.7
Indirect taxes account						
31 Indirect taxes	—	—	—	—	—	—
32 Import duties	—	—	—	—	—	—
Rest-of-the-world account						
33 Rest of the world	—	—	—	—	—	—
34 Total	44434.3	20947.0	14231.4	3077.5	3731.3	7441.8

TABLE 7-1 Disaggregated SAM, Colombia, 1970[a] (*Continued*)

	Factor Account			Institutional Current Account		
	7	8	9	10	11	12
Want account						
1 Food	—	—	—	11280.4	3461.9	1140.6
2 Nonfood	—	—	—	6433.6	1623.9	779.1
3 Housing	—	—	—	4837.8	953.8	567.6
4 Health	—	—	—	745.9	304.6	177.5
5 Education	—	—	—	1387.8	237.9	223.2
6 Other social services	—	—	—	2542.6	298.5	711.2
Factor account						
7 Urban labor rem.	—	—	—	—	—	—
8 Rural labor rem.	—	—	—	—	—	—
9 Gross profits	—	—	—	—	—	—
Institutional current account						
10 Urban employed	13259.4	—	16625.7	—	—	—
11 Urban worker	6866.2	—	—	—	—	—
12 Urban capitalist	1392.4	—	2694.9	—	—	—
13 Urban self-employed	9304.8	—	16419.1	—	—	—
14 Urban inactive	4528.7	—	6502.3	—	—	—
15 Rural employed	—	1208.7	958.1	—	—	—
16 Rural worker	—	5526.7	—	—	—	—
17 Rural capitalist	—	481.0	1178.5	—	—	—
18 Rural self-employed	—	5486.4	4304.2	—	—	—
19 Rural inactive	—	1271.1	822.3	—	—	—
20 Firms	—	—	15492.4	—	—	—
21 Government	—	—	1882.2	1767.9	148.3	490.8
Capital account						
22 Aggr. capital account	—	—	—	1130.2	−109.3	20.1
Activities account						
23 Agriculture	—	—	—	—	—	—
24 Mining	—	—	—	—	—	—
25 Processed coffee	—	—	—	—	—	—
26 Industry	—	—	—	—	—	—
27 Elect., gas, and water	—	—	—	—	—	—
28 Modern services	—	—	—	—	—	—
29 Personal services	—	—	—	—	—	—
30 Govt. Services	—	—	—	—	—	—
Indirect taxes account						
31 Indirect taxes	—	—	—	—	—	—
32 Import duties	—	—	—	—	—	—
Rest-of-the-world account						
33 Rest of the world	—	—	—	173.7	—	3.1
34 Total	35351.5	13973.9	66897.7	30299.7	6919.5	4113.2

TABLE 7–1 *Continued*

	Institutional Current Account					
	13	*14*	*15*	*16*	*17*	*18*
Want account						
1 Food	10680.1	4822.2	1036.6	3830.6	609.2	6016.0
2 Nonfood	5443.9	2240.2	472.8	1172.1	229.9	2156.1
3 Housing	3865.8	2456.4	170.8	353.8	96.3	730.7
4 Health	682.5	426.5	59.6	171.5	46.6	378.5
5 Education	1121.8	366.6	64.1	89.5	29.6	186.1
6 Other social services	2169.5	751.4	169.0	225.9	172.5	299.6
Factor account						
7 Urban labor rem.	—	—	—	—	—	—
8 Rural labor rem.	—	—	—	—	—	—
9 Gross profits	—	—	—	—	—	—
Institutional current account						
10 Urban employed	—	—	—	—	—	—
11 Urban worker	—	—	—	—	—	—
12 Urban capitalist	—	—	—	—	—	—
13 Urban self-employed	—	—	—	—	—	—
14 Urban inactive	—	—	—	—	—	—
15 Rural employed	—	—	—	—	—	—
16 Rural worker	—	—	—	—	—	—
17 Rural capitalist	—	—	—	—	—	—
18 Rural self-employed	—	—	—	—	—	—
19 Rural inactive	—	—	—	—	—	—
20 Firms	—	—	—	—	—	—
21 Government	1317.2	642.4	64.0	63.9	262.4	274.3
Capital account						
22 Aggr. capital account	583.3	856.7	136.8	−328.1	210.5	−154.6
Activities account						
23 Agriculture	—	—	—	—	—	—
24 Mining	—	—	—	—	—	—
25 Processed coffee	—	—	—	—	—	—
26 Industry	—	—	—	—	—	—
27 Elect., gas, and water	—	—	—	—	—	—
28 Modern services	—	—	—	—	—	—
29 Personal services	—	—	—	—	—	—
30 Govt. services	—	—	—	—	—	—
Indirect taxes account						
31 Indirect taxes	—	—	—	—	—	—
32 Import duties	—	—	—	—	—	—
Rest-of-the-world account						
33 Rest of the world	89.5	131.6	20.9	—	—	32.4
34 Total	25953.6	12694.0	2194.6	5579.2	1689.4	9886.6

Table 7-1   Disaggregated SAM, Columbia, 1970[a] (*Continued*)

	Institutional Current Account			Cap. Acc.	Activities Account	
	19	*20*	*21*	*22*	*23*	*24*
Want account						
1 Food	1556.7	—	—	—	—	—
2 Nonfood	395.5	—	—	—	—	—
3 Housing	198.6	—	—	—	—	—
4 Health	84.4	—	—	—	—	—
5 Education	24.6	—	—	—	—	—
6 Other social services	101.6	—	—	—	—	—
Factor account						
7 Urban labor rem.	—	—	—	—	2730.3	442.1
8 Rural labor rem.	—	—	—	—	7093.0	296.5
9 Gross profits	—	—	—	—	23233.6	2143.7
Institutional current account						
10 Urban employed	—	—	335.0	—	—	—
11 Urban worker	—	—	35.1	—	—	—
12 Urban capitalist	—	—	15.0	—	—	—
13 Urban self-employed	—	—	161.6	—	—	—
14 Urban inactive	—	—	1629.7	—	—	—
15 Rural employed	—	—	22.1	—	—	—
16 Rural worker	—	—	37.9	—	—	—
17 Rural capitalist	—	—	25.4	—	—	—
18 Rural self-employed	—	—	69.9	—	—	—
19 Rural inactive	—	—	307.0	—	—	—
20 Firms	—	—	1284.0	—	—	—
21 Government	148.3	3248.5	—	—	—	—
Capital account						
22 Aggr. capital account	−102.8	13527.9	7660.8	—	—	—
Activities account						
23 Agriculture	—	—	—	2636.0	724.5	22.8
24 Mining	—	—	—	55.7	18.1	43.9
25 Processed coffee	—	—	—	—	—	—
26 Industry	—	—	—	13250.1	4066.7	190.9
27 Elect., gas, and water	—	—	—	6.4	6.6	106.2
28 Modern services	—	—	—	12633.4	3573.2	725.6
29 Personal services	—	—	—	—	6.0	2.0
30 Govt. services	—	—	9961.6	78.8	23.0	10.9
Indirect taxes account						
31 Indirect taxes	—	—	—	—	−220.6	−346.3
32 Import duties	—	—	—	—	116.5	4.3
Rest-of-the-world account						
33 Rest of the world	—	—	58.9	—	910.3	43.4
34 Total	2406.8	16776.4	21604.1	28660.3	42281.2	3686.0

TABLE 7-1 *Continued*

	Activities Account					
	25	26	27	28	29	30
Want account						
1 Food	—	—	—	—	—	—
2 Nonfood	—	—	—	—	—	—
3 Housing	—	—	—	—	—	—
4 Health	—	—	—	—	—	—
5 Education	—	—	—	—	—	—
6 Other social services	—	—	—	—	—	—
Factor account						
7 Urban labor rem.	128.1	7718.4	576.5	12266.2	4592.8	6897.1
8 Rural labor rem.	28.6	1722.4	58.0	2465.7	923.2	1386.4
9 Gross profits	512.9	10811.8	754.9	28443.6	4571.1	—
Institutional current account						
10 Urban employed	—	—	—	—	—	—
11 Urban worker	—	—	—	—	—	—
12 Urban capitalist	—	—	—	—	—	—
13 Urban self-employed	—	—	—	—	—	—
14 Urban inactive	—	—	—	—	—	—
15 Rural employed	—	—	—	—	—	—
16 Rural worker	—	—	—	—	—	—
17 Rural capitalist	—	—	—	—	—	—
18 Rural self-employed	—	—	—	—	—	—
19 Rural inactive	—	—	—	—	—	—
20 Firms	—	—	—	—	—	—
21 Government	—	—	—	—	—	—
Capital account						
22 Aggr. capital account	—	—	—	—	—	—
Activities account						
23 Agriculture	5908.5	15041.5	3.6	412.8	701.3	249.8
24 Mining	3.1	1826.4	35.7	173.7	4.6	5.6
25 Processed coffee	549.0	—	—	—	224.5	47.1
26 Industry	81.0	24164.6	453.6	9202.3	3664.4	1594.9
27 Elect., gas, and water	4.9	576.1	43.5	221.1	85.3	55.7
28 Modern services	576.0	18371.7	112.1	12214.4	233.2	668.3
29 Personal services	1.1	90.7	9.8	416.9	79.2	162.0
30 Govt. services	3.3	158.0	4.0	88.9	11.4	9.9
Indirect taxes account						
31 Indirect taxes	3072.2	3486.7	−11.7	1169.0	113.0	9.6
32 Import duties	—	3160.3	—	8.1	—	3.6
Rest-of-the-world account						
33 Rest of the world	—	16851.3	—	2714.3	87.0	33.2
34 Total	10868.7	103979.9	204.0	69797.0	15291.0	11123.2

TABLE 7–1   Disaggregated SAM, Colombia, 1970^a (*Continued*)

	Indirect Taxes		R.O.W.	Total
	31	32	33	34
Want account				
1 Food	—	—	—	44434.3
2 Nonfood	—	—	—	20947.0
3 Housing	—	—	—	14231.4
4 Health	—	—	—	3077.5
5 Education	—	—	—	3731.3
6 Other social services	—	—	—	7441.8
Factor account				
7 Urban labor rem.	—	—	—	35351.5
8 Rural labor rem.	—	—	—	13973.9
9 Gross profits	—	—	−3591.9	66897.7
Institutional current account				
10 Urban employed	—	—	79.5	30299.7
11 Urban worker	—	—	18.2	6919.5
12 Urban capitalist	—	—	10.8	4113.2
13 Urban self-employed	—	—	68.1	25953.6
14 Urban inactive	—	—	33.3	12694.0
15 Rural employed	—	—	5.8	2194.6
16 Rural worker	—	—	14.6	5579.2
17 Rural capitalist	—	—	4.4	1689.4
18 Rural self-employed	—	—	26.0	9886.6
19 Rural inactive	—	—	6.3	2406.8
20 Firms	—	—	—	16776.4
21 Government	7271.9	3292.7	729.4	21604.1
Capital account				
22 Aggr. capital account	—	—	5229.4	28660.3
Activities account				
23 Agriculture	—	—	2321.5	42281.2
24 Mining	—	—	1393.4	3686.0
25 Processed coffee	—	—	9194.3	10868.7
26 Industry	—	—	2656.7	103979.9
27 Elect., gas, and water	—	—	—	204.0
28 Modern services	—	—	2932.2	69797.0
29 Personal services	—	—	—	15291.0
30 Govt. services	—	—	17.7	11123.2
Indirect taxes account				
31 Indirect taxes	—	—	—	7271.9
32 Import duties	—	—	—	3292.7
Rest-of-the-world account				
33 Rest of the world	—	—	—	21149.8
34 Total	7271.9	3292.7	21149.8	—

^{a}Cap. Acc., capital account; R.O.W., rest-of-the-world account; Rem., remuneration; Aggr., aggregated; Elect., electricity; Govt., government.

TRANSFORMING THE SAM
INTO A MODEL

Analytically, input–output tables and SAM tables are treated in very similar ways. Particularly in the context of a comparative analysis of the structural properties of different socioeconomic systems, which is the focus of this study, the SAM is an appropriate framework for conducting such comparisons in ways similar to comparative structural analysis of input–output tables (Chenery and Watanabe, 1958). For comparative analyses, the constancy of coefficients can be an advantage. Impact multipliers based on constant coefficients obtained from inverted input–output or social accounting coefficient tables have an advantage of being more country neutral in cross-country comparisons than flexible models, which involve nonuniformities in their treatment of individual case studies.

In input–output analysis, an endogenous vector of sectoral production, P, can be predicted from a matrix of input–output coefficients, A, and a vector of exogenous final demand, F, as in Equation (7-1).

$$P = AP + F = (I - A)^{-1}F \qquad (7\text{-}1)$$

The SAM can be used similarly. To transform the social accounting matrix into a predictive model along the above lines requires performing several steps.

First, the SAM accounts need to be subdivided into endogenous and exogenous components and regrouped accordingly, so that the exogenous accounts fall to the right and bottom of the endogenous accounts. Following an established convention, which coincides with the focus of this chapter, the endogenous accounts include four categories:

1. Wants, rows and columns 1 through 6
2. Factor incomes, rows and columns 7 through 9
3. Households and firms, rows and columns 10 through 20
4. Production activities, rows and columns 23 through 30.

These endogenous accounts form a 28×28 submatrix within the regrouped SAM, containing all the flows from endogenous accounts to endogenous accounts. The outgoings of other accounts constitute a 28×5 submatrix to the right, which contains flows of sectoral export and investment demands and income transfers from the rest of the world and government. These are exogenous outgoings and can be summed into one exogenous vector. To the bottom of the endogenous accounts is a submatrix that contains the outgoings of the endogenous accounts into the other accounts, that is, imports, taxes, and savings. These residual balances need not be treated further here.

Second, the flows in the endogenous accounts need to be expressed as average propensities of their corresponding column totals. Thus, each flow in the 28×28 matrix is divided by its respective column total to give the matrix of average propensities, denoted by A.

As a result of these manipulations, the SAM takes the form of Table 7-2. Note that the A matrix appears in a partitioned form to facilitate a decomposition of the multipliers in the next section. The vector of row totals, y, represents the endogenous variables, whereas the vector x represents the exogenous variables.

The vector of endogenous variables, y, can now be solved from Equation (7-2)

$$y = Ay + x = (I - A)^{-1}x = M_a x \qquad (7\text{-}2)$$

where M_a is the aggregate multiplier matrix.

TABLE 7-2   SAM in the Form of $y = Ay + x$

| | Expenditures | Endogenous Accounts | | | | Exogenous Account | |
		Wants *1*	Factors *2*	Institutions *3*	Activities *4*	Government, Capital, and Rest of World	Totals
Receipts							
Endogenous 1. Wants				A_{13}		X_1	Y_1
2. Factors					A_{24}	X_2	Y_2
3. Institutions			A_{32}	A_{33}		X_3	Y_3
4. Activities		A_{41}			A_{44}	X_4	Y_4
Exogenous Others							
				(residual balance)			
Totals		Y_1'	Y_2'	Y_3'	Y_4'		

Given A and x for 1970–1975, in constant 1970 prices, predicted values of the 28 endogenous variables for 1970–1975 are obtained. Using the SAM, we predict a 20 percent growth rate in total Gross Domestic Product (GDP) over 5 years, or about 3.7 percent per annum, compared to a realized growth of 4.9 percent per annum. We should note, of course, that macroeconomic forecasts for 1971–1975 have been particularly inaccurate for most countries. Predictions of the institutional incomes are underestimates, as well; however, the predicted growth differences between the household groups provide important information that is otherwise not available. In particular, it is noted that the rural households have benefited relatively more than the urban households. The same reasons for the poor ability of the traditional input–output model to predict the value added apply also for the SAM. Furthermore, the generation of additional endogenous accounts by making use of constant coefficients in the SAM reduce the ability of the SAM to function as a predictive tool.

MULTIPLIER ANALYSIS

The use of the SAM as an analytical tool rests less in its predictive ability than in the study of the underlying economic structure through an analysis of its inverse multipliers and their decomposition, which will be the focus of this section. Recalling Equation (7-2) the aggregate multiplier matrix M_a can be decomposed into three multiplier matrices M_1, M_2, and M_3, as in Equation (7-3).

$$y = Ay + x = (I - A)^{-1}x = M_a x = M_3 M_2 M_1 x \qquad (7-3)$$

In terms of the SAM, M_1, which is known as the transfer multiplier, captures effects resulting from direct transfers within the endogenous account, that is, between production activities. The open-loop effects, M_2, capture the interactions among the endogenous accounts, that is, from production to factors, institutions, and wants. The closed-loop effects, M_3, ensure that the circular flow of income is completed among endogenous accounts, that is, from production activities to factors to insitutions to wants and then back to activities in the form of consumption demand, and again and again.[1] Because the multiplier matrix M_a and its partition into M_1, M_2, and M_3 can be extensive, we limit the presentation to the aggregate and decomposed impacts of exogenous injections in sectoral activities. Of course, it is possible to pursue the impact of institutional transfers, but this is left for another occasion.

Table 7-3 gives the relevant aggregate multipliers within M_a. Specifically, they fall into four submatrices: $M_{a,14}$, $M_{a,24}$, $M_{a,34}$, and $M_{a,44}$, corresponding, respectively, to the impacts on wants (subindex 1), factors (subindex 2), institutions (subindex 3), and activities (subindex 4), from injections in activities (subindex 4).

Taking up the first submatrix in Table 7-3, rows 1 through 6, the impact of allocations to activities on the wants account (items 1 through 6), we note the relatively high impact of government services on food, which surpasses that of agriculture on food. The dominating impact of services, as compared to other sectors, is generally established for other wants categories, too.

In the second submatrix, rows 7 through 9, which relates to the impact of allocations on the factor accounts, we find that labor income is highly affected by expansion in services activities. Other sectors with significant effects are mining and agriculture. Capital income is mostly affected by expansion in the agricultural, mining, and service activities.

We can now analyze the third submatrix, the income effects, $M_{a,34}$. It is worth using decomposition analysis in tracing how the results are obtained in the third submatrix. The decomposition of $M_{a,34}$, into its transfer, open, and closed multiplier effects requires analyses of only three submatrices, as in Equation (7-3).

$$M_{a,34} = (M_{3,33})(M_{2,34})(M_{1,44}) \qquad (7\text{-}4)$$

$$\text{overall} = (\text{closed})(\text{open})(\text{transfer})$$

Tables 7-4, 7-5, and 7-6 show the $M_{1,44}$, $M_{2,34}$, and $M_{3,33}$ submatrices, respectively. Table 7-4 captures the well-known transfer within the input–output accounts. The first column of Table 7-4 shows that an initial injection in agriculture of 1.0 results in an addition in agriculture of 4.1 percent, mining 0.4 percent, industry 15.6 percent, electricity, water, and gas 0.2 percent, modern services 14.1 percent, personal services 0.1 percent, and government services 0.1 percent. The original injection of 1.0 leads to a total increase of 1.3459. These transfer effects will be traced through the rest of the system, $M_{2,34}$ and $M_{3,33}$, to illustrate how the system works.

Table 7-5, which presents $M_{2,34}$, captures the open-loop effects, the highest of which are those for rural households in the agriculture column. This pattern is the result of the high concentration of rural factor income in agriculture and the dominating link between rural factors and rural households. In a similar way, the mining sector benefits the urban employers and capitalists whereas the government sector benefits the other urban households.

The closed-loop multipliers as captured in $M_{3,33}$, Table 7-6, are associated with the consumption patterns of the households. The increases in income resulting from open-loop effects are used mainly to purchase consumer goods, which increases output, and, in turn, increases factor income that is paid out as institutional income.

---

1. The formal derivation of the decomposed multiplier is described in, among others, Pyatt and Roe (1977), Bulmer-Thomas (1982), Pleskovic and Treviño (1985), Cohen and Jellema (1986), and Round (Chapter 8, this volume).

TABLE 7-3 SAM Aggregate Multipliers by Type of Activity, Colombia, 1970

Sector/Institution	Agriculture 23	Mining 24	Processed Coffee 25	Industry 26	Electricity, Gas, and Water 27	Modern Services 28	Personal Services 29	Government Services 30
1 Food	0.8808	0.9411	0.6124	0.6252	0.8688	0.8059	0.8700	1.0221
2 Nonfood	0.4077	0.4460	0.2852	0.2962	0.4173	0.3855	0.4141	0.4846
3 Housing	0.2686	0.3022	0.1893	0.2004	0.2869	0.2639	0.2816	0.3275
4 Health	0.0597	0.0650	0.0417	0.0432	0.0608	0.0561	0.0605	0.0712
5 Education	0.0712	0.0802	0.0502	0.0531	0.0760	0.0700	0.0746	0.0865
6 Other social services	0.1437	0.1608	0.1011	0.1061	0.1510	0.1396	0.1482	0.1701
7 Urban labor remuneration	0.4983	0.6235	0.3634	0.4678	0.7529	0.6200	0.7571	1.1372
8 Rural labor remuneration	0.3474	0.2783	0.2262	0.1908	0.2177	0.2109	0.2549	0.3384
9 Gross profits	1.5329	1.7075	1.0747	1.0505	1.4194	1.4032	1.3411	1.1634
10 Urban employed	0.5680	0.6583	0.4035	0.4366	0.6352	0.5814	0.6173	0.7157
11 Urban worker	0.0968	0.1211	0.0706	0.0909	0.1462	0.1204	0.1470	0.2209
12 Urban capitalist	0.0814	0.0934	0.0576	0.0608	0.0868	0.0810	0.0839	0.0917
13 Urban self-employed	0.5075	0.5833	0.3595	0.3810	0.5466	0.5077	0.5285	0.5849
14 Urban inactive	0.2129	0.2459	0.1510	0.1621	0.2344	0.2159	0.2274	0.2588
15 Rural employed	0.0520	0.0485	0.0350	0.0316	0.0392	0.0383	0.0413	0.0459
16 Rural worker	0.1374	0.1101	0.0895	0.0755	0.0861	0.0834	0.1008	0.1338
17 Rural capitalist	0.0390	0.0397	0.0267	0.0251	0.0325	0.0320	0.0324	0.0321
18 Rural self-employed	0.2350	0.2191	0.1580	0.1425	0.1768	0.1731	0.1864	0.2077
19 Rural inactive	0.0504	0.0463	0.0338	0.0303	0.0373	0.0364	0.0397	0.0451
20 Firms	0.3551	0.3955	0.2490	0.2433	0.3288	0.3251	0.3107	0.2695
23 Agriculture	1.5737	0.6004	0.9710	0.5876	0.5835	0.5337	0.6379	0.6819
24 Mining	0.0348	1.0495	0.0248	0.0483	0.0560	0.0366	0.0384	0.0417
25 Processed coffee	0.0224	0.0241	1.0688	0.0160	0.0224	0.0208	0.0378	0.0308
26 Industry	1.6098	1.7025	1.1272	2.4351	1.7949	1.5808	1.8056	1.9301
27 Electricity, gas, and water	0.0336	0.0669	0.0243	0.0332	1.0581	0.0363	0.0410	0.0449
28 Modern services	0.9332	1.1483	0.7095	0.9055	0.9709	2.0243	0.9183	1.0742
29 Personal services	0.2901	0.3213	0.2038	0.2148	0.3056	0.2842	1.3023	0.3611
30 Government services	0.0195	0.0240	0.0140	0.0163	0.0219	0.0196	0.0204	1.0235

TABLE 7-4 $M_{1,44}$ Transfer Effects in Sectoral Accounts

	Agriculture 23	Mining 24	Processed Coffee 25	Industry 26	Electricity, Gas, and Water 27	Modern Services 28	Personal Services 29	Government Services 30
23 Agriculture	1.0414	0.0275	0.6002	0.2071	0.0524	0.0417	0.1077	0.0600
24 Mining	0.0036	1.0156	0.0030	0.0258	0.0245	0.0074	0.0070	0.0050
25 Processed coffee	0.0000	0.0001	1.0532	0.0001	0.0001	0.0001	0.0156	0.0047
26 Industry	0.1560	0.1299	0.1133	1.3908	0.3336	0.2279	0.3495	0.2241
27 Electricity, gas, and water	0.0016	0.0316	0.0018	0.0098	1.0249	0.0057	0.0083	0.0071
28 Modern services	0.1411	0.2754	0.1543	0.3262	0.1512	1.2676	0.1078	0.1293
29 Personal services	0.0012	0.0025	0.0012	0.0033	0.0062	0.0079	1.0062	0.0157
30 Government services	0.0010	0.0036	0.0010	0.0027	0.0028	0.0020	0.0015	1.0015
Total	1.3459	1.4862	1.9228	1.9658	1.5957	1.5603	1.6036	1.4474

TABLE 7-5 $M_{2,34}$ Open-Loop Effects from Sectors to Institutions

	Agriculture 23	Mining 24	Processed Coffee 25	Industry 26	Electricity, Gas, and Water 27	Modern Services 28	Personal Services 29	Government Services 30
10 Urban employed	0.1608	0.1896	0.0162	0.0537	0.1980	0.1672	0.1870	0.2326
11 Urban worker	0.0125	0.0233	0.0023	0.0144	0.0549	0.0341	0.0583	0.1204
12 Urban capitalist	0.0247	0.0282	0.0024	0.0071	0.0260	0.0233	0.0239	0.0244
13 Urban self-employed	0.1519	0.1743	0.0147	0.0451	0.1652	0.1463	0.1524	0.1632
14 Urban inactive	0.0617	0.0719	0.0061	0.0196	0.0722	0.0621	0.0675	0.0794
15 Rural employed	0.0224	0.0153	0.0009	0.0029	0.0078	0.0089	0.0095	0.0108
16 Rural worker	0.0663	0.0318	0.0010	0.0066	0.0112	0.0140	0.0239	0.0493
17 Rural capitalist	0.0155	0.0130	0.0009	0.0024	0.0075	0.0084	0.0073	0.0043
18 Rural self-employed	0.1012	0.0690	0.0041	0.0132	0.0350	0.0401	0.0429	0.0489
19 Rural inactive	0.0220	0.0145	0.0008	0.0028	0.0071	0.0082	0.0092	0.0113
20 Firms	0.1273	0.1347	0.0109	0.0241	0.0857	0.0944	0.0692	0.0000
Total	0.7663	0.7656	0.0603	0.1919	0.6706	0.6070	0.6565	0.7456

TABLE 7-6 $M_{3,33}$ Closed-Loop Effects between Institutions

	Urban Employed 10	Urban Worker 11	Urban Capitalist 12	Urban Self-Emp. 13	Urban Inactive 14	Rural Employed 15	Rural Worker 16	Rural Capitalist 17	Rural Self-Emp. 18	Rural Inactive 19
10 Urban employed	1.4689	0.5094	0.4650	0.4792	0.4543	0.4578	0.5220	0.3588	0.4952	0.4904
11 Urban worker	0.0983	1.1059	0.0988	0.1001	0.0945	0.0951	0.1066	0.0745	0.1017	0.0998
12 Urban capitalist	0.0652	0.0709	1.0645	0.0666	0.0632	0.0637	0.0729	0.0499	0.0691	0.0685
13 Urban self-employed	0.4088	0.4446	0.4047	1.4179	0.3965	0.3996	0.4567	0.3132	0.4329	0.4292
14 Urban inactive	0.1740	0.1891	0.1724	0.1778	1.1686	0.1699	0.1939	0.1332	0.1839	0.1822
15 Rural employed	0.0339	0.0374	0.0331	0.0348	0.0329	1.0338	0.0394	0.0264	0.0371	0.0369
16 Rural worker	0.0815	0.0908	0.0789	0.0839	0.0789	0.0822	1.0966	0.0640	0.0909	0.0905
17 Rural capitalist	0.0269	0.0295	0.0263	0.0276	0.0261	0.0266	0.0308	1.0208	0.0291	0.0290
18 Rural self-employed	0.1531	0.1690	0.1493	0.1573	0.1487	0.1526	0.1778	0.1192	1.1676	0.1669
19 Rural inactive	0.0325	0.0360	0.0317	0.0334	0.0316	0.0325	0.0379	0.0253	0.0357	1.0355
20 Firms	0.2600	0.2841	0.2555	0.2663	0.2532	0.2555	0.2947	0.2003	0.2785	0.2774
Total	2.8030	2.9667	2.7803	2.8449	2.7485	2.7743	3.0293	2.3856	2.9217	2.9063

Reading the rows of Table 7-6 and excluding the initial injections and a few exceptions, we see that the closed-loop multipliers are fairly constant. This can be interpreted as the result of similar expenditure and savings patterns over households. The closed-loop multipliers are generally much higher than either the transfer or open-loop multipliers, which reflects the fact that consumption is larger than other categories of final demand. An open-loop effect of 1.0 into any household creates between 2.3856 and 3.0293 of total institutional income. The national impact for transfer effects ranged between 1.3459 and 1.9658, whereas that for open-loop effects varied between 0.0603 and 0.7663, in Tables 7-4 and 7-5, respectively. Being higher than the other multipliers and given their low variance, the closed-loop multipliers tend to dampen the effects of the transfer and open-loop multipliers.

Table 7-7 summarizes these interactions in a compact form. Columns 1 and 2 give the combined effects on the incomes of rural worker households and all others of the transfer and open-loop multipliers following the exogenous initial injection in agriculture of one million pesos. Columns 3 and 4 complement the picture by introducing closed-loop effects. Column 5 gives the overall effects, which, when summed, result into the overall multiplier for rural workers, as was found in Table 7-3, $M_{a,34}$ (16, 21), that is, 0.137 units. Similarly, the overall multipliers can be obtained for other household groups and firms, resulting in a total overall multiplier effect of 2.335 units.

These results suggest that the marginal share of benefits to rural workers from agricultural expansion amounts to about 5.8 percent. Because the income share of rural workers in 1970 amounted to 3.5 percent, we can expect an injection in agriculture to enhance the relative position of rural workers in the income distribution. The results also suggest that the significant gains obtained in the factor account by one group (in the open-loop effects) are reduced by losses through consumption to other groups (in the closed-loop effects). For Columbia, therefore, the effect of an injection in agriculture has a progressive effect on income distribution. The mining multiplier points in the same direction but less significantly. The energy multiplier distributes relatively more to urban than to rural households. The government sector multiplier appears to benefit household groups in various degrees at the cost of firms.

Finally, the fourth submatrix of Table 7-3 gives the aggregate multipliers of

TABLE 7-7   Effects of +1 in Agricultural Activity on Institutional Incomes, Colombia[a]

| | Open-loop Coefficients (Agriculture) (1) | Sum of Open-Loop Effects (All Sectors) (2) | Closed-Loop effects | | Sum of Closed-Loop Effects (5) | Simulated (%) (6) | Actual 1970 (%) (7) |
			Rural Worker (3)	All Others (4)			
Rural worker	0.066	0.072	1.097	0.076	0.137	5.8	3.5
All others	0.7	0.765	1.792	2.704	2.198	94.1	96.5
Total	0.766	0.837	2.889	2.780	2.335	100.0	100.0

[a]Transfer effect coefficient for agriculture = 1.041.

injections in activities on activities. These aggregate multipliers can also be decomposed into their transfer, open-loop, and closed-loop effects, as in Equation (7-4). Because

$$M_{a,44} = (M_{3,44})(M_{2,44})\,(M_{1,44})$$
$$\text{overall} = (\text{closed})\,(\text{open})\,(\text{transfer})$$

(7-5)

$M_{a,44}$ does not have an impact on accounts other than its own account 4, the open-loop effects are not applicable here, and $M_{2,44}$ is an identity matrix. As a result, an analysis of the differences between the aggregate multiplier and that part forming the transfer effects is sufficient to appreciate the nature of the remaining part forming the closed-loop effects.

The aggregate multipliers of $M_{a,44}$ can be compared now with the previously discussed transfer effects of activities on activities, $M_{1,44}$, found in Table 7-4. The latter represents the Leontief open-model inverse. As expected, first, the SAM inverse contains more linkages than the Leontief open-model inverse, with the result that $M_{a,44}$ is substantially higher than $M_{1,44}$. Second, because of the heterogeneity of the linkages the structural pattern of $M_{a,44}$ is also different from $M_{1,44}$.

Sectors are ranked according to the Leontief open-model total column multipliers in the order of industry 1.97, mining 1.49, services 1.45, and agriculture 1.35. The contribution to production activity and their ranking are significantly different in the SAM total column multipliers: services 5.19, mining 4.94, agriculture 4.52, and industry 4.26.

INTERNATIONAL COMPARISONS

Greater analytical insight is gained if basically comparable social accounting matrices are constructed for the individual countries. With the exception of the SAMs for four countries, which have been constructed by the same investigators, the available SAMs for the other six selected countries are very diversified in content and hardly permit comparisons.[2] However, appropriate aggregation and modifications can result in bringing the various SAMs to a common base. In the process, we necessarily exclude some valuable information on some countries.

We limited the classification of activities to four large groups of sectors: agriculture, mining, industry, and services. For institutions, the distinction is done categorically among urban households, leading to the distinction between the three groups of employers, employees, and self-employed, and by size of land ownership among rural households, leading to three groups of large landowners, medium landowners, and small landless households.

Table 7-8, which gives the size of the $M_{a,34}$ and $M_{a,44}$ multipliers, shows that India and Pakistan have the highest income multipliers, $M_{a,34}$, 3.7, and 4.0, respectively, which is partly the result of a treatment of imports in their SAMs that does not consider leakage to the rest of the world fully. At the other extreme, Suriname, Egypt, and Kenya show the lowest income multipliers, 1.0, 1.1, and 1.3, respectively, reflecting low degrees of interdependence. For all countries together the

---

2. For an inventory of most of the available SAMs including the six other SAMs analyzed here see Pyatt and Round (1985). The SAMs for Colombia, Suriname, Korea, and Pakistan have been constructed by the author and several associates.

TABLE 7-8   Income and Output Multipliers: Column Sums of Multipliers $M_{a,34}$ and $M_{a,44}$, Respectively: Ten Countries

		Agriculture	Mining	Industry	Services	Average
Colombia	$M_{a,34}$	2.146	2.512	1.651	2.230	2.135
	$M_{a,44}$	4.447	4.952	4.287	4.678	4.591
Suriname	$M_{a,34}$	1.153	0.777	0.816	1.220	0.992
	$M_{a,44}$	1.967	1.871	1.849	1.911	1.899
Egypt	$M_{a,34}$	1.570	0.354	0.893	1.473	1.073
	$M_{a,44}$	2.897	1.721	2.537	2.997	2.538
Kenya	$M_{a,34}$	1.867	1.127	0.910	1.501	1.351
	$M_{a,44}$	3.514	3.994	3.198	3.766	3.618
India	$M_{a,34}$	4.427	3.384	3.328	3.599	3.685
	$M_{a,44}$	6.910	5.185	5.977	5.711	5.951
Indonesia	$M_{a,34}$	2.567	NC[a]	1.395	2.395	2.119
	$M_{a,44}$	4.176	NC	2.414	3.579	3.390
Iran	$M_{a,34}$	2.584	1.470	1.752	2.085	1.973
	$M_{a,44}$	4.358	3.025	3.576	3.595	3.639
Korea	$M_{a,34}$	1.883	2.080	1.144	1.809	1.729
	$M_{a,44}$	3.514	3.994	3.198	3.766	3.618
Pakistan	$M_{a,34}$	4.428	4.119	3.502	4.084	4.033
	$M_{a,44}$	9.463	8.924	8.110	8.610	8.777
Sri Lanka	$M_{a,34}$	2.289	NC	1.714	2.163	2.055
	$M_{a,44}$	3.334	NC	2.929	3.007	3.090

[a]NC, not computed.

size of the income multipliers $M_{a,34}$ is about half that of output multipliers $M_{a,44}$, the difference caused partly by intermediate deliveries and partly by government income and transactions with the rest of the world. For individual countries, we note that Columbia, Egypt, and Kenya extract a lower income proportion from output, around 0.45, whereas India, Indonesia, and Sri Lanka extract a higher proportion, around 0.64. In these countries, it takes less of an output effort to produce a unit of household income.

The income multipliers are highest for impulses in the agricultural sector, followed in 7 of the 10 countries by the services sector. Manufacturing ranks between third and fourth, whereas mining does not show a clear ranking. Although the output multipliers show a similar ranking pattern among the sectors, there are more exceptions here. It is noted that the five Asian countries of Iran, Pakistan, India, Sri Lanka, and Indonesia show a very homogeneous pattern of sectoral ranking regarding their income and output multipliers.

In reflecting on the distributional pattern of the income multipliers and their decomposition, we calculate the percentage distribution of the multiplier benefits on each household group. To assess the marginal effect of the multipliers on income distribution, we note that a higher multiplier percentage share than the actual share for the lowest income groups is representative of a distributional mechanism that promotes a more equal distribution of income.

Korea, Pakistan, and other Asian countries have in common a progressive redistributive effect from richer toward poorer household groups, following injections in agriculture or in industry. These effects are also present in Colombia but less

significantly. This is the result partly of open-loop effects, which are more discriminatory in the Asian countries than in Colombia, and partly of closed-loop effects, which
tend to shift resources from richer to both poorer groups and firms, reflecting self-
constrained consumption patterns among poorer household groups in Asian countries as compared to imitative consumption patterns in Colombia.

We turn now to the decomposition of output multipliers, $M_{a,44}$. Because open-
loop effects are not applicable here—see Equation (7-6)—an analysis of the
differences between the aggregate multiplier and that part forming the transfer effects
is sufficient to appreciate the nature of the remaining part forming the closed-loop
effects. In Table 7-9, we compare the aggregate multipliers of $M_{a,44}$ with those of
transfer effects of activities on activities, $M_{1,44}$, the latter representing the open-model
Leontief inverse.

The attractive position that industry occupies in a structural analysis based on
the Leontief open-model data as the foremost contributor to production activity from
an additionally allocated unit is taken over by the activities of services, agriculture,
and mining, which contribute individually more than manufacturing in a SAM
framework. These results are consistent for the 10 countries, with the open-model
multipliers being about one-third of the SAM multipliers, depending on the country
and the sector.

CONCLUSION

In addition to its use for purposes of calibrating economy-wide models, the SAM
forms an appropriate framework for appraising policy issues relating to growth and
distribution and for a comparative analysis of the structural properties of different
socioeconomic systems. In all 10 case studies, agricultural multipliers show more
progressive redistributive effects than manufacturing multipliers. We also showed that
the growth effect is higher for agriculture than for industry, so that as far as these two
sectors are concerned progressive redistribution and higher growth are not in conflict
with each other.

In general, the Asian countries we studied show more progressive mechanisms.
These results are the result partly of open-loop effects, which link particular sectoral
activities to particular factor incomes and particular household groups in the Asian
context as compared to relatively weaker correspondence between activities, factors,
and households elsewhere, and partly of closed loop-effects, which tend to shift
relatively more resources from richer to poorer groups than vice versa, reflecting more
self-oriented consumption patterns among poorer household groups in the Asian
context as compared to more similar consumption patterns among rich and poor
household groups elsewhere. Furthermore, the SAM multipliers obtained in all 10
case studies differ appreciably in value and rank from those derived from that part of
the SAM inverse that corresponds to the open-model Leontief inverse.

For an effective analysis of development mechanisms and problems in different
socioeconomic settings, it is necessary to construct and make available social
accounting matrices for many more countries and for more years. Difficulties in the
way of standardization and comparability will take some time to solve, although the
multiplier analysis as presented here may provide clues as to which SAM classifications, entries, and analytical designs are more meaningful and operational in a
comparative analysis of socioeconomic systems and their implications for global
issues in policy making.

TABLE 7-9 Total Column Multipliers in the SAM and the Leontief Inverses: Ten Countries

Sector	Colombia 1970		Suriname 1979		Egypt 1976		Kenya 1976		India 1968/69	
	SAM	Leontief	SAM	Leontief	SAM	Leontief	SAM	Leontief	SAM	Leontief
Agriculture	4.447	1.478	1.968	1.218	2.898	1.321	2.871	1.160	6.910	1.350
Mining	4.953	1.499	1.871	1.385	1.722	1.348	3.099	2.118	5.184	1.240
Manufacturing	4.287	1.985	1.849	1.316	2.537	1.575	2.540	1.755	5.977	1.936
Services	4.679	1.558	1.912	1.121	2.997	1.353	2.934	1.615	5.711	1.411

Sector	Indonesia 1975		Iran 1970		Korea 1979		Pakistan 1979		Sri Lanka 1970	
	SAM	Leontief	SAM	Leontief	SAM	Leontief	SAM	Leontief	SAM	Leontief
Agriculture	4.176	1.584	4.357	1.396	3.515	1.388	9.463	1.865	3.335	1.378
Mining	NC[a]	NC	3.025	1.454	3.995	1.451	8.924	1.888	NC	NC
Manufacturing	2.414	1.345	3.576	1.668	3.198	1.847	8.110	2.187	2.929	1.524
Services	3.579	1.240	3.594	1.344	3.767	1.619	8.610	1.671	3.007	1.193

[a]NC, not computed.

REFERENCES

Bulmer-Thomas, Victor. 1982. *Input-Output Analysis in Developing Countries.* New York: John Wiley.

Chenery, Hollis B., and T. Watanabe. 1958. "International Comparisons of the Structure of Production." *Econometrica.* Vol. 26, pp. 487–521.

Cohen, Solomon I., P. A. Cornelisse, E. Thorbecke, and R. Teekens, eds. 1984. *The Modelling of Socio-Economic Planning Processes.* Aldershot, Hants, UK: Gower Publishing Company.

Cohen, Solomon I., and T. Jellema. 1986. "Social Accounting and Development Analysis." Discussion Paper No. 77, Centre for Development Planning, Erasmus University Rotterdam, Rotterdam, The Netherlands.

Pleskovic, Boris, and Gustavo Treviño. 1985. *The Use of a Social Accounting Framework for Public Sector Analysis: The Case Study of Mexico.* Ljubljana, Yugoslavia: International Centre for Public Enterprises in Developing Countries.

Pyatt, Graham, and Alan Roe. 1977. *Social Accounting for Development Planning.* Cambridge, England: Cambridge University Press.

Pyatt, Graham, and Jeffery I. Round. 1985. *Social Accounting Matrices.* Symposium Series, The World Bank Publications Department, Washington, D.C.

III

EXTENDED MODELS AND MULTIPLIER DECOMPOSITIONS

8

Decomposition of Input–Output and Economy-Wide Multipliers in a Regional Setting

JEFFERY I. ROUND

The concept of the multiplier, particularly multisectoral and multidimensional versions, still dominates much of the current literature in regional science and regional economics. Until fairly recently, analyses have focused on the application of the open static input–output model at the regional level. However, during the past 10 years, many analysts have made interesting extensions to the basic model that help us to understand more about the nature of linkages within a regional system as well as to create a more workable model for assessing the impact of external shocks. I refer particularly to the contributions by Schinnar (1976), Batey and Madden (1981), Madden and Batey (1983), Batey (1985), and more generally to even more comprehensive systems, such as that outlined by Brouwer et al. (1983). The purpose of the present chapter is to review and extend some related work that has emanated from the development economics literature in recent years, particularly concerning multiplier decompositions and the nature of system linkages, based on the construction and use of social accounting matrices. Finally, I set both strands of research in a more general context in which I aim to identify more clearly the link between economic and demographic models.

A REGIONAL SAM FRAMEWORK

At the heart of the extended multiplier analysis described in subsequent sections of this chapter is a social accounting matrix (SAM) framework set out in a regional context. Many writers have discussed the appropriate structure of regional accounting systems and the many practical and conceptual problems associated with them. In a previous paper (Round, 1986), I reviewed some of these contributions, and I presented a matrix framework that combines certain conceptual merits with practical expendiency. It is based on an idea put forward by Stone (1961) and further developed by Barnard (1969) and Czamanski (1973), but, in it, I take account of at least some of Richardson's (1978, p. 83) trenchant criticisms of regional social accounting by anticipating the well-established inherent difficulties of measurement, particularly those relating to interregional transactions and transfers.

A simplified version of the two-region SAM I propose to adopt is shown in schematic form in Table 8-1. A number of accounts have been suppressed in order to highlight the multiplier analysis presented in subsequent sections. Accounts are divided into endogenous and exogenous accounts, which are discussed later. The endogenous accounts for each region consist of production accounts, factor income and outlay accounts, and household current accounts. All of the other basic economic accounts are consolidated into a single exogenous account. At an aggregate level, the exogenous account would include a corporate enterprises' current account, a government (central, state, and local) current account, a consolidated capital account, a rest of the world current and capital account, plus an account to accommodate indirect taxes and subsidies. It is important to recognize these as the near minimum set of accounts necessary to describe an economic system. Table 8-1 is complicated only to the extent that certain transactions and transfers between two regions are treated explicitly so that it becomes an interregional system. In particular, trade in goods and services between the two regions are portrayed by the diagonal matrices, $\hat{t}_1$, with superscripts showing the geographical direction of flow. Similarly, interregional factor remittances are recorded in $\hat{t}_2$ and household income transfers in $\hat{t}_3$. Clearly, these are not the only interregional transactions and transfers but, in this instance, all others are subsumed within the exogenous accounts x and v. An empirical example of an extended version of this regional system based on a social accounting matrix for the Malaysian economy has been shown in Round (1986).

Because the relationship of conventional input–output accounts and multipliers with the regional framework displayed in Table 8-1 will become central to later discussions, more detail is shown for the production accounts. This will also counter the impression that the framework portrays an oversimplified view of the real world, whereas, in fact, it is a scheme fully capable of combining realism with a wide range of analytical uses. Table 8-2 is taken from Table 8-1. It shows the production accounts of one region in more detail, with all accounts for the "other" region now consolidated for expositional convenience. In the production accounts, production activities are now distinguished from commodities. The commodity accounts are further disaggregated between those commodities produced locally and those wholly imported. However, not all commodities classified as "local" commodities are produced locally, because local supplies might be augmented by imported close substitutes. Commodity imports from the other region therefore potentially appear as two row vectors t'_{L1} and t'_{M1} and, in the way we have defined them, are conventionally referred to, respectively, as competitive and complementary imports. In principle, we do not need to maintain such a sharp distinction between these two kinds of imports, because complementary imports can be viewed as those associated with zero substitution elasticities and a zero base-year local supply. Competitive imports would comprise all of the remainder. In a strict input–output context, however, it is sometimes useful to distinguish between the two. The subscripts A, L, and M therefore maintain the distinction between the three types of production accounts, but in all other ways the notation is similar to that already shown in Table 8-1. Furthermore, the basic structure of the transactions between the accounts in Table 8-1 is maintained in Table 8-2, so that, for instance,

TABLE 8-1 A Schematic SAM for a Two-Region System[a]

| | Endogenous Accounts | | | | | | Exogenous Accounts (Outlays) | Total |
| | Region 1 | | | Region 2 | | | | |
	Production	Factors	Households	Production	Factors	Households		
Exogenous accounts								
Region 1								
Production	T_{11}^1		T_{13}^1	$\hat{t}_1^{12}$			x_1^1	y_1^1
Factors	T_{21}^1				$\hat{t}_2^{12}$		x_2^1	y_2^1
Households		T_{32}^1	T_{33}^1			$\hat{t}_3^{12}$	x_3^1	y_3^1
Region 2								
Production	$\hat{t}_1^{21}$			T_{11}^2		T_{13}^2	x_1^2	y_1^2
Factors		$\hat{t}_2^{21}$		T_{21}^2		T_{33}^2	x_2^2	y_2^2
Household			$\hat{t}_3^{21}$		T_{32}^2	T_{33}^2	x_3^2	y_3^2
Exogenous accounts (incomings)	$v_1^{1'}$	$v_2^{1'}$	$v_3^{1'}$	$v_1^{2'}$	$v_2^{2'}$	$v_3^{2'}$	θ	θ
Total	$y_1^{1'}$	$y_2^{1'}$	$y_3^{1'}$	$y_1^{2'}$	$y_2^{2'}$	$y_3^{2'}$	θ	

[a]Prime (') represents a transpose matrix; circumflex ($\hat{}$) represents a diagonal matrix.

TABLE 8-2 A Schematic Regional SAM, Emphasizing the Production Accounts

	Production			Factors	Households	Other Region	All Other Accounts	Total
		Commodities						
	Activities	Local	Imported					
Production								
Activites		T_{AL}						y_{1A}
Commodities								
Local	T_{LA}				T_{1L3}	t_{1L}	x_{1L}	y_{1L}
Imported	T_{MA}				T_{1M3}		x_{1M}	y_{1M}
Factors	T_{21}					t_2^a	x_2	y_2
Households				T_{32}	T_{33}	t_3^a	x_3	y_3
Other region		t'_{L1}	t'_{M1}	t'_2	t'_3			
All other accounts	v'_1	b	b	v'_2	v'_3			
Total	y'_{1A}	y'_{1L}	y'_{1M}	y'_2	y'_3			

[a] These are transfers out of the region and are likely to differ from transfers into the region, although shown by the same symbol in the table.

[b] Commodity imports from the rest of the world should appear here and be correspondingly deducted from v_1.

input–output transactions in commodities shown as T_{11} now has the following form

$$T_{11} = \begin{bmatrix} 0 & T_{AL} & 0 \\ T_{LA} & 0 & 0 \\ T_{MA} & 0 & 0 \end{bmatrix} \tag{8-1}$$

with correspondingly detailed structures for T_{13} and T_{21}.

The most important feature of the SAM as portrayed in Table 8-1 from the point of view of the regional accounting structure is the distinction between functional flows and geographical flows. Interregional transactions and transfers are therefore seen as taking place in two stages: first, the purely geographical transfer (of goods, income, or capital) from an account in one region to a similar account in the other region, and second, the functional (or economic) transactions that take place between accounts but within a region. This means that, in principle, the interregional flows are all diagonal matrices. In practice, however, spatial transfers, particularly of goods, are not costless to tranship, so that t_1^{12} and t_1^{21} are likely to contain some off-diagonal elements. The accounting details of this system are discussed more fully by Round (1986).

The final point to make about Table 8-1 is to highlight the nature and significance of the accounts and flows chosen to be endogeneous to the system. The designation of endogenous and exogenous accounts is necessary as we move from an accounting system and toward a model structure. In principal, the SAM from which Table 8-1 is derived is comprehensive and is therefore essentially a "general equilibrium" data system. However, a particularly interesting multiplier analysis can be derived from it by restricting attention to a set of linkages between production, the generation of factor incomes and their subsequent receipt by households, and the expenditure behavior of households. It will also help for the purpose of extending the discussion toward demographic issues, which are dealt with later. Clearly, these endogenous relationships capture the main elements of the circular flow of income, even though other potentially important interdependencies, such as savings, capital formation, and the flow of funds, are all excluded. A fuller discussion of the features of the endogenous behavior we have included here, and particularly the role of the factor accounts in the relationships, has been included in Pyatt and Thorbecke (1976), Pyatt and Roe et al. (1977), and Pyatt and Round (1977, 1985), as well as in earlier papers on decomposing multipliers based on a SAM framework, such as Pyatt and Round (1979) and Round (1985). The main point to note in this context is that "people" enter the economic accounts in two ways: first, as members of defined household groups, and second, as members of the labor force who receive factor incomes in return for the labor services they provide.[1] The existence of these two distinct economic roles that individuals play indicates the need to include both factor and household accounts in the SAM for modeling purposes. Put another way, it enables us to distinguish between the activities of individuals in the labor (and other factor) markets and their activities in the commodity markets. If the factor accounts are excluded then the role of the factor markets is lost and so is the key to the link between demographic and economic models. As it stands therefore, the structure of the endogenous transactions matrix, T,

---

1. Note that this immediately begs the question as to where those who are not members of the labor force, or who are unemployed, would be included. They would appear as members of household groups but they would not ordinarily receive factor income payments.

shows input–output transactions in T_{11}, factor payments in T_{21}, the distribution of factor payments to households in T_{32}, household expenditures in T_{13}, whereas T_{33} shows the interhousehold transfer payments, which form part of the transfer income and which augment labor income by households of different types. Unemployment benefits (transfers from government) and distributed profits (transfers from companies) form part of the exogenous income receipts, shown as x_3 in Tables 8-1 and 8-2; however, the possibility of endogenizing these and other transfer payments is briefly discussed later.

DECOMPOSING MULTIPLIERS FOR A REGIONAL ECONOMY

The endogenous structure of the SAM, shown in Tables 8-1 and 8-2, leads to the derivation of some interesting ex post accounting multipliers. This derivation has previously been set out and extensively discussed by Pyatt and Round (1979), as well as by Stone (1978), following the original version of it by us, which was published as Chapter 4 in Pyatt and Roe et al. (1977). More recently, there have been many studies implementing these decompositions for a variety of economies, including Defourny and Thorbecke (1984), Pleskovic and Treviño (1985), and Cohen (Chapter 7, this volume).

The ex post accounting structure of the endogenous transactions may be defined as a set of coefficient matrices in which

$$A_{ij} = T_{ij}\hat{y}_j^{-1} \tag{8-2}$$

so that

$$A = \begin{bmatrix} A_{11} & 0 & A_{13} \\ A_{21} & 0 & 0 \\ 0 & A_{32} & A_{33} \end{bmatrix} \tag{8-3}$$

where i, j refers to the three endogenous groups of accounts referred to as the production, factor, and household accounts. Thus, if the endogenous account totals represented by y are expressed in terms of exogenous injections x, then

$$y = Ay + x$$
$$= (I - A)^{-1}x$$
$$= Mx \tag{8-4}$$

where M is a multiplier matrix in the sense that $M \geq I$. Of particular interest is to show that M can be decomposed to bring out more clearly the different kinds of linkages in the system. Thus, we can show that

$$y = Mx$$
$$= M_3 M_2 M_1 x \tag{8-5}$$

where M_1, M_2, and M_3 are multiplier matrices that capture different kinds of effects that take place in the system. M_1 contains the effects that injections into one group of accounts have on itself through interdependencies within the group. These will include the input–output multipliers, but they also include the multiplier effects of household transfers in so far as these exist. M_1 is referred to as the "transfer" or "own direct effects" multiplier. M_3 also depicts own-direct effects, but these are the effects resulting from the circular flow of income between groups of accounts. In this sense, we refer to it as the "closed-loop" or "own-indirect effects" multiplier. The final matrix M_2 is the "open-loop," or "cross-effects" multiplier, which shows the effects that an injection into one group of accounts has upon some other group, after allowing for the own-account effects in M_1 and M_3.

A better understanding of this decomposition can be obtained by specifying M_1, M_2, and M_3 in detail. Pyatt and Round (1979) have shown that if the diagonal blocks in A (represented by $\hat{A}$) are subtracted from A, then a (block) circular permutation matrix $(A - \hat{A})$ of order 3 remains. Furthermore, if we define A^* to be $(I - \hat{A})^{-1}(A - \hat{A})$, then A^* is also of circular permutation form, and this leads to the required result where

$$M_1 = (I - \hat{A})^{-1}; \qquad M_2 = (I + A^* + A^{*2}); \qquad M_3 = (I - A^{*3})^{-1}$$

The precise structures of these matrices are as follows:

$$M_1 = \begin{bmatrix} (I - A_{11})^{-1} & 0 & 0 \\ 0 & I & 0 \\ 0 & 0 & (I - A_{33})^{-1} \end{bmatrix}$$

$$M_2 = \begin{bmatrix} I & A_{13}^* A_{32}^* & A_{13}^* \\ A_{21}^* & I & A_{21}^* A_{13}^* \\ A_{32}^* A_{21}^* & A_{32}^* & I \end{bmatrix}$$

$$M_3 = \begin{bmatrix} (I - A_{13}^* A_{32}^* A_{21}^*)^{-1} & 0 & 0 \\ 0 & (I - A_{21}^* A_{13}^* A_{32}^*)^{-1} & 0 \\ 0 & 0 & (I - A_{32}^* A_{21}^* A_{13}^*)^{-1} \end{bmatrix}$$

Hence, M_1, M_2, and M_3 are multiplier matrices and capture the distinct and separable effects in the system, as indicated earlier. The transfer multipliers matrix, M_1, contains input–output multipliers $(I - A_{11})^{-1}$ and the household transfers multipliers $(I - A_{33})^{-1}$ but excludes all those effects that would be induced from one class of accounts to another. On the other hand, the closed-loop multiplier matrix, M_3, contains all induced effects that emanate from an injection in one account and, after going around the system, feed back to itself. Having accounted for all own-account effects in this way, M_2 picks up all the remaining cross-effects in the system.

Before proceeding to the specifically regional aspects of these multipliers, we briefly explore the similarities and differences between the above (Pyatt–Round) multipliers and the many other kinds of multisectoral multipliers that have figured so prominently in regional analysis. Not surprisingly, as it turns out, all the multisectoral (input–output based) multipliers are closely related to one another and differ only in their emphasis on different parts of the system, the degree of system closure, or the form of endogenous behavior specified. Therefore, restricting our attention to a system in which production and household income and expenditure behavior are endogenous, the Pyatt–Round multipliers are comparable with those set out by Miyazawa (1976), which have been the focus of recent attention by Batey (1985) and Rose and Beaumont (Chapter 10, this volume).

In one sense, we can consider the framework on which the Miyazawa multipliers are based as a partially reduced form of the SAM-based Pyatt–Round multipliers. In particular, there are no institution accounts in the Miyazawa multipliers, so that factor incomes are spent directly on goods and services in the Kalecki tradition. This means that the three links in the basic circular flow of income, described earlier, are reduced to two, and it also means that the stage in the "income propagation process" that involves institutions will be lost. A further consequence is that Miyazawa's reduced-form system will exclude transfer incomes between household groups and other institutions from the set of endogenous transactions.

A second difference between the two multiplier models stems from their respective approaches to decomposition. If we disregard the household accounts and interhousehold transfers, then, of course, the starting point for multiplier decomposition, the matrix M, is identical in both systems. Rows and columns of M may be partitioned into production activities and factors, which leads Miyazawa to decompose M into quadrants. Each quadrant has a specific interpretation and much of the interest in computing Miyazawa-type multipliers at the national and regional level [for example, Rose and Beaumont (1988; and Chapter 10, this volume)] has been directed toward particular components, such as the "interrelational multiplier." In fact, however, the Pyatt–Round framework offers a broader opportunity for studying linkage, from which many Miyazawa multipliers, and, in particular, the interrelational multipliers, may be obtained as particular components or special cases.

It is worth noting in this context that the Type I, II, and III multipliers (Miernyk, 1965) are related measures of system linkage, but, in the sense of Leontief, Keynes, and Kalecki, are not strictly multipliers at all. They are ratios of various income multipliers normalized with respect to direct income effects and do not, therefore, measure income or output effects of exogenous impulses on the system. Furthermore, although a close relationship exists, they are not directly analogous to the decomposed multipliers M_1, M_2, and M_3.[2]

An obvious distinguishing feature of the decomposition of the overall multiplier into M_1, M_2, and M_3 from all previous decompositions is that it is multiplicative. It is very clear that the multiplicative approach has a distinct appeal as a decomposition procedure for "multipliers." The degree of linkage in the system can therefore be observed from the degree of departure of each matrix M_1, M_2, or M_3 from I, but the total contribution of each multiplier, in absolute terms, is dependent on the size of the other two, and this remains true of the additive version proposed by Stone (1978).

Finally, on a similar theme, Defourny and Thorbecke (1984) have proposed an alternative to multiplier decomposition based on structural path analysis. They recognize the usefulness of the multiplicative decomposition in establishing the nature of linkage in the system, but they claim that their method is of more direct help to a policymaker in breaking down the "channels of influence;" however, it is a more micro-oriented approach and consequently reveals less about whole system linkage.

At a practical level, in a number of studies for developing countries, these decompositions have been shown to be effective ways of analyzing the interrelationship between production structure and income distribution. To carry out such an exercise, the principal data requirement is, of course, to have a SAM with a detailed

---

2. Editors' Note: In a number of studies, for example, Jordan and Polenske (1988), analysts incorporate another component of final demand and value added, such as government expenditures and taxes, to form another version of Type III multiplier.

disaggregation of factor and household groups as well as a number of production sectors. However, the size of the SAM and the number of accounts are not nearly as important as the classifications of households and types of labor and other factors that they embrace. A household usually comprises several individuals, often with very different characteristics. The members of households who are employed receive income in return for the labor services they provide, and this mapping is determined by A_{12} in the multiplier model. Households with members who are unemployed or otherwise inactive may receive unemployment or welfare benefits, but this would be transfer income, not a part of the domestic product, and therefore would be shown as part of x_3 in the multiplier model.

The problem of choosing appropriate classifications for commodities and production activities has long been recognized in input–output analysis at both the national and regional levels. What is often not so well recognized is the existence of similar problems in distinguishing between households of different types, classifying labor, hence identifying labor markets. An important question is, therefore, how should one characterize households of different types? Household classification by the level of household income is one possibility. This has frequently been used in closed input–output models, such as by Miernyk et al. (1967) and Miyazawa (1976), although it is fraught with problems of identifying target households that might move between income groups as policy changes. The geographical location of the household is another possibility and is particularly useful in distinguishing between households in subregional areas, for example, urban/rural or metropolitan/suburban/rural areas. However, beyond these obvious examples, it may not be possible to choose characteristics that describe all members of a household in exactly the same way. Households most frequently contain more than one individual and their characteristics, particularly their employment status or other labor force characteristics, may vary considerably. Usually, a household is classified by the characteristics of a principal member, say, the household head or the main earner,[3] but "individual-specific" characteristics should be avoided. Hence, almost any classification geared to employment status is likely to be an imperfect way of classifying households and should serve to caution us in distinguishing between "employee" and "employer" households, "employed" and "unemployed" households, or even "active" and "inactive" households.

DECOMPOSING MULTIPLIERS FOR AN INTERREGIONAL ECONOMY

The multiplier decompositions just outlined take no account of spatial linkages, and, in this sense, they are not particularly good for describing interrelationships in a true regional setting. I have previously discussed this issue in Round (1985), in which a similar multiplier decomposition analysis was extended to linked regional systems. In this section, I shall summarize these results and integrate the multipliers so derived with those obtained in the previous section. Once again the SAM already shown in Table 8-1 serves as the basis for the analysis.

In simplified notation Table 8-1 can be represented in partitioned form as

3. These are not always the same individual.

follows:

$$\begin{bmatrix} y^1 \\ y^2 \end{bmatrix} = \begin{bmatrix} T^{11} & \hat{t}^{12} \\ \hat{t}^{21} & T^{22} \end{bmatrix} i + \begin{bmatrix} x^1 \\ x^2 \end{bmatrix} \tag{8-6}$$

where the superscripts refer to the two regions concerned, and, as before, i represents the unit vector. As in the earlier decomposition analysis, we define coefficient matrices so as to develop ex post regional multipliers. In order to capture the interregional multiplier linkages, we now enlarge the endogeneity in the system to embrace those flows between regions relating to commodity trade and factor and household transfers. Thus,

$$B_{ii} = T^{ii}(\hat{y}^i)^{-1} \quad \text{and} \quad \hat{b}_{ij} = \hat{t}^{ij}(\hat{y}^j)^{-1}$$

so that

$$\begin{bmatrix} y^1 \\ y^2 \end{bmatrix} = \begin{bmatrix} B_{11} & \hat{b}_{12} \\ \hat{b}_{21} & B_{22} \end{bmatrix} \begin{bmatrix} y^1 \\ y^2 \end{bmatrix} + \begin{bmatrix} x^1 \\ x^2 \end{bmatrix} \tag{8-7}$$

which may be solved as

$$\begin{bmatrix} y^1 \\ y^2 \end{bmatrix} = \begin{bmatrix} (I - B_{11})^{-1} & 0 \\ 0 & (I - B_{22})^{-1} \end{bmatrix} \left\{ \begin{bmatrix} 0 & \hat{b}_{12} \\ \hat{b}_{21} & 0 \end{bmatrix} \begin{bmatrix} y^1 \\ y^2 \end{bmatrix} + \begin{bmatrix} x^1 \\ x^2 \end{bmatrix} \right\} \tag{8-8}$$

Now, defining $D_{ij} = (I - B_{ii})^{-1}\hat{b}_{ij}$ Equation (8-8) becomes

$$\begin{bmatrix} y^1 \\ y^2 \end{bmatrix} = \begin{bmatrix} I & -D_{12} \\ -D_{21} & I \end{bmatrix}^{-1} \begin{bmatrix} (I - B_{11})^{-1} & 0 \\ 0 & (I - B_{22})^{-1} \end{bmatrix} \begin{bmatrix} x^1 \\ x^2 \end{bmatrix} \tag{8-9}$$

which may be written as

$$y = M_{rx}M_{r1}x \tag{8-10}$$

where M_{rx} and M_{r1} are representations of the multiplying matrices in Equation (8-8). Both are multiplier matrices because $M_{rx} \geq I$ and $M_{r1} \geq I$, but they have interesting individual interpretations. M_{r1} is the intraregional multiplier matrix: it depicts the linkage effects between endogenous accounts wholly within each region, whereas M_{rx} picks up the multiplier effects one region has on the other and is therefore the interregional multiplier. It should be noted that the key elements here are the interregional trade and transfer vectors b_{ij}, which determine D_{ij}. We can easily show that the interregional multiplier matrix may be further decomposed to give

$$M_{rx} = \begin{bmatrix} (I - D_{12}D_{21})^{-1} & 0 \\ 0 & (I - D_{21}D_{12})^{-1} \end{bmatrix} \begin{bmatrix} I & D_{12} \\ D_{21} & I \end{bmatrix} \tag{8-11}$$

$$= M_{r3}M_{r2}$$

where M_{r3} and M_{r2} represent the matrices in expression (8-11) and are once again multiplier matrices in the same sense as before. M_{r3} is block diagonal, and it shows the "closed-loop" multiplier effects in a spatial dimension. That is, in an ex post sense, it shows the effects an injection in one region has on itself through the endogenously defined linkages with the other region, remembering that all own-region (internal) linkage effects have been removed already and subsumed within M_{r1}. On the other hand, M_{r2} is the interregional "open-loop" multiplier matrix, which captures the effects one region has upon the other after accounting for all "own-region" effects.

The total multiplier effect can be expressed as a combination of expressions (8-10) and (8-11) giving

$$y = M_{r3} M_{r2} M_{r1} x \tag{8-12}$$

However, the analysis of the previous section has shown that M_{r1} can be further decomposed into multipliers that take account of the functional relationships between and within the production sectors, factors, and households. In particular, M_{r1} can easily be seen to comprise the following:

$$
\begin{aligned}
M_{r1} &= \begin{bmatrix} M_3^1 M_2^1 M_1^1 & 0 \\ 0 & M_3^2 M_2^2 M_1^2 \end{bmatrix} \\
&= \begin{bmatrix} M_3^1 & 0 \\ 0 & M_3^2 \end{bmatrix} \begin{bmatrix} M_2^1 & 0 \\ 0 & M_2^2 \end{bmatrix} \begin{bmatrix} M_1^1 & 0 \\ 0 & M_1^2 \end{bmatrix} \\
&= \hat{M}_3 \hat{M}_2 \hat{M}_1 \tag{8-13}
\end{aligned}
$$

where $\hat{M}_k$ is the block diagonal matrix of intraregional multipliers of type k. Thus, the combination of Equations (8-12) and (8-13) gives the sense in which the whole system of functional and spatial endogeneity can be expressed as a multiplicative compounding of separable multiplier effects. The closer a multiplier matrix is to the identity matrix, the weaker is that particular multiplier effect. None of the previous attempts, such as by Miyazawa (1976) and Miller (1986) to capture these effects through block-partitioned matrices and additive decompositions, shows the nature and degree of linkage at each stage at this level of detail or, indeed, in this way.

Let us now consider the purely regional features of those decomposed multipliers. The interregional "closed-loop" multiplier matrix M_{r3} is of special interest and ties in closely with continuing interest in interregional feedback effects.[4] Bearing in mind the broader degree of endogeneity, we see that M_{r3} contains more than input–output feedback multipliers and will typically include feedbacks arising through interregional household transfers and migrant remittances. If all these effects are weak and M_{r3} is near to I, then M_{r2} will be nearly decomposable, thereby showing weak open-loop effects in one direction or the other, leading to the conclusion that the principal contributions to the total multiplier would be intraregional rather than interregional. For two regions, this is as far as the decompositions can be carried, but for three or more regions several further loops can be extracted. This is more generally discussed in Round (1985).

EXTENDING MULTIPLIERS FOR AN INTERREGIONAL ECONOMY

In deriving the multipliers and their decompositions, I provided no justification for moving from ex post (or accounting) multipliers to their use as ex ante impact multipliers. The use of fixed input–output coefficients is now commonplace, and the efficacy of using ex post coefficients in an ex ante sense has been extensively discussed in the literature already. However, there are obvious additional difficulties in regional and interregional systems, because the assumption must be extended to interregional trade patterns. This has also been exhaustively discussed, and the limitations are well

4. See Miller (1986) and Gillen and Guccione (1980).

known. At the subnational level, when we are dealing with regions using a common currency and subject to fixed exchange rates, the problem is less severe than at the supranational level. Nevertheless, the use of production and trade coefficients represented by average propensities is, in any case, best limited to fixed-price models. If relative prices are allowed to change, then even the production module would become far less defensible than at present.

As the endogeneity of the system is broadened to include factors and household behavior, the nature of the assumptions must be considered more carefully. One purpose of the exercise is to close the system to show the two-way dependence between production structure and the distribution of income across households. That is, it closes the income–expenditure–production loop, which is fundamental to any economic system. However, it is still a demand-led system, and it is an implicit assumption that there will be an adequate factor supply (as well as sufficient production capacity) in order to meet the factor demands. Although substitutions between factors are likely to take place, the use of constant coefficients A_{21}, ex ante, will largely depend upon the classification of types of labor and capital we adopt. The same would be true of the coefficients mapping factoral income into households A_{32}, in which, ex ante, we are assuming that households supply the same proportions of incremental factor supplies as they do, on average, ex post. Perhaps the least defensible assumption of all would be that the expenditure propensities of households are the same at the margin as they are on average. In a fixed-price model, all that we require to know in order to relax this assumption is a set of income elasticities for each commodity. This would allow us to adjust the ex post coefficients accordingly, hence to replace average by marginal propensities.[5]

With these considerations as background, the multipliers derived in this paper may be viewed in two senses. In the first place, as a description of ex post structure, the decompositions show the degree of system linkage as it existed in the accounting period from which the multipliers were constructed. A second perspective is to consider the use of these decomposed multipliers to study economic impacts. For this purpose, it is arguable that, under certain conditions and with some modifications of the coefficients, the multipliers could be considered adequate, but it is a basic requirement for describing endogenous behavior that outlays bear some relation to account totals. This gives us some clue as to the possibilities for incorporating more endogenous accounts into the system. Let us consider, in turn, the accounts currently subsumed within the set of exogenous accounts. These include the remaining institution current account activities (companies and government), all capital account transactions (savings and investment), and the external accounts.

The household sector includes all unincorporated businesses, because it is frequently impossible to distinguish between returns to labor (wages) and returns to capital (profits) for small traders and small business enterprises. However, the corporate sector is the institution that receives profits as a return to corporate capital and that makes payments of distributed profits to shareholders, tax payments to government, besides retaining profits as part of capital finance. Similarly, the government sector receives income mainly in the form of taxes of various kinds and

---

5. This is not to preclude the possibility that for some household groups the marginal expenditure propensities would be the average propensities, for example, for immigrant households (Miernyk et al., 1967).

spends some of this on goods and services as well as making transfer payments to households (as, say, unemployment and welfare payments) and to other institutions. The existence of these transfers is not in question, rather, it is whether we can reasonably endogenize corporate and government incomes and outlays in fixed coefficients terms. As ex post relationships, these may represent past linkage. However, government outlays are more of a policy than a behavioral link, and it is therefore highly questionable whether this would be a good basis to generate sensible ex ante multipliers. Nevertheless, if the endogenous accounts were to include a broader institutional group rather than just households, we note that the structure of endogenous flows represented by the A matrix would remain intact. Indeed, the institutional transfer matrix T_{33}, hence A_{33}, would, in a sense, be more informative, for it would endogenously determine all transfers in the regional system rather than only those between household groups. The only remaining accounts to consider are capital and external transactions, but these are notoriously difficult to endogenize in a simple, yet meaningful, way.

Before leaving the question of further extending the multipliers and their decompositions, we relate this discussion to the recent and burgeoning literature on linked economic and demographic systems. The raison d'être for much of this work is captured by Schinnar's remark that

> there is abundant evidence pointing to the fact that demographic variations have been induced by manipulations or movements in economic variables and, conversely, that demographic changes have important "feedback" effects on economic matters. (Schinnar, 1976, p. 455)

The essence of Schinnar's approach is to use an open, static input–output model to determine labor demands, which then get mapped into cohort and occupational categories. After allowing for the unemployed, the total labor force is determined and subsequently grows over time through a separate demographic loop. The effects of the mix and size of the population then affect the economic model through expenditures on commodities in a final phase. Similar economic and demographic links have been incorporated in a series of models for developing countries, referred to as the BACHUE models.[6] Contrary to the criticism of Batey and Madden (1981) all of these models incorporate feedbacks from the demographic to the economic components of the model. Indeed, and particularly in the BACHUE models, the income/consumption loop is handled in a detailed way, using, for example, expenditure functions based on both household composition and household income. Notwithstanding these similarities, there are also many differences between the Schinnar and BACHUE models, particularly in the way in which the labor market in general is treated, and market clearing in particular.

For these reasons we must be clear about the true nature of the "demographic" loop in a demographic–economic model, and the kind of feedbacks that have been incorporated. Part of the problem has to do with terminology, but I would contend that a model embracing different types of labor, labor markets, and their effects on household income, expenditure, and general well-being of the population is

6. See, for example, Rodgers et al. (1978) and Moreland (1984) for two BACHUE studies. The series of BACHUE studies were conducted under the auspices of the International Labour Organization, Geneva, and are named after the Colombian goddess of "love, fertility, and harmony between nature and man."

"economic." Only when we incorporate specifically "noneconomic" population factors, particularly (though not exclusively) as they affect labor supply, such as births, deaths, fertility, and migration, do we have a true "demographic" model. As already indicated, there are some good examples of these models, including those enunciated by Madden and Batey (1983) and Brouwer et al. (1983). Certainly, we can claim that the multiplier decompositions discussed earlier, and the SAM structure inclusive of factor accounts on which they are based, bring out many of the economic features inherent in an explicit recognition of segmented labor markets and of households that comprise individuals with very different characteristics, including those who do not participate in the labor market. In this sense, SAM-based models, such as those developed earlier in this chapter, already incorporate some of the feedbacks identified by Schinnar.

To go further with the demographic links requires us to specify a more representative labor market model, particularly at the regional level at which regional migration might well play an important additional role. As a depiction of ex ante multipliers, the present model, in common with Schinnar, Madden, and Batey, and most other household augmented input–output models, assumes away the complexities of the labor market. It is unrealistic to assume unemployment rates are exogenous (Schinnar) or that the price mechanism plays no part in the labor markets (Batey and Madden). Some interesting possibilities on this have been suggested by Ledent and Gordon (1981) using the Harris–Todaro model of migration, which has been used in a number of similar instances to augment labor supply submodels and which figures in the ambitious BACHUE models for some developing countries.

CONCLUSION

The SAM approach to the design and construction of macroeconomic data bases and the subsequent development of fixed price (multiplier) and flexiprice (computable general equilibrium) models has proved to be a useful way of assessing the degree of linkage in an economy, particularly with regard to a range of questions to do with poverty alleviation and income distribution in developing countries. This has been shown to have a direct relationship with recent work in regional analysis on linked demographic and economic systems. In conclusion, however, the achievements must be seen against some current limitations. The decomposition of fixed price multipliers set out in this chapter shows insights into basic structural linkage and has a direct bearing on the specification of economic–demographic linkages. However, the usefulness of fixed-price relationships is limited, and there is much scope for future research in this area.

ACKNOWLEDGMENTS

The author wishes to thank Graham Pyatt and Sir Richard Stone for their inspiration and help on an earlier version of this chapter.

REFERENCES

Barnard, J. R. 1969. "A Social Accounting System for Regional Development Planning." *Journal of Regional Science.* Vol. 9, pp. 109–115.

Batey, P. W. J., and M. Madden. 1981. "Demographic–Economic Forecasting within an Activity-Commodity Framework: Some Theoretical Considerations and Empirical Results." *Environment and Planning A.* Vol. 13, pp. 1067–1083.

Batey, P. W. J. 1985. "Input–Output Models for Regional Demographic–Economic Analysis: Some Structural Comparisons." *Environment and Planning A.* Vol. 17, pp. 73–99.

Brouwer, F., J. P. Hettelingh, and L. Hordijk. 1983. "An Integrated Regional Model for Economic–Ecological–Demographic–Facility Interactions." *Papers of the Regional Science Association.* Vol. 52, pp. 87–103.

Czamanski, S. 1973. *Regional and Interregional Social Accounting.* Lexington, MA: Lexington Books.

Defourny, J., and E. Thorbecke. 1984. "Structural Path Analysis and Multiplier Decomposition within a Social Accounting Matrix Framework." *Economic Journal.* Vol. 94, pp. 111–136.

Gillen, W. J., and A. Guccione. 1980. "Interregional Feedbacks in Input–Output Models: Some Formal Results." *Journal of Regional Science.* Vol. 20, pp. 477–482.

Jordan, P. G., and K. R. Polenske. 1988. "A Multiplier Impact Study of Fishing Activities in New England and Nova Scotia." In *Input–Output Analysis: Current Developments,* edited by Maurizo Ciaschini. London: Chapman & Hall, Ch. 20.

Ledent, J., and P. Gordon. 1981. "A Framework for Modelling Interregional Population Distribution and Economic Growth." *International Regional Science Review.* Vol. 6, pp. 85–90.

Madden, M., and P. W. J. Batey. 1983. "Linked Population and Economic Models: Some Methodological Issues in Forecasting, Analysis, and Policy Optimization." *Journal of Regional Science.* Vol. 23, pp. 141–164.

Miernyk, W. H. 1965. *Elements of Input–Output Analysis.* New York: Random House.

Miernyk, W. H., E. R. Bonner, J. H. Chapman, and K. Shellhammer. 1967. *Impact of the Space Program on a Local Economy.* Morgantown, WV: West Virginia University Library.

Miller, R. E. 1986. "Upper Bounds on the Size of Interregional Feedbacks in Multiregional Input–Output Models." *Journal of Regional Science.* Vol. 26, pp. 285–306.

Miyazawa, K. 1976. *Input–Output Analysis and the Structure of Income Distribution.* Berlin: Springer–Verlag.

Moreland, R. S. 1984. *Population, Development, and Income Distribution—A Modelling Approach (BACHUE—International).* London and Aldershot, Hants, UK: Martin's and Gower.

Pleskovic, B., and G. Treviño. 1985. *The Use of a Social Accounting Matrix Framework for Public Sector Analysis: The Case Study of Mexico.* Ljubljana, Yugoslavia: International Center for Public Enterprises in Developing Countries.

Pyatt, G., and J. I. Round. 1977. "Social Accounting Matrices for Development Planning." *Review of Income and Wealth.* Series 23, pp. 239–364.

Pyatt, G., and J. I. Round. 1979. "Accounting and Fixed Price Multipliers in a SAM Framework." *Economic Journal.* Vol. 89, pp. 850–873.

Pyatt, G., and J. I. Round. 1985. *Social Accounting Matrices: A Basis for Planning.* Washington, D.C.: The World Bank.

Pyatt, G., and E. Thorbecke. 1976. *Planning Techniques for a Better Future.* Geneva: International Labour Organization.

Pyatt, G., and A. R. Roe with J. I. Round, R. M. Lindley, and others. 1977. *Social Accounting for Development Planning.* Cambridge, England: Cambridge University Press.

Richardson, H. W. 1978. *Regional and Urban Economics.* Harmondsworth, Middlesex, UK: Penguin.

Rodgers, G. B., M. J. D. Hopkins, and R. Wery. 1978. *Population, Employment, and Inequality (BACHUE—Philippines).* Farnborough, UK: Saxon House.

Rose, A., and P. Beaumont. 1988. "Interrelational Income Distribution Multipliers for the West Virginia Economy." *Journal of Regional Science.* Vol. 28, pp. 461–475.

Round, J. I. 1985. "Decomposing Multipliers for Economic Systems Involving Regional and World Trade." *Economic Journal.* Vol. 95, pp. 383–399.

Round, J. I. 1986. "Social Accounting for Regional Economic Systems." In *Integrated Analysis of Regional Systems,* edited by P. Batey and M. Madden. London: Pion, pp. 90–106.

Schinnar, A. P. 1976. "A Multidimensional Accounting Model for Demographic and Economic Planning Interactions." *Environment and Planning A*. Vol. 8, pp. 455–475.

Stone, J. R. N. 1961. "Social Accounts at the Regional Level." In *Regional Economic Planning*, edited by W. Isard and J. Cumberland. Paris: Organization for European Co-operation and Development, pp. 263–296.

Stone, J. R. N. 1978. "The Disaggregation of the Household Sector in the National Accounts." Paper presented at World Bank Conference on Social Accounting Methods in Development Planning, Cambridge, England, reprinted in Pyatt and Round,1985, pp. 145–185.

9

The Effects of Household Disaggregation in Extended Input–Output Models

PETER W. J. BATEY and MELVYN J. WEEKS

Input–output analysis at the regional level has traditionally focussed upon interindustry linkages. Analysts have used it to trace the pattern of direct and indirect economic linkages within a region, enabling assessments to be made of the extent to which a change in demand in one industry is transmitted to other industries within the same economy.

A major defect of much of the work in this field has been the relative neglect of the household sector, hence of demographic–economic linkages. Analysts have treated household income and expenditures—generally more significant at the regional level than at the national level (Hewings, 1986)—in a cursory manner, usually as a single row and column within the input–output table. In the past 10 years, however, analysts have become increasingly aware of the need to improve the specification of households in such models (Madden and Batey, 1980; Oosterhaven, 1981; Hewings and Jensen, 1986). This has led to a variety of different approaches to household disaggregation, reflected in a range of extended input–output models (Batey, 1985).

Our aim in the present chapter is twofold. The first is methodological and concerns the issue of model design. We intend to investigate some of the forms of household disaggregation that are available by focusing on four specific input–output models. We shall demonstrate that the task of disaggregation can be viewed as a simple process of model elaboration, in which particular stages are included or omitted according to local circumstances.

The second aim is to establish how far the results of an economic impact analysis are likely to be influenced by the choice of household disaggregation scheme. Using data from the Greater Cork region in the Irish Republic, we present a systematic comparison of the impacts measured by each of the four types of model. In the empirical analysis, we will examine the relative importance of interindustry structure and household income and consumption in determining the size of impacts and will measure the changes in these impacts that occur as the input–output model is progressively extended. Our focus throughout will be on income and employment impacts and on any differences between these impacts.

HOUSEHOLD DISAGGREGATION IN REGIONAL INPUT–OUTPUT MODELS

In this section, we examine a sequence of model elaboration, starting with the simplest form of model, in which households are treated exogenously, outside the Leontief inverse, and leading eventually to a comprehensive extended model in which three distinct types of household income and expenditure are included. Each model will be represented as a system of simultaneous equations expressed in the form of an activity–commodity framework (Batey and Madden, 1981), consisting of a square matrix of coefficients postmultiplied by a vector of activity levels (unknowns), with the result set equal to a vector of constraints (input variables). The system of equations is solved by inverting the matrix of coefficients and a determinate solution is obtained.

The sequence may, for convenience, be divided into four stages. As a starting point, we take the simple, one-region static input–output model in which household consumption is treated as a component of final demand, and household income is a component of primary inputs. The activity–commodity framework for this model is shown in Equation (9-1):

$$(I - A)x_I = d_I \tag{9-1}$$

where

$I - A$ is a square matrix, consisting of a technical coefficients matrix A subtracted from an identity matrix;

x_I is a column vector of industrial gross output; and

d_I is a column vector of industrial final demand.

With this model, we can assess the impact of household spending on industrial output, but we cannot account for the effect that a change in industrial output might have on household income and expenditure. In other words, we ignore the induced effect of households.

The conventional response to this problem has been to enlarge the input–output model by adding a single row and column to the matrix of coefficients. We can then treat the household sector endogenously, on the same basis as industrial sectors. The activity–commodity framework now becomes

$$\begin{bmatrix} I - A & -h_c \\ -h_r & 1 \end{bmatrix} \begin{bmatrix} x_I \\ x_H \end{bmatrix} = \begin{bmatrix} d_I \\ d_H \end{bmatrix} \tag{9-2}$$

where

h_c is a column vector of household consumption propensities;

h_r is a row vector of income from employment coefficients;

x_H is household income, a scalar;

d_H is exogenous household income, that is, income received by residents living in the study area from sources outside the area.

(Other notation has already been defined.)

Several criticisms can be made of this form of model. The first arises from the assumption of a linear and homogeneous consumption function: we assume that households of whatever kind have the same wage rate and consumption propensities. Second, we implicitly assume that these propensities apply exclusively to employed households. If considered at all, we treat consumption by unemployed households as part of final demand. It is not influenced by the consumption of employed households. Third, we make no explicit assumption about the source of newly employed workers: are they recruited from the local labor market or are they migrants? There is the implication that, before taking up employment, these workers (or, more precisely, their consumption) had no impact upon our regional economy. In effect, therefore, they are in-migrants to the region.

The issue of a linear and homogeneous consumption function is one that was discussed in detail in a pioneering exercise by Miernyk et al. (1967) as part of a study of the impact of the space program upon Boulder, Colorado. Following Tiebout (1969),[1] Miernyk and his colleagues assumed that changes in personal income in a region could be divided into two types: extensive and intensive. They defined extensive growth as an increase in output and employment without any increase in per capita income. Intensive growth occurs as a result of increases in productivity. They assumed that in-migrants receive the same wage rates as indigenous workers (extensive income), and they identified the difference between this and total income growth as intensive income, reflecting increases in productivity among the indigenous workforce.

They also assumed that indigenous and in-migrant workers have different consumption propensities. In the Boulder model, the analysts assumed that new residents consume according to the average propensity, and they associated the consumption arising from increased per capita incomes with the marginal propensity. To circumvent the problem of linearity, they divided existing workers into a number of income groups, each with a different propensity to consume within the regional economy. Elsewhere, Madden and Batey (1983) have shown that this quasi-nonlinear relationship between income and consumption can be incorporated within a linear equation system.

Miernyk's Boulder model and a later formulation by Blackwell (1978) provide the impetus for the third stage in our sequence of model elaboration. Batey et al. (1987) have shown that this model can be represented as three blocks of simultaneous equations:

$$
\begin{bmatrix} I - A & -h_c^m & -h_c^a \\ h_r^{a-m} & 1 & 0 \\ h_r^m & 0 & 1 \end{bmatrix}
\begin{bmatrix} x_I \\ x_H^i \\ x_H^e \end{bmatrix}
=
\begin{bmatrix} d_I \\ d_H^i \\ d_H^e \end{bmatrix}
\tag{9-3}
$$

where superscripts i and e denote intensive income and extensive income, respectively.

We find it instructive to compare this model with the earlier household endogenous model given by Equation (9-2). We note that the single row vector of income from employment coefficients, h_r, has been replaced by two separate row vectors, denoted here by h_r^m and h_r^{a-m}. Row vector h_r^m defines, for each industrial sector, the proportion of that sector's gross output accounted for by income payments by in-migrants (extensive income growth), whereas h_r^{a-m} is the proportion of sectoral gross output accounted for by payments to indigenous workers for increased productivity (intensive income growth). Blackwell (1978) and Batey et al. (1987) give the precise method of calculating these coefficients.

---

1. Miernyk took the lead from the earlier unpublished version of Tiebout's paper.

We now subdivide household consumption, previously denoted by a single column vector of consumption propensities, into two vectors: average consumption propensities, h_c^a, linked with extensive income, and marginal propensities, h_c^m, associated with intensive income.

The model specified in Equation (9-3) overcomes some of the criticisms that analysts have made of the conventional household endogenous model. In particular, we can relax the assumption of homogeneity. The form of disaggregation we adopted, distinguishing between indigenous and in-migrant households, is no doubt appropriate for cases in which there is the expectation of rapid regional growth, accompanied by a shortage of suitable workers in the local labor market. The model is clearly less applicable in declining regions in which there is a substantial pool of unemployed workers. We now turn to an extension of Equation (9-3), in which we model explicitly the income and consumption of unemployed households. This model, given by Equation (9-4), represents the fourth stage in the process of elaboration:

$$
\begin{bmatrix}
I - A & -h_c^m & -h_c^a & -sh_c^u \\
-h_r^{a-m} & 1 & 0 & 0 \\
-h_r^m & 0 & 1 & 0 \\
l\hat{\rho} & 0 & 0 & 1
\end{bmatrix}
\begin{bmatrix}
x_I \\
x_H^i \\
x_H^e \\
u
\end{bmatrix}
=
\begin{bmatrix}
d_I \\
d_H^i \\
d_H^e \\
p
\end{bmatrix}
\qquad (9\text{-}4)
$$

where

l is a row vector of employment/gross output ratios, specified by industrial sector;

$\hat{\rho}$ is a diagonal matrix containing probabilities, indicating the proportion of vacancies filled by previously unemployed indigenous workers;

s is a scalar, indicating the unemployment benefit rate;

h_c^u is a column vector of consumption propensities for unemployed households;

u is a scalar, measuring the unemployment level (expressed as number of workers); and

p is a scalar, measuring the level of labor supply.

The aspects of particular interest in Equation (9-4) are all associated with the final row and column of the matrix of coefficients. Three features merit special attention. First, we note that in this model we can fill employment vacancies both by workers drawn from the regional unemployment pool and by in-migrants from outside the region: the precise combination for each industrial sector is determined by the value of parameter ρ_i. Second, unemployed workers are paid a fixed rate of benefit, denoted by s, and their consumption propensities are given by h_c^u. The product of s and h_c^u will therefore yield a column vector denoting the consumption of specific industrial commodities per unemployed worker. Finally, for every employment vacancy filled by an unemployed indigenous worker, there is a corresponding reduction in the unemployment level u. This is determined by the fourth block of equations in (9-4) that serves as an accounting identity:

$$
l\hat{\rho}x_I + u = p \qquad (9\text{-}5)
$$

In this equation, employment opportunities available to indigenous workers $(l\hat{\rho}x_I)$ are added to unemployment, u, and the result set equal to labor supply, p.

In Equation (9-4), we have a model in which three types of household income and

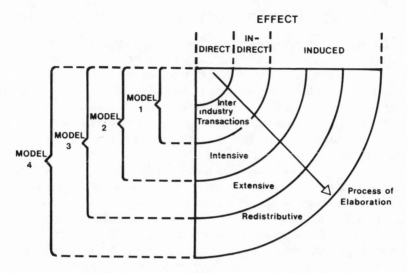

FIGURE 9-1   Sequence of model elaboration (the "onionskin" model).

expenditure are represented, reflecting the behavior of indigenous employed workers, in-migrant workers, and indigenous unemployed workers.

The models represented by Equations (9-1) to (9-4) provide a flexible structure, which should satisfy the needs of most regional impact analyses. Now that each of the models has been described, we reflect briefly on the process of model elaboration. We have seen that each stage in the process involved building on the previous one, rather like successive layers of onionskin. This is illustrated in Figure 9-1, which summarizes the sequence of elaboration, while at the same time enabling each of the four models to be clearly identified.

In Figure 9-1, a distinction is made between direct, indirect, and three different types of induced effects of a change in final demand. Direct effects can, of course, be established from the matrix of coefficients. *Model* 1 serves to measure direct and indirect effects; *Model* 2 measures direct, indirect, and *intensive* induced effects;[2] *Model* 3 measures direct, indirect, and *intensive and extensive* induced effects; and *Model* 4 measures direct, indirect, and *intensive, extensive, and redistributive* induced effects. Here redistributive income is defined as the unemployment benefit payments foregone by indigenous unemployed workers when they move into paid employment. It will serve to reduce the overall size of extensive income.

The process of model elaboration should not be seen as rigid: in certain circumstances, it may be desirable to omit particular stages. In regions in which the unemployment rate is at a consistently low level, for example, it may be appropriate to remove the final "onionskin" and ignore the effect of redistributive income; in other cases, it may not be worthwhile to retain the distinction between intensive and extensive income. In the next section, we shall examine empirical evidence for one region—Greater Cork in Ireland—to gauge the relative importance of each of the various model extensions discussed here.

2. Potentially there are three versions of Model 2; as well as the version described here, the model can be specified with extensive income or with intensive and extensive income aggregated [as in Equation (9-2)].

MEASURING THE EFFECTS OF DISAGGREGATION

If regional input–output models are to provide a useful source of guidance to decision-makers on the likely income and employment impacts of development proposals, it is important that the choice of which model to use is not made lightly. There needs to be a clear understanding of how the results of an economic impact analysis are affected by model structure. Our review of the various ways of extending the input–output model leads us to expect that there will be variations in impact multipliers, depending on which household disaggregation scheme is employed.

The purpose of this section is to present an empirical analysis in which two basic questions about the effects of disaggregation are analyzed. First, we shall examine the four main types of model in order to compare the income and employment multipliers from each. What range of impact magnitudes can we expect, and does a more elaborate model enable us to make more precise estimates? Second, we intend to focus on the induced effects of household income and expenditure. Which are the most important components of the induced effect, and how does their size compare with that of the indirect effect, which stems from interindustry transactions?

We use a 1973 survey-based input–output table for the Greater Cork region for the analysis. Cork is the second largest city in the Irish Republic, and at the time of the input–output study, the region had a population of approximately 135,000. The region contains a substantial amount of manufacturing industry (42% of total employment) and provides an important service function, particularly in relation to education and medicine.

The original Cork input–output study included 39 industrial sectors. To these we added two household sectors, representing indigenous and in-migrant households. Blackwell (1976, 1978) has described how the data assembled in the study were used to construct an extended input–output model, based on Miernyk's Boulder model.

The household component of the Cork model has been modified for the purpose of the present study. The first change involves the specification of a third household sector, to represent the income and consumption of the unemployed, whereas the second concerns the internal composition of each household sector. Rather than define households on the basis of the employment status of their head, we have reconstituted these sectors so that all workers of the same employment status are grouped within one household sector. We adopt the approach described in detail in Batey (1982) and Weeks (1985), which we used in an earlier study of the Merseyside economy (Batey and Madden, 1983). It has the advantage that it allows a clearer analysis of the effects of income and expenditure: in particular, the difference between consumption propensities will be more sharply defined. Data for these modifications were obtained from the 1973 Household Budget Survey for the Irish Republic.

The model obtained from this extension of the initial Cork model is equivalent to that defined by Equation (9-4). We assume a flat rate of unemployment benefit(s) of £9.75 per week, midway between the benefit payable to a single unemployed man (£7.80) and that payable to a family man with two children (£12.00). We set the parameter ρ, which denotes the probability of vacancies being filled by workers drawn from the region's unemployment pool, to 0.8 for all industrial sectors.[3]

---

3. The effects of varying s and ρ on multiplier values are analyzed in Batey and Weeks (1987a), in which empirical evidence is presented for the Strathclyde Region.

It is a simple matter to convert this model to Models 1, 2, and 3, defined by Equations (9-1)–(9-3). We merely reverse the process of model elaboration, at each stage removing a household row and column from the matrix of coefficients.

EMPIRICAL RESULTS

We present the results of the empirical analysis in two parts, corresponding to each of the basic questions about disaggregation that we introduced earlier. We begin by considering the multipliers obtained from each of the four main types of model. Table 9-1 shows the results for income multipliers, whereas Table 9-2 gives the equivalent results for employment multipliers. Both tables assume a direct change of 1000 units: £ of household income in the case of Table 9-1 and jobs in Table 9-2. Our interest lies not so much in the overall change, but rather in the additional quantities of income or employment that are generated as a consequence of the initial impact. Hence, the tables show only the income and employment that form the indirect and induced effects.

We present the results for 9 of the 39 industrial sectors in the Cork input–output study. These sectors were chosen by us to represent three distinct categories of industry, defined on the basis of wage rate and employment/gross output ratio:

1. Labor intensive/high wage   Wholesale machinery, hardware, and electrical goods;
   Communications;
   Professional services.

2. Labor intensive/low wage   Clothing and footwear manufacturing;
   Wood and wood products;
   Personal services: hotels and restaurants.

3. Capital intensive/high wage   Chemical and rubber products manufacturing;
   Energy;
   Insurance, banking, and financial services.

The models we used are those defined by Equations (9-1)–(9-4), except for Model 2, which we modified to include a single row of total income from employment coefficients and a single column of average consumption propensities. This enables us to make useful comparisons with the disaggregated household structures in Models 3 and 4.

Several important points emerge from Table 9-1. The Model 2 economic impacts are consistently the largest and, as we would expect, the lowest economic impacts are given by Model 1. We find that the differences between the results of Models 2 and 3 are very slight: in general Model 1 impacts exceed those measured of Model 3 by about 5 percent. There is a small amount of variation in the Model 3/Model 2 ratio from one sector to another, but this is hardly significant when compared with the overall scale of impact. In fact, on the basis of this evidence, we cannot justify the extra effort required to construct Model 3, in terms of household disaggregation.

The results of Model 4 are more promising. In this model three types of household are included/indigenous employed, in-migrants, and indigenous unemployed. We find that by introducing the unemployed household sector, the income

TABLE 9-1 Comparison of Income Impacts Measured by Four Types of Input–Output Models

Industrial Sector	1 Model 1	2 Model 2	3 Model 3	4 Model 4	Column 4 ÷ Column 2 (%)	Column 3 ÷ Column 2 (%)
Wholesale machinery, hardware, and electrical goods	179	595	583	470	79.0	98.0
Communications	35	401	390	278	69.8	97.3
Professional services	25	387	370	259	66.9	95.6
Clothing and footwear manufacturing	156	564	552	467	82.8	97.9
Wood and wood products	253	695	682	593	85.3	98.1
Personal services: hotels and restaurants	386	876	851	828	94.5	97.3
Chemicals and rubber products manufacturing	165	577	565	442	76.6	97.9
Energy	151	557	527	397	71.3	94.6
Insurance, banking, and financial services	345	819	782	614	75.0	95.5

TABLE 9-2 Comparison of Employment Impacts Measured by Four Types of Input–Output Models

Industrial Sector	1 Model 1	2 Model 2	3 Model 3	4 Model 4	Column 4 ÷ Column 2 (%)	Column 3 ÷ Column 2 (%)
Wholesale machinery hardware, and electrical goods	137	599	584	449	75.0	97.5
Communications	34	501	486	359	71.7	97.0
Professional services	30	605	577	443	73.2	95.4
Clothing and footwear manufacturing	94	399	389	269	67.4	97.5
Wood and wood products	175	515	503	376	73.0	97.7
Personal services: hotels and restaurants	204	557	538	401	72.0	96.6
Chemicals and rubber products manufacturing	153	719	701	556	77.3	97.5
Energy	209	1099	1025	853	77.6	93.3
Insurance, banking, and financial services	154	766	746	597	77.9	97.4

multiplier is affected significantly, and, for two of the three categories of industrial sector, the income impacts fall by as much as 20–35 percent. However, a different pattern is found among the labor-intensive/low-wage sectors. Here, we observe that the Model 4 income multiplier is much closer to its Model 2 counterpart. Two factors appear to be working in combination to create this result. The first lies in the term used to calculate the direct effect, the denominator of the income multiplier. In the case of Model 4, this term becomes much smaller, when the sector employment: gross output ratio is high and the wage rate in that same sector is low, that is, in situations when comparatively large numbers of workers move into employment at wage rates not much higher than the unemployment benefit they were receiving previously. The second factor concerns the relatively strong pattern of interindustry linkages for this group of industrial sectors, as reflected in the large indirect effect measured by Model 1. This large indirect effect has consequences for the size of the numerator of the income multiplier. For Model 4, it tends to reduce the influence of a low wage rate and high employment/gross output ratio in the particular sector whose multiplier is being calculated, with the result that the numerator is higher than it otherwise would be. The prime example is the personal services sector in which wages are particularly low and in which the indirect effect is at its highest among the nine industrial sectors. In this case, the Model 4 income impact comes within 6 percent of its Model 2 equivalent.

In Table 9-2, we find the comparable set of results for employment impacts. Again, we see that the intensive/extensive income distinction embodied in Model 3 produces impacts that are very similar to those obtained from the more straightforward Model 2: in no case is the difference greater than 7 percent.

An interesting contrast appears when we compare the results from Models 2 and 4. As expected, the impacts measured by Model 4 are consistently lower than those from Model 2 but there is much less intersectoral variation than observed for income multipliers. This reflects the simpler form of calculation used for employment multipliers and the reliance on elements of the vector of employment/gross output ratios, for the measurement of direct effects in both Models 2 and 4. We note that in the Cork example, the use of Model 2 instead of the more elaborate Model 4 is likely to lead to the overestimation of employment impacts by between 22 and 33 percent.

We turn now to Tables 9-3 and 9-4. Here, we decompose income and employment multipliers in order to establish the relative importance of indirect and induced effects and, more specifically, the contributions that extensive, intensive, and redistributive extensions make to the overall induced effect. We compiled these tables by following the sequence of model elaboration outlined earlier, comparing the results of each model extension with those obtained from its immediate predecessor.

The results for income impacts are shown in Table 9-3. As with Table 9-1, the impacts represent the consequences of an initial, direct change of 1000 units of income. The total (direct, indirect, and induced) impact is given in the final column, for each of the nine selected industrial sectors. The first point to note is that in all sectors the induced effect exceeds the indirect effect. This confirms the general importance of modeling the household sector in regional models of this kind, as well as interindustry linkages. When the induced effect is examined in detail, we find that a consistent pattern emerges: the extensive income effect has the greatest impact in all sectors, and, in most cases, the intensive income and redistributive income effects are rather evenly matched. In fact, because they have opposite signs, in all but two sectors, the effects cancel each other out. This suggests that in the Cork example, a good approximation

TABLE 9-3 Relative Importance of Indirect and Induced Effects in the Measurement of Income Impacts

Industrial Sector	Indirect Effect	Induced Effect				Total Effect
		Total	Intensive	Extensive	Redistributive	
Wholesale machinery, hardware, and electrical goods	179	291	120	284	−113	1470
Communications	35	243	88	267	−112	1278
Professional services	25	234	88	268	−111	1259
Clothing and footwear manufacturing	156	311	102	294	−85	1467
Wood and wood products	253	340	118	311	−89	1593
Personal services: hotels and restaurants	386	442	123	342	−23	1828
Chemicals and rubber products manufacturing	165	277	129	271	−123	1442
Energy	151	246	34	342	−130	1397
Insurance, banking, and financial services	156	270	115	280	−125	1426

TABLE 9-4 Relative Importance of Indirect and Induced Effects in the Measurement of Employment Impacts

Industrial Sector	Indirect Effect	Induced Effect				Total Effect
		Total	Intensive	Extensive	Redistributive	
Wholesale machinery, hardware, and electrical goods	137	312	62	385	−135	1449
Communications	34	325	61	391	−127	1359
Professional services	30	413	118	429	−134	1443
Clothing and footwear manufacturing	94	175	21	274	−120	1269
Wood and wood products	175	201	46	282	−127	1376
Personal services: hotels and restaurants	204	197	80	254	−137	1401
Chemicals and rubber products manufacturing	165	403	75	473	−145	1556
Energy	209	644	304	512	−172	1853
Insurance, banking, and financial services	154	443	86	506	−149	1597

of income impacts may be obtained by using a model in which only extensive income is specified.

Table 9-4 presents the equivalent results for employment impacts, in which the initial change is 1000 jobs. We can again observe that induced effects are larger than indirect effects: the only exception is the personal services sector in which the two effects are very similar. The composition of the induced effect differs substantially from that for income impacts. In eight of nine sectors, the intensive income effect is much smaller than either the extensive income or the redistributive income effects. The extensive income effect is invariably the largest, but is modified significantly when the redistributive income effect is introduced. The results in Table 9-4 suggest that, in contrast to income multipliers, there is considerable benefit in using a model in which the household sector is represented in detail, at least including extensive and redistributive income and related consumption.

CONCLUSION

In this chapter we have shown that household disaggregation in input–output analysis can be represented as a simple process of model elaboration. We have characterized this process as an "onionskin" model, each stage constituting an additional "skin" of household income and expenditure. The process is flexible, allowing stages to be omitted if the analyst regards particular characteristics of household income and expenditure as being of little importance for the impact study at hand.

We have concentrated on four models, the most elaborate of which included three types of household: the indigenous employed, the in-migrant, and the indigenous unemployed. There is no doubt, however, that we could carry the process of elaboration further. One example of how this might be achieved is to be found in a recent paper by van Dijk and Oosterhaven (1986). They build their model on the foundations of Model 4 described here to include more detail about facets of the local labor market: on job vacancy chains, on trends in labor productivity, and on economically inactive households. Elsewhere, we have demonstrated that by introducing four simplifying assumptions, the van Dijk–Oosterhaven model can be converted to Model 4 (Batey and Weeks, 1987b).

The empirical study based on the Greater Cork region allows several conclusions to be drawn about the effects of household disaggregation. We first compared the income and employment multipliers from the four input–output models. In all the industrial sectors examined, the differences between impacts measured by Models 2 and 3 were very small, suggesting that there is little to be gained by building an input–output model including intensive and extensive household income as separate sectors.

Our comparison of Models 2 and 4 indicated that the introduction of redistributive income and consumption had a significant effect on multiplier values. Indeed, in the case of employment multipliers, we found that Model 2—the conventional household endogenous model—was consistently overestimating impacts by more than 20 percent. The results for income multipliers were more uneven, and in labor-intensive/low-wage sectors, the differences between Model 2 and Model 4 impacts were only slight.

Our analysis of the induced effect produced some particularly interesting findings. The first concerned the size of the induced effect compared with the indirect effect: for both income and employment impacts, the induced effect was consistently more important than the indirect effect, reinforcing the general argument we made at the beginning of the chapter about the need to pay more attention to household specification than has hitherto been done.

When the composition of the induced effect was examined, we found that the largest component was the result of extensive income. In the study of income impacts, intensive and redistributive income effects came close to cancelling each other out, which leads us to suggest that a model based solely on extensive income may suffice in many cases. However, very different results were obtained for employment impacts. Here, there was a clear gradation of effects: extensive effects were the largest, but these were modified substantially by redistributive effects. Intensive effects had scarcely any impact.

ACKNOWLEDGMENTS

The research presented here was supported by the Economic and Social Research Council under grant D.00232051. Helpful comments on an earlier draft of the paper were received from G. J. D. Hewings, R. Jensen, G. R. West, R. Powell, J. Oosterhaven, P. Phibbs, M. Madden, and A. Trigg.

REFERENCES

Batey, P. W. J. 1982. "Reconstructing the Merseyside Demographic–Economic Forecasting Framework Along the Lines of Schinnar's Economic–Demographic Accounting Model." Working Note 11, Department of Civic Design, University of Liverpool, Liverpool, UK.

Batey, P. W. J. 1985. "Input–Output Models for Regional Demographic–Economic Analysis: Some Structural Comparisons." *Environment and Planning A*. Vol. 17, pp. 73–99.

Batey, P. W. J. 1987. "Comprehensive Extended Input–Output Models: Some Notes." Working Note 58, Department of Civic Design, University of Liverpool, Liverpool, UK.

Batey, P. W. J., and M. Madden. 1981. "Demographic–Economic Forecasting Within an Activity–Commodity Framework: Some Theoretical Considerations and Empirical Results." *Environment and Planning A*. Vol. 13, pp. 1067–1083.

Batey, P. W. J., and M. Madden. 1983. "The Modelling of Demographic–Economic Change within the Context of Regional Decline: Analytical Procedures and Empirical Results." *Socio-Economic Planning Sciences*. Vol. 17, pp. 315–328.

Batey, P. W. J., M. Madden, and M. J. Weeks. 1987. "Household Income and Expenditure in Extended Input–Output Models: A Comparative Theoretical and Empirical Analysis." *Journal of Regional Science*. Vol. 27, pp. 341–356.

Batey, P. W. J., and M. J. Weeks. 1987a. "An Extended Input–Output Model Incorporating Employed, Unemployed, and In-migrant Households." *Papers of the Regional Science Association*. Vol. 62, pp. 93–115.

Batey, P. W. J., and M. J. Weeks. 1987b. "A Comprehensive Extended Input–Output Model: Theoretical Development and an Empirical Example." Working Note 55, Department of Civic Design, University of Liverpool, Liverpool, UK.

Blackwell, J. 1976. "Greater Cork Area Input–Output Study: Principal Results," Working Paper No. 50, Department of Town Planning, Cork Corporation, 1976.

Blackwell, J. 1978. "Disaggregation of the Household Sector in Regional Input–Output Analysis: Some Models Specifying Previous Residence of Workers." *Regional Studies*. Vol. 12, pp. 367–377.

Hewings, G. J. D. 1986. "Problems of Integration in the Modelling of Regional Systems." In *Integrated Analysis of Regional Systems. London Papers in Regional Science 15*, edited by P. W. J. Batey and M. Madden. London: Pion, pp. 37–53.

Hewings, G. J. D., and R. C. Jensen. 1986. "Regional, Interregional, and Multiregional Input–Output Analysis." In *Handbook of Regional and Urban Economics: Vol. 1 Regional Economics*, edited by P. Nijkamp. Amsterdam: North Holland, pp. 293–355.

Madden, M., and P. W. J. Batey. 1980. "Achieving Consistency in Demographic–Economic Forecasting." *Papers of the Regional Science Association*. Vol. 44, pp. 91–106.

Madden, M., and P. W. J. Batey. 1983. "Linked Population and Economic Models: Some Methodological Issues in Forecasting Analysis and Policy Optimisation." *Journal of Regional Science*. Vol. 23, pp. 141–164.

Miernyk, W. H., et al. 1967. *Impact of the Space Program on a Local Economy: An Input–Output Analysis*. Morgantown, WV: West Virginia University Library.

Oosterhaven, J. 1981. *Interregional Input–Output Analysis and Dutch Regional Policy Problems*. Aldershot, Hants, UK: Gower.

Tiebout, C. M. 1969. "An Empirical Regional Input–Output Projection Model: The State of Washington 1980." *Review of Economics and Statistics*. Vol. 51, pp. 334–340.

Van Dijk, J., and J. Oosterhaven. 1986. "Regional Impacts of Migrants' Expenditure: An Input–Output/Vacancy Chain Approach." In *Integrated Analysis of Regional Systems. London Papers in Regional Science 15*, edited by P. W. J. Batey and M. Madden. London: Pion, pp. 122–147.

Weeks, M. J. 1985. "The Construction of Personal Consumption Propensities Using the Irish Household Budget Survey (1973)." Working Note 34, Department of Civic Design, University of Liverpool, Liverpool, UK.

10

Interrelational Income Distribution Multipliers for the U.S. Economy

ADAM Z. ROSE and PAUL BEAUMONT

The multiplier concept has proven to be a very useful tool. It captures the relationship between an initial stimulus and its repercussions, thereby making it possible to calculate the total output, employment, and income impacts of economic phenomena or policies. Although not unique to input–output analysis, there has been prevalent use of the multiplier within this framework over the past three decades. The "matrix multiplier" is particularly adept at revealing both the interdependence and the diversity within an economy by virtue of its ability to demonstrate the direct and higher order contributions of each sector.

Less well known, however, are multiplier concepts relating to income distribution, in spite of the extensive application of input–output analysis to this subject in recent years (Golladay and Haveman, 1976; Paukert et al., 1981; Leontief, 1986; Rose et al., 1988). Examples are the "matrix multiplier of income formation" (Miyazawa, 1976) and the "distributional impact vector" (Rose et al., 1982), which reflect the impact of sectoral growth on income generation and distribution. The conceptual analog of the standard output multiplier, however, is Miyazawa's "interrelational multiplier," which measures the effect of one income group upon another. This multiplier can yield great insight into intergroup dynamics of income formation and the equity implications of various policies. Unfortunately, a dearth of distributional data on both the income and expenditure side has prevented the calculation of interrelational multipliers.

The purpose of this chapter is to present and analyze the first set of interrelational multipliers for a national economy. Each element of the multiplier matrix measures how a direct change in the income of one income bracket results in a total (direct, indirect, and induced) income change in another bracket. The usefulness of the multipliers will be illustrated by applying them to an examination of the constancy of the size distribution of income in the United States and the viability of the "trickle-down" theory.

THE MIYAZAWA INTERRELATIONAL MULTIPLIER

The interrelational multiplier is derived by Miyazawa from a closed input–output model of the following form:

$$X = AX + CVX + F \tag{10-1}$$

where

> X = vector of gross output ($n \times 1$)
> A = matrix of technical production coefficients ($n \times n$)
> C = matrix of personal consumption coefficients, disaggregated by income class ($n \times r$)
> V = matrix of factor payment coefficients, disaggregated by income class ($r \times n$)
> F = vector of final demand minus personal consumption ($n \times 1$).

The term CVX is the core of a three-part, income-propagation process. Changes in the product mix alter the distribution of income, which, in turn, alters the pattern of consumption, which then further alters the interindustry mix, thus beginning the process over again (though subsequent rounds are of progressively smaller scales).

Letting $B = (I - A)^{-1}$, we can express the solution to the Miyazawa system as

$$X = B(I + CKVB)F \tag{10-2}$$

where

$$K = (I - L)^{-1} \tag{10-3}$$

$$L = VBC \tag{10-4}$$

Both K and L are ($r \times r$) matrices focusing explicitly on the distributional aspects of the income propagation process. Miyazawa defines L as the "matrix of interincome group coefficients," and K as the "interrelational multiplier of income groups." Each coefficient of L represents the *direct* increase in the income of one group as a result of the expenditure from an additional unit of income by another group. Each coefficient of K represents the *total* (direct, indirect, and induced) increase in the income of one group as a result of the expenditure from an additional unit of income by another group.

The interrelational multiplier concept is an example of the intersection of two new directions in input–output research. The first of these is the "extended" input–output model, which goes beyond the traditional emphasis on the structural, or A, matrix to include demographic (Batey, 1985) and institutional (Rose et al., 1988) variables. When the institutions themselves become sectors, the model becomes a social accounting matrix (Pyatt and Roe, 1977). The second direction is that of "multiplier decomposition," which involves the disaggregation of various components of the multiplier process (Round, 1985; Batey, 1985). Note also that interrelational multipliers need not be confined to linear models. A (nonlinear) econometric model could be used to compute them in a manner similar to the computation of interregional or international trade multipliers (Sawyer, 1979; Hickman and Filatov, 1983).

EMPIRICAL ESTIMATION

Economic accounting methods were used to estimate the income payment and consumption distribution quadrants of our model (Polenske, 1980; Jaszi, 1986). Economic accounting is essentially a deterministic approach, that is, one based on the tabulation of the universe of primary data or the "scale-up" of samples to control totals, with no inherent stochastic properties assumed. We briefly describe the estimation of the extended portion of the input–output model. For a more detailed discussion, the reader is referred to Rose et al. (1988) and Beaumont (1986).

Income Distribution Matrix

The $1,915.9 billion of Adjusted Gross Income (AGI) received by households in the United States in our benchmark year, 1982, includes 14 income types (Internal Revenue Service, 1984a).[1] Wages and salaries comprise 81.7 percent of AGI; however, since several of the types are characterized by a high variance across income classes, they have a significant effect on the overall distribution.

Survey-based data were accessed and refined for wages/salaries (U.S. Bureau of the Census, 1983), dividends (New York Stock Exchange, 1984), and seven of the more minor income types (Internal Revenue Service, 1984a, 1984b).[2] The remaining income components, for which primary data do not exist, were estimated as generalizations of these survey-based data sets. The process was eased substantially by the fact that several categories of income stem only from household financial activities and, therefore, do not involve any multisectoral data needs.

For example, after an exhaustive search, we deemed a New York Stock Exchange (1984) survey of stock holders to be the best source of data on dividend income that would be compatible with an input–output methodology. The data were used to generate a multisector stock ownership matrix, which was then premultiplied by a diagonal matrix of dividend–price ratios to yield a preliminary dividend flow matrix.[3] Finally, the preliminary matrix was balanced by the biproportional matrix adjustment (RAS) method to make it conform to control totals from the *Statistics of Income* table of dividends by adjusted gross income brackets (Internal Revenue Service, 1984a).

To transform the matrix of income flows into a useful model, we invoked the standard input–output assumption of proportionality—in this case, a fixed relationship between the distribution of each type of income and output in every sector. In the case of wage and salary income, we cite evidence of the stability of occupational requirements (Freeman, 1980). To this we must add the reasonable assumption that wage and salary rates are relatively stable in the short run. The fixed coefficient assumption is also reasonable for most types of capital-related income. Royalties are typically a flat rate per unit of production and associated with long-term contracts, and many rental agreements are long term as well. That portion of profits paid as dividends is likely to be stable given long-run motivations. Moreover, dividends are

1. We analyze the size distribution of AGI, rather than the more often used Personal Income (PI) for two major reasons. First, the AGI definition is considered by the authors to be a superior measure of "net income," because it excludes most moving expenses, employee business expenses, etc. Second, the distributional information in the U.S. Internal Revenue Service data base is considered superior to that in the U.S. Bureau of the Census data base on PI. AGI is on average about 3 percent lower than PI, with only a modest variation in this proportion across income groups.

2. Some of the individual income type data are collected on an individual basis and had to be converted to our preferred unit of analysis—the household. A mapping based on U.S. Bureau of the Census data involved several important steps that are discussed in Rose et al. (1988). Also, our definition of "households" is in actuality the number of filers of federal income tax returns, which differs from the Census definition by about 3 percent.

3. Theory and empirical verification have established that price–dividend ratios vary across income classes because of the relatively lower risk aversion and greater marginal tax bracket of upper income earners. However, much of the variation in the dividend return may be caused by differential investment across sectors. Even if there is some remaining variation in percentage dividend levels across income groups within sectors, changes in these levels may very well be uniform.

paid on a per share basis, and the number of shares outstanding does not fluctuate significantly from year to year. On the other hand, interest rates have been subject to major fluctuations in recent years.

Income distribution coefficients are presented in Table 10-1 for a sample of sectors.[4] Note that the coefficients are based on income flows that are part of the "endogenous" income generation/receipt/expenditure stream, in the true spirit of the multiplier process. In addition to deleting taxes and savings, we must make a minor reduction for income payments to government employees and to and from foreign countries (Rose and Stevens, 1988). The distribution of returns varies significantly across the sectors presented in Table 10-1 and across all 81 sectors of the U.S. input–output table in general. For example, Gini coefficient values (not shown) range from 0.235 in Lodging and Personal Services to 0.639 for Livestock (the economy-wide average Gini is 0.477). The relative skewness of returns across sectors is dependent on factors such as the skill level requirements of the labor force, the industry risk environment, and the capital–labor ratio. Thus, it is not surprising to find that service sectors generally have a relatively even distribution of income payments, and that sectors such as petroleum refining have income distributions that are relatively skewed in favor of upper income groups.

Consumption Coefficient Matrix

The Consumer Expenditure Survey (CES) from the U.S. Bureau of Labor Statistics (1985) was deemed the best data set available on which to base the estimation of the matrix of personal consumption coefficients—the C matrix—because of its extensive commodity and consumer income detail. Unlike earlier Bureau of Labor statistics (BLS) consumption surveys, the new CES is an ongoing survey with rotational panels of respondents being interviewed on a continuous basis. The 1980–1981 CES, which offers the closest temporal comparison with our income and output data, includes approximately 5000 consumer units (essentially households) in the complete panel rotation. Using very strict rules for full reporting of income and expenditures, we reduced the sample to 1798 consumer units.

The raw tabulation of the personal consumption coefficients from the CES must be adjusted to account for sampling idiosyncrasies and sector classification differences between the BLS and Bureau of Economic Analysis (BEA) commodity codes. Because these adjustments are described in detail in Beaumont (1986) and Rose and Beaumont (1986), only a brief description of the major adjustments will be given here.

First, we adjusted the expenditure shares computed from the CES to obtain direct estimates of expenditures for omitted categories. For example, there is no item in the BLS classification scheme that corresponds to the trade margin on consumption goods, yet the retail and wholesale trade margin is 16.8 percent of total personal consumption expenditure in the 1982 U.S. input–output table.

The second major adjustment entailed a reconciliation of a matrix of consumption flows derived from the consumption shares with independent control totals for total consumption expenditure by income class and total consumption

---

4. The final income distribution matrix is of the order 81 (sectors) × 10 (income groups). Some of the submatrices for individual income groups were originally of smaller order, but were disaggregated by a weighting scheme based on sectoral gross outputs. The complete matrix is presented in Rose et al. (1988).

TABLE 10-1 Income Distribution Coefficients for Selected Sectors of the U.S. Economy, 1982[a]

Income Class	Food and Kindred	Apparel	Glass and Glass Products	Utility Services	Auto Repair	Amusements	Health and Education
0–$ 5,000	0.001	0.004	0.006	−0.003	0.002	0.008	0.011
$5,000–$9,999	0.011	0.014	0.018	0.015	0.011	0.022	0.026
$10,000–$14,999	0.014	0.020	0.026	0.019	0.015	0.026	0.032
$15,000–$19,999	0.011	0.022	0.025	0.021	0.014	0.022	0.030
$20,000–$24,999	0.011	0.022	0.028	0.026	0.017	0.022	0.032
$25,000–$34,999	0.021	0.038	0.055	0.040	0.032	0.041	0.053
$35,000–$49,999	0.021	0.029	0.052	0.045	0.033	0.049	0.062
$50,000–$74,999	0.011	0.009	0.020	0.019	0.011	0.025	0.034
$75,000+	0.007	0.006	0.015	0.038	0.006	0.024	0.052

Source: Adapted from Rose et al. (1988).
[a]All coefficients are net of exogenous income.

expenditure by sector. We took the latter (row control totals) from the 1982 U.S. input–output table "personal consumption expenditures," which are also consistent with the National Income and Product Accounts (NIPA). The column control totals, total expenditures by income class, were derived by multiplying the average propensity to consume (APC) for each income bracket by an estimate of total disposable income for the bracket. We computed the APCs from the CES, and we calculated the disposable income figure by applying the ratio of pre- and posttax income from the BLS survey to total adjusted gross income (Internal Revenue Service, 1984a). The total expenditures by income class were proportionally adjusted to match the sum of the row control totals, since it was based on the more accurate NIPA.

Again, we adjusted expenditures to account for the deletion of exogenous flows on the income and expenditure sides. Finally, we applied an RAS matrix-balancing routine to the sectoral consumption flows, derived by multiplying the adjusted preliminary shares by the revised total consumption expenditure figures.

Revised personal consumption coefficients were computed from adjusted and balanced consumption flow matrices. These average propensity to consume (APC) vectors for selected sectors are shown in Table 10-2. Most of the patterns of coefficients across rows are either nearly monotonic or nearly quadratic. On the whole, the final C matrix gives reasonable estimates of the APCs, and yields patterns across income groups that are consistent with a priori expectations.

Although the APCs are adequate for the analysis of the basic income structure of the economy, in many applications, such as policy analyses involving significant income changes, the marginal propensity to consume (MPC) becomes more relevant. The estimation of the MPCs, however, is significantly more difficult than the estimation of the APCs (Tyrrell and Mount, 1982; Devine, 1983). In our analyses, we assume that the APCs offer good first-order approximations for the MPCs. This assumption is more likely to be true for normal goods—particularly in the middle-income groups—than for luxury goods and inferior goods.[5]

EMPIRICAL INTERRELATIONAL MULTIPLIERS

We combined the V and C matrices, described in the previous section, with an A matrix to compute the interrelational multipliers, the K matrix, as in Equation (10-3). The A matrix in this computation is based on the 1982 Impact Analysis System for Planning (IMPLAN) update of the official U.S. BEA input–output table (U.S. Forest Service, 1986). The matrix of interrelational multipliers for the U.S. economy in 1982 is reported in Table 10-3. Each element in the table measures the total income payments (direct, indirect, and induced) received by households in the income bracket indicated at the left as a result of a direct income increase to households in the income bracket indicated in the column heads. For example, a $1 direct increase in income to households in the $15,000–$20,000 bracket will result in a total increase in income of $1.052 for those same households ($1 in direct effects and 5.2 cents in indirect and induced effects) and a 3.8 cent indirect and induced effect for households in the $5,000–$10,000 income bracket.

The last row in Table 10-3 represents the column sums of the interrelational

5. Only in the special case in which the APCs are equal for all income classes and there is no constant term in the Engle curve will the APC equal the MPC. See Devine (1983) for a complete description of a piecewise linear expenditure system that is consistent with our method of analysis.

TABLE 10-2 Adjusted Consumption Coefficients for the U.S. Economy, 1982[a]

Sector	Below $5,000	$5,000–$9,999	$10,000–$14,999	$15,000–$19,999	$20,000–$24,199	$25,000–$34,999	$35,000–$49,999	$50,000–$74,999	$75,000 and over
Food and kindred	0.163	0.104	0.084	0.079	0.082	0.061	0.055	0.050	0.031
Tobacco	0.014	0.011	0.011	0.009	0.009	0.007	0.006	0.005	0.002
Apparel	0.014	0.015	0.017	0.019	0.020	0.017	0.019	0.021	0.018
Drugs	0.044	0.027	0.015	0.013	0.009	0.008	0.007	0.003	0.005
Rubber and miscellaneous	0.002	0.003	0.004	0.003	0.004	0.003	0.003	0.003	0.001
House appliances	0.004	0.003	0.003	0.005	0.004	0.004	0.003	0.002	0.002
Utility services	0.067	0.042	0.035	0.034	0.032	0.026	0.023	0.020	0.012
Auto repair	0.012	0.017	0.017	0.019	0.023	0.018	0.018	0.018	0.015
Amusements	0.003	0.005	0.008	0.010	0.010	0.010	0.013	0.014	0.014
Health and education	0.156	0.133	0.127	0.138	0.127	0.121	0.122	0.124	0.153

[a]All coefficients are net of spending out of exogenous income and net of imports.

TABLE 10-3 Interrelational Multipliers for the U.S. Economy, 1982

Income Brackets	Below $5,000	$5,000–$10,000	$10,000–$15,000	$15,000–$20,000	$20,000–$25,000	$25,000–$35,000	$35,000–$50,000	$50,000–$75,000	$75,000+	Total
$0–$5,000	1.010	0.009	0.009	0.009	0.009	0.010	0.010	0.008	0.008	1.082
$5,000–$10,000	0.046	1.040	0.038	0.038	0.038	0.038	0.037	0.032	0.029	1.336
$10,000–$15,000	0.061	0.052	1.050	0.050	0.049	0.049	0.048	0.042	0.038	1.440
$15,000–$20,000	0.064	0.055	0.052	1.052	0.051	0.051	0.050	0.043	0.039	1.457
$20,000–$25,000	0.070	0.059	0.056	0.055	1.054	0.054	0.053	0.046	0.041	0.489
$25,000–$35,000	0.133	0.113	0.107	0.105	0.103	1.103	0.100	0.086	0.077	1.927
$35,000–$50,000	0.133	0.112	0.107	0.105	0.103	0.104	1.101	0.087	0.078	1.931
$50,000–$75,000	0.072	0.059	0.055	0.053	0.052	0.051	0.050	1.043	0.038	1.472
$75,000+	0.083	0.068	0.062	0.059	0.057	0.056	0.054	0.047	1.042	1.530
Total	1.672	1.567	1.538	1.526	1.516	1.516	1.503	1.434	1.390	

multipliers or the total effect across all income brackets of an increase in income for the income bracket at the head of the column. The total effects decline monotonically from a high of 1.672 for the $5,000 and under bracket to a low of 1.390 for the $75,000 and over bracket. This pattern should be expected since the lower income brackets are characterized by relatively higher APCs (lower tax and savings rates).

The column sums in Table 10-3 are smaller than input–output analysts might have expected for two reasons. First, the column sums actually represent a disaggregation, by income classes, of the traditional aggregate Keynesian income multiplier. In other words, these multipliers represent the total change in income divided by a one unit direct change in income. Input–output income multipliers are traditionally defined as the total income change divided by the direct income change associated with a one unit change in final demand that stimulated it.[6] We can recover these input–output multipliers by dividing the column sums in Table 10-3 by the column sums of the direct, or first-round, effects matrix—the L matrix of Equation (10-4). This calculation results in multipliers that range from 3.723 for the lowest income bracket to a 5.353 for the highest income bracket. For the purposes of analysis and interpretation, we prefer the multiplier concept underlying the results in Table 10-3.[7]

A second reason that our multipliers appear to be small is because we view the multiplier process in a very strict sense as only legitimately including endogenous elements of the income formation, distribution, and spending process. Subtracting taxes, savings, transfers, government payrolls, and a few minor categories reduces our original $1,915.9 billion income figure by more than 50 percent for the purpose of our computations. The result is a somewhat conservative estimate of the magnitude of the multipliers. However, we emphasize that since the focus of this chapter is on distribution, it is the relative proportions of the multipliers (both within rows and within columns) that is important. These proportions are relatively stable in spite of our "endogeneity" adjustment.

As we move down the columns of Table 10-3, it is apparent that, aside from the own-group direct effect, the greatest gains from a spending increase in any income bracket are received by the $25,000–$35,000 and $35,000–$50,000 income brackets. This is somewhat misleading since these two income brackets contain, by a wide margin, the largest number of households. Of course, if we are interested in aggregate results, Table 10-3 is reporting precisely the correct information. For purposes of analysis, however, we find it best to normalize the interrelational multipliers by dividing each element in Table 10-3 by the number of households in the corresponding row of that element. We also rescale the elements to indicate the total income received by each household in an income class from a one billion dollar increase in income to all households in the income class indicated by the column heading. The results of this normalization are reported in Table 10-4. Note that the diagonal elements in Table 10-4 distinguish between the indirect and induced effects (the top number) and the direct, indirect, and induced effects (the number in parentheses below). For most analyses, the former number is the more useful.

6. The "direct" income change (or first-round effect) is thus considerably less than one unit.

7. This positive correlation between multiplier size and income is misleading because it is solely the result of a progressively shrinking direct income base. The multipliers presented in Table 10-3 are superior in portraying the relative ability of an income class to generate income throughout the economy because these multipliers all have the same base—one unit of income.

TABLE 10-4 Interrelational Multipliers for the United States, 1982 (per Household Basis)

	Below $5,000	$5,000–$10,000	$10,000–$15,000	$15,000–$20,000	$20,000–$25,000	$25,000–$35,000	$35,000–$50,000	$50,000–$75,000	$75,000+
$0–$5,000	0.53 (56.23)	0.51	0.51	0.51	0.51	0.54	0.54	0.46	0.44
$5,000–$10,000	2.71	2.33 (61.02)	2.24	2.25	2.21	2.21	2.18	1.89	1.72
$10,000–$15,000	4.28	3.65	3.51 (73.40)	3.50	3.44	3.44	3.38	2.93	2.66
$15,000–$20,000	6.10	5.20	4.97	4.92 (99.84)	4.83	4.85	4.75	4.09	3.67
$20,000–$25,000	7.95	6.73	6.40	6.27	6.15 (119.75)	6.15	6.01	5.19	4.65
$25,000–$35,000	10.61	8.98	8.53	8.33	8.17	8.20 (87.87)	8.00	6.87	6.12
$35,000–$50,000	13.74	11.65	11.11	10.91	10.71	10.75	10.49 (114.13)	9.01	8.10
$50,000–$75,000	23.40	19.39	18.06	17.25	16.85	16.73	16.20	13.98 (341.10)	12.48
$75,000+	57.75	47.05	43.23	40.97	39.83	38.86	37.45	32.80	29.43 (722.91)

As we read down the columns of Table 10-4, we note that higher income households gain considerably more from an income increase by any income group than lower income households. For instance, a one billion dollar increase to households in the $25,000–$35,000 bracket results in an income increase of $38.86 for the highest income bracket and just 54 cents for the lowest income bracket. In fact, as we read down any of the columns, the numbers are strictly monitonically increasing. Qualitatively, this result is not too surprising. After all, we have performed an income disaggregated analysis of the income formation process, and the average income distribution coefficients are skewed toward higher income groups. Quantitatively, however, these results are surprising. If households in the $5,000–$10,000 income bracket receive an additional one billion dollars, then individual households in the lowest income bracket will receive an additional 51 cents in income, whereas households in the highest income bracket will receive an additional $47.05 apiece in indirect and induced spending effects.

Reading along the rows of Table 10-4, we note that households tend to gain more from equivalent income increases to the low-income brackets than from equivalent increases in the high-income brackets. For example, households in the $25,000–$35,000 income row receive $10.61 from a one billion dollar spending increase by the lowest income bracket but only $6.12 if an equivalent increase in spending is made by households in the highest income bracket. Thus, a rich person will benefit more from the income gain of a poor person than from that of another rich person. A careful examination of the income and personal consumption coefficient matrices offers one explanation. Low-income groups buy a higher proportion of goods whose production results in income disbursements skewed toward higher income households than do high-income groups. For example, a high percentage of low-income groups' expenditures is for rental property, the proceeds of which tend to accrue to high-income households. On the other hand, high-income households spend a much greater proportion of their budgets on entertainment than do low-income households, and expenditures in this industry tend to generate receipts fairly evenly across all income groups. Of course, we cannot forget that the propensity to consume is higher for low-income groups than for high-income groups. We should also note that our analysis does not account for what the high-income groups do with their additional savings. It is not likely, however, that these savings could be invested in a way that would significantly change these results in the short-term.

POLICY IMPLICATIONS

Our results yield some important implications. For example, they provide insight into the constancy of income disparities over time (Rivlin, 1975; Reynolds and Smolensky, 1978; Blinder, 1980; Atkinson, 1983). Reading down the column, an extra billion dollars of income, through tax reform, transfer payments, or job creation, flowing to the lowest income group results in an average increase (direct and indirect and induced) of about $56 per household for this group (see the entry in parentheses in column one of Table 10-4), whereas it results in an (indirect and induced) increase of $58 per household for the highest income group, and significant rewards for several of the other brackets. Thus, income maintenance programs for the lower income brackets will yield benefits to other brackets that will partially offset the direct distributional improvement.

Another reason there is so much inertia in the U.S. distribution of income is the limited difference of the interrelational multipliers, as one reads along the rows. This is caused in part by the relative regularity of consumption patterns across income brackets. It is reinforced by the higher order effects of income formation, distribution, and consumption. Because commonality of the set of suppliers increases during successive rounds of production, sectoral distinctions in both the distribution of income and consumption expenditures are further narrowed.

Also, our results cast some doubt on the relevance of the "trickle-down" theory in the U.S. setting. A $1 billion increase in the income of the highest income bracket results in a direct and indirect $723 increase per household for this group, but less than $1 for the $0–$5,000 bracket! The term "trickle" is intended to describe a *process* by which gains at the top flow to the bottom, though it appears best to describe a result, at least in the short run. In the long run, the dynamics of the savings/investment process in stimulating growth may reveal a significantly greater diffusion of income as a result of the activities of those in higher brackets.

CONCLUSION

We have presented the first set of empirical interrelational multipliers of income distribution for the United States. They were calculated from an extended input–output model whose income-differentiated payments and consumption components are based almost entirely on survey-based data.

We take the consistency between many of our results and a priori expectations as one indication of their reliability. At the same time, we do not view these results as redundant, but as adding precision to an important area of economic inquiry. Reference to general trends or tendencies may be adequate in highly aggregated models, but a basic rationale for input–output models is that detail matters. This is as true in the income and consumption sectors as in the intermediate sectors. With an extended multisector model we can go beyond trying to add and subtract tendencies, and perform numerical estimation. Yet, with the interrelational multiplier concept, this need not be an arduous task once such a model is constructed. The interrelational multiplier offers the potential to analysts to compute total income distribution impacts as readily as they have computed total output, employment, and income impacts using more standard multipliers over the past few decades.

ACKNOWLEDGMENTS

The authors wish to thank Wassily Leontief, Anne Carter, Faye Duchin, Mark Henry, Karen Polenske, Robert Strauss, Roger Bezdek, and Jeffery Round for their helpful comments. We are grateful to Thomas Juster and Eva Jacobs for help regarding the data used. We also wish to acknowledge computer programming assistance from Mostafa Aleseyed and Shih-Mo Lin, and the general support services of the West Virginia University Regional Research Institute, with which both authors were affiliated when this study was carried out. Earlier versions of this chapter were presented at the 1986 North American Regional Science Association Meetings and the 1986 American Economic Association Meetings.

REFERENCES

Atkinson, Anthony B. 1983. *The Economics of Inequality.* (2nd ed.) London: Oxford University Press.

Batey, Peter W. J. 1985. "Input–Output Models for Regional Demographic–Economic Analysis." *Environment and Planning A.* Vol. 17, pp. 73–99.

Beaumont, Paul. 1986. "Personal Consumption Coefficients by Income Class: Estimates from the 1980–81 Consumer Expenditure Survey" (mimeo). Morgantown, WV: Regional Research Institute, West Virginia University.

Blinder, Alan S. 1980. "The Level and Distribution of Economic Well-Being." In *The American Economy in Transition,* edited by Martin Feldstein. Chicago: University of Chicago Press.

Devine, Paul. 1983. "Forecasting Personal Consumption Expenditures from Cross-Section and Time Series Data." Ph.D. dissertation. College Park, MD: University of Maryland, Department of Economics.

Freeman, Richard. 1980. "An Empirical Analysis of the Fixed Coefficients Manpower Requirements Models." *Journal of Human Resources.* Vol. 15, pp. 176–199.

Golladay, Frederick L., and Robert H. Haveman. 1976. "Regional and Distributional Effects of a Negative Income Tax." *American Economic Review.* Vol. 66, pp. 629–641.

Hickman, Bert, and Victor Filatov. 1983. "A Decomposition of International Income Multipliers." In *Global Econometrics,* edited by F. G. Adams and B. Hickman. Cambridge, MA: MIT Press.

Internal Revenue Service. 1984a. *Statistics of Income. 1982.* Washington, D.C.: U.S. Government Printing Office.

Internal Revenue Service. 1984b. *Statistics of Income, Corporation Income Tax Returns, 1982.* Washington, D.C.: U.S. Department of the Treasury.

Jaszi, George. 1986. "An Economic Accountant's Audit." *American Economic Review.* Vol. 76, pp. 411–417.

Leontief, Wassily. 1986. "Technological Change, Prices, Wages, and Rates of Return on Capital in the U.S. Economy." In *Input–Output Economics.* (2nd ed.) New York: Oxford University Press.

Miyazawa, Kenichi. 1976. *Input–Output Analysis and the Structure of Income Distribution.* New York: Springer-Verlag.

New York Stock Exchange. 1984. *Shareownership,* 1983, New York Stock Exchange.

Paukert, Felix, Jiri V. Skolka, and Jef Maton. 1981. *Income Distribution, Economic Structure and Employment.* London: Croom Helm.

Polenske, Karen R. 1980. *The United States Multiregional Input–Output Accounts and Model.* Lexington, MA: Lexington Books.

Pyatt, Graham, and Alan Roe. 1977. *Social Accounting for Development Planning.* Cambridge, England: Cambridge University Press.

Reynolds, Morgan, and Eugene Smolensky. 1978. "The Fading Effect of Government on Inequality." *Challenge.* Vol. 21, pp. 32–37.

Rivlin, Alice. 1975. "Income Distribution—Can Economists Help?" *American Economic Review.* Vol. 65, pp. 1–15.

Rose, Adam, and Paul Beaumont. 1986. "Interrelational Income Distribution Multipliers for the U.S. Economy." Paper presented at the North American Regional Science Association Meetings, Columbus, OH.

Rose, Adam, and Benjamin H. Stevens. 1988. "Transboundary Income Flows in Regional Input–Output Models" (mimeo). Regional Research Institute, West Virginia University.

Rose, Adam, Benjamin Nakayama, and Brandt Stevens. 1982. "Modern Energy Region Development and Income Distribution: An Input–Output Approach." *Journal of Environmental Economics and Management.* Vol. 9, pp. 149–164.

Rose, Adam, Brandt Stevens, and Gregg Davis. 1988. *Natural Resource Policy and Income Distribution*. Baltimore, MD: Johns Hopkins University Press.

Round, Jeffery I. 1985. "Decomposing Multipliers for Economic Systems Involving Regional and World Trade." *Economic Journal*. Vol. 95, pp. 383–399.

Sawyer, J. A., ed. 1979. *Modelling the International Transmission Mechanism*. Amsterdam: North-Holland.

Tyrrell, Timothy, and Timothy Mount. 1982. "A Nonlinear Expenditure System Using a Linear Logit Specification." *American Journal of Agricultural Economics*. Vol. 64, pp. 539–546.

U.S. Bureau of the Census. 1983. *Detailed Population Characteristics*. Washington, D.C.: U.S. Department of Commerce.

U.S. Bureau of Economic Analysis. 1984. "U.S. Input–Output Table, 1977." *Survey of Current Business*. Vol. 64, pp. 42–84.

U.S. Bureau of Labor Statistics. 1985. "Consumer Expenditure Survey: Interview Survey, 1980–81." Bulletin No. 2225. Washington, D.C.: U.S. Government Printing Office.

U.S. Forest Service. 1986. "U.S. Input–Output Table: 1982." Rocky Mountain Experiment Station, Ft. Collins, Colorado.

11

Labor Quality and Productivity Growth in the United States: An Input–Output Growth-Accounting Framework

EDWARD N. WOLFF and DAVID R. HOWELL

Much recent research has focused on the productivity slowdown that has afflicted most of the industrialized world since the late 1960s (see Maddison, 1982, 1987). In spite of this effort, there has been limited success in developing a comprehensive and convincing explanation for the slowdown (see, for example, Denison, 1979, 1984; Wolff, 1985a, 1985b). The post-1967 period is also characterized by a slowdown in output growth, an intensifying international competition, and rapid changes in production technology—most notably toward the use of programmable automation in both factories and offices. The consequences of these changes for the labor force have been immense, with much higher than normal unemployment rates, a reduction in job security, an increase in part-time work, and changes in the skill requirements of work. This chapter focuses on the last of these—changes in skill requirements—and explores its significance for the productivity slowdown.

The measure and explanation of productivity growth should take into account changes in the quality of inputs over time. In the case of labor, change in quality will reflect the evolution of both the skill content of jobs and the mix of jobs. If changes in skill content and job mix result in an upgrading (downgrading) of skill requirements, effective labor input per hour worked will increase (decrease). Thus, the quality of labor employed (and the way quality is measured) can have, at least potentially, a major effect on the measured rate of productivity growth. In previous productivity studies, labor input has been measured by the use of undifferentiated quantities (hours or employees) of labor. In some recent studies, these quantities have been adjusted using an index of relative earnings. Only under extremely strong assumptions, however, will earnings offer a reliable guide to the quality (skill levels) of employed labor. In the analysis presented in this chapter, we replace relative earnings with alternative measures of job-skill requirements derived from the Dictionary of Occupational Titles (U.S. Department of Labor, 1977).

In prior work (Wolff, 1985b), a standard input–output accounting system was modified in order to analyze the effects of changes in final output composition on overall productivity growth in the economy. A growth-accounting framework was developed whereby changes in overall productivity growth could be decomposed into

148

various sources. In Wolff (1985b), three sources were considered: (1) changes in the rate of technical changes on the sectoral level, (2) changes in the Leontief inverse matrix, and (3) changes in the sectoral composition of final demand. In this chapter, we extend the framework to incorporate changes in the skill composition of the labor force.

This chapter consists of three primary sections. In the first, we develop a growth-accounting framework from a standard input–output system to analyze three sources of overall productivity growth in the U.S. economy: sectoral technical change, changes in the composition of final output, and changes in the skill composition of the labor force.

In the second section, we consider some issues surrounding the measurement of labor skills and describe our approach. At the end of this section, we present results on changes in skill requirements for the U.S. economy and for each of 10 large industry sectors.

In the third section, we present results on the sources of productivity growth in the United States from 1958 to 1977. This analysis is distinguished by the use of alternative measures of both productivity growth (unadjusted for labor quality) and labor input (reflecting various measures of skill requirements). Particular attention is paid to the sources of the productivity slowdown that occurred after 1967.

GROWTH-ACCOUNTING FRAMEWORK

Because we are primarily interested in skill changes and their effect on productivity growth, we develop a growth-accounting framework for labor productivity growth,[1] beginning with a standard input–output accounting framework. Unless otherwise noted, all components are in constant dollar terms. Let

X_t = (column) vector of gross output by sector at time t.
Y_t = (column) vector of final demand by sector at time t.
a_t = matrix of interindustry technical coefficients at time t.
l_t = (row) vector of labor coefficients at time t, showing employment per unit of output.
p_t = (row) vector of prices at time t, showing the price per unit of output of each industry.

In addition, let us define the following scalars:

$y_t = p_t Y_t$ = total final output valued at current prices p.
$L_t = l_t X_t$ = total employment at time t.

Furthermore, let us also introduce the technical inverse coefficient matrix q as[2]

$$q = (I - a)^{-1} \qquad (11\text{-}1)$$

and define the total labor requirements vector λ as

---

1. See Wolff (1985b) for the derivation of an analogous growth-accounting framework for total factor productivity growth.

2. It should be noted that we are treating depreciation as exogenous in this framework. See Wolff (1985b) for the case in which depreciation is treated as endogenous and, more generally, in which capital is treated as a produced means of production.

$\lambda = lq =$ (row) vector, showing the direct plus indirect labor requirements per unit of output.

It follows directly that in the case in which labor is the only factor of production, the vector λ is also the vector of relative prices:

$$p_t = \lambda_t \tag{11-2}$$

We can now define the rate of growth of overall or economy-wide unadjusted labor productivity, ρ, in conventional fashion as

$$\rho \equiv pdY/y - dL/L \tag{11-3}$$

On the sectoral level, we introduce an analogous concept, the rate of unadjusted "total labor productivity" (TLP) growth, defined as

$$\pi_j \equiv -d\lambda_j/p_j = -d\lambda_j/\lambda_j = \text{rate of unadjusted TLP growth in sector } j.$$

It then follows directly that[3]

$$\rho = \pi\hat{p}Y/y \tag{11-4}$$

We can now introduce a labor-quality index into the framework as follows. Let

$m_t =$ matrix of occupational coefficients by industry, such that $\sum m_{ij} = 1$.

Then, define

$\sigma_t =$ (row) vector showing the skill score of each occupation i at time t (each skill index will lead to a different vector σ).

Then

$s_t = \sigma_t m_t =$ (row) vector, showing the average skill level of each industry j at time t.

Skill-adjusted labor input can now be defined as

$l^* = (\sigma m)\hat{l} = s\hat{l} =$ (row) vector of quality-adjusted direct labor coefficients by industry, showing direct quality-adjusted employment per unit of output.

---

3. This can be shown as follows.

$$\pi\hat{p}Y/y = -(d\lambda)Y/y$$
$$= -[ldq + (dl)q]Y/y$$

since, by definition, $\lambda = lq$. Then,

$$\pi\hat{p}Y/y = [-l(dq)Y - (dl)X]/y$$
$$= \{-l(dq)Y + ldX - [ldX + (dl)X]\}/y$$
$$= [-l(dq)Y + ldX - dL]/y$$

since $L = lX$. Moreover, since $X = qY$,

$$\pi\hat{p}Y/y = [-l(dq)Y + l(dq)Y + lqdY - dL]/y$$
$$= (\lambda dY - dL)/y$$

But $p_t = \lambda_t$. Hence, $y_t = p_t Y_t = \lambda_t Y_t = L_t$, and

$$\pi\hat{p}Y/y = pdY/y - dL/L$$

This completes the proof.

Total quality-adjusted labor input, L^*, is then given by

$$L^* = l^* X \tag{11-5}$$

We can now derive quality-adjusted rates of labor productivity growth. First, define

$\lambda^* = s\hat{lq} = s\hat{\lambda} =$ (row) vector of total (direct plus indirect) quality-adjusted labor requirements per unit of output.

Then,

$\pi_j^* = -d\lambda^*_j/\lambda_j^* =$ rate of quality-adjusted total labor productivity (TLP) growth for each sector j.

But, by definition,

$$\pi_j^* = -d\lambda_j/\lambda_j - ds_j/s_j$$

Define

$\theta_j \equiv ds_j/s_j =$ rate of increase of average skill requirements in sector j.

Then,

$$\pi_j^* = \pi_j - \theta_j \tag{11-6}$$

A growth-accounting framework can now be developed from this approach. Because we are interested in identifying the sources of change in conventionally measured labor productivity growth, we first take the discrete time differential of Equation (11-4). If we ignore second-order terms, then the change in the rate of growth of overall unadjusted labor productivity is given by

$$\Delta\rho \cong \pi(\Delta\beta) + (\Delta\pi)\beta \tag{11-7}$$

where $\beta_j \equiv p_j Y_j/y =$ the value share of sector j in total final output. From Equation (11-6), it now follows that

$$\Delta\rho \cong \pi(\Delta\beta) + (\Delta\pi^*)\beta + (\Delta\theta)\beta \tag{11-8}$$

This decomposition allows us to separate the change in overall unadjusted labor productivity growth into three effects, corresponding to the three terms on the right-hand side of Equation (11-8). The first is the final output composition effect, which shows the change in overall productivity growth that would occur if sectoral rates of productivity growth remained unchanged over time but final output shares shifted as they did in actuality. Here, β measures value shares, not real shares, and $\Delta\beta$ reflects, in part, relative price changes. The second is the technical change effect, which shows the change in overall labor productivity that would occur if final output shares remained constant over time but sectoral rates of TLP growth, adjusted for changes in labor quality, changed as they had in actuality. The third is the skill effect, which shows the effect of changes in average skill levels by industry on the change in overall TFP growth, assuming that all other factors remained constant. This last term is of particular interest for the post-1967 period, because it will indicate what portion (if any) of the slowdown in overall labor productivity growth is attributable to changes in the quality of the labor force.

MEASUREMENT OF LABOR QUALITY

Several recent studies (Gollop and Jorgenson, 1980; Chinloy, 1980, 1981) have developed measures of labor input that reflect the relative compensation received by workers. This standard approach is based on the view that, as Gollop and Jorgenson (1980) stated, "A worker's average compensation per hour provides a good approximation to the worker's marginal productivity" (p. 48). In a competitive labor market, earnings differentials among individuals will reflect relative skills, effort, and job attractiveness. Using this approach, Darby (1984, p. 303) computes the quality of an hour of labor by females under the age of 25 as 41 percent of an hour of male workers over 25. The relative quality of female labor rises to 57 percent for women in the over 25 age group.

Virtually every analyst who conducted a major productivity study that adjusted labor hours for changes in quality has adopted this marginal productivity approach. Yet, it requires some very strong assumptions about the character of the postwar United States economy. For example, production must be characterized by neither increasing nor decreasing returns; the effects of monopoly power in product markets (employer ability to pay high wages), union power, regulation, and discriminatory behavior must be negligible, and workers and firms must be well-informed maximizers whose decisions ensure that current wages reflect only the current (rather than future) provision of labor services. Only if these (and other) assumptions are good approximations can we rely on current wage differentials to reflect the current quality of labor inputs.

The consistent findings in wage studies of significant wage effects of capital intensity, concentration, firm size, union status, race, and gender raise substantial doubts about this reliability (Krueger and Summers, 1987). For instance, the standard earnings-based approach suggests that an hour of an unskilled automobile assembly-line worker's labor (typically male) is about three times the quality of a sewing machine operator's hour (typically female), a result that is manifestly open to question. Should the ratio of assembly-line workers to sewing machine operators increase, the work force as a whole will appear to be undergoing an upgrading of skills. With no change in output or employment, productivity growth will appear to have slowed as more labor inputs (skill units) appear to be used in production.

Years of schooling and experience are alternative labor-embodied measures of skills. Like relative earnings, the reliability of these measures is problematic: the quality of schooling varies greatly over time and among regions, and there may have been inflationary trends in credential and certification requirements. Concerning experience, there is the problem of the conflation of skills developed on the job with years of experience. Does a janitor with 15 years of experience have three times the skills of a janitor with 5 years of experience?

Because of these difficulties with labor-embodied skill measures, we have chosen to adjust labor input by direct job-based measures of labor-skill requirements. These are measures of the skills required for adequate performance of tasks, not measures of the skill residing in a given worker independently of the job.

Job-Based Measures of Skill Requirements

The development of such job-related skill measures for industries was accomplished by weighting occupational employment by occupation skill requirements. The analysis of changes in skill levels over several decades required Census employment data, and because occupation and industry classifications change with every decennial Census, a major part of this project involved the development of consistent occupation by industry employment matrices for 1960, 1970, 1980 and 1985. Thus, our industry skill measures are based on employment matrices at the 267 occupation and 64 industry level.

The best sources of detailed, economy-wide measures of the skill requirements of jobs for the postwar period are the second (1949), third (1965), and fourth (1977) editions of the Dictionary of Occupational Titles (DOT). Based on over 75,000 on-site visits between 1966 and 1974, the fourth edition provides a variety of measures of job content, including the required levels of General Educational Development (GED), Specific Vocational Preparation (SVP), Data (intelligence, verbal and numerical), and Temperament (adaptability to performing repetitive work) that are required. Roos and Treiman (Miller et al., 1980) reclassified the DOT occupations to 591 1970 Census occupations and calculated the values of a number of DOT variables for each of these Census occupations.

Our measures of job-skill requirements capture three fundamental dimensions of skills: cognitive, interactive, and motor. Two variables are used to measure cognitive skills: general educational development (GED) and substantive complexity (SC). GED is employed in part because it has been the most frequently used DOT variables in past studies of skill change. It also serves as a check for the SC measure. SC is derived from a factor analytic test of a large number of DOT variables. Using the 4th edition scores for 1970 Census occupations, Roos and Treiman (Miller et al., 1980, Appendix F) conducted a factor analysis of 46 DOT variables to determine whether an underlying factor might be identified as "substantive complexity." The results provided strong support for the existence of such a factor: it was highly correlated with GED, Specific Vocational Preparation, Data (synthesizing, coordinating, and analyzing), and other measures of cognitive skills (p. 339).[4]

Interactive skills are measured by the DOT "People" variable, which, on a scale of 0–8, identifies whether the job requires mentoring (0), negotiating (1), instructing (2), supervising (3), diverting (4), persuading (5), speaking–signaling (6), serving (7), or taking instructions (8). For comparability with the other measures, we reversed the order of this scale to run from low to high skills.

Motor skills (MS) can be represented by another factor-based variable (Miller et al., 1980, p. 339). High MS scores reflect job requirements such as setting up machines, precision working, and operating/controlling. Lower scores reflect tending and feeding machines and handling materials.

A final measure, Total (TOT) Skills, can be created to capture all three fundamental dimensions of job skills by summing the Substantive Complexity, People (scaled to a 0–10 range), and Motor Skills measures.

Skill Change, 1960–1985

Table 11-1 presents the percentage change in job-based skill levels for both total employees and nonsupervisory workers for 1960–1970, 1970–1980, and 1980–1985.

4. A strong case for the use of factor-based scales is made by Miller et al. (1980). They conducted a series of reliability tests and concluded that "the more reliable indicators of the features of occupations tapped by the worker traits and worker functions variables could be created by developing factor-based multiple-item scales to represent the various dimensions revealed by factor analysis. Such scales would have the advantage of greater internal reliability and consistency than single indicators" (p. 188).

TABLE 11-1   Percentage Change in Economy-Wide Skill Levels, 1960–1985

Skill Measure	1960–1970 (%)	1970–1980 (%)	1980–1985 (%)
SC	7.1	4.7	1.2
	(4.3)[a]	(1.9)	(0.6)
GED	3.6	2.2	0.6
	(1.9)	(0.6)	(0.3)
PS	2.6	2.2	0.0
	(0.7)	(1.0)	(0.0)
MS	0.7	−1.7	−0.6
	(2.0)	(−0.4)	(0.2)
TOT[b]	4.7	2.5	0.3
	(3.2)	(1.3)	(0.3)

[a]Figures for nonsupervisory personnel are in parentheses.
[b]The measure TOT is defined as TOT = SC + PS + MS.

As noted earlier, our measures of job-embodied skill requirements are based upon data collected between 1966 and 1974. As a result, changes in industry skill levels from 1960 to 1985 reflect only changes in employment among our 267 occupations within each industry. This table shows negligible or small changes for Motor Skills (MS) and People Skills (PS), but larger changes for the cognitive skills variables (SC and GED) for all three periods. For both SC and GED, the percentage increase in total employee skill levels in the 1970–1980 decade was only about two-thirds as large as the change between 1960 and 1970. If the 1980–1985 figures are doubled to get rough decade-equivalent figures, the increase in these skill measures was again considerably smaller (about half) than the previous decade.

For nonsupervisory (NS) workers, defined as all occupations except professional, technical, and kindred workers and managers and administrators, the change in SC and GED for both the 1960–1970 and the 1970–1980 periods was substantially lower than the change for total employees. Further, the percentage decline between the growth in SC levels in the 1960s and the growth in the 1970s for NS workers (from 4.3 to 1.9, a decline of about 56 percent) was much larger than the decline for all workers (from 7.1 to 4.7, a decline of about 34 percent). The results for GED requirements are similar. Thus, our indices of cognitive skills increased more slowly for the least skilled both within and between each of these decades.

Table 11-2 presents mean SC and people skill (PS) levels for 10 large industry groups in 1970 and the percentage change in these levels over the 1960s and the 1970s. The highest skill levels in 1970, by both measures, were recorded in other services (business, professional, medical, and educational) and FIRE (finance, insurance, and real estate). The nondurable manufacturing sector had the lowest SC level in 1970, whereas the lowest PS levels were recorded in the construction and durable manufacturing sectors. During the 1960s, the largest increases in SC levels occurred in three relatively low-skill sectors—mining, nondurable manufacturing, and durable manufacturing—as well as in other services, a high-skill sector. Mining and the two manufacturing sectors also had substantially larger increases in PS requirements over

TABLE 11-2 Mean SC and PS Skill Levels by Major Industry Group and Percentage Change over Time, 1960–1980

	Substantive Complexity (SC)			People Skills (PS)		
	SC Level 1970	Change 1960–1970 (%)	Change 1970–1980 (%)	PS Level 1970	Change 1960–1970 (%)	Change 1970–1980 (%)
1. Agriculture	3.85	−1.00	0.0	1.85	0.14	0.51
2. Mining	3.93	13.80	5.60	1.63	20.93	13.01
3. Construction	4.20	5.50	2.70	1.44	9.35	6.08
4. Nondurable manufacturing	3.39	8.33	4.75	1.54	8.26	11.01
5. Durable manufacturing	3.84	7.37	1.93	1.45	13.00	8.02
6. Transportation, communications, utilities	3.68	6.17	3.60	1.95	3.83	6.26
7. Trade	4.01	0.85	4.72	2.20	−3.83	4.90
8. Finance, insurance, real estate	5.24	4.02	1.14	3.01	6.66	2.37
9. Other services	4.86	7.44	3.96	3.53	7.38	1.90
10. Government	4.44	3.90	4.24	2.54	2.05	9.81

the 1960–1980 period than the other sectors. These results suggest an inverse relationship between skill levels and skill change, a hypothesis that is supported by correlation analysis.

Our data also suggest a negative relationship between skill change and employment growth. Thus, although the service sectors (numbers 6 through 10 in Table 11-2) have seen the most rapid increases in employment, average skill increases have been moderate. This may be accounted for by evidence that a large portion of service sector employment growth has occurred among low-skilled occupations. In contrast, although the goods-producing sectors have shown much slower employment growth, they have had major changes in occupation mix, as low-skilled production workers are eliminated and managers, professionals, and technical workers increase their share of employment.

SOURCES OF PRODUCTIVITY GROWTH, 1958–1977

We begin the analysis with a comparison of alternative measures of overall labor productivity growth from 1958 to 1977.[5] In deriving the growth-accounting framework, we used the total labor requirements vector λ as the relative price vector, thus as the weights for the sectoral components of final output to arrive at total final output, y. This was necessary to arrive at Equation (11-4). However, this is a somewhat unconventional choice of prices to compute total final output. As a check, we compared more conventional measures of overall labor productivity growth with those computed using λ.

The results are shown in Table 11-3. The first line shows estimates of annual rates of overall unadjusted labor productivity growth. Economy-wide labor productivity growth averaged 2.6 percent per year over the 1958–1967 period, 1.2 percent per year from 1967 to 1977, and 1.9 percent per year over the whole 1958–1977 period. The change in labor productivity growth between 1958–1967 and 1967–1977 was -1.4 percentage points. The second line shows similar calculations using current market prices (p_m). Productivity growth estimates are higher for both periods, but the change in productivity growth between the two periods is almost the same as in line 1.

Constant sectoral market prices are used in lines 3 and 4. The results are very similar to those using λ. In line 5, we use the average market price in each period to weight the components of final demand. This index produces the largest decline in labor productivity growth between the two periods. Lines 6 and 7 use constant total labor requirement price indices, and the results are quite similar to those of line 1. In the last line, we use the average value of λ over the period as the price index, and the resulting decline in labor productivity growth between the two periods is somewhat higher than that of line 1.

Summary measures for the eight price indices are presented at the bottom of

5. See Wolff (1985b) for details on sources and methods for the input–output data. The occupation-by-industry matrices were merged with the input–output tables on a 47-industry level. The concordance between the 87-sector Bureau of Economic Analysis (BEA) industry classification scheme for the input–output data and the 64-industry classification scheme used for the occupation-by-industry matrices can be obtained from the authors. Because the occupation-by-industry matrices were for different years than the input–output data, geometric interpolation of the industry skill scores for the Census years was used to impute industry skill scores to the input–output data.

TABLE 11-3   Alternative Estimates of the Annual Rate of Growth of Overall Unadjusted Labor Productivity Growth, 1958–1977

Price Index	1958–1967 (%)	1967–1977 (%)	1958–1977 (%)	Change from 1958–1967 to 1967–1977 (%)
1. Current lambda (λ_t)	2.59	1.23	1.92	−1.36
2. Current market price (p_{mt})	2.97	1.70	2.34	−1.27
3. Constant 1972 prices	2.69	1.27	1.95	−1.42
4. Constant prices, 1958–1977 average	2.74	1.24	1.95	−1.50
5. Average price for period $[(p_{mt} + p_{mt-1})/2]$	2.82	1.16	1.90	−1.66
6. Constant 1967 lambda	2.47	1.15	1.77	−1.32
7. Constant lambda, 1958–1977 average	2.46	1.09	1.73	−1.37
8. Average lambda for period $[(\lambda_{mt} + \lambda_{mt-1})/2]$	2.51	0.98	1.68	−1.53
Average of eight measures (%)	2.66	1.23	1.90	−1.43
Standard deviation of the eight measures (%)	0.17	0.20	0.19	0.12
Ratio of standard deviation to average	0.065	0.162	0.100	−0.083

Table 11-3. The variation among the eight indices is small relative to the average value of these indices. Thus, measures of overall productivity growth appear to be insensitive to the particular price indices employed to weight the final output components. Moreover, estimates of labor productivity growth using our measure λ fall almost in the midpoint of this range of estimates, suggesting considerable reliability for this index.

Table 11-4 presents results on total labor productivity growth (TLP) for 10 large industry groups using unadjusted labor hours (π) and skill-adjusted labor hours (π^*). It is, perhaps, helpful to begin with the last line of the table, which shows the overall measures. As noted above, overall unadjusted TLP grew by 2.6 percent per year between 1958 and 1967. The average skill level of the labor force, as measured by GED, increased by 0.4 percent per year over this period. As a result, TLP, adjusted by GED level, grew by 2.2 percent per year (2.6–0.4 percent). Likewise, the average skill level of the employed labor force, as measured by SC scores, increased by 0.7 percent per year, and SC-adjusted TLP growth increased at 1.9 percent per year, 0.7 percentage points less than unadjusted labor productivity growth.

Both unadjusted and adjusted TLP growth declined between 1958–1967 and 1967–1977. The unadjusted measure fell from 2.6 to 1.2 percent per year. GED-adjusted TLP grew by 1.0 percent per year in the second period, compared to 2.2 percent in the 1958–1967 period, whereas SC-adjusted TLP grew by 0.8 percent per year, down from 1.9 percent in the first period. The rate of increase in the average skill level of the work force also declined between the two periods. The GED-weighted skill level slowed from an annual rate of increase of 0.4 percent in 1958–1967 to 0.2 percent

TABLE 11-4 Annual Rates of Total Labor Productivity Growth, by Sector and Period, Using Unadjusted and Adjusted Labor Hours

Sector	1958–1967 (%)			1967–1977 (%)			1958–1977 (%)			Change from 1958–1967 to 1967–1977 (%)		
	Unadjusted	GED	SC	Unadjusted	GED	SC	Unadjusted	GED	SC	Unadjusted	GED	SC
1. Agriculture	3.47	3.37	3.35	4.23	4.02	3.89	3.85	3.70	3.62	0.76	0.65	0.54
2. Mining	0.76	0.43	0.09	-1.90	-2.22	-2.50	-0.57	-0.89	-1.21	-2.66	-2.65	-2.59
3. Construction	3.54	3.26	3.08	-0.40	-0.57	-0.74	1.57	1.34	1.17	-3.94	-3.83	-3.82
4. Nondurable manufacturing	4.05	3.80	3.59	1.30	1.02	0.74	2.68	2.41	2.16	-2.75	-2.78	-2.85
5. Durable manufacturing	3.81	3.55	3.31	0.72	0.56	0.38	2.27	2.05	1.85	-3.09	-2.99	-2.93
6. Transportation, communication, utilities	3.94	3.67	3.41	2.30	2.16	1.94	3.12	2.92	2.68	-1.64	-1.51	-1.47
7. Trade	2.69	2.63	2.58	0.30	0.34	0.28	1.49	1.48	1.43	-2.39	-2.29	-2.30
8. Finance, insurance, real estate	2.50	2.20	1.99	3.05	2.74	2.44	2.77	2.47	2.22	0.55	0.54	0.45
9. Other services	2.08	1.69	1.33	-0.20	-0.35	-0.60	0.94	0.67	0.37	-2.28	-2.04	-1.93
10. Government	0.52	0.34	0.17	-0.31	-0.50	-0.72	0.10	-0.08	-0.27	-0.83	-0.84	-0.89
Overall	2.59	2.24	1.91	1.23	1.02	0.77	1.92	1.63	1.34	-1.36	-1.22	-1.13

in 1967–1977, whereas the annual rate of increase in the SC-weighted skill level slowed from 0.7 to 0.4 percent.

In our accounting, the crucial variable is the *change* over time in the *difference* between the skill-weighted and the unadjusted rates of labor productivity growth (cf. Equation 11-8). This difference narrowed between the two periods, from 0.35 in 1958–1967 to 0.21 in 1967–1977 for the GED-based measure and from 0.68 to 0.46 for the SC-based index (see the last row of Table 11-4). As a result, overall skill-adjusted TLP growth fell *less* than unadjusted TLP growth between the 1958–1967 and the 1967–1977 periods. Unadjusted TLP growth fell by 1.36 percentage points between the two periods, whereas GED-adjusted TLP growth fell by 1.22 percentage points and SC-adjusted TLP growth fell by 1.13 percentage points. The direct implication of this is that part of the slowdown in overall unadjusted TLP growth is the result of the slowdown in the rate of growth in employee skill levels. In terms of Equation (11-8), the $\Delta\theta$ term is negative.

Results are similar on the industry level. Because average skill scores increased in all industries from 1958 to 1967, rates of skill-adjusted TLP growth are correspondingly lower than unadjusted TLP growth in every sector. The differences are quite substantial in all sectors except agriculture and trade. Similar results are apparent for 1967–1977. Skill-adjusted rates of TLP growth were uniformly smaller than the unadjusted rates, with the exception of the GED-adjusted index in the trade sector. With the exception of the trade sector, differences between the unadjusted and adjusted TLP growth rates were again fairly large.

As Table 11-4 shows, the annual rate of unadjusted TLP growth fell between 1958–1967 and 1967–1977 in all sectors except agriculture and FIRE. In construction and durable manufacturing, unadjusted TLP growth fell by more than three percentage points, and in mining, nondurable manufacturing, trade, and other services by more than two percentage points between these periods. Among the eight sectors with lower productivity growth in 1967–1977 than 1958–1967, unadjusted TLP growth fell by more than GED-adjusted TLP growth in each except nondurable manufacturing and government, and fell by more than SC-adjusted TLP growth in each except nondurable manufacturing. The sectoral results indicate that for most, but not all, sectors, the slowdown in skill growth helped account for part of the sectoral slowdown in unadjusted TLP growth.

Table 11-5 shows the decomposition of the change in overall unadjusted TLP growth into three sources: (1) final output composition effect, (2) sectoral technical change effect, and (3) skill change effect. The decomposition is based directly on Equation (11-8) and was performed at the 47-sector level. About 10 percent of the slowdown in overall productivity growth was the results of changes in the composition of final output. This estimate is consistent with the earlier estimates reported in Wolff (1985b). The skill-change effect varies considerably depending on the skill measure used. On the basis of the substantive complexity (SC), motor skill (MS), and composite (TOT) indices, about one-sixth of the productivity slowdown was accounted for by the slowdown in the growth of skill requirements and about three-fourths by the slowdown in the rate of sectoral technical change. Based on GED, skill changes accounted for about 10 percent of the productivity slowdown, whereas on the basis of the people skill (PS) index, skill changes explained virtually none of the productivity slowdown.

TABLE 11-5   Percentage Decomposition of Change in Overall Unadjusted Labor Productivity Growth between 1958–1967 and 1967–1977[a]

Measure and Weights	Final Output Effect (%)	Technical Change Effect (%)	Skill Change Effect (%)	Sum Of Three Effects (%)
1. SC measure				
a. First period weights	11.4	70.2	16.1	97.7
b. Average period weights	10.0	76.3	15.2	101.5
2. GED measure				
a. First period weights	11.4	77.1	9.6	98.1
b. Average period weights	10.0	82.3	9.1	101.5
3. PS measure				
a. First period weights	11.4	84.3	2.8	98.5
b. Average period weights	10.0	88.8	2.6	101.5
4. MS measure				
a. First period weights	11.4	69.2	17.1	97.7
b. Average period weights	10.0	75.3	16.1	101.5
5. TOT measure				
a. First period weights	11.4	71.3	15.1	97.8
b. Average period weights	10.0	77.2	14.2	101.5

[a]The three effects may not sum to unity because of the exclusion of second-order terms and rounding errors.

CONCLUSION

To explore the changes in the skill content of labor inputs and to determine the implications of these changes for the measurement and analysis of productivity growth, we have employed a variety of measures of job-skill requirements from the Dictionary of Occupational Titles. These measures were chosen to capture the cognitive, interactive, and motor skills dimensions of job requirements.

Based upon changes in occupation mix alone, our results indicate a general upgrading of the skill content of labor inputs from 1960 to 1985, with the greatest increases occurring from 1960 to 1970. Although these results are broadly consistent with earlier studies using DOT data (Rumberger, 1981; Spenner, 1983), ours apply to a more recent period. More importantly, our employment matrices have enabled us to calculate these changes for individual industries.

The productivity analysis produced three principal results. First, the growth in skill requirements accounts for a substantial portion of the growth in unadjusted TLP from 1958 to 1977. Thus, unadjusted TLP growth averaged 1.92 percent per year, whereas GED-adjusted TLP growth was 1.63 percent and SC-adjusted TLP growth was just 1.34 percent. At the 10-sector level, skill-adjusted TLP growth was lower than the unadjusted rate for each sector. The differences were quite substantial, except for trade. This indicates that skill upgrading was responsible for a considerable portion of the productivity gains of each of the major sectors except trade.

Second, overall productivity growth fell by over one percentage point between 1958–1967 and 1967–1977. Moreover, TLP growth slowed down in all sectors of the economy, except agriculture and trade. In seven sectors, unadjusted TLP growth declined by more than two percentage points. The data also show that the rate of increase in skill levels fell between the two periods. As a result of the slowdown in growth of skill requirements, the gap between the skill-adjusted and unadjusted rates narrowed between 1958–1967 and 1967–1977 in 8 of the 10 sectors. In equivalent terms, the contribution of skill growth to sectoral productivity growth fell between the two periods in almost all industries.

Third, on the basis of our input–output growth-accounting framework, we find that the slowdown in the rate of increase in job-skill requirements helps account for a portion of the slowdown in overall labor productivity growth between 1958–1967 and 1967–1977. For three of five of our skill indices, about one-sixth of the productivity slowdown of the 1970s is attributable to the decline in the rate of increase in skill requirements of workers. This is a rather significant finding, particularly in light of previous literature on the sources of the productivity slowdown in the United States, which have failed to consider the effects of changes in direct measures of labor quality. Studies that have used indirect measures of labor quality, such as education and age (Denison, 1979a), have failed to attribute a significant portion of the productivity slowdown to changes in labor quality.

ACKNOWLEDGMENTS

An earlier version of this chapter was presented at the Eighth International Conference on Input–Output Techniques in Sapporo, Japan, in August 1986. We would like to thank those present at the conference for their comments. We would particularly like to acknowledge Karen R. Polenske for her comments and suggestions, Wayne Farel for his able research assistance, and the C. V. Starr Center for Applied Economics for its financial support of this work.

REFERENCES

Chinloy, Peter. 1980. "Sources of Quality Change in Labor Input." *American Economic Review.* Vol. 70, pp. 108–119.

Chinloy, Peter. 1981. *Labor Productivity.* Cambridge, MA: Abt Books.

Darby, Michael R. 1984. "The U.S. Productivity Slowdown: A Case of Statistical Myopia." *American Economic Review.* Vol. 74, pp. 301–322.

Denison, Edward F. 1979. "Explanations of Declining Productivity Growth." *Survey of Current Business.* Vol. 59, pp. 1–24.

Denison, Edward F. 1984. "Accounting for Slower Economic Growth: An Update." In *International Comparisons of Productivity and the Causes of the Slowdown*, edited by John Kendrick. Cambridge, MA: Ballinger Publishing Co.

Gollop, Frank M., and Dale W. Jorgenson. 1980. "U.S. Productivity Growth by Industry, 1947–73." In *New Developments in Productivity Measurement and Analysis*, edited by John Kendrick and Bea Vaccara. Chicago: University of Chicago Press.

Krueger, Alan B., and Lawrence H. Summers. 1987. "Reflections on the Interindustry Wage Structure." In *Unemployment and the Structure of Labor Markets*, edited by Kevin Lang and Jonathan S. Leonard. New York: Basil-Blackwell, pp. 17–47.

Maddison, Angus. 1982. *Phases of Capitalist Development.* Oxford: Oxford University Press.

Maddison, Angus. 1987. "Growth and Slowdown in Advanced Capitalist Economies: Techniques of Quantitative Assessment." *Journal of Economic Literature.* Vol. 25, pp. 649–698.

Miller, Ann R., Donald J. Treiman, Pamela S. Cain, and Patricia A. Roos. 1980. Work, Jobs and Occupations: A Critical Review of the Dictionary of Occupational Titles. Washington, D.C.: National Academy Press.

Rumberger, Russell W. 1981. "The Changing Skill Requirements of Jobs in the U.S. Economy." *Industrial and Labor Relations Review.* Vol. 34, pp. 578–591.

Spenner, Kenneth I. 1983. "Deciphering Prometheus: Temporal Changes in Work Content." *American Sociological Review.* Vol. 48, pp. 824–837.

U.S. Department of Labor. 1977. "Dictionary of Occupational Titles." 4th ed. Washington, D.C.: U.S. Government Printing Office.

Wolff, Edward N. 1985a. "The Magnitude and Causes of the Recent Productivity Slowdown in the U.S." In *Productivity Growth and U.S. Competitiveness*, edited by Kenneth McClennan and William Baumol. New York: Oxford University Press.

Wolff, Edward N. 1985b. "Industrial Composition, Interindustry Effects, and the U.S. Productivity Slowdown." *Review of Economics and Statistics.* Vol. 67, pp. 268–277.

IV

REGIONAL, INTERREGIONAL, AND INTERNATIONAL ISSUES

12

Effects of Tariff Reductions on Trade in the Asia–Pacific Region

YASUHIKO TORII, SEUNG-JIN SHIM, and YUTAKA AKIYAMA

The purpose of the present study is to simulate the effect of tariff reduction as an instrument of regional cooperation among the major Pacific Rim countries. Changes in the flow of trade and growth of Gross Domestic Product (GDP) induced by alternative types of tariff reductions are estimated for Japan, Korea, the five ASEAN countries,[1] and the United States.

Regional cooperation in the Pacific region is becoming an urgent issue. Throughout the 1970s and 1980s, the member countries in the region have attained a rapid rate of growth through favorable international trade, direct investment, and economic cooperation. Since 1983, however, the slowdown of growth is becoming more serious, partly because of the world depression and partly because of the disharmony created by protectionism. In order to recover the growth and harmony necessary for the long-term expansion of the world economy, some new treatment of regional adjustment by promoting more open trade and cooperation is necessary.

In practice, from the late 1970s, some constructive ideas have been proposed for regional cooperation in the region, such as the Pacific Economic Cooperation Conference (PECC), the Pacific Basin Economic Council (PBEC), and the Pacific Trade and Development Conference (PAFTAD).

Theoretically, regional cooperation is conceivable through a partial free trade area, customs unions, a common market, and so on, among which one possible way is the revision and reduction of tariffs. In the present study, we draw a basic design for regional adjustments of tariffs. Unlike the general adjustments, such as the Kennedy Round and the Tokyo Round, the regional reduction of tariffs has proved to be feasible for solving problems peculiar to the region, which includes many member countries at different stages of economic development. It is urgent for these countries to encourage international transactions of goods, services, and capital.

For the present study, we combine a multisectoral linear programming model with an international regional input–ouput model to simulate the effects of alternative tariff reductions in the region. First, an overview of the issues is presented. Second, we recompile the international input–output table of the Pacific countries originally

---

1. The Association of Southeast Asia Nations (ASEAN) is composed of Indonesia, Malaysia, the Philippines, Singapore, Thailand, and Brunei, among which Brunei is omitted from our study.

compiled by the Institute of Developing Economies (IDE) and valued at prices after customs clearance, by revaluing transactions at FOB (free on board) prices in order to introduce tariff rates explicitly, and construct a linear programming model using the recompiled table. Third, the data are briefly described, and five alternative scenarios of tariff reduction and their effects are simulated. Fourth, results of the simulation are presented. Fifth, some concluding remarks are provided.

OVERVIEW OF ISSUES

Partial equilibrium models for assessing effects of tariff reduction on social welfare were originally proposed by Viner (1950), mainly in the theory of customs unions, followed by Meade (1955) and Lipsey (1960). Recent literature indicates a rapidly growing interest in general equilibrium trade policy modeling to investigate impacts of tariff protection, or trade liberalization, on social welfare using an input–output framework inaugurated by Evans (1971, 1972), who made a model of Australia as an open economy. A number of studies on welfare impacts of tariff protection were made by Bruno (1973), Bhagwati and Srinivasan (1973), Taylor and Black (1974), Staelin (1976), and Helpman (1978). The linear programming technique was applied to evaluate the effects of tariff protection by Lage (1970).

Numerical general equilibrium models are being used to analyze effects of various trade policy options for a number of developed and developing countries and of proposals for multilateral trade liberalization in the negotiations under the General Agreement on Trade and Tariffs (GATT). Models were constructed and empirical studies were conducted by Brown and Whalley (1980), Dixon et al. (1986), Harrison (1986), Deardorf and Stern (1986), and Whalley (1986). A study of interregional effects of tariff reductions was done by Harrison and Kimbell (1985), who estimated and applied a numerical general equilibrium model of 10 Pacific Basin countries to study the nature and extent of their economic interdependence with respect to trade liberalization.

The model presented in this chapter is a type of general equilibrium model. We assume that intermediate inputs are substitutable between domestic products and imports with respect to relative input prices, employing a Leontief-type technology. In this study, we have focused only on the effect of the tariff reduction, although there are many other important issues. Direct export subsidies, production subsidies, discriminatory pricing, and investment subsidies, for example, are urgent and important for present world trade.

We have concentrated only on tariff reduction in this chapter because first, alternative policies other than tariff reduction are mostly applied on an industry basis, whereas tariff reduction is a measure to adjust overall international trade structures. In other words, tariff reduction is applied uniformly to all traded goods. Second, tariff reduction is the central issue in the now-proceeding multilateral trade negotiations, which was initiated in the Montevideo Assembly in 1986. In the coming New Round, or Uruguay Round, the assessment of tariff cooperation should be the key issue together with other aspects, such as service trade and nontariff barriers.

MODEL

Our model includes three member countries and one region, namely Japan, Korea, the United States, and the five ASEAN countries with an exogenous block for the rest of the world. For the study, data for the five ASEAN countries are consolidated into the subtotal for the ASEAN region.

For the member countries and region, the following equations are used. The superscripts r and s in each equation denote any pair of partner countries and region, and superscript rs denotes the direction of flow from country r to country s.

The demand and supply balance in country r for commodity i is defined in Equation (12-1) at producer's prices.

$$\sum_s^m \sum_j^n A_{ij}^{rs} X_j^s + \sum_s^m F_i^{rs} Y^s + E_i^r = X_i^r, \qquad r = 1, 2, \ldots, m; \; i = 1, 2, \ldots, n \qquad (12\text{-}1)$$

where

A_{ij}^{rs} = matrix of intermediate input coefficients,
F_i^{rs} = matrix of final demand coefficients,
Y^r = vector of final demands,
E_i^r = vector of exports to the rest of the world,
X_i^r = vector of total products,

Flows of domestic transactions of each member country are the diagonal blocks of the $A_{ij}^{rs} X_j^r$ matrix, whereas flows of international trade of intermediate goods among member countries are the off-diagonal blocks. Imports from the rest of the world are defined in Equation (12-2).

$$M_i^r = \sum_j^n Mm_{ij}^r X_j^r + Mf_i^r Y^r, \qquad r = 1, 2, \ldots, m; \; i = 1, 2, \ldots, n \qquad (12\text{-}2)$$

where

Mm_{ij}^r = matrix of coefficients of intermediate imports from the rest of the world, $r = 1, 2, \ldots, m$

Mf_i^r = matrix of coefficients of final imports from the rest of the world, $r = 1, 2, \ldots, m$.

Theoretically, intermediate trade and final trade, $A_{ij}^{rs} X_j^s$ and $F_i^{rs} Y^s$, respectively, in Equation (12-1), are to be valued at FOB prices, but, in the international input–output table that was compiled by IDE, they are valued at prices after customs clearance, or CIF (cost, insurance, and freight) prices plus import duties. Therefore, there are the following relations between the observed input coefficients, $\mathbb{A}_{ij}^{rs}$, and real input coefficients, A_{ij}^{rs}.

$$\mathbb{A}_{ij}^{rs} = A_{ij}^{rs} \qquad\qquad \text{when } r = s \qquad (12\text{-}3a)$$

$$\mathbb{A}_{ij}^{rs} = A_{ij}^{rs}(1 + t_i^s + h_i^{rs}) \qquad \text{when } r \neq s \qquad (12\text{-}3b)$$

where

t_i^s = weighted average of tariff rates of sector i in country $s, s = 1, 2, \ldots, m$
h_i^{rs} = freight and insurance on international trade of commodity i from country r to $s, r, s = 1, 2, \ldots, m$.

Analogous relations exist with observed final trade coefficients, $\mathbb{F}_i^{rs}$, intermediate import coefficients, Mm_{ij}^r, and final import coefficients, Mf_i^r:

$$F_i^{rs} = F_i^{rs} \qquad\qquad \text{when } r = s \qquad\qquad (12\text{-}4a)$$

$$= (1 + t_i^s + h_i^{rs})F_i^{rs} \qquad \text{when } r \neq s \qquad\qquad (12\text{-}4b)$$

$$Mm_{ij}^r = (1 + t_i^r + h_i^{rs})Mm_{ij}^r \qquad\qquad\qquad (12\text{-}5)$$

$$Mf_i^r = (1 + t_i^r + h_i^{rs})Mf_i^r \qquad\qquad\qquad (12\text{-}6)$$

Thus, Equation (12-1) is converted into the equation using coefficients at the value after custom clearance, A_{ij}^{rs} and F_i^{rs} as follows:

$$\sum_s^m \sum_j^n A_{ij}^{rs}X_j^s + \sum_s^n F_i^{rs}Y^s + E_i^r - (T_i^r + H_i^r) = X_i^r \qquad r = 1, 2, \ldots, m$$

$$i = 1, 2, \ldots, n \qquad (12\text{-}7)$$

and

$$M_i^r = \sum_j^n Mm_{ij}^r X_j^r + Mf_i^r Y^r \qquad\qquad (12\text{-}8)$$

with the following adjustment factors,

$$T_i^r = \sum_s^m (t_i^s/\theta_i^s)\left(\sum_j^n A_{ij}^{rs}X_j^s + F_i^{rs}Y^s\right), \qquad r \neq s \qquad (12\text{-}9)$$

$$H_i^r = \sum_s^m (h_i^{rs}/\theta_i^s)\left(\sum_j^n A_{ij}^{rs}X_j^s + F_i^{rs}Y^s\right), \qquad r \neq s \qquad (12\text{-}10)$$

$$\theta_i^s = (1 + t_i^s + h_i^{rs})$$

where

T_i^r = aggregate tariff on imported composite commodity i from specific exporter country r to all countries s, $r, s = 1, 2, \ldots, m$

H_i^r = aggregate freight insurance on imported composite commodity i from all specific exporter country r to all countries $s, r, s = 1, 2, \ldots, m$.

The set of Equations (12-7)–(12-10) presents the international input–output model in terms of value after custom clearance, or CIF prices plus import duties, in the form of an Isard-type model, with noncompetitive intermediate imports.

Now, we assume that input coefficients, A_{ij}^s, are constant, and that there can be substitution between domestic productions and imports, as follows:

$$A_{ij}^s = \sum_r^m A_{ij}^{rs} + Mm_{ij}^s = \text{constant} \qquad\qquad (12\text{-}11)$$

When tariffs are reduced, the coefficients A_{ij}^{rs}, Mm_{ij}^r, and Mf_i^r are subject to the following adjustment:

$$A_{ij}^{rs'} = (1 + \Delta P_i^{rs}\varepsilon_i^s)A_{ij}^{rs} \qquad r, s, = 1, 2, \ldots, m, \text{ when } r \neq s \qquad (12\text{-}12)$$

$$Mm_{ij}^{s'} = (1 + \Delta P_i^{rs}\varepsilon_i^s)Mm_{ij}^s \qquad\qquad (12\text{-}13)$$

where

$$\Delta P_i^{rs} = \frac{(1 + t_{i1}^s + h_i^{rs}) - (1 + t_{i0}^s + h_i^{rs})}{(1 + t_{i0}^s + h_i^{rs})} \qquad \text{when } r \neq s \qquad (12\text{-}14)$$

where

t_{i0}^s = tariff rate on commodity i for the base year, $s = 1, 2, \ldots, m$

t_{i1}^s = tariff rate on commodity i for the target year, $s = 1, 2, \ldots, m$

ε_i^s = price elasticity of import of commodity i in importing country s, $s = 1, 2, \ldots, m$.

Because A_{ij}^s is constant, domestic input coefficients can be written as follows:

$$A_{ij}^{ss'} = A_{ij}^s - \left(\sum_r^m A_{ij}^{rs'} + Mm_{ij}^{s'} \right), \qquad \text{when } r \neq s \qquad (12\text{-}15)$$

In the same way, final demand can be written as follows:

$$F_i^s = \sum_r^m F_i^{rs} + Mf_i^s = \text{constant} \qquad (12\text{-}16)$$

where

$$F_i^{rs'} = (1 + \Delta P_i^{rs} \varepsilon_i^s) F_i^{rs} \qquad r, s = 1, 2, \ldots, m, \text{ when } r \neq s \qquad (12\text{-}17)$$

$$Mf_i^{s'} = (1 + \Delta P_i^{rs} \varepsilon_i^s) Mf_i^s \qquad (12\text{-}18)$$

$$F_i^{ss'} = F_i^s - \left(\sum_r^m F_i^{rs'} + Mf_i^{s'} \right), \qquad \text{when } r \neq s \qquad (12\text{-}19)$$

Therefore, the observed input coefficients, $\mathbb{A}_{ij}^{rs'}$ and $\mathbb{F}_i^{rs'}$, after tariff reduction may be written as

$$\mathbb{A}_{ij}^{rs'} = (1 + t_i^s + h_i^{rs})(1 + \Delta P_i^{rs} \varepsilon_i^s) A_{ij}^{rs}, \qquad \text{when } r \neq s \qquad (12\text{-}20)$$

$$\mathbb{A}_{ij}^{ss'} = A_{ij}^s - \left(\sum_r^m \mathbb{A}_{ij}^{rs'} + \mathbb{M}m_{ij}^{s'} \right), \qquad \text{when } r \neq s \qquad (12\text{-}21\text{a})$$

$$\mathbb{M}m_{ij}^{s'} = (1 + t_i^s + h_i^{rs})(1 + \Delta P_i^{rs} \varepsilon_i^s) Mm_{ij}^s \qquad (12\text{-}21\text{b})$$

$$\mathbb{F}_i^{rs'} = (1 + t_i^s + h_i^{rs})(1 + \Delta P_i^{rs} \varepsilon_i^s) F_i^{rs}, \qquad \text{when } r \neq s \qquad (12\text{-}22)$$

$$\mathbb{F}_i^{ss'} = F_i^s - \left(\sum_r^m \mathbb{F}_i^{rs'} + \mathbb{M}f_i^{s'} \right), \qquad \text{when } r \neq s \qquad (12\text{-}23\text{a})$$

$$\mathbb{M}f_i^{s'} = (1 + t_i^s + h_i^{rs})(1 + \Delta P_i^{rs} \varepsilon_i^s) Mf_i^s \qquad (12\text{-}23\text{b})$$

In our multisectoral linear-programming model, tariff rates are specified as exogenously conforming to the tariff reduction scheme. Our linear programming model is as follows. The objective function is to maximize total GDP of member countries.

$$\sum_s^m V^s = \sum_s^m \sum_j^n v_j^s X_j^s \qquad (12\text{-}24)$$

subject to the following constraints:

$$\sum_s^m \sum_j^n \mathbb{A}_{ij}^{rs'} X_j^s + \sum_s^m \mathbb{F}_i^{rs'} Y^s + E_i^r - (T_i^{r'} + H_i^r) \leqslant X_i^r \qquad (12\text{-}25)$$

$$T_i^{r'} = \sum_s^m (t_i^s/\theta_i^s) \left(\sum_j^n \mathbb{A}_{ij}^{rs'} X_j^s + \mathbb{F}_i^{rs'} Y^s \right) \qquad (12\text{-}26)$$

$$H_i^{r'} = \sum_s^m (h_i^{rs}/\theta_i^s) \left(\sum_j^n \mathbb{A}_{ij}^{rs'} X_j^s + \mathbb{F}_i^{rs'} Y^s \right) \qquad (12\text{-}27)$$

$$\sum_j^n l_j^r X_j^r \leqslant \bar{L}^r \qquad (12\text{-}28)$$

$$X_j^r \leqslant \bar{X}_j^{ru} \qquad (12\text{-}29)$$

$$\bar{C}^{rl} \leqslant C^r \leqslant \bar{C}^{ru}, \qquad G^r = \bar{G}^r, \qquad I^r = \bar{I}^r, \qquad E^r = \bar{E}^r \quad (12\text{-}30)$$

$$Y^r = C^r + G^r + I^r \qquad (12\text{-}31)$$

$$v_j^s = 1 - \left(\sum_r^m \sum_i^n \mathbb{A}_{ij}^{rs} + \sum_i^n \mathbb{M} m_{ij}^s \right) \qquad (12\text{-}32)$$

Nonnegativity is assumed for all variables. Final demands, C, G, and I, are aggregate private consumption, government expenditure, and fixed capital formation, respectively; L and l are labor supply and labor coefficient, respectively; V is value added, and v is the coefficient of value added.

Equation (12-25) is the demand–supply balance constraint. Constraints on labor supply and production capacity are introduced in Equations (12-28) and (12-29), respectively. Upper bounds on X and C are imposed, without which the country tends to specialize completely in some commodities.

This model makes it possible to analyze endogenous changes in imports and exports within the region and to simulate changes on the total GDP of the member countries, trade flows of each industry in each country, and the trade balance of payments of each country.

DATA AND ALTERNATIVE SCENARIOS OF TARIFF REDUCTIONS

This study is based on the *International Input–Output Table of the ASEAN Countries* *1975*, compiled by the Institute of Developing Economies (1982). The table has 56 sectors for each of the eight member countries (five ASEAN countries, Japan, Korea, and the United States) and the rest of the world.

In the original table, domestic transactions are valued at producers' prices, intermediate and final trade at FOB prices, and imports from the rest of the world at CIF prices. For the purpose of our study, all trade data were converted into basic values, that is, CIF plus custom duties, according to the definition of Equations (12-4)–(12-6). Estimated freight and insurance and import duties were added to the original transactions. Weighted averages of tariff rates, labor coefficients, and price elasticities of imports were estimated for each sector and country and are available from the authors. The given variables $\bar{C}$, $\bar{G}$, and $\bar{I}$ of each country were collected from International Financial Statistics (International Monetary Fund, 1986), and exports, $\bar{E}$, were estimated from U.N. trade statistics (United Nations, 1980).

Three cases of simulations have been conducted for five alternative formulas of tariff reduction for 1985. Observed 1975 input–output coefficients, in money terms, are used instead of those for 1985. Alternative schemes of tariff reduction are presented in Table 12-1. Each of the simulations includes three cases: Case 1, reduction only by Japan; Case 2, reduction by Japan, the United States, and Korea; and Case 3,

TABLE 12-1   Tariff Reduction Formulas

Cutting Formula	Scenario Number	Tariff Type[a]	Tariff Liberalization Nation		
			Case 1	Case 2	Case 3
Linear	I	$t_1 = t_0 - 0.2t_0$	Japan	United States,	All
cutting	II	$t_1 = t_0 - 0.5t_0$	only	Japan,	countries
	III	$t_1 = t_0 - 0.8t_0$		Korea	
Harmonization	IV	$t_1 = 0.14t_0/(0.14 + t_0)$	Japan	United States,	All
cutting	V	$t_1 = 0.09t_0/(0.09 + t_0)$	only	Japan,	countries
				Korea	

[a]t_0 is the initial tariff rate. t_1 is the tariff rate after tariff liberalization.

reduction by all member countries including ASEAN. The scheme of linear reduction had been actually adopted in the Kennedy Round in 1964–1967. The scheme of harmonizing reduction had been adopted in the Tokyo Round in 1973–1979.

RESULTS OF SIMULATIONS

We divided our simulation results into three categories: effects on GDP, effects on trade flows, and effects on trade balances.

Effects on GDP of Member Countries

Effects of tariff reduction on the GDP of member countries are presented in Table 12-2. Scenarios I, II, and III present simulations of linear formulas of tariff reduction by 20, 50, and 80 percent, respectively. Generally, the larger the rates of reduction, the larger the positive impacts induced on the GDP of member countries.

If only Japan were to reduce tariffs (Cases I-1, II-1, and III-1), the tariff reduction might induce relatively small increases of GDP in Japan, with a slight decrease in other member countries. If Japan, Korea, and the United States were to have a linear reduction simultaneously (Cases I-2, II-2, and III-2), it might create a more optimistic scenario of substantial increases of the GDP in Korea, Japan, and the United States and a slight decrease in the ASEAN region. If all member countries were to reduce their tariffs simultaneously (Cases I-3, II-3, and III-3), the GDP of all member countries might increase, with a particularly large increase of the GDP in Korea and the ASEAN region. Results of scenarios IV and V of the harmonization type of tariff reduction are shown in Table 12-2. Like the cases of linear reduction, only the harmonizing reduction by Japan generates pessimistic scenarios, whereas the reduction by Japan, Korea, the United States, and all member countries tends to give more optimistic scenarios. The harmonizing reductions by Japan, Korea, and the United States (Cases IV-2 and V-2) induce an increase of the GDP in Korea, Japan, and the United States and a slight decrease in the ASEAN region. Harmonizing reductions by all member countries (Cases IV-3 and V-3) create increases of the GDP in all member countries, particularly in Korea and the ASEAN region.

Three important conclusions can be drawn. First, the tariff reduction may be

TABLE 12-2 Percentage Change in GDP and Trade Flows within Member Countries

	Percentage Change in GDP					Percentage Change in Trade Flows within Member Countries		
	ASEAN	Japan	Korea	United States	Total	Member Countries	Rest of the World	World
Scenario I (20 percent linear reduction: $t_1 = t_0 - 0.2t_0$)								
Case I-1 Japan only	−0.0154	0.0420	−0.0111	−0.0004	0.0088	0.4279	0.0118	0.1094
Case I-2 Japan, Korea, United States	−0.0311	0.0295	0.4231	0.0060	0.0159	1.1236	0.3570	0.5569
Case I-3 All member countries	0.2150	0.0261	0.4201	0.0060	0.0240	1.7608	−0.2367	0.2321
Scenario II (50 percent linear reduction: $t_1 = t_0 - 0.5t_0$)								
Case II-1 Japan only	−0.0386	0.1060	−0.0269	−0.0009	0.0222	1.0699	0.1143	0.3385
Case II-2 Japan, Korea, United States	−0.0782	0.0753	1.1213	0.0162	0.0417	2.8070	−0.1192	0.5675
Case II-3 All member countries	0.5875	0.0673	1.1144	0.0160	0.0640	4.3989	−0.5753	0.5920
Scenario III (80 percent linear reduction: $t_1 = t_0 - 0.8t_0$)								
Case III-1 Japan only	−0.0616	0.1738	−0.0420	−0.0015	0.0365	1.7115	0.2910	0.6244
Case III-2 Japan, Korea, United States	−0.1232	0.1250	1.8935	0.0268	0.0698	4.5784	−0.5983	0.6165
Case III-3 All member countries	1.0215	0.1132	1.8830	0.0265	0.1087	7.1157	−0.0765	1.6113
Scenario IV [Harmonizing reduction: $t_1 = 0.14t_0/(0.14 + t_0)$]								
Case IV-1 Japan only	−0.0304	0.0745	−0.0237	−0.0007	0.0154	0.6752	0.2232	0.3293
Case IV-2 Japan, Korea, United States	−0.0621	0.0462	1.5094	0.0070	0.0343	2.3722	−0.3696	0.2739
Case IV-3 All member countries	0.8451	0.0359	1.4997	0.0068	0.0649	4.4207	−0.8268	0.4046
Scenario V [Harmonizing reduction: $t_1 = 0.09t_0/(0.09 + t_0)$]								
Case V-1 Japan only	−0.0387	0.0969	−0.0294	−0.0009	0.0200	0.8825	0.2099	0.3678
Case V-2 Japan, Korea, United States	−0.0782	0.0623	1.7525	0.0102	0.0430	2.9028	−0.6848	0.1571
Case V-3 All member countries	0.9771	0.0509	1.7418	0.0099	0.0788	5.2399	−0.2162	1.0642

more effective when more member countries (we might hope all member countries) join the reduction; second, larger rates of reduction may induce larger increases of the GDP; third, harmonizing reduction seems to be more effective than linear reduction.

Effects on Trade Flows of Member Countries

Effects of tariff reduction on trade flows within member countries are presented in Table 12-2. First, the tariff reduction only by Japan induces fewer effects than the reduction by the three major countries and/or by all member countries. Second, tariff reduction may induce substantial increases of trade among member countries, while it decreases the trade with the rest of the world. In other words, trade-creation effects are larger than trade-diversion effects. Third, in each formula, the larger the rates of reduction, the larger the import increases.

Table 12-3 presents effects of tariff reduction on imports by origin and destination countries. Among the scenarios of linear reduction (Cases I, II, and III), Cases I-2, II-2, and III-2 show significant increases of imports by Korea from Japan and from the United States, and imports by the United States from Korea. If all member countries were to reduce their tariffs simultaneously (Cases I-3, II-3, and III-3), imports of the ASEAN region from the other member countries may increase. In ASEAN countries, import increases are larger than export increases, partly because initial tariff rates in the ASEAN region are the highest in the member countries.

Effects on the Trade Balance

In Table 12-4, effects of the tariff reduction on the trade balance are presented. In Cases I-1, II-1, and III-1, in which only Japan reduces tariffs, the Japanese trade surplus tends to decrease gradually. However, it decreases by no more than 7 percent, even in the case of an 80 percent tariff reduction. This fact indicates that trade imbalance is caused not only by tariff barriers, but also by other factors, such as industrial structure, input structure, and nontariff barriers.

If Japan, Korea, and the United States were to reduce their tariffs simultaneously (Cases I-2, II-2, and III-2), the trade balance of the ASEAN region would be improved significantly. If all member countries were to reduce tariffs according to a linear formula (Cases I-3, II-3, and III-3), the trade balance of the ASEAN region would deteriorate significantly. In the case of the harmonizing reduction by all member countries (Scenarios IV and V), the trade balance of the ASEAN region would deteriorate even more.

SUMMARY AND CONCLUSION

The contribution of this study to the methodology of analyzing the effect of tariff reduction is that the tariff rates and freight and insurance rates have been explicitly introduced into the international input–output coefficients; a linear programming model, the objective function of which maximizes the GDP, was adopted to analyze effects of tariff reduction in the Asia–Pacific Region.

From this study, we conclude that tariff reductions within the member countries in the Asia–Pacific region would increase trade within the region as well as trade with the rest of the world, induce a positive impact, both directly and indirectly, on GDP,

TABLE 12-3 Percentage Change in Imports for Each Country by Origin Country

Scenario I: 20 Percent Linear Reduction[a]

Origin Countries	Case I-1 Japan only				Case I-2 Japan, Korea, United States				Case I-3 All member countries			
	ASEAN	Japan	Korea	United States	ASEAN	Japan	Korea	United States	ASEAN	Japan	Korea	United States
ASEAN	—	1.44	0.03	-0.00	—	1.45	0.49	0.73	—	1.45	0.48	0.73
Japan	-0.00	—	0.02	-0.00	0.01	—	3.50	1.03	4.56	—	3.50	1.03
Korea	-0.01	1.55	—	-0.00	0.01	1.57	—	2.43	3.88	1.58	—	2.43
United States	-0.00	1.03	0.02	—	0.01	1.05	1.86	—	3.65	1.05	1.87	—
Rest of the world	-0.00	1.13	0.01	-0.50	0.01	1.11	0.01	0.06	0.14	1.10	0.03	-0.90
Total	-0.00	1.15	0.02	-0.42	0.01	1.14	1.54	0.22	1.82	1.13	1.54	-0.58

Scenario II: 50 Percent Linear Reduction

Origin Countries	Case II-1 Japan only				Case II-2 Japan, Korea, United States				Case II-3 All member countries			
	ASEAN	Japan	Korea	United States	ASEAN	Japan	Korea	United States	ASEAN	Japan	Korea	United States
ASEAN	—	3.61	0.07	-0.00	—	3.61	1.21	1.81	—	3.62	1.19	1.81
Japan	-0.01	—	0.06	-0.00	0.02	—	8.72	2.58	11.39	—	8.23	2.57
Korea	-0.02	3.88	—	-0.00	0.03	3.93	—	6.08	9.67	3.96	—	6.08
United States	-0.01	2.59	0.06	—	0.02	2.61	4.64	—	9.12	2.62	4.65	—
Rest of the world	-0.01	1.27	0.01	-0.40	0.02	0.26	0.05	-0.32	0.34	0.29	0.06	-1.09
Total	-0.01	1.75	0.04	-0.34	0.02	1.03	3.84	0.16	4.53	1.04	3.85	-0.49

Scenario III: 80 Percent Linear Reduction

Origin Countries	Case III-1 Japan only				Case III-2 Japan, Korea, United States				Case III-3 All member countries			
	ASEAN	Japan	Korea	United States	ASEAN	Japan	Korea	United States	ASEAN	Japan	Korea	United States
ASEAN	—	5.77	0.11	-0.00	—	5.78	1.76	2.90	—	5.79	1.75	2.90
Japan	-0.02	—	0.09	-0.01	0.04	—	15.01	4.12	18.21	—	14.93	4.11
Korea	-0.03	6.21	—	-0.00	0.40	6.35	—	9.72	15.83	6.39	—	9.72
United States	-0.01	4.14	0.09	—	0.04	4.18	8.07	—	14.58	4.20	8.03	—
Rest of the world	-0.01	1.42	0.02	-0.19	0.02	0.37	0.41	-1.15	0.55	1.39	0.39	-0.84
Total	-0.01	2.36	0.06	-0.16	0.03	1.61	6.75	-0.28	7.25	2.35	6.70	-0.02

Scenario IV: 14 Percent Harmonizing Reduction

Origin Countries	Case IV-1 Japan only				Case IV-2 Japan, Korea, United States				Case IV-3 All member countries			
	ASEAN	Japan	Korea	United States	ASEAN	Japan	Korea	United States	ASEAN	Japan	Korea	United States
ASEAN	—	1.91	0.04	-0.00	—	1.92	1.37	1.14	—	1.93	1.35	1.14
Japan	-0.01	—	0.05	-0.00	0.02	—	12.80	1.62	14.93	—	12.73	1.62
Korea	-0.01	3.08	—	-0.00	0.38	3.18	—	4.84	14.04	3.21	—	4.84
United States	-0.01	1.75	0.05	—	0.02	1.78	6.73	—	11.28	1.79	6.70	—
Rest of the world	-0.01	1.18	0.01	-0.19	0.01	0.18	0.49	-0.69	0.42	0.18	0.47	-1.47
Total	-0.01	1.38	0.03	-0.16	0.02	0.66	5.78	-0.30	5.84	0.66	5.74	-0.95

TABLE 12-3   Percentage Change in Imports for Each Country by Origin Country (*Continued*)

Scenario V: 9 Percent Harmonizing Reduction

Origin Countries	Case V-1 Japan only				Case V-2 Japan, Korea, United States				Case V-3 All member countries			
	ASEAN	Japan	Korea	United States	ASEAN	Japan	Korea	United States	ASEAN	Japan	Korea	United States
ASEAN	—	2.56	0.06	-0.00	—	2.58	1.59	1.47	—	2.58	1.58	1.47
Japan	-0.01	—	0.06	-0.00	0.03	—	14.37	2.09	16.96	—	14.29	2.09
Korea	-0.02	3.91	—	-0.00	0.38	4.02	—	6.15	15.58	4.06	—	6.15
United States	-0.01	2.26	0.06	—	0.03	2.30	7.59	—	13.01	2.31	7.55	-0.51
Rest of the world	-0.01	1.20	0.02	-0.22	0.02	0.22	0.49	-1.22	0.49	0.20	0.47	-0.51
Total	-0.01	1.55	0.04	-0.18	0.02	0.85	6.47	-0.66	6.67	0.84	6.43	-0.06

[a]Destination countries.

TABLE 12-4   Effects on Balance of Trade[a]

		ASEAN	Japan	Korea	United States
No tariff reduction	ASEAN	—	2874.4	788.4	5010.2
	Japan	−2874.4	—	4630.9	11029.7
	Korea	−788.4	−4630.9	—	−2117.6
	United States	−5010.2	−11029.7	2117.6	—
Case I-1	ASEAN	—	3131.8	788.7	5010.4
Japan only	Japan	−3131.8	—	4569.2	10865.5
	Korea	−788.7	−4569.2	—	−2119.1
	United States	−5010.4	−10685.5	2119.1	—
Scenario I: 20 percent linear reduction					
Case I-2	ASEAN	—	3130.1	793.9	5102.7
Japan	Japan	−3130.1	—	4872.0	11129.7
Korea	Korea	−793.9	−4872.0	—	−2143.1
United States	United States	−5102.4	−11129.7	2134.1	—
Case I-3	ASEAN	—	2451.0	781.0	4818.1
All member countries	Japan	−2451.2	—	4872.0	11128.1
	Korea	−781.0	−4872.0	—	−2134.1
	United States	−4818.1	−11128.1	2134.1	—
Scenario II: 50 percent linear reduction					
Case II-1	ASEAN	—	3517.9	789.2	5010.7
Japan only	Korea	−789.2	−4476.5	—	−2121.2
	United States	−5010.7	−10182.2	2121.2	—
Case II-2	ASEAN	—	3514.0	801.9	5240.9
Japan	Japan	−3514.0	—	5230.9	11292.1
Korea	Korea	−801.9	−5230.9	—	−2157.8
United States	United States	−5240.9	−11292.1	2157.8	—
Case II-3	ASEAN	—	1817.8	769.9	4530.6
All member countries	Japan	−1817.8	—	5231.0	11286.3
	Korea	−769.9	−5231.0	—	−2158.6
	United States	−4530.6	−11288.3	2158.6	—
Scenario III: 80 percent linear reduction					
Case III-2	ASEAN	—	3903.9	789.7	5011.0
Japan only	Japan	−3903.9	—	4383.7	9679.0
	Korea	−789.7	−4383.7	—	−2133.3
	United States	−5011.0	−9679.3	2123.3	—
Case III-2	ASEAN	—	3897.8	806.9	5379.4
Japan	Japan	−3897.8	—	5681.3	11454.8
Korea	Korea	−806.9	−5681.3	—	−2222.2
United States	United States	−5379.4	−11454.8	2222.2	—
Case III-3	ASEAN	—	1185.8	755.8	4243.4
All member countries	Japan	−1185.8	—	5673.0	11449.3
	Korea	−755.8	−5673.0	—	−2219.8
	United States	−4243.4	−11449.3	2219.8	—
Scenario IV: 14 percent harmonizing reduction					
Case IV-1	ASEAN	—	3216.4	789.0	5010.5
Japan only	Japan	−3216.4	—	4508.3	10454.3
	Korea	−789.0	−4508.3	—	−2120.7
	United States	−5010.5	−10454.3	2120.7	—
Case IV-2	ASEAN	—	3213.8	802.5	5154.5
Japan	Japan	−3213.8	—	5618.5	11148.5
Korea	Korea	−802.5	−5618.5	—	−2336.0
United States	United States	−5154.5	−11148.5	2336.0	—

TABLE 12-4   Effects on Balance of Trade[a] (*Continued*)

		ASEAN	Japan	Korea	United States
Case IV-3	ASEAN	—	989.8	757.3	4274.5
All member countries	Japan	−989.8	—	5611.0	11144.5
	Korea	−757.3	−5611.0	—	−2333.8
	United States	−4274.5	−11144.5	2333.8	—
Scenario V: 9 percent harmonizing reduction					
Case V-1	ASEAN	—	3332.6	789.2	5010.7
Japan only	Korea	−789.2	−4475.4	—	−2121.5
	United States	−5010.7	−10286.5	2121.5	—
Case V-2	ASEAN	—	3329.2	805.0	5196.1
Japan	Japan	−3329.2	—	5721.3	11185.7
Korea	Korea	−805.0	−5721.3	—	−2336.3
United States	United States	−5196.1	−11185.7	2336.3	—
Case V-3	ASEAN	—	801.4	754.8	4181.6
All member countries	Japan	−801.4	—	5713.0	11181.1
	Korea	−754.8	−5713.0	—	−2333.8
	United States	−4181.6	−11181.1	2333.8	—

[a]Million dollars.

and improve the balance of trade in each country. Furthermore, the positive impacts on trade, GDP, and the balance of trade would become larger as the rates of reduction become higher.

In order to make our model more realistic, exports to the rest of the world, which were assumed to be exogenous, could be treated endogenously. Moreover, different schemes of tariff reduction by import items may be desirable rather than the uniform linear and harmonizing reduction formulas used in this study.

REFERENCES

Bhagwati, J. N., and T. N. Srinivasan. 1973. "The General Equilibrium Theory of Effective Protection and Resource Allocation." *Journal of International Economies.* Vol. 3, pp. 259–281.

Brown, F., and J. Whalley. 1980. "General Equilibrium Evaluation of Tariff-Cutting Proposals in the Tokyo Round and Comparisons with More Extensive Liberalization of World Trade." *Economic Journal.* Vol. 90, pp. 838–866.

Bruno, M. 1973. "Protection and Tariff Change under General Equilibrium." *Journal of International Economics.* Vol. 3., pp. 205–225.

Deardorff, A. V., and R. M. Stern. 1986. *The Michigan Model of World Production and Trade.* Cambridge, MA: MIT Press.

Dixon, P. B., B. R. Parmenter, and R. J. Rimmer. 1986. "ORANI Projections of the Short-Run Effects of a 50% Across-the-Board Cut in Protection Using Alternative Data Base." In *General Equilibrium Trade Policy Modeling*, edited by T. N. Srinivasan and J. Whalley. Cambridge, MA: MIT Press, pp. 33–60.

Evans, H. D. 1971. "Effects of Protection in a General Equilibrium Framework." *Review of Economics and Statistics.* Vol. 53, pp. 147–156.

Evans, H. D. 1972. *A General Equilibrium Analysis of Protection: The Effects of Protection in Australia.* Amsterdam: North-Holland.

Harrison, G. 1986. "A General Equilibrium Analysis of Tariff Reduction." In *General Equilibrium Trade Policy Modelling*, edited by T. N. Srinivasan and J. Whalley. Cambridge, MA: MIT Press, pp. 101–124.

Harrison, G., and L. Kimbell. 1985. "Economic Interdependence in the Pacific Basin: A General Equilibrium Approach." In *New Developments in Applied General Equilibrium Analysis*, edited by J. Piggott and J. Whalley. Cambridge, England: Cambridge University Press, pp. 143–174.

Helpman, E. 1978. "The Exact Measurement of Welfare Losses Which Result from Trade Taxes." *International Economic Review*. Vol. 19, pp. 157–163.

Institute of Developing Economies. 1982. *International Input–Output Table for ASEAN Countries, 1975*. IDE Statistical Data Series No. 39. Tokyo: Asian Economic Press.

International Monetary Fund. 1986. *International Financial Statistics*.

Lage, G. M. 1970. "A Linear Programming Analysis of Tariff Protection." *Western Economic Journal*. Vol. 18, pp. 167–185.

Lipsey, R. G. 1960. "The Theory of Customs Unions: A General Survey." *Economic Journal*. Vol. LXX, No. 279 (September), pp. 496–514.

Meade, J. E. 1955. *The Theory of Customs Unions*. Amsterdam, North-Holland.

Staelin, C. P. 1976. "A General Equilibrium Model of Tariffs in a Non-Competitive Economy." *Journal of International Economics*. Vol. 6, pp. 39–63.

Taylor, L., and S. L. Black. 1974. "Practical General Equilibrium Estimation of Resource Pulls under Trade Liberalization." *Journal of International Economics*. Vol. 4, pp. 37–58.

United Nations. 1980. *Yearbook of International Trade Statistics*.

Viner, J. 1950. *The Customs Unions Issue*. New York: Carnegie Endowment For International Peace.

Whalley, J. 1986. *Trade Liberalization Among Major World Trading Areas*. Cambridge, MA: MIT Press.

13

Structural Change in Interregional Input–Output Models: Form and Regional Economic Development Implications

WILLIAM B. BEYERS

Although it has been a half-century since Leontief's publication of the first input–output model of the United States economy (Leontief, 1936), it has also been a third of a century since Leontief and Isard's pioneering statements on spatial and temporal dimensions of input–output models (Isard, 1951; Leontief, 1953). In this time, the input–output model has been widely adopted for use in regional settings. Interestingly, the spatial and temporal conceptualizations proposed by Leontief and Isard in the early 1950s have been less frequently measured. We have few subnational regions with input–output models for more than one time period, thereby allowing analyses of structural change. Interregional models are still rare, and analyses of structural change in interregional input–output systems are almost nonexistent. This chapter focuses on the latter of these long-neglected topics.

From a regional development perspective, changing interregional interdependence structures are manifested in changing levels of feedback relationships between regions, changing spatial patterns of income payments and receipts, and shifting geographies of final demand structures. There is talk today of an increasingly interdependent economy and this is frequently illustrated by data on the proportional growth of international trade as a fraction of gross national product (Clairmonte and Cavanagh, 1984). But, what about trade at the intranational level? How are regions, such as states, or the set of Bureau of Economic Analysis (BEA) urban-focused regions in the United States, changing in terms of their interdependence over time? As the economy exhibits a shift in output and employment toward a broad variety of services, including many sectors that are becoming deregulated or influenced by information-exchange technologies that encourage greater long-distance spatial interaction, how is the spatial structure of the economy changing?

Most regional input–output analysts have estimated data for a single region for a point in time. Richardson's recent extensive review of input–output multipliers illustrates this research focus (Richardson, 1985); references to interregional and intertemporal issues and models are almost absent from this review.

We argue that there is evidence that can be used to help construct macro-structural views (e.g., general structural properties) of interregional systems. Our argument is that these macrostructural views, when coupled with analyses of regional structural change, provide us with enough information to draw conclusions about likely characteristics of change in the structure of interregional input–output systems in advanced economies.

This chapter is organized as follows. The next section provides evidence on macrostructural characteristics of some survey-based state input–output models in the United States, followed by a brief review of empirical work on feedback relationships in interregional input–output models. Then some data are presented on structural change in regional input–output models, followed by a discussion of spatial structure, and interregional structural change. Some concluding comments are offered in the final section.

MACROSTRUCTURES AND FEEDBACK

Exchange relationships between producers and consumers classified in various sectors are the heart of the input–output model. The exchange relations between industrial sectors lead to multipliers defined in or through the use of the Leontief inverse matrix. In the regional version of this system of accounts, linkages to local components of the final payments system have also been found empirically to be an important basis for multiplier effects, through the regional disposition of these final payments as categories of regional final demand (Miernyk, 1966; Thomas, 1972; Beyers, 1974). In particular, linkages between the income generation process and local personal consumption expenditures, governmental outlays, and investment processes have been found to have propulsive impacts as strong as or stronger than those tied to the interindustry linkage system at the region level.

To illustrate these macrostructural relationships, Table 13-1 shows aggregated data calculated from the Washington, Georgia, and West Virginia regional survey-

TABLE 13-1   Input–Output Macrostructures for Selected States

	Direct Requirements		Direct, Indirect, and Induced Requirements	
	(1)	(2)	(3)	(4)
	Intermediate	PCE	Intermediate	PCE
Washington				
Intermediate	0.227	0.366	1.846	0.737
Value added	0.579	0.084	1.167	1.558
Imports	0.194			
Georgia				
Intermediate	0.274	0.310	1.835	0.666
Value added	0.498	0.147	1.071	1.560
Imports	0.228			
West Virginia				
Intermediate	0.200	0.309	1.451	0.519
Value added	0.310	0.138	0.522	1.346
Imports	0.491			

Sources: Bourque and Conway (1977), Schaffer et al. (1972), and Miernyk et al. (1970), respectively.

based input–output models. The direct intermediate requirements (column 1) shown in Table 13-1 represent the regional and import purchase components from the various sectors, and the value-added payments of these sectors. Personal consumption expenditures (PCE) are here expressed as a function of total value added (column 2). Using the Georgia data as an example, we find that intermediate purchases by all sectors in the Georgia economy from Georgia sectors are 0.274 per dollar of output, value-added payments are 0.498 per dollar of output, and imports amounted to 0.228 per dollar of output. Using the intrastate interindustry coefficients in Table 13-1 to calculate direct and indirect requirements coefficients, we obtain output multipliers of 1.294 for Washington, 1.379 for Georgia, and 1.25 for West Virginia. If value added and PCE are made endogenous, these output multipliers rise dramatically to 1.846, 1.835, and 1.451, respectively (column 3, Table 13-1), illustrating the relative significance of the induced effects linkage system in regional input–output models.

Although regional linkages to the income payments–income disposition sectors have been identified as a key source of "power" in the regional input–output model, we note that there are significant interregional linkages within these systems as well. Producers in a region make payments to shareholders located elsewhere, or profits "leak" from a plant in a region that is part of a corporate organization headquartered in another region or nation. Regional producers pay taxes to central governments located in other regions. Households purchase goods and services imported from other regions. In a typical region, the value of goods sold to local households (as measured in the PCE account) imported from other regions exceeds the value of regionally produced goods. Although most household service purchases are from local sellers, imported services, such as tourist, investment, or long-distance telephone, are significant. The typical state economy has various sectors exporting goods and services with a value much greater than the level of imports needed to sustain this level of exports, and this "trade surplus" tends to be offset by imports flowing to consumers, local governments, and used in the capital formation process. Table 13-2 shows data for the Washington, Georgia, and West Virginia economies illustrating this general structural characteristic of state economies, although we note that there is not a balance in the external trade account for any one of these states.

TABLE 13-2   State-Level Export–Import Relations[a]

Category	Washington	Georgia	West Virginia
Industrial exports	9246.9	14091.3	4347.0
Less			
Industrial imports	5037.7	8159.2	2903.0
Balance	4209.2	5932.1	1444.0
Less			
Imports to households	3384.4	3777.8	1039.4
Imports to investment	931.9	802.1	331.4
Imports to state and local government and federal when estimated	195.5	254.6	174.9
Net trade balance	(302.6)	1097.6	(101.7)

Sources: Bourque and Conway (1972); Schaffer et al. (1972), and Miernyk et al. (1970).
[a]Million dollars.

Although the local induced-effects linkage system has been found to have relatively strong multiplier power at the regional scale, analysts through survey research have also found that backward interindustry linkages from a given region to other regions are typically as strong as intraregional linkages. Table 13-3 presents data illustrating these linkage structures to the remainder of the United States (O.U.S. for Other U.S.), again for the Washington, Georgia, and West Virginia economies.

For Washington and Georgia, interregional interindustry purchases are about as large as regional purchases, whereas for West Virginia imported intermediate purchases substantially exceed local intermediate purchases. In each case, the author's estimates of intermediate inputs required from each state by the balance of the national economy are rather small proportionally, a reflection of the modest size of a given state economy in comparison to the size of the national economy. The direct and indirect inverse matrices for these states are shown in Table 13-3. Intrastate multipliers are slightly larger than those reported above (as a result of feedback effects—for example, Washington, 1.294 versus 1.298); however, O.U.S. output requirements (linked to state final demand and to O.U.S. final demand) can be seen to be much larger than direct requirements coefficients (for example, Georgia, 0.228 in Table 13-1 versus 0.669 in Table 13-3).

Some efforts have been devoted to the estimation of interregional models (Moses, 1955). However, little progress has been made in the United States in estimating these models through survey research because of the very high cost involved in the measurement of these structures. Other less costly modeling systems have been developed, most commonly of a multiregional, rather than interregional, nature (Bolton, 1980), just as most regional models have been developed through the use of some low-cost simulation procedure, rather than through field measurement. The notable efforts of Polenske and associates in developing a multiregional U.S. model based on the states should be acknowledged as having shed light on differences in regional interindustry and industrial structure (Polenske, 1980). However, this work does not lead to explicit estimates of interregional interdependence structures and

TABLE 13-3   Interregional Models

	Direct Requirements		Direct and Indirect Requirements	
	Washington	*O.U.S.*	*Washington*	*O.U.S.*
Washington	0.227	0.006	1.298	0.015
O.U.S.	0.194	0.502	0.505	2.012
	Georgia	*O.U.S.*	*Georgia*	*O.U.S.*
Georgia	0.274	0.009	1.386	0.024
O.U.S.	0.228	0.499	0.629	2.005
	West Virginia	*O.U.S.*	*West Virginia*	*O.U.S.*
West Virginia	0.200	0.004	1.256	0.009
O.U.S.	0.490	0.504	1.239	2.023

interregional flow information is largely based on Census of Transportation data, with service activity flows only roughly estimated.

A subtle distinction should be drawn at this point between multiregional and interregional input–output models. We are concerned with the latter, which explicitly identify flows between regions, in contrast to the former, which specify regional structure and (consistent) pooled estimates of import and export activity by sector (Bolton, 1980).

Feedback relations in interregional input–output models have been investigated by Miller in an extensive body of research. Miller has defined feedback as output occurring in a region because of the backward linkages that it has with other regions (Miller, 1966, 1969, 1985). Essentially, the notion advanced by Miller is similar to that of indirect effects within a region in the single-region input–output model. Miller and others have generally found intraregional feedback effects to be weak, a conclusion verified by data in Tables 13-1 and 13-3.

From another viewpoint, feedback in the interregional input–output model takes on greater significance. Consider again the data in Table 13-3. Although the intraregional consequences of interregional linkages may have small impacts on regional output, large impacts occur in interregional output (Beyers, 1983). Strong interregional direct requirements lead to strong interregional indirect requirements, which can be seen by comparing off-principal-diagonal elements in the direct and direct and indirect matrices in Table 13-3. These are feedback relations in the same sense of the term as used by Miller, but in the case of off-principal-diagonal elements the focus is on the interregional consequences of regional final demand. This openness of economic structure suggests that an interregional input–output model is needed if we want to measure geographically specific impacts of the interindustry linkage system found in a given regional economy.

REGIONAL STRUCTURAL CHANGE

The dearth of survey-based input–output models estimated for more than one time period in a given region limits our knowledge of regional dimensions of structural change in input–output models. The pioneering work at the national level of Leontief (Leontief, 1953) and Carter (1970) has not been matched widely at the regional scale. The data most often used for these analyses in the United States are the Washington State data, utilizing the three well-known, survey-based input–output tables developed for the years 1963, 1967, and 1972 (Bourque and Weeks, 1969; Beyers et al., 1970; Bourque and Conway, 1977). The general approach used in analyzing structural change in the Washington models has paralleled that of Carter and Leontief: evaluation of changes in interindustry requirements embodied in the Leontief inverses for different time periods.

The Washington input–output models produce results that mirror Carter's national scale analyses, with aggregate stability found in the proportion of output accounted for by intermediate demand, and a general tendency for aggregate multipliers to be sufficiently stable over time for Conway to conclude that

> this evaluation of the multipliers of the Washington State input–output model over time should cause regional analysts to reassess the need for updating models frequently, particularly when their primary use is for impact studies. (Conway, 1977, p. 213)

Conway found relatively more stability in the overall interindustry linkage system than in the induced effects system. Over the time period of the first three Washington models, he found that the share of income accruing to personal consumption expenditures fell, and that the share of personal consumption expenditures made on regionally produced output also declined.

Beyers also analyzed changes in regional interindustry structure, through a reformulation of the Washington input–output models into versions for the central Puget Sound region (about two-thirds of the employment in Washington state is located in the central Puget Sound area) for a somewhat different time span: 1958–1977. This was a period of very rapid growth for the Puget Sound region, potentially leading to major structural changes. However, we found very slight changes in the aggregate structure of industrial markets over this 20-year time period, and individual sectors aggregate purchase structure did not change significantly. The expansion of the public sector was the most evident structural change; it represented a growing market for local industry, and was a growing source of income. The larger fraction of income accruing to the public sector could be part of the reason for the decline in the regional strength of consumption functions noted by Conway. Household expenditures became slightly more externalized, whereas new investment was related to much larger levels of imported goods in 1977 than in 1958.

Structural change within the intermediate purchases system in these Puget Sound region models was also analyzed; the pattern of change was similar to that observed by Carter at the national scale. Many service sectors showed increases in demands for their output as a fraction of total purchases, whereas primary and materials purchasing sectors showed decreasing requirements. Our discussion of regional structural change has thus far focused on the changing linkage structure within the system of direct requirements coefficients. It is also important to note differences in relative growth rates of output in various sectors. The services were found to display generally a strong growth in their share of production, and services share of the regional export base (as measured in dollar value of sales to export customers) was also estimated to have expanded significantly over this time period, from 17.6 percent of total export sales in 1958 to 27.9 percent in 1977. Hence, services output grew because of expanded regional demands, and relative expansions in external demand.

From a structural perspective, this trend toward services increasing their share of output has impacts of the following nature. Services imports per dollar of output are much smaller than manufacturing, as indicated in Table 13-4. As the overall structure of output/exports shifts toward the services, leakages from the regional economy needed to support production would decline, ceteris paribus. Within the regional economy, if service sectors are purchasing somewhat more services from regional and

TABLE 13-4   Puget Sound Region Linkage Structures[a]

	Manufacturing	*Services*
Local purchases	15.5	18.6
Imports	39.6	6.6
Value added	44.9	74.8

[a]Cents worth of inputs per dollar of output.

other imported sources to produce their output, it may be that value added per dollar of services output would also tend to fall.

INTERREGIONAL STRUCTURAL CHANGE

Let us now turn to likely characteristics of interregional structural change. We have noted:

1. At the regional level, aggregate backward linkage strength appears to be fairly stable in the Washington state economy over time, but service inputs have grown to be more important. A new Washington input–output model for the year 1982 (Bourque, 1987) shows increased regional interdependence, at the expense of value-added payments (bringing the ratio of value added to output in Washington nearer to the national proportion), but more important was particularly strong growth in the proportional importance of foreign exports and imports.
2. External linkages of individual regions are strong and lead to larger *inter*regional multiplier effects than *intra*regional multiplier effects, per dollar of final demand.
3. Regional linkages are typically stronger to value added than to the interindustry linkage system, and these linkages lead to strong regional induced effects on output and on income.
4. Changes in regional structure appear to mirror national structural change, at least with respect to increased use of "general inputs."
5. The Puget Sound and Washington data suggest tendencies toward a more open system over time, within the consumption sector, and recently in the interindustry linkage system. Declining shares of earnings originating as wage and salary payments open opportunities for income to move interregionally—as dividends, royalties, or rents, or as transfer payments (Beyers, 1979).

Although data of the type shown in Tables 13-1, 13-2, and 13-3 indicate the openness of regional economies, there is relatively little survey data on the spatial structure of interregional trade. Beyers (1983) showed that this structure could be approximated by a gravity model. Recent survey work on markets of producer services firms in the Puget Sound region also leads to a similar view of spatial market structure (Beyers and Alvine, 1985). Comparable results were obtained by Sakai in analyses of Japanese input–output data (Sakai, 1972).

Let us now look at some survey data on changes in interregional linkage structures. These findings suggest that analyses of interregional structural change cannot be undertaken just with respect to the interindustry component of the interregional input–output model, but need to encompass final demand and final payments systems as well. Beyers has engaged in some survey research, which indicates general changes in the spatial structure of markets and sources of supply in these linkage systems. Figure 13-1 shows regions identified in a sample of manufacturers in Washington State as places in which they expected their markets to grow. Each dot in Figure 13-1 shows a state or region in which a firm in a survey of about 160 medium-sized Washington state manufacturers anticipated market expansion over a 5-year period, and it can be seen that growth in distant markets was a common expectation. The locations of expected market growth were distant from the locations of the current markets of firms in this sample (Beyers, 1983). Not shown in Figure 13-1 is the fact that very few firms anticipated contractions in the spatial pattern of their markets.

FIGURE 13-1 Expected change in sales, next 5 years.

Although the survey data on sales reported above indicate a general trend toward more spatially extensive sales patterns, survey data on purchases do not support the same spatial extension of interdependence structures, as shown in Table 13-5. About half of the firms surveyed anticipated no changes in sales relations, but three-fourths saw no changes in purchase relations. On the other hand, of those anticipating a change in sales or purchases locations, many more regions were identified as anticipated new sales locations than anticipated new purchases locations.

Can it be that interdependence structures are becoming spatially more extensive with these asymmetries in survey results? One possibility is that the survey data are flawed. Compositional explanations are also possible for these apparent contradictions. One compositional issue has to do with the stability of the population being sampled. Input–output models based on data gathered at different points in time are sampling a varying population of establishments. Expectations of changing market shares may not be realized if firms go out of business. Therefore, the dynamics of firm populations must be taken into account, and recent research by scholars, such as

TABLE 13-5   Survey Data on Sales and Purchases Locations[a]

	Sales Locations		Purchases Locations	
	No Change	*Change*	*No Change*	*Change*
Past 5 years	47	53	77	23
Next 5 years	46	54	76	24

[a]Percentage of responses.

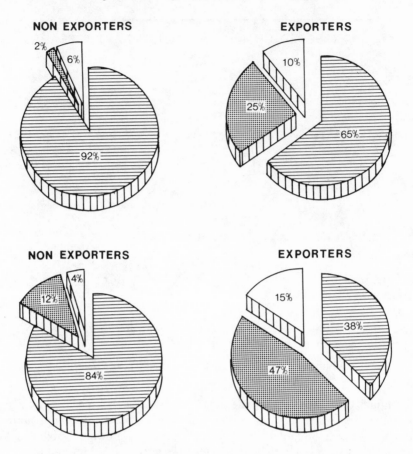

FIGURE 13-2   Original (top) and current (bottom) geographic strategy.

Birch (1984), has highlighted the fact that a sizable proportion of operating businesses ceases operations in this country each year—maybe on the order of 8–10 percent of establishments. These cessations are offset by about a 10–12 percent rate of formation of new enterprises in a given year, thus leading to a net gain of new enterprises of about 2 percent per annum.

This constant layering of new establishments into the economy may lead to differences in perceived and actual changes in spatial interaction patterns. One possibility is that there is a firm "spatial market life cycle," as suggested in Figure 13-2. This figure shows data on the changing market focus of a sample of Puget Sound region producer service firms; it is evident that their marketing effort shifted from dominantly a local market focus early in their company histories toward a more externalized marketing focus as they have aged (Beyers et al., 1986). Figure 13-3 shows results from the same survey, indicating that the youngest cohort of firms had the most externalized market focus. Hence, it may be that firms in the aggregate have a market orientation that is gradually becoming more spatially extensive, and that new entrants into the population of establishments have an initial external orientation that is also growing over time. Thus, the aggregate regional spatial linkage structure will

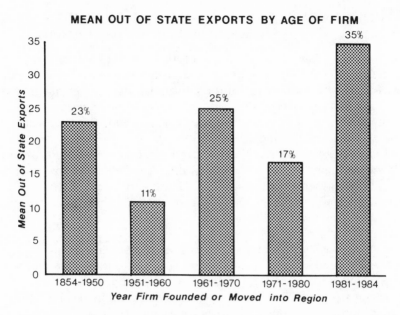

FIGURE 13-3   Mean out-of-state exports by age of firm.

change as a function of the mix of establishments with these different market orientations.

Mix changes in the relative size of sectors could also produce apparent changes in aggregate regional market orientation. If a set of sectors grew in relative importance at the same time as their import requirements grew, while another set of sectors had declining import requirements and a decreasing share of regional output, it is possible that aggregate regional interdependence would appear to remain stable.

Organizational structural change in business enterprises may also be leading to more complex spatial structures, where the transmission of interregional linkages is manifested in the final payments system in addition to the interindustry linkage system. The question of how organizational structures and changes in these structures are represented in the Leontief model is an issue for research (Jackson, 1987). Interregional payments of profits, or more generally gross returns from branch (office) operations and other interregional financial flows are largely undocumented. If wage and salary payments are still declining as a share of value added (Beyers, 1979), then the need is even greater to document the spatial structure of the nonwage component of the income stream.

With respect to changes in the spatial structure of final demand, we need to distinguish between the various categories. The Washington data seem to suggest more extensive spatial relations in personal consumption expenditure and investment outlays over time. The growth of the public sector—state, local, and federal—has certainly been a major structural phenomenon in this country since the Great Depression era. However, from an empirical standpoint, the representation and statistical documentation of interregional input–output relations in the public sector is insufficiently understood at this juncture to discuss spatial structural change in this linkage system.

CONCLUSIONS AND REGIONAL DEVELOPMENT IMPLICATIONS

In this chapter we have tried to bring together interregional and intertemporal characterizations of the input–output model at the subnational level, emphasizing characteristics of structural change at the subnational level in the United States. We argued that although direct evidence is not available on changes in interregional input–output structure, proximate evidence exists that allows us to speculate on the direction of change in time and space.

Indicators presented in this chapter suggest that intraregional interdependence systems are becoming weaker over time, although they have powerful linkages structures through the induced expenditures framework at any given point in time. The evidence seems to point to increasing spatial interdependence over time, on interindustry account, within the final payments system, and for categories of final demand.

From a regional economic development perspective, this apparent integration of interregional production (and ownership) structures means that dependence of given regions on markets in other given regions is being replaced by a more diverse spatial market structure. This spatial diversification means individual regions could be gaining more stable market bases, but the other side of such extensions/diversifications of market structures is that the integrated multiregional system is "in the same boat together" to a greater extent than may have been the case historically. This type of mutual interdependence relationship is also promoted by organizational changes taking place in modern economies, including growing levels of multiregional and international multiestablishment office and manufacturing organizations, and a panoply of governmental bodies at the international, national, and regional scale all promoting development, interaction, and loosening of barriers to interregional and international trade.

The phenomenal growth of the service economy in recent years presents measurement challenges for those interested in interregional input–output models. The linkage systems associated with these sectors are often "invisible," making their estimation difficult from secondary sources, such as transportation census data. Studying flows of people on airlines, of information exchanges made by (overnight) express mail systems or intraurban bicycle carriers, of word and data transmission between places on the ground or by satellites (or the heavenly bodies used as communication dishes) has now become a necessity if we are to document the interregional structures for these rapidly growing information service sectors. Flanked by an ever more efficient manufacturing sector, the new service economy may hasten the interregional integration process that has been an ongoing feature of manufacturing production systems through long-term decreases in transportation costs.

Although the evidence presented in this chapter seems to point in the direction of interregional structural change as outlined earlier, these arguments need to be seen as tentative, needing verification at various spatial levels. If intertemporal relationships in interregional input–output models are changing as we have suggested, then research on this topic should not languish. We need to develop better micro-level knowledge of interregional firm linkage change, and macro-level documentation of interregional input–output models for various years to be able to document spatial structural adjustments in industrial production systems, systems of final payments, and the structure of final demands.

ACKNOWLEDGMENTS

The financial support of the National Science Foundation, the Economic Development Administration, and the State of Washington for the measurements reported in this chapter are gratefully acknowledged. The opportunity to assist the Central Puget Sound Economic Development District in research on the services has also helped crystallize ideas presented in this chapter, an opportunity for which I am very grateful.

REFERENCES

Beyers, W. B. 1974. "On the Structure of Growth Center Linkage Systems." *Economic Geography.* Vol. 50, pp. 203–218.

Beyers, W. B. 1979. "Contemporary Trends in the Regional Economic Development of the United States." *Professional Geographer.* Vol. 31, pp. 34–44.

Beyers, W. B. 1983. "The Interregional Structure of the U.S. Economy." *International Regional Science Review.* Vol. 8, pp. 213–231.

Beyers, W. B., and M. J. Alvine. 1985. "Export Services in Postindustrial Society." *Papers of the Regional Science Association.* Vol. 57, pp. 33–45.

Beyers, W. B., P. J. Bourque, W. Seyfried, and E. Weeks. 1970. *Input–Output Tables for the Washington Economy, 1967.* Graduate School of Business Administration, University of Washington, Seattle, WA.

Beyers, W. B., J. M. Tofflemire, H. Stranahan, and E. Johnsen. 1986. *The Service Economy: Understanding Growth of the Producer Services in the Central Puget Sound Region.* Central Puget Sound Economic Development District, Seattle, WA.

Birch, D. 1984. "The Changing Rules of the Game: Finding a Niche in the Thoughtware Economy." *Economic Development Commentary.* National Council for Urban Economic Development. Vol. 8, pp. 12–16.

Bolton, R. 1980. "Multiregional Models: an Introduction to a Symposium." *Journal of Regional Science.* Vol. 20, pp. 131–142.

Bourque, P. J. 1987. *The Washington State Input–Output Study for 1982.* Graduate School of Business Administration, University of Washington.

Bourque, P. J., and R. S. Conway, Jr. 1977. *The 1972 Washington Input–Output Study.* Graduate School of Business Administration, University of Washington.

Bourque, P. J., and E. Weeks. 1969. *Detailed Input–Output Tables for Washington State, 1963.* Washington Agricultural Experiment Station Circular 508, Washington State University.

Carter, A. 1970. *Structural Change in the American Economy.* Cambridge MA: Harvard University Press.

Clairmonte, F. F., and J. H. Cavanagh. 1984. "Transnational Corporations and Services: The Final Frontier." *Trade and Development.* UNCTAD. No. 5, pp. 215–273.

Conway, R. S., Jr. 1977. "The Stability of Regional Input–Output Multipliers." *Environment and Planning A.* Vol. 9, pp. 197–214.

Isard, W. 1951. "Interregional and Regional Input–Output Analysis: A Model of a Space Economy." *Review of Economics and Statistics.* Vol. 33, pp. 318–328.

Jackson, Randall. 1987. "Conjoining Interindustry and Ownership Data: An Empirical Example." Paper presented at the Association of American Geographers meetings, Portland, OR (April).

Leontief, W. 1936. "Quantitative Input and Output Relations in the Economic System of the United States." *Review of Economics and Statistics.* Vol. 18, pp. 105–125.

Leontief, W. 1953. *Studies in the Structure of the American Economy.* New York: Oxford University Press.

Miernyk, W. 1966. *Elements of Input–Output Analysis.* New York: Random House.

Miernyk, W., et al. 1970. *Simulating Regional Economic Development.* Lexington, MA: Heath Lexington.

Miller, R. E. 1966. "Interregional Feedback Effects in Input–Output Models: Some Preliminary Results." *Papers of the Regional Science Association*. Vol. 17, pp. 105–125.

Miller, R. E. 1969. "Interregional Feedback Effects in Input–Output Models: Some Experimental Results." *Western Economic Journal*. Vol. 7, pp. 41–50.

Miller, R. E. 1985. "Upper Bounds on the Size of Interregional Feedbacks in Multiregional Input–Output Models." *Journal of Regional Science*. Vol. 26, pp. 285–306.

Moses, L. 1955. "The Stability of Interregional Trading Patterns and Input–Output Analysis." *American Economic Review*. Vol. 45, pp. 803–832.

Polenske, K. 1980. *The U.S. Multiregional Input–Output Accounts and Model*. Lexington MA: Lexington Books.

Richardson, H. W. 1985. "Input–Output and Economic Base Multipliers: Looking Backward and Forward." *Journal of Regional Science*. Vol. 25, pp. 607–661.

Sakai, H. 1972. "The Center-Periphery Dichotomy in the Japanese Economy: A Study in Distance and Spatial Interaction." Unpublished Ph.D. dissertation, Columbia University.

Schaffer, W., L. A. Laurent, and E. M. Sutter, Jr. 1972. *The Georgia Economic Model*. Atlanta: Georgia Department of Industry and Trade.

Thomas, M. D. 1972. "Growth Pole Theory: An Examination of Its Basic Concepts." In *Growth Centers in Regional Development*, edited by Niles M. Hansen. New York: Free Press.

14

Spatial Interaction and Input–Output Models: A Dynamic Stochastic Multiobjective Framework

PETER NIJKAMP and AURA REGGIANI

Input–output analysis has a long history in the field of regional economics. As a result of the pathfinding work of Leontief and Isard in the 1950s and 1960s, input–output analysis has become a major analytical tool for spatial interactions and allocations in the field of commodity flows, not only at a national (or international) but also at a regional (or interregional) scale. Extensions toward environmental and energy analysis in the 1970s are also noteworthy in the framework of spatial–sectoral allocation analysis.

The estimation of the entries of a matrix in allocation analysis, given (changes in) row and column totals, has received much attention in the past decades. The conventional transportation model in linear programming, the Koopmans–Beckmann quadratic assignment model, the RAS-updating method in input–output analysis, the entropy-based spatial interaction model, and the minimum information principle are all examples of assessment methods of matrix cells, when direct information on the values of these cells is lacking. These methods have often played an important role in input–output analysis (Batten and Boyce, 1986).

Various attempts have been made to provide a synthesis of such methods based on different methodologies. For example, it has been shown by Coelho and Wilson (1977), Erlander (1977), and Evans (1973) that a linear cost-minimizing model in spatial interaction analysis may be regarded as a special limit case of the entropy approach. In general, however, it is clear that the use of different assessment principles implies essentially the use of different (i.e., conflicting) objective functions. This case of multiple objective models in spatial interaction analysis has recently been introduced in an interesting article by Hallefjord and Jörnsten (1986).

The latter situation is also extremely important in an interregional input–output framework, as sometimes cost-minimizing principles (e.g., the Leontief–Strout model) are applied, whereas in other cases information-theoretic or gravity-based principles are used. Thus, the potential offered by multiple objective models deserves closer analysis.

In spite of the rigor and consistency achieved in input–output analysis, usually a basic flaw remains, that is, its essentially static character. Fully dynamic input–output models are still very rare. This is particularly surprising, because in the related field of spatial interaction analysis, various attempts have been made at designing dynamic models (Nijkamp and Reggiani, 1989). It is a well-known fact (Batten, 1983) that regional and interregional input–output analyses are particular types of spatial interaction analyses: both approaches deal with the assessment of the entries of a matrix, given its row and column totals. Therefore, it may be interesting to use recent achievements in the area of spatial interaction analysis as a "model" for exploring the possibilities of designing fully dynamic input–output models, as it is clear that dynamic spatial interaction models may be regarded as generalized input–output models. If the recorded marginal transactions are subject to a dynamic change pattern, results from a dynamic spatial interaction theory may be helpful. In particular, the use of optimal control principles may be relevant in this context. This would also provide a framework for endogenizing the technical structure, which is usually imposed as a fairly rigid framework in input–output analyses. In this sense, technological change or changes on the demand side, for instance, may also be dealt with, so that indirect implications for the spatial allocation of commodities can be more properly analyzed.

A third aspect of allocation and input–output analyses, which has up to now received far less attention, is the potential stochasticity of these models. Various elements in dynamic models cannot plausibly be regarded to be deterministic in nature, so that it is worth exploring the field of stochastic allocation models. This problem has in the past received some attention in input–output analysis (Gerking, 1976), in allocation problems based on the master equation analysis (De Palma and Lefèvre, 1984; Haag and Weidlich, 1986; Kanaroglou et al., 1986; Weidlich and Haag, 1983) and in random utility theory (De Palma and Lefèvre, 1983; Leonardi, 1985), but in the broader context of spatial interaction analyses, this issue has often been neglected.

In the light of the previous remarks, this chapter will focus on three issues in (spatial) allocation analysis: multiple objectives, dynamics, and stochasticity. An attempt will be made at providing a coherent framework for analyzing these three issues simultaneously. Therefore, the chapter is organized as follows. In the next section, the problem of multiple objectives in (spatial) allocation analysis is discussed, followed by a presentation of a simple dynamic model based on optimal control analysis and another section devoted to stochasticity, particularly in the framework of optimal control models. Then, a synthesis containing a new formal approach to multiple objective, dynamic, and stochastic models for allocation analysis is presented; the chapter concludes with a research outlook.

MULTIPLE OBJECTIVE SPATIAL INTERACTION ANALYSIS

In the present section, we will start with some standard results from conventional static spatial interaction analysis (Nijkamp and Reggiani, 1989). The usual spatial interaction model based on the minimum information principle (or maximum entropy principle) can be reformulated in the context of multiple objective programming analysis as follows:

$$\max_{\text{s.t.}} \omega = -\frac{1}{\beta}\sum_i \sum_j T_{ij}(\ln T_{ij} - 1) - \sum_i \sum_j c_{ij}T_{ij}$$

$$\sum_j T_{ij} = O_i \qquad \forall i$$

$$\sum_i T_{ij} = D_j \qquad \forall j \qquad (14\text{-}1)$$

where T_{ij} is the flow from i to j, c_{ij} its corresponding unit cost, O_i the origin total, and D_j the destination total. These flows may represent commodity flows in input–output analysis, transport flows in transportation analysis, migration flows in demoeconomic analysis, etc. The parameter β acts as a distance friction coefficient, as it can easily be demonstrated (Wilson et al., 1981) that the solution of (14-1) is equal to

$$T_{ij} = A_i B_j O_i D_j \exp(-\beta c_{ij})$$

with A_i and B_j balancing factors defined as

$$A_i = \exp(-\beta \lambda_i)/O_i \qquad (14\text{-}2)$$

and

$$B_j = \exp(-\beta \mu_j)/D_j \qquad (14\text{-}3)$$

where λ_i and μ_j are the Lagrange multipliers associated with O_i and D_j, respectively.

Model (14-1) may also be presented as a multiple objective model with two objective functions:

$$\max_{\text{s.t.}} \omega = -\alpha_1 \sum_i \sum_j T_{ij}(\ln T_{ij} - 1) - \alpha_2 \sum_i \sum_j c_{ij} T_{ij}$$

$$\sum_j T_{ij} = O_i$$

$$\sum_i T_{ij} = D_j$$

where the weight coefficients α_1 and α_2 satisfy the usual addition conditions:

$$\alpha_1 + \alpha_2 = 1$$

This is obviously a model with two conflicting objectives, that is, maximization of interactivity (measured by the entropy) and minimization of total interaction costs (Hallefjord and Jörnsten, 1986). Now, it is easily seen that instead of (14-2) and (14-3), we have the following solution for the balancing factors:

$$A_i = \exp(-\lambda_i/\alpha_1)/O_i$$

$$B_j = \exp(-\mu_j/\alpha_1)/D_j$$

$$\beta = \alpha_2/\alpha_1$$

It is clear that the above-mentioned model can easily be extended with alternative objective functions, although in that case it is generally impossible to derive elegant analytical solutions. However, by means of interactive numerical procedures, a final solution is in principle still possible (for further details, see Rietveld, 1980).

What is the meaning of the above-mentioned multiple objective model in the context of input–output analysis? The use of this model in an input–output framework would imply a compromise between the conventional Leontief–Strout gravity trade model and a cost-minimizing pooling model for input–output flows. The first component of (14-1) is in agreement with a gravity (or entropy) specification and hence consistent with an information-theoretic methodology. The second component emerges from a linear programming approach assuming cost minimization. Consequently, the use of this multiobjective approach in estimating (changes in) input–output coefficients is more flexible and general than conventional unidimensional estimation criteria.

DYNAMIC MULTIPLE OBJECTIVE SPATIAL INTERACTION ANALYSIS

The previous multiple objective programming analysis can be extended by including a dynamic systems equation describing the evolution of the spatial system concerned over time. It is evident that various ways for specifying a dynamic spatial interaction model geared to (14-1) can be chosen. In general, however, it is then extremely cumbersome to derive manageable analytical results. Let us consider here the following dynamic model:

$$\dot{O}_i = \gamma_i O_i + \delta_i \left(\sum_j T_{ji} - \sum_j T_{ij} \right) \tag{14-4}$$

where γ_i is the natural growth rate of place i, and δ_i is a parameter. It is assumed that O_i is a state variable whose dynamic evolution is linearly dependent on the net push-out and pull-in effects of origin i. It should be noted that model (14-4) is among others a member of the family of dynamic migration models proposed by Okabe (1979) and Sikdar and Karmeshu (1982), which can be specified as follows:

$$\dot{P}_i = \gamma_i P_i + \sum_j T_{ji} - \sum_j T_{ij} \tag{14-5}$$

where $P_i = P_i(t)$ is the population size of place i. In fact, if we assume that the total push-out effects from origin i are linearly dependent (through the parameter δ_i) on the population size in i, we obtain

$$O_i = \delta_i P_i \tag{14-6}$$

or

$$\dot{O}_i = \delta_i \dot{P}_i \tag{14-7}$$

In the context of the previous general dynamic model, we may again raise the question of the relevance of such a model in the framework of input–output analysis. As mentioned before, a basic flaw of many input–output models is the static nature of both the technical relationships and the column and row totals. In our present model, the assumption is essentially made that the column (or row) totals are not only determined by external forces, but also by internal dynamics of the cell entries. In other words, the change in these totals is inter alia a function of the cells estimated in a previous period. This change is then the result of attraction and repulsion effects (either between regions or between sectors). Clearly, a model of this nature leads to a highly dynamic input–output pattern, which may be further analyzed by means of dynamic programming or optimal control methods.

Next by substituting (14-6) and (14-7) into (14-5), we clearly obtain the dynamic Equation (14-4). The general idea of (14-4) is that the rate of change of marginal totals in a given place is influenced by its own state value and by the net push–pull effects exerted on that specific place. Then we may specify the following optimal control model (with T_{ij} as control variables) with two conflicting objective functions:

$$\max \omega_1 = \int_0^T - \sum_i \sum_j T_{ij}(\ln T_{ij} - 1)\, dt$$

$$\max_{\text{s.t.}} \omega_2 = \int_0^T - \sum_i \sum_j c_{ij} T_{ij}\, dt$$

$$\sum_j T_{ij} = O_i$$

$$\sum_i T_{ij} = D_j$$

$$\sum_i O_i = \sum_j D_j$$

$$\dot{O}_i = \gamma_i O_i + \delta_i \left(\sum_j T_{ji} - \sum_j T_{ij} \right) \qquad (14\text{-}8)$$

Obviously, the constraints in (14-8) are assumed to hold for each time period. It is also assumed that $\gamma_i < \delta_i$. It is a well-known fact that maximization of the first objective function will generate more dispersion among the cell values of an interaction matrix, whereas maximization of the second function will lead to an orientation toward a limited number of corner solutions (Nijkamp, 1977).

Multiple objective programming theory indicates that the solution of (14-8) has to be located on the efficiency frontier of the two objective functions. The set of efficient solutions can (in principle) be generated by a linear parameterization of these objective functions (Nijkamp, 1980), so that the following Hamiltonian H and Lagrangean function L can be obtained for a constrained optimal control model:

$$H = \varepsilon_1 \left[- \sum_i \sum_j T_{ij}(\ln T_{ij} - 1) \right] + \varepsilon_2 \left(- \sum_i \sum_j c_{ij} T_{ij} \right) + \sum_i \Psi_i \dot{O}_i \qquad (14\text{-}9)$$

where Ψ_i represents the costate variable (associated with O_i), and

$$L = H + \sum_i \lambda_i \left(O_i - \sum_j T_{ij} \right) + \sum_j \mu_j \left(D_j - \sum_i T_{ij} \right) + \rho \left(\sum_j D_j - \sum_i O_i \right)$$

The first-order conditions for a constrained maximum are

$$\frac{\partial L}{\partial T_{ij}} = 0$$

$$\frac{\partial L}{\partial O_i} = -\dot{\Psi}_i \qquad (14\text{-}10)$$

$$\frac{\partial H}{\partial \Psi_i} = \dot{O}_i$$

whereas the first-order optimality conditions related to the first set of conditions in (14-10) are

$$\frac{\partial L}{\partial T_{ij}} = -\varepsilon_1 \ln T_{ij} - \varepsilon_2 c_{ij} - \lambda_i - \mu_j - \delta_i \Psi_i + \delta_j \Psi_j = 0$$

so that we find

$$T_{ij} = \exp[(-\lambda_i - \mu_j - \delta_i\Psi_i + \delta_j\Psi_j - \varepsilon_2 c_{ij})/\varepsilon_1] \qquad (14\text{-}11)$$

Now it is straightforward to derive

$$T_{ij} = A_i G_i^{-1} O_i B_j G_j D_j \exp(-\beta c_{ij})$$

where

$$A_i = \exp(-\lambda_i/\varepsilon_1)/O_i$$
$$B_j = \exp(-\mu_j/\varepsilon_1)/D_j$$
$$G_i = \exp(\delta_i\Psi_i/\varepsilon_1)$$
$$G_j = \exp(\delta_j\Psi_j/\varepsilon_1)$$
$$\beta = \varepsilon_2/\varepsilon_1 \qquad (14\text{-}12)$$

By redefining

$$\bar{A}_i = A_i G_i^{-1}$$
$$\bar{B}_j = B_j G_j \qquad (14\text{-}13)$$

we can derive the following elegant standard solution:

$$T_{ij} = \bar{A}_i \bar{B}_j O_i D_j \exp(-\beta c_{ij}) \qquad (14\text{-}14)$$

which is equivalent to the following logit form:

$$p_{ij} = \frac{T_{ij}}{O_i} = \frac{\bar{B}_j D_j \exp(-\beta c_{ij})}{\sum_j \bar{B}_j D_j \exp(-\beta c_{ij})} \qquad (14\text{-}15)$$

with p_{ij} representing the probability of a move from i to j. Solution (14-14) of our optimal control problem is unique, as we are dealing with a concave integrand.

The parameter β functions also as a weight factor according to (14-12): if, for instance, $\beta \to 0$, then $\varepsilon_2 \to 0$ so that in case of a negligible distance friction the contribution of the corresponding cost function also vanishes, and vice versa. It should be noted that if we consider the optimal control problem (14-8) without the standard constraints on origin and destination (i.e., exclusively a model with the dynamic equation for O_i), we will obtain an unconstrained spatial interaction model of the following type:

$$T_{ij} = G_i^{-1} G_j \exp(-\beta c_{ij})$$

where G_i and G_j may be interpreted as potential attractors of i and j, respectively.

The previous optimal control approach (14-8) can again be extended by introducing general dynamic objective functions, but then less tractable analytical results will emerge (Nijkamp and Reggiani, 1988).

STOCHASTIC DYNAMIC MULTIPLE-OBJECTIVE SPATIAL INTERACTION ANALYSIS

In the present section, an attempt will be made at introducing stochasticity into the model just described. First, following Arnold (1974) and Arnold and Lefever (1981), we define a "stochastic process" as a "differential equation for random functions," so that dynamics is implicitly embodied in the concept of stochasticity. In particular, we assume that the originally deterministic model (14-4) has a random component of the so-called "white noise" type, representing the statistical uncertainty on the marginal totals of our dynamic spatial interaction model (caused, for example, by stochastic external growth processes).

It is well known (Arnold, 1974) that this "white noise" is a "very useful mathematical idealization for describing random influences that fluctuate rapidly and hence are virtually uncorrelated for different instants of time." In this context, instead of our dynamic Equation (14-4), we assume a stochastic differential equation that obeys a continuous Wiener or Brownian motion process (related to the "white noise"), which can be represented as follows (Kamien and Schwartz, 1981; Kushner, 1971; Malliaris and Brock, 1982):

$$dO_i = \left[\gamma_i O_i + \delta_i \left(\sum_j T_{ji} - \sum_j T_{ij} \right) \right] dt + O_i \sigma_i \, dz_i$$

$$= g_i \, dt + O_i \sigma_i \, dz_i \qquad (14\text{-}16)$$

where dz_i is the incremental change in a stochastic process z that satisfies a Wiener process. It is clear that (14-16) is a time-dependent process, which should essentially be written as

$$dO_i(t) = g_i(t) \, dt + O_i(t) \sigma_i(t) \, dz \qquad (14\text{-}17)$$

The formal expression (14-17) is called Itô's stochastic differential equation [with initial condition $O_i(0) = O_i^*$], where σ_i is the diffusion component of the stochastic process. Clearly, in a deterministic context, $\sigma_i = 0$.

The latter specification indicates that the expected rate of change ("drift") is in fact represented by $g_i(t)$, but in this case there is also a stochastic disturbance term, which we have assumed to be proportional to the origin size O_i. It should be noted that—although Wiener processes modeling stochasticity have been used before in economics, physics, and biology—the addition of a stochastic term to the differential equations describing the dynamics of a spatial model has been proposed so far only by Sikdar and Karmeshu (1982) for a nonlinear gravity migration model and by Vorst (1985) for an urban retail model. It is a well-known result that, for a Wiener process z and for any partition t_0, t_1, t_2 of the time interval, the random variables $z(t_1) - z(t_0)$, $z(t_2) - z(t_1)$, $z(t_3) - z(t_2), \ldots$ (i.e., the incremental changes) are independently and normally distributed with mean zero and variances $t_1 - t_0$, $t_2 - t_1$, $t_3 - t_2, \ldots$, respectively.

As far as this approach in the framework of input–output analysis is concerned, it is worth noting that the source and nature of stochasticity in input–output models are fraught with uncertainties. The specification of a conventional probability distribution for uncertain elements is then a less meaningful approach. By using a general Wiener process, we are able to incorporate random changes in both the average pattern of column or raw totals and in their dispersion.

Next, it can be shown (see Appendix 14-A) that without further constraints the solution of (14-16) is equal to

$$O_i = G(t, z) = O_i^* \exp \left\{ (-\delta_i - \sigma_i^2/2)t + \sigma_i z_i + \left[\gamma_i + (\delta_i/O_i) \sum_j T_{ji} \right] t \right\} \qquad (14\text{-}18)$$

so that (14-18) is the optimal trajectory of the state variable O_i.

Assuming again two objective functions (that is, an entropy function and a cost function), we may specify the following parametrized optimal control model, in which the mathematical expectation E of the weighted objective functions has to be maximized:

$$\omega = \max_{\text{s.t.}} E \int_0^T -\left[\varepsilon_1 \left\{ \sum_i \sum_j T_{ij}(\ln T_{ij} - 1) \right\} + \varepsilon_2 \sum_i \sum_j c_{ij} T_{ij} \right] dt$$

$$\sum_j T_{ij} = O_i$$

$$\sum_i T_{ij} = D_j \qquad\qquad (14\text{-}19)$$

$$\sum_i O_i = \sum_j D_j$$

$$dO_i = \left[\gamma_i O_i + \delta_i \left(\sum_j T_{ji} - \sum_j T_{ij} \right) \right] dt + O_i \sigma_i \, dz_i = g_i \, dt + O_i \sigma_i \, dz_i$$

We will now analyze the latter model by first regarding the constraints on the control variables T_{ij}. Following Malliaris and Brock (1982), we may write the Hamilton–Jacobi–Bellman equation associated with (14-19) as

$$-\frac{\partial \omega}{\partial t} = \max_{T_{ij}} \left(-\left\{ \varepsilon_1 \left[\sum_i \sum_j T_{ij}(\ln T_{ij} - 1) \right] + \varepsilon_2 \sum_i \sum_j c_{ij} T_{ij} \right\} + \sum_i \frac{\partial \omega}{\partial O_i} g_i + 1/2 \sum_i \frac{\partial^2 \omega}{\partial O_i^2} \left(\sum_j T_{ij} \right)^2 \sigma_i^2 \right)$$

$$(14\text{-}20)$$

where the assumption is made that O_i is uncorrelated with O_j. Equation (14-20) can now also be written as

$$-\frac{\partial \omega}{\partial t} = \max_{T_{ij}} H^*$$

where H^* is the functional form of the expression in brackets at the right-hand side of (14-20).

Next, if we define the costate variable $\Psi_i^*(t)$ as follows:

$$\Psi_i^*(t) = \frac{\partial \omega}{\partial O_i}$$

we may write H^* as

$$H^* = -\left\{ \varepsilon_1 \left[\sum_i \sum_j T_{ij}(\ln T_{ij} - 1) \right] + \varepsilon_2 \sum_i \sum_j c_{ij} T_{ij} \right\} + \sum_i \Psi_i^* g_i + 1/2 \sum_i \frac{\partial \Psi_i^*}{\partial O_i} \sigma_i^2 \left(\sum_j T_{ij} \right)^2$$

$$(14\text{-}21)$$

Then by comparing (14-21) with (14-9), we can derive

$$H^* = H + 1/2 \sum_i \frac{\partial \Psi_i^*}{\partial O_i} \sigma_i^2 \left(\sum_j T_{ij} \right)^2 \qquad (14\text{-}22)$$

where the last term at the right-hand side of (14-22) thus represents the stochastic part of the dynamic process concerned.

Now, we will introduce the constraints on the control variables. Then, it is straightforward (Chow, 1979) to define the following Lagrangean expression, L^*:

$$L^* = H^* + \sum_i \lambda_i \left(O_i - \sum_j T_{ij} \right) + \sum_j \mu_j \left(D_j - \sum_i T_{ij} \right) + \rho \left(\sum_j D_j - \sum_i O_i \right) \quad (14\text{-}23)$$

In the latter case, we may apply the Pontryagin Stochastic Maximum Principle (Malliaris and Brock, 1982). This principle states that for an optimal control variable T_{ij}^* that maximizes the Lagrangean (14-23), the following conditions hold: (1) the costate function Ψ_i^* satisfies the following stochastic differential equation:

$$d\Psi_i^* = -\frac{\partial L^*}{\partial O_i} dt + \sum_i \frac{\partial \Psi_i^*}{\partial O_i} O_i \sigma_i \, dz_i \quad (14\text{-}24)$$

(2) the following transversality condition holds:

$$\Psi_i^*[O_i(T), T] = \frac{\partial \omega}{\partial O_i} [O_i(T), T] \geq 0$$

$$\Psi_i^*(T) O_i(T) = 0 \quad (14\text{-}25)$$

Furthermore, it is easily seen that the optimal solution T_{ij}^* is equal to

$$T_{ij}^* = \exp\left[\left(-\lambda_i - \mu_j - \delta_i \Psi_i^* + \delta_j \Psi_j^* - \varepsilon_2 c_{ij} + O_i \sigma_i^2 \frac{\partial \Psi_i^*}{\partial O_i} \right) \Big/ \varepsilon_1 \right]$$

This expression leads to the interesting result that—apart from the last stochastic term—the same formal outcome is obtained as in (14-11), so that the final solution is

$$T_{ij}^* = A_i^* O_i Z_i B_j^* D_j \exp(-\beta c_{ij}) \quad (14\text{-}26)$$

where A_i^* and B_j^* have formal definitions similar to that in (14-13):

$$A_i^* = A_i \exp(\delta_i \Psi_i^*/\varepsilon_1)^{-1}$$

$$B_j^* = B_j \exp(\delta_j \Psi_j^*/\varepsilon_1)$$

and where Z_i is equal to

$$Z_i = \exp\left(O_i \sigma_i^2 \frac{\partial \Psi_i^*}{\partial O_i} \Big/ \varepsilon_1 \right)$$

It should be noted that here A_i^* and B_j^* are stochastic terms as they incorporate the costate variable Ψ_i^* satisfying (14-24) and (14-25). Obviously, Ψ_i^* does not have an explicit solution owing to the difficulties involved in the calculations of (14-20) and (14-24). It should also be added that the term Z_i is stochastic because it incorporates the diffusion component σ_i^2 of the stochastic Wiener process z_i.

It is also interesting to see that the stochastic solution (14-26) can formally be transformed into a logit form as follows:

$$p_{ij}^* = \frac{T_{ij}^*}{O_i} = Z_i \frac{B_j^* D_j \exp(-\beta c_{ij})}{\sum_j B_j^* D_j \exp(-\beta c_{ij})} \quad (14\text{-}27)$$

which is in agreement with standard results from conventional spatial interaction analysis. In fact, if $\sigma_i = 0$, Equation (14-27) yields as a special case the logit form (14-

15) obtained from the deterministic approach. Consequently, introduction of a stochastic white noise process in interaction and input–output analysis is in principle possible and does not affect the basic structure of a gravity type of solution.

CONCLUSION

The main result emerging from the previous analysis is that stochastic fluctuations tend to destabilize a spatial interaction system. This result is fully in agreement with a recent stochastic analysis of a spatial interaction problem, proposed by Sikdar and Karmeshu (1982), where, however, the stochastic process is solved by a so-called Stratonovic prescription. In particular, the introduction of random perturbations of the "white noise" type in the rate of change of the exits O_i sheds new light on stochastic process models analyzed so far (for interesting reviews, see Pickles, 1980; Kanaroglou et al., 1986). If we consider the dynamic probability p_{ij}^* as a transition probability from a state i to a state j, as given by Equation (14-27) it can be decomposed (Cordey-Hayes and Gleave, 1974; Tomlin, 1979) into an "escape frequency" (determined by the term Z_i) and a "capture probability" (determined by the stochastic logit form). In our context, the "escape frequency" is a function depending on the variance σ_i^2 which, according to Cordey-Hayes and Gleave's hypothesis, might be caused by generic factors such as age distribution of population and variation of income with time (or, in the case of input–output analyses, by sectoral developments); the "capture probability" incorporates implicitly the stochasticity with the term B_j^*.

From a theoretical viewpoint, the above concept might have some resemblance to fluctuations in biological models. Here, it is well-known (Maynard Smith, 1974) that the effect of the environmental (external) fluctuations is to change the level prevailing in a deterministic framework (for example, the case of very strong fluctuations causing the extinction of a population).

Another important result emerging from our analysis is that the solution is formally compatible with a logit expression in both a deterministic and a stochastic approach. On the one hand, this confirms also the descriptive and explanatory power of logit models (and hence implicitly also of macro approaches related to the maximization of entropy) in a dynamic context (Nijkamp and Reggiani, 1989). On the other hand, this may offer particularly appealing perspectives in the field of empirical applications. In this context, it is interesting to recall the contribution by Haag (1986), who introduces stochasticity through a master equation approach and ends with the same structure of the stationary flow distribution as static random utility theory.

Finally, in the framework of multiple objective analysis, Equation (14-27) shows which are the efficient (stochastic) solutions, emerging from two conflicting objectives varying over time and subject to a stochastic evolution of the state variables. Although multiobjective analysis has been used in dynamics before (see, for instance, Nijkamp, 1977, 1979, 1980), its use in a stochastic context is still limited (Ermoliev and Leonardi, 1981); the analysis presented in the previous section tries to make a new theoretical effort in the field of spatial interaction and input–output analysis.

The merger of the above-mentioned classes of input–output models and spatial interaction models appears to lead to new theoretical insights regarding the stability of spatial–economic systems. At the more practical level of empirical input–output analysis, it is worth mentioning that the use of a more general multiobjective method for estimating (changes in) cells consequent upon changes in column or row totals may lead to a higher flexibility and a plausible range of estimates (instead of single point estimates). This is also extremely important to test the long-term stability of results of input–output models, as was shown in our optimal control approach. And finally, the use of white noise random processes allows the researcher to include stochastic processes in a more flexible way than is being done in conventional probabilistic approaches.

In conclusion, we may stress the importance of stochasticity in the evolution of a spatial interaction system by showing, through Equation (14-27), how the fluctuations may influence the standard results, in both a theoretical and empirical respect. In this context, input–output models can be represented in a generalized structural form incorporating stochastic dynamics.

APPENDIX 14-A. PROOF OF THE SOLUTION OF A WIENER PROCESS FOR A DYNAMIC SPATIAL INTERACTION MODEL

By starting with (14-18) and using Itô's theorem, we have

$$dF(z, t) = F_t \, dt + F_z \, dz + 1/2 F_{zz}(dz)^2 \qquad (14A\text{-}1)$$

and

$$\begin{array}{c|cc} & dz & dt \\ \hline dz & dt & 0 \\ dt & 0 & 0 \end{array} \qquad (14A\text{-}2)$$

so that

$$F_t = (-\delta_i - \sigma_i^2/2 + \gamma_i)O_i + \delta_i \sum_j T_{ji} \qquad (14A\text{-}3)$$

$$F_{z_i} = O_i \sigma_i \qquad (14A\text{-}4)$$

$$F_{z_i z_i} = O_i \sigma_i^2 \qquad (14A\text{-}5)$$

By substituting (14A-2), (14A-3), (14A-4), and (14A-5) into (14A-1), we can easily check that (14-16) is consistent with the original Wiener process:

$$\begin{aligned} dO_i &= \left[-O_i \delta_i - (\sigma_i^2/2)O_i + (\sigma_i^2/2)O_i + \gamma_i O_i + \delta_i \sum_j T_{ji} \right] dt + O_i \sigma_i \, dz_i \\ &= \left[\gamma_i O_i + \delta_i \left(\sum_j T_{ji} - O_i \right) \right] dt + O_i \sigma_i \, dz_i \\ &= \left[\gamma_i O_i + \delta_i \left(\sum_j T_{ji} - \sum_j T_{ij} \right) \right] dt + O_i \sigma_i \, dz_i \end{aligned}$$

QED.

ACKNOWLEDGMENT

A. R. gratefully acknowledges the C.N.R. grant, number 88.0306310, which supported her part of this research project.

REFERENCES

Arnold, L. 1974. *Stochastic Differential Equations: Theory and Applications.* New York: John Wiley.

Arnold, L., and R. Lefever. 1981. *Stochastic Nonlinear Systems in Physics, Chemistry and Biology.* Berlin: Springer-Verlag.

Batten, D. F. 1983. *Spatial Analysis of Interacting Economies.* Dordrecht, The Netherlands: Martinus Nijhoff.

Batten, D. F., and D. E. Boyce. 1986. "Spatial Interaction, Transportation, and Interregional Commodity Flow Models." In *Handbook in Regional Economics*, edited by P. Nijkamp. Amsterdam: North-Holland, pp. 357–406.

Chow, G. C. 1979. "Optimum Control of Stochastic Differential Equation Systems." *Journal of Economic Dynamics and Control.* Vol. 1, pp. 143–175.

Coelho, J. D., and A. G. Wilson. 1977. "Some Equivalence Theorems to Integrate Entropy Maximizing Sub-models within overall Mathematical Programming Frameworks." *Geographical Analysis.* Vol. 9, pp. 160–173.

Cordey-Hayes, H., and D. Gleave. 1974. "Migration Movements and the Differential Growth of City Regions in England and Wales." *Papers of the Regional Science Association.* Vol. 33, pp. 99–123.

De Palma, A., and C. Lefèvre. 1983. "Individual Decision-Making in Dynamic Collective Systems." *Journal of Mathematical Sociology.* Vol. 90, pp. 103–124.

De Palma, A., and C. Lefèvre. 1984. "The Theory of Deterministic and Stochastic Compartmental Models and Its Applications: The State of Art." *Sistemi Urbani.* No. 3, pp. 281–323.

Erlander, S. 1977. "Entropy in Linear Programming—An Approach to Planning." Linkoping Institute of Technology, Report LITH-Mat-R-77-3, Linkoping, Sweden.

Ermoliev, Y., and G. Leonardi. 1981. "Some Proposals for Stochastic Facility Location Models." *Sistemi Urbani.* No. 3, pp. 455–470.

Evans, S. 1973. "A Relationship between the Gravity Model for Trip Distribution and the Transportation Problem in Linear Programming." *Transportation Research.* Vol. 7, pp. 39–61.

Gerking, S. 1976. *Estimation of Stochastic Input–Output Models.* Dordrecht/Boston: Martinus Nijhoff.

Haag, G. 1986. "A Stochastic Theory for Residential and Labour Mobility Including Travel Networks." In *Technological Change, Employment, and Spatial Dynamics*, edited by P. Nijkamp. Berlin: Springer-Verlag, pp. 340–357.

Haag, G., and W. Weidlich. 1986. "A Dynamic Migration Theory and Its Evaluation for Concrete Systems." *Regional Science and Urban Economics.* Vol. 16, pp. 57–80.

Hallefjord, A., and K. Jörnsten. 1986. "Gravity Models with Multiple Objectives: Theory and Applications." *Transportation Research B.* Vol. 20B, pp. 19–39.

Kamien, M. I., and N. L. Schwartz. 1981. *Dynamic Optimization: The Calculus of Variations and Optimal Control in Economics and Management.* Amsterdam: North-Holland.

Kanaroglou, P., K. L. Liaw, and Y. Y. Papageorgiou. 1986. "An Analysis of Migratory Systems: 1. Theory." *Environment and Planning A.* Vol. 18, pp. 913–928.

Kushner, H. 1971. *Introduction to Stochastic Control.* New York: Holt, Rinehart & Winston.

Leonardi, G. 1985. "A Stochastic Multi-Stage Mobility Choice Model." In *Optimization and Discrete Choice in Urban Systems*, edited by G. Hutchinson, P. Nijkamp, and M. Batty. Berlin: Springer-Verlag, pp. 132–147.

Malliaris, A. G., and W. A. Brock. 1982. *Stochastic Methods in Economics and Finance.* Amsterdam: North-Holland.

Maynard Smith, J. 1974. *Models in Ecology.* London: Cambridge University Press.

Nijkamp, P. 1977. *Theory and Application of Environmental Economics.* Amsterdam: North-Holland.

Nijkamp, P. 1979. "A Theory of Displaced Ideals: An Analysis of Interdependent Decisions via Nonlinear Multiobjective Optimization." *Environment and Planning A*. Vol. 11, pp. 1165–1178.

Nijkamp, P. 1980. *Environmental Policy Analysis: Operational Methods and Models*. Chichester, New York: John Wiley.

Nijkamp, P., and A. Reggiani. 1988. "Analysis of Dynamic Spatial Interaction Models by Means of Optimal Control." *Geographical Analysis*. Vol. 20, pp. 18–30.

Nijkamp, P., and A. Reggiani. 1989. "Spatial Interaction and Discrete Choice: Statics and Dynamics." In *Contemporary Development in Quantitative Geography*, edited by J. Hauer, H. Timmermans, and N. Wrigley. Dordrecht, The Netherlands: Reidel.

Okabe, A. 1979. "Population Dynamics of Cities in a Region: Conditions for a State of Simultaneous Growth." *Environment and Planning A*. Vol. 11, pp. 609–628.

Pickles, A. 1980. "Models of Movement: A Review of Alternative Methods." *Environment and Planning A*. Vol. 12, pp. 1383–1404.

Rietveld, P. 1980. *Multiple Decision Methods and Regional Planning*. Amsterdam: North-Holland.

Sikdar, P. K., and S. Karmeshu. 1982. "On Population Growth of Cities in a Region: A Stochastic Nonlinear Model." *Environment and Planning A*. Vol. 14, pp. 585–590.

Tomlin, S. G. 1979. "A Kinetic Theory of Urban Dynamics." *Environment and Planning A*. Vol. 11, pp. 97–105.

Vorst, A. C. F. 1985. "A Stochastic Version of the Urban Retail Model." *Environment and Planning A*. Vol. 17, pp. 1569–1580.

Weidlich, W., and G. Haag. 1983. *Concepts and Models of a Quantitative Sociology: The Dynamics of Interacting Populations*. Berlin: Springer-Verlag.

Wilson, A. G., J. D. Coelho, S. M. Macgill, and H. C. W. L. Williams. 1981. *Optimization in Locational and Transport Analysis*. New York: John Wiley.

V

MEASUREMENT ERROR
AND DATA SCARCITY

15

Perspectives on Probabilistic Input–Output Analysis

RANDALL W. JACKSON and GUY R. WEST

Throughout its first half-century, the input–output model has led, in one respect, a charmed existence. Unlike any other economic model, its statistical properties have received only token attention, whereas the more practical applications and theoretical extensions have received great emphasis. It is curious that analysts have not focused on the statistical character of such a widely used economic modeling framework. One possible explanation lies in Leontief's own early aversion toward the pursuit of such knowledge:

> One might as well be resigned to the fact that the economic system can be adequately described and its operation satisfactorily explained only in terms of a conceptual scheme involving a very large and *statistically irreducible* number of operationally distinct but mutually dependent variables. (Leontief, 1955, pp. 12–13, italics ours)

There are, however, scattered through the massive input–output literature, attempts to capture the stochastic nature of the input–output modeling framework. These contributions have been so widely dispersed that a clear view of stochastic input–output modeling has not emerged, which brings us to the twofold purpose of this chapter. First, the analysis of probabilistic error structure in input–output models is reviewed in its historical context. In so doing, the state of the art becomes clear, so that the second purpose of identifying the missing links and potentially fruitful research directions may be served.

We have attempted a thorough review of the literature, but have no doubt overlooked and omitted important contributions. In many respects, the entire literature on coefficient change, reconciliation procedures, regionalization of data bases, and aggregation issues is of relevance, and could therefore rationally be included. It is, of course, well beyond the scope of this chapter to chronicle the entire evolution of input–output research.

Much detail has been put aside in return for greater coverage. We have attempted to provide nonmathematical interpretations; those interested in more specific mathematical detail are encouraged to consult the original sources. In studies in which the effects of error structures formed the focus, we have attempted to extract from each a common set of critical information, including

1. The nature of the approach: Is the analysis primarily theoretical/analytical or simulation based?
2. The nature of the research question: Where is the emphasis?
   a. On direct or on indirect coefficients?
   b. On output distributions?
   c. On multipliers?
3. The kind of error structure considered:
   a. Additive (absolute) or multiplicative (percentage)?
   b. Symmetric or asymmetric distributions?
4. Significant conclusions and contributions.

The rest of this chapter is presented in two major sections. The first presents a chronological review of the contributions to stochastic input–output analysis, and the second section discusses some potentially fruitful current and future research directions.

REVIEW

Although in the late 1940s and early 1950s we saw a variety of studies aimed at the properties of "an inverse," Sherman and Morrison's (1950) solution for the adjustment of an inverse matrix given a change in one element of a matrix may well have been the harbinger. Given a limited number of known changes in the original matrix, the method could be applied *ad seriatum* to arrive at a new inverse without ever having to invert the new table. This was, for its time, a significant development, because most calculations were obtained by hand. This method was later to serve not only as a method of analysis, but also as an heuristic device in the conceptual development of stochastic input–output.

Perhaps the most direct early contribution to input–output error analysis can be found in the analytical/theoretical work of Evans (1954), who began by questioning the contribution of matrix errors to errors in the column vector of activity level estimates. He was primarily concerned with cumulative versus noncumulative errors in the interindustry framework, and he was among the first to show that the error in using a structural matrix for time t in conjunction with a forecasted final demand vector depends on the degree to which the forecasted vector differs from a scalar multiple of the initial final demand vector. Simulation experiments were used to analyze stochastic error, based on symmetric, multiplicative error structure. In his evaluation, errors in structural matrices are not only noncumulative, but compensating in effect.

In similar early work, Christ (1955) applied small absolute errors to the direct coefficients, based on the mathematical formulation of Dwyer and Waugh (1953). Christ believed that errors were compensating and that the "errors in the inverse . . . are probably not as much as an order of magnitude larger than their parent errors in the input–output matrix" (Christ, 1955, pp. 157–158).

Quandt (1958, 1959) provided the next major contributions. His 1958 paper was a comprehensive, analytical/theoretical treatment, explicitly stating that the errors in coefficients will have stochastic properties. He rejected the notion of "true" coefficients because "they would exhibit variations even if they were obtained by taking exhaustive samples every time" (Quandt, 1958, p. 156). Quandt's research questions presage those of a host of scholars to follow and merit enumeration:

1. Can analysts theoretically attach confidence limits to the solution?
2. Is it possible to calculate the moments of the distribution of the solution?
3. How are the moments of the distribution of the input coefficients related to the moments of the distributions of the elements of the inverse or of the solution?
4. What, if anything, can be said about the distribution of the input coefficients?
5. What is the meaning of the solution of a probabilistic Leontief system?

Quandt assumed symmetrical, additive, independent errors structures with zero means, and he performed a simulation of a hypothetical, two-sector region. Among his significant contributions is the analytical derivation of confidence intervals around gross output solutions for a two-sector model.

Quandt's 1959 paper was a largely nontheoretical work, based on the assumption of additive error structure for a three-sector model. His conclusions were that errors in gross output tended to be skewed, and that the lognormal distribution provides an adequate description of the solution, irrespective of the distribution of the original (symmetrical) errors.

As perhaps the sole direct contributor of the 1960s, Theil (1966) analyzed the relationship of coefficient errors to errors in output vectors. In his formulation, the observed matrix is equal to the "true" matrix plus a matrix of error terms. He expressed additive errors in the original matrix as additive errors in the Leontief inverse. Park (1973) carried this type of analysis further in considering errors in Type I and Type II output multipliers from additive errors in the augmented input coefficient matrix. Each concluded that errors in the output vectors and multipliers are linear combinations of errors in the various components of the original model.

A second major attempt of the early 1970s to extend probabilistic analysis to input–output multipliers was by McCamley et al. (1973). Using Rao's (1952) variance approximation method, they derived a formula for the variance of sectoral income multipliers. By assuming row coefficient independence, they obtained an analytical approximation based on the distribution of total outputs, the values of the Leontief inverse, and the covariance among elements in the same column of the direct coefficients table. Error distributions were not analyzed, but the approach was demonstrated empirically.

The prime motivation for studies of the probabilistic attributes of input–output models has clearly been the question of accuracy. A collective contribution in these terms is found in the regional modeling perspective of Morrison and Smith (1974), McMenamin and Haring (1974), and Malizia and Bond (1974). Following the lead of Czamanski and Malizia (1969) and Schaffer and Chu (1969), Round (1978) assessed the accuracy of nonsurvey techniques vis-à-vis survey-based models. For the first time, attention was focused on measures of the distance between two interindustry matrices (for a recent contribution, see Knudsen and Fotheringham 1986). Although McMenamin and Haring (1974) studied the accuracy of technical coefficients, total final demand, value added, total intermediate input and output, imports and exports, and multiplier estimates, they did not focus directly on the accuracy of the total requirements coefficients either on a partitive cell-by-cell basis or at the "holistic" level (Jensen, 1980).

In the spirit of the debate on regionalization and reconciliation methods, Gerking and Miernyk's well-known contributions and exchanges appeared (Gerking, 1976a, 1976b, 1979; Gerking and Pleeter, 1977; Miernyk, 1976, 1979). Following from early work of Briggs (1957), Gerking focused on statistical estimation methods for direct coefficients, whereas Miernyk supported methods based only on survey data and professional judgment. Gerking's evaluations of his methods were based on comparisons of traditionally calculated and statistically estimated direct coefficient tables. These exchanges prompted considerable discussion (e.g., Brown and Giarratani, 1979; Hanseman and Gustafson, 1981; Hanseman, 1982) and increased interest and activity in stochastic input–output analysis.

In what would become more than a decade of input–output research, another group of scholars began to focus on the properties of the interindustry framework. Among the earliest of these is Sebald's (1974) study of the sensitivity of large-scale input–output models to parametric uncertainties. Sebald first studied worst case percentage tolerances on solution elements, given uncertainty characteristics on model parameters. Negative tolerances were smaller on average than the positive tolerances even though the perturbations were of the same magnitude, and tolerance amplification (greater uncertainty on the solution than on the model parameters) is predominant.

Of particular interest is Sebald's attention to the "Most Important Parameter" (MIP) concept. "Given a model solution and a known or assumed uncertainty on each parameter," the MIP problem seeks to "identify the model parameters whose uncertainty is responsible for a significant uncertainty in any element of the solution" (Sebald, 1974, pp. 3–4). A parameter is inverse important if "reasonable variations in its value can affect the solution in some significant way" (Sebald, 1974, p. 23). Sebald's work is particularly significant in focusing the sensitivity analysis directly upon the inverse coefficients.

Bullard and Sebald (1977) next assessed uncertainty in the 1967 Bureau of Economic Analysis (BEA) accounts at various levels of aggregation. They specified distributions of system parameters that would simulate the activities involved in compiling the table. Lognormal, normal, or "folded normal" distributions were used, based on the characteristics of the mean and the level of certainty attributed to various parameters. The error structure captured most closely resembled a multiplicative structure, hence, a mixture of error symmetry was obtained. Varying levels of aggregation produced "effectively no change in the simulation output uncertainties" (Bullard and Sebald, 1977, p. 37).

Initially motivated by more pragmatic issues, West (1981, 1982) developed a method to rank the technical coefficients in order of their importance. Analysts with limited budgets would thus have a method of allocating scarce resources for generating or updating input–output data. For multiplicative error terms, the absolute error in the jth column multiplier is a function not only of the size of the jth output multiplier, but also of the magnitude of the output multiplier corresponding to the row sector in which the original error lies. Further, the error over all output multipliers from an error in one coefficient a_{ij} is the error in that coefficient weighted by the ith output multiplier and the jth row total of the inverse.

Two other studies of the 1970s are particularly significant: Simonovits (1975) and Goicoechea and Hansen (1978). Following Quandt and Evans, Simonovits analytically compared the expected value of the Leontief matrix with the expected value of its inverse. If all the elements of A are independent, random, and symmetrically distributed, then the $E(I - A)^{-1} \geqslant [I - E(A)]^{-1}$, that is, the expected value of the Leontief inverse is underestimated by what Simonovits termed the "practical estimator." These conclusions support Evans' assertion of compensating error effects.

The contribution of Goicoechea and Hansen is significant, yet it has received much less attention than might have been expected. Technology coefficients and demand variables of the input–output framework are treated as random variables. Each equation is transformed into a probabilistic inequality, asserting "that the number of times (expressed as a percentage) interindustry use and final consumption are less than or equal to the output of sector i is $1 - \alpha_i$" (Goicoeachea and Hansen, 1978, p. 286), where α_i is an error probability. The coefficients for each industry may have any (known) probability density function, and, in their presentation, they are arbitrarily ascribed exponential density functions to ensure nonnegativity conditions. Inequalities are transformed into a set of deterministic equivalents, resulting in a system of nonlinear equations. Although the source and nature of the error structure receive little attention, this approach enables statements to be made about system structure, explicitly related to industry specific conditions, which are not possible under any of the earlier formulations.

Interest in errors in regional nonsurvey input–output models continued in the work of Stevens and Trainer (1980), Park et al. (1981), Garhart (1985), and more recently Giarratani (1986). Stevens and Trainer conducted a series of simulation experiments based on multiplicative error structures and directed toward the relative contribution of errors in technical coefficients and regional purchase coefficients to impacts on multipliers. Whereas Stevens and Trainer based their experiments on hypothetical matrices, Park et al. used an empirical table. Both sets of analysts concluded that errors in regional purchase coefficients (RPCs) were of greater significance than those in technical coefficients in affecting regional output multipliers.

Garhart (1985) also analyzed the relative contribution to multiplier error of RPCs, but under conditions of either purely additive error or a combination of additive and multiplicative error. Garhart concluded that analysts should interpret the results of Stevens and Trainer and Park et al. with caution, and he called for at least equal attention to technical coefficients as to regional purchase coefficients.[1]

Recent studies more directly aimed at stochastic input–output include West (1986) and Lahiri and Satchell (1986), whose work follows closely the concerns of Simonovits (1975). Lahiri and Satchell reexamined the relationship between the expected value of the Leontief inverse and its true value when the direct coefficients table is a stochastic input–output matrix. A misinterpretation of Simonovits theoretical formulation led to a badly needed, but largely unsuccessful, attempt at unraveling terminology. In short, there is a notable imprecision that results from using the terms *true* and *expected* interchangeably.

Lahiri and Satchell (1986) continued by generalizing some early results and providing some new ones. Specifically, they demonstrated at least one case in which Simonovits' assertion of underestimation (which is overestimation in Lahiri's framework) holds when the assumption of independence of error terms is relaxed (i.e., biproportionally stochastic, multiplicative, error terms). Further, the combination of

---

1. Giarratani's (1986) tests of the relative contribution to direct coefficient error of RPCs and technical coefficients, but based on empirical data, supported Garhart's conclusions.

over- and underestimation (compensating effects) given row constraints is shown to hold true when considering either flows or technical coefficients tables, a general result not offered by Simonovits. Although these studies are significant, the probability density function of the inverse is still unknown. To calculate the confidence limits of the solution, we must know more about the error structure, in particular the probability density function of the direct coefficient errors, ε_{ij}.

West (1986) directly confronted the problem of approximating multiplier density functions and moments. Assuming coefficient independence and small, normally distributed error terms, West derived a formal expression for the probability density of the deviations from an observed multiplier, given an estimate of the standard error of the input coefficient. His formulation demonstrates that the expected value of this error term is positive and the multiplier distribution is positively skewed. More importantly, his results provide the first derivation of theoretical multiplier confidence intervals.

The two papers that best represent the state of stochastic input–output research are those of Lahiri and Satchell (1986) and West (1986). Lahiri and Satchell offer the broadest generalizations concerning over- and underestimation. West's contribution is most significant in terms of its practical utility and culminates more than three decades of work in stochastic input–output analysis.

There remains, of course, a great deal to be accomplished. With the exception of conclusive, but poor, results concerning over- and underestimation (poor in light of restrictive row constraints), coefficient interdependence has not received adequate attention. The nonlinearity of inversion introduces immense complexity when coefficient interdependence is allowed. The strongest justification for the independence assumption, offered by Quandt (1958), was that coefficient column sums of (less than) unity do not necessarily imply interdependence. Although the assumption of interindustry (or cross-industry) independence is much less objectionable, each of us must cringe a bit when column coefficient independence is accepted. Quandt himself was unwilling to defend this assumption strongly, as evidenced by a qualifying footnote in the first of his two papers (Quandt, 1958, p. 157).

Not unrelated is the question of synergy in input–output models; a change in the total system attributes generally exceeds the sum of the changes in the direct coefficients. Clearly, any method that examines the importance of single coefficients will capture only limited effects on the system.

Next there is the question of temporal relationships. Suppose, for example, that coefficient $a_{k1}(t)$ is ranked as the most important coefficient at time t. Following the updating procedure based on the initial coefficient rankings, $a_{k1}(t + 1)$ may rank considerably lower. In the extreme, suppose that on the basis of coefficient rankings we scrutinize the top 30 percent of the coefficients from time t. After updating, and using the same algorithm, the now top ranked coefficient was not among the original 30 percent. How is inverse importance for each time interval related? Can changes in inverse importance be modeled?

Can the results of Lahiri and Satchell or West be extended to generalizations about aggregation error? How does the error that results from aggregation resemble error structures assumed in other error sensitivity analyses? The distinction between error analysis in the deterministic model and error analysis in the stochastic model is very cloudy. What will the implications be if the error structure is found to be asymmetrical? Will the inverse solution be affected?

CURRENT AND FUTURE RESEARCH DIRECTIONS

Quandt's initial research questions provide the means to summarize the state of the art and to identify some potentially fruitful directions for research. Taken in the order presented, we can attach theoretical confidence limits to the solution of the Leontief system. The two most direct methods derive from Goicoechea and Hansen (1978) and West (1986). In response to both the second and third questions, we can show that the moments of the distributions of the solution are calculable and that the relationship is specified in terms of the moments of the distributions of the input coefficients. The last two research questions, however, are not so clearly answered and point to future research. What can be said about the distribution of the input coefficients? Surprisingly, a partial justification for this research direction is found in Leontief:

> Mathematical statistics will, however, become very useful, nay indispensable...
> after all the principal parts of the analytical structure have been erected and one
> can turn to a more precise fitting and mutual adjustment of its originally rough-
> hewn components. (Leontief, 1955, p. 13)

One area of research in the last half decade has focused on the nature of the direct coefficient and the relationships it represents. In addition to offering further justification for distributions of error terms around direct coefficients, an alternative perspective on variation in production coefficients is evolving. Expected, systematic variation within the population represented by each average production coefficient is increasingly the focus.

Wibe (1982) was among the first to suggest that even within a single industry category, there are reasons to expect a wide variety of production schedules (empirically observed input cost shares). Based on a sample of Sweden's industrial establishments, Wibe showed that the average labor coefficient for the most profitable establishments is only 73 percent of the industry average, whereas the same coefficient for the least profitable establishments was 130 percent of the average. Further, Wibe's data suggest that establishments that are efficient in gross profit share are not only efficient in labor, but also in the use of intermediates. If increases in final demand are met by the most efficient establishments and declines in final demand impact the least efficient establishments, a range of effects will result from perturbations of equal magnitude but opposite sign.

Jackson (1986) applied a similar logic in a simulation-based analysis of full probability distributions for input–output coefficients. An alternative to viewing the error problem as one of a lack of statistical coherence among true value, observed value, and estimator is to consider the full distribution of direct establishment level coefficients for each $i–j$ combination. Although there is a true (if unknown) coefficient for any time period past, in the absence of other information, the best option for future intervals is to approximate these industry aggregates on the basis of the characteristics of the underlying distributions. Further, if we expect systematic variation within the populations of industry aggregates, then asymmetric distributions may be the norm.

One justification for expected asymmetry in these distributions lies in the temporal characteristics of the production process. Following Hicks (1973), assume that streams of inputs produce streams of outputs. Input streams must commence prior to streams of outputs, because nothing is produced from nothing. The generic form of a production process under these conditions appears in Figure 15-1. The two

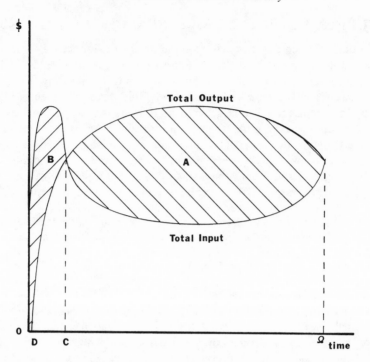

FIGURE 15-1   Process life curves.

curves represent appropriately capitalized values of total inputs and total output over the life of the process.

The input curve is characterized by an initial "hump" that represents startup costs that tail off after the physical plant is in place and after labor training costs have been borne. Input costs reach a minimum at some point of maximum process efficiency, then begin to rise again as maintenance costs rise as a result of physical plant aging, and as resource or input quality begins to fall. Likewise, as production begins, output rises from zero to some maximum level that may be maintained for some interval, then begins to decline due, *inter alia*, to decreased efficiency of aging capital.

The viability of this process depends on the relationship between the two shaded areas, A and B; A must be greater than or equal to B. Using Hicks' notation, the process $[a(t), b(t)]$ is a mortal one, defined for $t = [0, \Omega]$. Net output, $q(t)$, equals total output, $b(t)$, less total input, $a(t)$. Capital value of the process at time $t = 0$, $k(0)$, equals

$$\int_{0}^{\Omega} q(t)e^{-\sigma(t)}\, dt$$

where σ is the instantaneous rate of interest, and must clearly be nonnegative. If the process is viable, $k(t)$ must also be nonnegative for any interval $[v, \Omega]$ where $0 \leqslant v < \Omega$.

Although capital value must be positive for all intervals that terminate at Ω, the same cannot be said for all other intervals. Figure 15-1 demonstrates that, in fact, $k(t) < 0$ for all intervals in $[0, C]$. Moreover, the instantaneous ratio of inputs to outputs (aggregate cost share, ACS) derived directly from Figure 15-1 and shown in

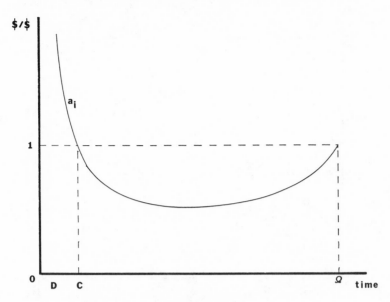

FIGURE 15-2   Lifetime aggregate cost share.

Figure 15-2 can take on any value in $(0, \infty)$. This temporal variation in the input–output ratio is present even in the absence of changes in technology, prices, or interest rates. A regional industry comprised of one establishment will exhibit systematic variation in that industry's ACS throughout its life cycle.

The volatility and directional change tendencies for the temporal ACS will be a function of the type and size of the establishment (Mills and Schumann, 1985) and the particular process, that is, the functions $a(t)$ and $b(t)$. The value of inputs is a function of the enabling technology and prices of inputs, whereas the value of outputs is a function of input factor prices and demand for output and quantity produced. Although constant input prices for a single plant have been implicitly assumed, spatial price variation has not been restricted.

Spatially variant input prices imply spatially variant $a(t)$. Hence, even if all processes are of the same vintage across regions, input–output ratios across places will be expected to vary with input price variations. Alternatively, prices could be held constant across and within regions, allowing only the age of capital stock to vary. Either within or across regions, input–output ratios would be expected to vary with age of process. In both instances, technology has been held constant. Ages of capital stock, input prices, and technologies will all generally vary from place to place. Although these variations strongly support additional systematic variation in input–output ratios, it will be useful to return to the assumptions of equal and constant input prices and production functions, allowing only the ages of an identical process to vary across establishments in a single industry in a single region.

Figure 15-3 presents a general form for process mortality rates for establishments of different vintage. Mortality is low at process inception and at very early stages of development, rises as poor planning and/or management take its toll, is typically highest among businesses 2–5 years of age, and tapers off dramatically as firms survive this critical period (Vaden, 1984). The rate generally remains at a low level for some duration, then rise again as processes, plants, and or products approach the ends of

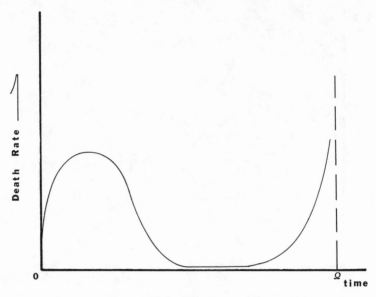

FIGURE 15-3   Process mortality.

their life spans. Figure 15-4 depicts corresponding frequencies of ages of plants for a typical industry under relatively constant rates of market entry.

Figures 15-2 and 15-4 can be combined to form the pdf for an industry's distribution of ACS shown in Figure 15-5. Because the process age distribution is presented as a probability density, the derived curve in Figure 15-5 is itself a density function. The area under this curve bounded on the left by zero and on the right by a_i represents the probability of any plant in the industry having an aggregate cost share less than or equal to a_i.

Because the denominator of individual coefficients is the same as that for the ACS, only inputs whose costs are constant proportions of total output value for the entire life of the process will have invariant coefficients. Not all individual input factors can be of this type, for no additive combination of such input–output coefficients could generate the derived aggregate cost share curve. Intuitively, every

FIGURE 15-4   Probability density for establishment age, one industry.

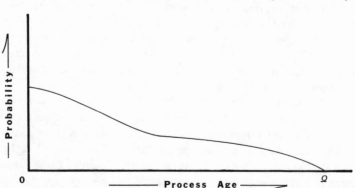

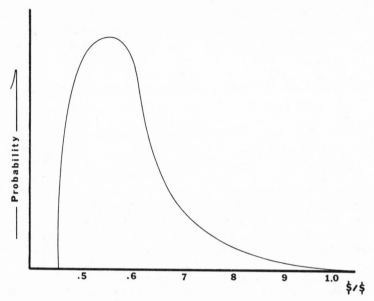

FIGURE 15-5   Probability density for aggregate cost share.

individual coefficient would be expected to display some variation. Hence, in response to Quandt's fourth question, we can characterize input coefficients by distributions that are generally asymmetric and skewed right.

Quandt's last question concerned the meaning of the solution of a probabilistic Leontief system. For those analysts who have viewed stochastic input–output models with respect to impacts of random error structure derived from measurement and sampling, aggregation, or sales/purchases reconciliation methods, the meaning is easily generalized. Given an inability to gather precise data and to define and categorize activities adequately, we will always have a measure of imprecision in an input–output data base. Estimates of the character of this embedded imprecision enable us to make mathematical statements about the precision of the inverse solution.

From the alternative perspective, the analyst's primary interest lies in the probability distribution of outcomes from future changes in the structure of final demand. The probability assessment is based on a knowledge and description of the full distributions of variables underlying the traditional industry aggregates. Thus, tools developed in stochastic input–output studies provide a strong foundation on which to build the probabilistic perspective.

REFERENCES

Briggs, F. E. 1957. "On Problems of Estimation in Leontief Models." *Econometrica.* Vol. 25, pp. 444–455.
Brown, D. M., and F. Giarratani. 1979. "Input–Output as a Simple Econometric Model: A Comment." *Review of Economics and Statistics.* Vol. 61, pp. 621–623.

Bullard, C. W., and A. R. Sebald. 1977. "Effects of Parametric Uncertainty and Technological Change on Input-Output Models." *Review of Economics and Statistics.* Vol. 59, pp. 75–81.

Christ, Carl F. 1955. "A Review of Input–Output Analysis." In *Input–Output Analysis: An Appraisal.* Studies in Income and Wealth, National Bureau of Economic Research, Vol. 18. Princeton, NJ: Princeton University Press, pp. 137–169.

Czamanski, S., and E. E. Malizia. 1969. "Applicability and Limitations in the Use of National Input–Output Tables for Regional Studies." *Papers of the Regional Science Association.* Vol. 23, pp. 65–77.

Dwyer, P. S., and F. V. Waugh. 1953. "On Errors in Matrix Inversion." *Journal American Statistical Association.* Vol. 68, pp. 289–319.

Evans, W. D. 1954. "The Effect of Structural Matrix Errors on Interindustry Relations Estimates." *Econometrica.* Vol. 22, pp. 461–480.

Garhart, R. E., Jr. 1985. "The Role of Error Structure in Simulations on Regional Input–Output Analysis." *Journal of Regional Science.* Vol. 25, pp. 353–366.

Gerking, Shelby D. 1976a. "Reconciling 'Rows Only' and 'Columns Only' Coefficients in an Input–Output Model." *International Regional Science Review.* Vol. 1, pp. 30–46.

Gerking, Shelby D. 1976b. "Input–Output as a Simple Econometric Model." *Review of Economics and Statistics.* Vol. 58, pp. 274–282.

Gerking, Shelby D. 1979. "Reconciling Reconciliation Procedures in Regional Input–Output Analysis." (With reply by W. H. Miernyk.) *International Regional Science Review.* Vol. 4, pp. 23–36, and pp. 38–40.

Gerking, Shelby D., and S. Pleeter. 1977. "Minimum Variance Sampling in Input–Output Analysis." *Review of Regional Studies.* Vol. 7, pp. 60–80.

Giarratani, F. 1986. "Evidence on the Structure of Errors." Paper presented to the British Section Regional Science Association, September, Bristol.

Goicoechea, A., and D. R. Hansen. 1978. "An Input–Output Model with Stochastic Parameters." *AIIE Transactions.* Vol. 10, pp. 285–291.

Hanseman, D. 1982. "Stochastic Input–Output Analysis: A Simulation Study." *Environment and Planning A.* Vol. 14, pp. 1425–1435.

Hanseman, D., and E. Gustafson. 1981. "Stochastic Input–Output Analysis: A Comment." *Review of Economics and Statistics.* Vol. 63, pp. 468–470.

Hicks, J. 1973. *Capital and Time.* London: Oxford University Press.

Jackson, Randall W. 1986. "The 'Full Distribution' Approach to Aggregate Representation in the Input–Output Modeling Framework." *Journal of Regional Science.* Vol. 26, pp. 515–530.

Jensen, Rod C. 1980. "The Concept of Accuracy in Regional Input–Output Models." *International Regional Science Review.* Vol. 5, pp. 139–154.

Jensen, Rod C., and Guy R. West. 1980. "The Effects of Relative Coefficient Size on Input–Output Multipliers." *Environment and Planning A.* Vol. 12, pp. 659–670.

Knudsen, D. C., and A. S. Fotheringham. 1986. "Matrix Comparison, Goodness-of-Fit, and Spatial Interaction Modeling." *International Regional Science Review.* Vol. 10, pp. 127–148.

Lahiri, S., and S. Satchell. 1986. "Properties of the Expected Value of the Leontief Inverse: Some Further Results." *Mathematics for Social Science.* Vol. 11, pp. 69–82.

Leontief, Wassily. 1955. "Some Basic Problems of Empirical Input–Output Analysis." *Input–Output Analysis: An Appraisal.* Studies in Income and Wealth, National Bureau of Economic Research, Vol. 18. Princeton, NJ: Princeton University Press, pp. 9–22.

Malizia, Emil, and Daniel L. Bond. 1974. "Empirical Tests of the *RAS* Method of Interindustry Coefficient Adjustment." *Journal of Regional Science.* Vol. 14, pp. 355–365.

McCamley, F., D. Schreiner, and G. Muncrief. 1973. "A Method for Estimating the Sampling Variances of Multipliers Derived from a From-To-Model." *Annals of Regional Science.* Vol. 7, pp. 81–89.

McMenamin, D. G., and J. V. Haring. 1974. "An Appraisal of Nonsurvey Techniques for Estimating Regional Input–Output Models." *Journal of Regional Science*. Vol. 14, pp. 191–205.

Miernyk, William H. 1976. "Comments on Recent Developments in Input–Output Analysis." *International Regional Science Review*. Vol. 1, pp. 47–55.

Miernyk, William H. 1979. "Reply to Reconciling Reconciliation Procedures in Regional Input–Output Analysis." *International Regional Science Review*. Vol. 4, pp. 36–38.

Mills, D. E., and Schumann, L. 1985. "Industry Structure with Fluctuating Demand." *American Economic Review*. Vol. 75, pp. 758–767.

Morrison, W. I., and P. Smith. 1974. "Non-Survey Input–Output Techniques at the Small Area Level: An Evaluation." *Journal of Regional Science*. Vol. 14, pp. 1–14.

Park, S. 1973. "On Input–Output Multipliers with Errors in Input–Output Coefficients." *Journal of Economic Theory*. Vol. 6, pp. 399–403.

Park, S., M. Mohtadi, and A. Kubursi. 1981. "Errors in Regional Nonsurvey Input–Output Models: Analytical and Simulation Results." *Journal of Regional Science*. Vol. 21, pp. 321–340.

Quandt, Richard. 1958. "Probabilistic Errors in the Leontief Systems." *Naval Research Logistics Quarterly*. Vol. 5, pp. 155–170.

Quandt, Richard. 1959. "On the Solution of Probabilistic Leontief Systems." *Naval Research Logistics Quarterly*. Vol. 6, pp. 295–305.

Rao, C. R. 1952. *Advanced Statistical Methods in Biometric Research*. New York: Hafner Press.

Round, Jeffery I. 1978. "An Interregional Input–Output Approach to the Evaluation of Nonsurvey Methods." *Journal of Regional Science*. Vol. 18, pp. 179–194.

Schaffer, W. A., and K. Chu. 1969. "Nonsurvey Techniques for Constructing Regional Interindustry Models." *Papers of the Regional Science Association*. Vol. 23, pp. 83–101.

Sebald, A. V. 1974. "An Analysis of the Sensitivity of Large Scale Input–Output Models to Parametric Uncertainties." Center for Advanced Computation Document No. 122. Urbana, II: University of Illinois at Urbana–Champaign.

Sherman, J., and W. J. Morrison. 1950. "Adjustment of an Inverse Matrix Corresponding to a Change in One Element of a Given Matrix." *Annals of Mathematical Statistics*. Vol. 21, pp. 124–127.

Simonovits, A. 1975. "A Note on the Underestimation and Overestimation of the Leontief Inverse." *Econometrica*. Vol. 43, pp. 493–498.

Stevens, Benjamin H., and Glynnis A. Trainer. 1980. "Error Generation in Regional Input–Output Analysis and Its Implication for Non-Survey Models." In *Economic Impact Analysis: Methodology and Application*, edited by Saul Pleeh. Boston: Martinus Nijhoff, pp. 68–84.

Theil, Henri. 1966. *Applied Economic Forecasting*. Amsterdam, The Netherlands: North Holland.

Vaden, R. 1984. "Business 'Births' Long-Run Employment Impact." *New Jersey Economic Indicators*. (March 9), pp. 4–9.

West, Guy R. 1981. "An Efficient Approach to the Estimation of Regional Input–Output Tables." *Environment and Planning, A*. Vol. 13, pp. 857–867.

West, Guy R. 1982. "Sensitivity and Key Sector Analysis in Input–Output Models." *Australian Economic Papers*. Vol. 21, pp. 365–378.

West, Guy R. 1986. "A Stochastic Analysis of an Input–Output Model." *Econometrica*. Vol. 54, pp. 363–374.

Wibe, S. 1982. "The Distribution of Input Coefficients." *Economics of Planning*. Vol. 2, pp. 65–70.

16

Qualitative Input–Output Analysis

RANKO BON

The demand-side input–output model can be used to forecast sectoral outputs on the basis of known tables of intersectoral transactions for a base year and final demand forecasts for the desired year. Similarly, the supply-side input–output model can be used to forecast sectoral inputs with the known transaction tables for a base year and value added projections for the desired year. The former model was introduced by Leontief (1936), whereas the latter was suggested by Ghosh (1958). Input–output models have been extended in many directions, and include regional models (see, for example, Isard et al., 1960; Polenske, 1980).

The application of input–output analysis and its extensions is often hampered by the unavailability or unreliability of data. This holds for transaction tables, as well as for final demand or value-added projections. Data problems are particularly severe in the construction of input–output models for developing countries and in the construction of multiregional input–output (MRIO) or interregional input–output (IRIO) models in both developed and developing countries. Qualitative reasoning, developed in the field of the so-called naive physics, a subfield of artificial intelligence (AI), offers a partial solution to these problems (see, for example, Bobrow, 1985). Qualitative input–output (QIO) analysis offers a new set of concepts for theoretical exploration of economic structure and process.

Heretofore, QIO has relied on concepts and methods developed in the theory of directed graphs, as exemplified by Harary et al. (1965) and Busacker and Saaty (1965). Czayka (1970) and Holub and Schnabl (1985), among others, explore the relationship between economic structure and process, using many fruitful results from the theory of directed graphs. However, this chapter draws from the qualitative reasoning formalisms, which can be realized in computer programs that manipulate symbols rather than numbers.

According to Forbus (1985, p. 164), "the features which make qualitative models useful for physical reasoning... should be useful in other domains, especially in domains where numerical data is unreliable or hard to come by." However, he cautions that

> [t]here seems to be no real agreement on what mathematical descriptions are appropriate in economics, hence it will be hard to judge whether a qualitative model is correct. In addition, the very structure of the domain can change with time.... These factors make modeling economics much harder than modeling physics.

Indeed, many controversies in economics are not about facts, but about inter-preting mathematical descriptions of facts as they appear in economic models. The mathematical foundations of input–output analysis are fortunately not under significant dispute; this makes it an excellent candidate for the application of qualitative models.

This chapter is divided into five parts. First, some fundamentals of qualitative matrix algebra (QMA) are introduced rather informally, and a theorem concerning the derivation of qualitative inverses is proved. Second, some fundamentals of QIO analysis are introduced. Third, qualitative multiregional input–output (QMRIO) models are briefly discussed. Fourth, a potential limitation of QIO is pointed out. Fifth, a number of conclusions concerning both theory and application are suggested, together with a proposal for further research in QIO analysis.

SOME FUNDAMENTALS OF QUALITATIVE MATRIX ALGEBRA

Let $[Z]$ stand for the qualitative transaction table, in which the existence of a flow between two sectors is denoted by " +," and its nonexistence is denoted by "0." For reasons of stability, $[Z]$ must be q-nonnegative or q-positive, that is, it must contain only pluses and zeroes, or only pluses, respectively. Furthermore, let $[A]$ stand for the qualitative direct-input (production) and $[B]$ stand for direct-output (allocation) coefficient matrices in which the existence of a coefficient is denoted by " +," and its nonexistence is denoted by "0." These two matrices are associated, respectively, with demand-side and supply-side input–output models (see, e.g., Miller and Blair, 1985, pp. 317–322; Bon, 1986). It is obvious that $[Z] \equiv [A] \equiv [B]$. Although the topolog-ical properties of the three matrices are identical, the distinction between the two types of input–output models does not vanish, as will be shown below.

Finally, let $[(I - A)^{-1}]$ stand for the qualitative inverse of $(I - A)$, in which the existence of a direct path or an indirect path of minimal topological length between two sectors is denoted by " +," and its nonexistence is denoted by "0." It is obvious that the topological length of the longest minimal path is $n \leqslant m - 1$, where m is the rank of matrix A. Note that $[(I - A)^{-1}] \equiv [(I - B)^{-1}]$, since $[A] \equiv [B]$. Also, the coefficients of the inverse in the demand-side (supply-side) model represent partial derivatives of output with respect to changes in final demand (inputs with respect to changes in value added), and the elements of the qualitative inverse therefore represent the signs of these partial derivatives. In fact, the direction of change is the crucial idealization in qualitative reasoning.

Topologically speaking, the inversion procedure generates interindustry linkages in which indirect links exist between sectors. In terms of logic, this can be interpreted as a rule: if sector P is directly linked to sector Q, and sector Q is directly linked to sector R, then sector P is indirectly linked to sector R. The inversion procedure can therefore be expressed in terms of logical implications that can be easily realized in qualitative reasoning formalisms. The details of such formalisms will not be discussed here, though some operations of qualitative algebra will be introduced informally.

The qualitative inverse can be obtained on the basis of two operations of qualitative algebra—addition and multiplication. These two operations are defined as follows for qualitative scalars, denoted by $[p]$ and $[q]$:

$[p] + [q]$	+	0	−
+	+	+	?
0	+	0	−
−	?	−	−

$[p] \times [q]$	+	0	−
+	+	0	−
0	0	0	0
−	−	0	+

in which ambiguities are denoted by "?." In the case of qualitative addition, unambiguous results require additional information about the relative magnitudes, or partial ordering, of $[p]$ and $[q]$. However, ambiguities do not arise in qualitative multiplication; in fact, they may vanish under multiplication, because $(?)(0) = 0$. (The treatment of ambiguities is one of the major features that distinguishes this approach to QIO from the previous ones, as will be shown below.) These operations can be applied to qualitative matrix multiplication using the standard conventions of matrix algebra. For example,

$$[0 \quad 0 \quad +] \begin{bmatrix} 0 \\ + \\ + \end{bmatrix} = (0)(0) + (0)(+) + (+)(+) = +$$

Using these QMA concepts, the qualitative inverse is obtained as follows.

THEOREM: $[(I - A)^{-1}] = [A^n]$, where $n \leqslant m - 1$, and where m is the rank of A.

PROOF: Because the approximation inverse is defined as $(I - A)^{-1} = I + A + A^2 + \cdots + A^k$, where k is sufficiently large so that A^{k+1} is sufficiently close to zero, it follows that $[(I - A)^{-1}] = [I + A + A^2 + \cdots + A^k]$. As each round of qualitative powers can replace zeroes only by pluses, it follows that $[A^k] = [I + A + A^2 + \cdots + A^k]$. However, the pattern of pluses cannot change for $k \geqslant n$. Therefore, the addition of successive powers of $[A]$ beyond $[A^n]$ is redundant.   QED.

For example,

$$[I] = \begin{bmatrix} + & 0 & 0 \\ 0 & + & 0 \\ 0 & 0 & + \end{bmatrix}; \quad [A] = \begin{bmatrix} + & + & 0 \\ 0 & + & + \\ 0 & 0 & + \end{bmatrix}; \quad [A^2] = [A^3] = \cdots = \begin{bmatrix} + & + & + \\ 0 & + & + \\ 0 & 0 & + \end{bmatrix}$$

where, denoting the elements of $[A^2] = [(I - A)^{-1}]$ by $[a_{ij}^*]$,

$$[a_{11}^*] = (+)(+) + (+)(0) + (0)(0) = (+) + (0) + (0) = +$$

$$[a_{12}^*] = (+)(+) + (+)(+) + (0)(0) = (+) + (+) + (0) = +$$

- -

$$[a_{33}^*] = (0)(0) + (0)(+) + (+)(+) = (0) + (0) + (+) = +$$

The unchanging pattern of pluses is reached for $n = 2$; therefore, in this case $n = m - 1$, as $m = 3$. In other words, for $n \geqslant 2$, $[A^n]$ is q-idempotent. It is obvious that $[I] + [A] + [A^2] = [A^2]$, the qualitative inverse of $[A]$. Note that n represents the longest minimal topological path between two sectors. Also, each new plus generated by the powering process indicates the existence of a path between two sectors, the topological length of which is given by the exponent itself.

Unlike inversion, the power-series solution shows the impact of a change in final demand or value added in the form of a propagation process. The initial exogenous impact can be studied in stages, from one time-instant to another. The underlying model of time is topological in character because the precedence relations between time instants are ordinal. Inversion hides this process, as it treats it as instantaneous; the whole process is compressed in a single time instant. The relationship between structure and process is explained by Holub and Schnabl (1985), for instance, who use similar concepts in the study of the "velocity" and "completeness" of the propagation process.

It should be borne in mind that the qualitative inverse may be identical to the qualitative coefficient matrix, in which case $n = 1$. For example:

$$[A] = [A^2] = \cdots = \begin{bmatrix} + & 0 & + \\ 0 & + & + \\ 0 & 0 & + \end{bmatrix}$$

Therefore, in this case $[(I - A)^{-1}] = [A]$, that is, $[A]$ is q-idempotent. In such cases, there are no indirect links between sectors, and the powering process fails to generate any changes in the pattern of pluses. The scope of this chapter does not permit further investigation of the properties of the qualitative inverse or of other operations of QMA needed for QIO analysis that may be defined in a similar fashion.

SOME FUNDAMENTALS OF QUALITATIVE INPUT–OUTPUT ANALYSIS

The qualitative inverse can be used to obtain the qualitative projection of changes in output, ΔX, on the basis of a qualitative projection of changes in final demand, ΔY, because $[\Delta X] = [(I - A)^{-1}][\Delta Y]$. Consider the following example:

$$[A] = \begin{bmatrix} + & + & 0 \\ 0 & + & + \\ 0 & 0 & + \end{bmatrix}; \quad [\Delta Y] = \begin{bmatrix} 0 \\ + \\ 0 \end{bmatrix}$$

Therefore, using the inverse obtained above,

$$[\Delta X] = \begin{bmatrix} + & + & + \\ 0 & + & + \\ 0 & 0 & + \end{bmatrix} \begin{bmatrix} 0 \\ + \\ 0 \end{bmatrix} = \begin{bmatrix} + \\ + \\ 0 \end{bmatrix}$$

where

$$[\Delta x_1] = (+)(0) + (+)(+) + (+)(0) = (0) + (+) + (0) = +$$
$$[\Delta x_2] = (0)(0) + (+)(+) + (+)(0) = (0) + (+) + (0) = +$$

and

$$[\Delta x_3] = (0)(0) + (0)(+) + (+)(0) = (0) + (0) + (0) = 0$$

This approach allows for negative changes in qualitative final demand projections as well. However, if positive and negative changes are combined in a qualitative final demand projection, ambiguities may arise. For example,

$$
\begin{bmatrix} ? \\ + \\ + \end{bmatrix} = \begin{bmatrix} + & + & + \\ 0 & + & + \\ 0 & 0 & + \end{bmatrix} \begin{bmatrix} - \\ 0 \\ + \end{bmatrix}
$$

where

$$[\Delta x_1] = (+)(-) + (+)(0) + (+)(+) = (-) + (0) + (+) = ?$$

$$[\Delta x_2] = (0)(-) + (+)(0) + (+)(+) = (0) + (0) + (+) = +$$

and

$$[\Delta x_3] = (0)(-) + (0)(0) + (+)(+) = (0) + (0) + (+) = +$$

To eliminate ambiguities, an analyst may proceed in two directions. On the one hand, these ambiguities can be eliminated by providing additional assumptions about relative magnitudes of the coefficients in the inverse and the corresponding components of final demand. For example, if $|\Delta y_1| > |\Delta y_3|$ and $a_{11}^* > a_{13}^*$, then $[\Delta x_1] = -$. On the other hand, the ambiguities may be used to generate multiple scenarios, which may be more appealing from the point of view of practical applications of QIO analysis in economic policy and planning exercises. More specifically, ambiguities lead to alternative possible futures. For example, $[\Delta x_1] = +$ if $|\Delta y_1| < |\Delta y_3|$ and $a_{11}^* < a_{13}^*$, $|\Delta y_1| = |\Delta y_3|$ and $a_{11}^* < a_{13}^*$, $|\Delta y_1| < |\Delta y_3|$ and $a_{11}^* = a_{13}^*$, etc.

The same qualitative inverse can be used to obtain the qualitative projection of changes in inputs, $\Delta X'$, on the basis of a qualitative projection of changes in value added, $\Delta W'$, because $[\Delta X'] = [\Delta W'][(I - B)^{-1}]$ and because $[(I - A)^{-1}] \equiv [(I - B)^{-1}]$. Note, however, that $[(\Delta X)']$ is generally not equal to $[\Delta X']$ for $[(\Delta Y)'] = [\Delta W']$. Consider the following example:

$$
[B] = \begin{bmatrix} + & + & 0 \\ 0 & + & + \\ 0 & 0 & + \end{bmatrix}; \qquad [\Delta W'] = [0 \quad + \quad 0]
$$

Therefore, using again the inverse obtained above,

$$
[\Delta X'] = [0 \quad + \quad 0] \begin{bmatrix} + & + & + \\ 0 & + & + \\ 0 & 0 & + \end{bmatrix} = [0 \quad + \quad +]
$$

In other words, the stimulation of demand for the goods of the second sector (demand-side) and the provision of more abundant resources for the same sector (supply-side) will lead to a different pattern of changes in outputs and inputs for the system as a whole. The former policy will not affect the third sector, whereas the latter policy will not affect the first sector.

QUALITATIVE MULTIREGIONAL
INPUT–OUTPUT ANALYSIS

This procedure can be easily extended to the qualitative multiregional input–output (QMRIO) models. In the Chenery–Moses (or demand-side) QMRIO model, given by $[\Delta X] = [(I - C\hat{A})^{-1}][C\Delta Y]$, where $[\Delta X]$ is the qualitative column vector of changes in regional output, $[C]$ is the qualitative diagonal-block regional trade matrix, $[\hat{A}]$ is the qualitative block-diagonal regional technology matrix, and $[C\Delta Y]$ is the column vector of trade-adjusted changes in regional final demand. The smallest such system has two sectors and two regions. Consider the following example:

$$
[C] = \left[\begin{array}{cc:cc} + & 0 & 0 & 0 \\ 0 & + & 0 & + \\ \hdashline 0 & 0 & + & 0 \\ 0 & 0 & 0 & + \end{array}\right]; \quad
[\hat{A}] = \left[\begin{array}{cc:cc} + & + & 0 & 0 \\ 0 & + & 0 & 0 \\ \hdashline 0 & 0 & + & 0 \\ 0 & 0 & + & + \end{array}\right]; \quad
\text{and } [\Delta Y] = \left[\begin{array}{c} + \\ - \\ \hdashline 0 \\ + \end{array}\right]
$$

Therefore,

$$
[C\hat{A}] = [C] \times [\hat{A}] = \left[\begin{array}{cc:cc} + & + & 0 & 0 \\ 0 & + & + & + \\ \hdashline 0 & 0 & + & 0 \\ 0 & 0 & + & + \end{array}\right]
$$

The qualitative inverse, $[(I - C\hat{A})^{-1}]$, is obtained as follows:

$$
[(C\hat{A})^2] = [(C\hat{A})^3] = \cdots = \left[\begin{array}{cc:cc} + & + & + & + \\ 0 & + & + & + \\ \hdashline 0 & 0 & + & 0 \\ 0 & 0 & + & + \end{array}\right]
$$

Furthermore,

$$
[C\Delta Y] = [C] \times [\Delta Y] = \left[\begin{array}{cc:cc} + & 0 & 0 & 0 \\ 0 & + & 0 & + \\ \hdashline 0 & 0 & + & 0 \\ 0 & 0 & 0 & + \end{array}\right]\left[\begin{array}{c} + \\ - \\ \hdashline 0 \\ + \end{array}\right] = \left[\begin{array}{c} + \\ ? \\ \hdashline 0 \\ + \end{array}\right]
$$

And finally,

$$
[\Delta X] = \left[\begin{array}{cc:cc} + & + & + & + \\ 0 & + & + & + \\ \hdashline 0 & 0 & + & 0 \\ 0 & 0 & + & + \end{array}\right]\left[\begin{array}{c} + \\ ? \\ \hdashline 0 \\ + \end{array}\right] = \left[\begin{array}{c} ? \\ ? \\ \hdashline 0 \\ + \end{array}\right]
$$

Both $[\Delta x_3]$ and $[\Delta x_4]$ are examples of the case in which the ambiguity vanishes under multiplication, that is, $(0)(?) = 0$, as mentioned above. For example:

$$[\Delta x_3] = (0)(+) + (0)(?) + (+)(0) + (0)(+)$$

$$= (0) + (0) + (0) + (0) = 0$$

Consider next a policy exercise concerning the impact of a change in the regional trade structure. For example, keeping everything else unchanged in the above model, let $[c_{13}] = +$. It can be shown that the qualitative inverse remains unchanged. This exercise thus establishes that this particular change in the structure of regional trade does not affect the output structure. Exercises such as this can be used in the exploratory stages of policy and planning studies.

Mutatis mutandis, the procedures introduced here can be used with the Bon–Polenske (or supply-side) QMRIO model (Bon, 1988), given by $[\Delta X'] = [\Delta W'R][(I - \hat{B}R)^{-1}]$, where $[\Delta X']$ is the qualitative row vector of changes in regional inputs, $[R]$ is the qualitative diagonal-block regional trade matrix, $[\hat{B}]$ is the qualitative block-diagonal regional technology matrix, and $[\Delta W'R]$ is the row vector of trade-adjusted changes in regional value added. Clearly, $[\hat{A}] \equiv [\hat{B}]$ and $[C] \equiv [R]$. Note, however, that $[C\hat{A}]$ will not in general be equal to $[\hat{B}R]$. Consequently, the demand-side and supply-side QMRIO models will in general have different inverses.

The model presented above is of the MRIO variety (Polenske, 1980) rather than of the IRIO variety (Isard et al., 1960) because of the significant difference between the data requirements of the two underlying accounting systems. More specifically, for n sectors and m regions, MRIO models require $n^2m + nm^2$, whereas IRIO models require n^2m^2 pieces of data. For example, for a system with 10 sectors and 10 regions, MRIO models require 2,000 pieces of data, whereas IRIO models require 10,000. This is a considerable difference even in the case of qualitative regional models. Moreover, it is often convenient to compile the information on trade and technology independently, as the two types of information are likely to come from different groups of experts and to require updating at different periods of time.

A word of caution QIO analysis has one potentially significant limitation. If $[(I - A)^{-1}]$ is q-positive, that is, if $(I - A)^{-1}$ is positive, all projections of ΔX on the basis of ΔY will become trivial. In other words, ΔX itself will always be q-positive or q-negative. (If $[A]$ is q-positive, its inverse will be q-positive as well.) Therefore, as introduced here, QIO analysis is of practical value only if $[(I - A)^{-1}]$ is strictly q-nonnegative. This condition is likely to be satisfied only in economies at a very low stage of development, as well as for highly disaggregated input–output systems. It is precisely in such cases that data unavailability and unreliability are likely to be an important issue, however. Of course, q-nonpositive and q-negative matrices are excluded from consideration on standard stability grounds.

The practical implications of the above limitation of QIO analysis must remain an empirical issue. However, it is worthwhile to consider briefly the a priori grounds for believing that the q-nonnegativity condition on inverses will not present a problem with highly disaggregated input–output systems. Production systems exhibit a *sui generis* directionality. Some goods undoubtedly flow back to their producers after a number of transformations, but it is reasonable to conjecture that this happens more often at a lower level of disaggregation. A good is more likely to "return" to the manufacturing sector, for example, than to the petrochemicals industry. The closer we come to the individual firm, the less likely it is that such cycles will occur. Therefore, the q-nonnegativity condition on inverses may be least binding in cases in which QIO analysis would be needed most.

CONCLUSION

First, it is of theoretical interest that QIO analysis does not distinguish between some features of demand-side and supply-side input–output models, represented by [A] and [B], respectively. For instance, a single inverse can be used in both models. QIO analysis is clearly reductionist in nature, but it offers a common foundation for both types of models, which represent two fundamental economic principles: demand determines output and supply determines input. As Bon (1986) argues, these two principles are interrelated in terms of the circular flow between sectors.

Second, QIO analysis offers new tools for the study of those properties of economic systems that are purely topological in character, that is, those properties that do not depend on the magnitudes of coefficients, but on their existence only. As Solow (1952, p. 41) writes:

> The particular nature of these properties is illustrated by the fact that they can be investigated with no knowledge of the value of a_{ij} other than which ones are zero and which are not. To test whether an a-matrix [here A matrix] is decomposable one needs only the matrix with the a_{ij} replaced by, say, + and 0.

An argument to this effect is also made by Chakravarty (1969, p. 144), as well as by Bon (1984, pp. 807 and 812). This indicates a direction for further research.

Third, QIO analysis offers a powerful practical tool to circumvent the problem of unavailable or unreliable data at the cost of higher levels of abstraction. QIO analysis may be used in early stages of policy and planning exercises to evaluate the impact of some fundamental assumptions about the direction of change in key policy and planning variables. This may be particularly important when a large number of alternatives must be considered. Once the most promising alternatives are found, they may be evaluated in more detail through quantitative analysis.

The qualitative transaction tables could be compiled by panels of industrial experts (and panels of regional trade experts in the case of regional studies) who could also suggest plausible future changes in the pattern of interindustry linkages. This form of data gathering would be particularly useful for developing countries and for regional studies, regardless of the level of development.

Furthermore, the value of input–output tables is limited because they are often compiled over protracted periods. Because timeliness is of the essence in economics, abstraction and simplification may become necessary and acceptable. As Hicks (1984, p. 245) argues,

> in practice, we must simplify quickly. Our special concern is with facts of the present world; but before we can study the present, it is already past. In order to say useful things about what is happening, before it is too late, we must select, even select quite violently.

QIO analysis offers the possibility of more timely information on interindustry transactions, albeit in a more abstract form. There is an inherent tradeoff between timeliness and quantitative precision.

Some computational methods of AI provide practical tools for the implementation of QMA and QIO (Bobrow, 1985). Symbolic or logic programming is a case in point. Clearly, it is possible to achieve logically equivalent results by means of standard numerical analysis on the basis of numbers of arbitrary magnitude, but it requires unnecessary artificiality and cumbersome interpretation.

Fourth, further research should focus on both QMA needed for QIO analysis and on applications of QIO analysis in the area of economic policy and planning. Research on QMA should emphasize the results exemplified by the qualitative inverse theorem presented here. The properties of the qualitative inverse should be investigated in greater detail. The study of applications should focus on scenario development methodologies based on QIO analysis. The primary purpose of this chapter is to suggest that these methodologies could offer a systematic framework for the analysis of possible futures rather than forecasts *sensu stricto*.

ACKNOWLEDGMENTS

The author thanks Ronald E. Miller, Lorris Mizrahi, and Karen R. Polenske for their constructive comments on a previous draft of this chapter.

REFERENCES

Bobrow, D. C., ed. 1985. *Qualitative Reasoning about Physical Systems*. Cambridge, MA, and London: The MIT Press.

Bon, Ranko. 1984. "Comparative Stability Analysis of Multiregional Input–Output Models: Column, Row, and Leontief–Strout Gravity Coefficient Models." *Quarterly Journal of Economics*. Vol. 99, pp. 791–815.

Bon, Ranko. 1986. "Comparative Stability Analysis of Demand-Side and Supply-Side Input–Output Models." *International Journal of Forecasting*. Vol. 2, pp. 231–235.

Bon, Ranko. 1988. "Supply-Side Multiregional Input–Output Models." *Journal of Regional Science*. Vol. 28, pp. 41–50.

Busacker, R. G., and T. L. Saaty. 1965. *Finite Graphs and Networks: An Introduction with Applications*. New York: McGraw-Hill.

Chakravarty, S. 1969. *Capital and Development Planning*. Cambridge, MA, and London: The MIT Press.

Czayka, L. 1972. *Qualitative Input–Output Analysis*. Meisenheim am Glan, Federal Republic of Germany: Verlag Anton Hain.

Forbus, K. D. 1985. "Qualitative Process Theory." In *Qualitative Reasoning about Physical Systems*, edited by D. C. Bobrow. Cambridge, MA, and London: The MIT Press, pp. 85–168.

Ghosh, A. 1958. "Input–Output Approach to an Allocation System." *Economica*. Vol. 25, pp. 58–64.

Harary, F., R. Z. Norman, and D. Cartwright. 1965. *Structural Models: An Introduction to the Theory of Directed Graphs*. New York, London, and Sydney: Wiley.

[Hicks, J.] 1984. *The Economics of John Hicks*. Oxford: Basil Blackwell.

Holub, H. W., and H. Schnabl. 1985. "Qualitative Input–Output Analysis and Structural Information." *Economic Modeling*. Vol. 2, pp. 67–73.

Isard, W., et al. 1960. *Methods of Regional Analysis*. New York: The Technology Press of M.I.T. and Wiley.

Leontief, Wassily. 1936. "Quantitative Input–Output Relations in the Economic System of the United States." *Review of Economics and Statistics.* Vol. 18, pp. 105–125.

Miller, Ronald E., and Peter D. Blair. 1985. *Input–Output Analysis: Foundations and Extensions.* Englewood Cliffs, NJ: Prentice-Hall.

Polenske, Karen R. 1980. *The U.S. Multiregional Input–Output Accounts and Model.* Lexington, MA: Lexington Books.

Solow, Robert. 1952. "On the Structure of Linear Models." *Econometrica.* Vol. 20, pp. 29–46.

17

Error and Sensitivity
Input–Output Analysis: A New Approach

MICHAEL SONIS and GEOFFREY J. D. HEWINGS

In this chapter, we review some of the earlier debates about the nature and importance of coefficient change to provide the stage for a discussion of a new approach, termed "a field of influence," that we believe will enable us to analyze the problem in a more general way. This approach may also be used in the identification of what we have referred to elsewhere as the Fundamental Economic Structure (FES) (Jensen et al., 1988a). In turn, this FES may provide us with the ability to develop a taxonomy of regional economic systems using the input–output model as a major contributor (Jensen et al., 1988b). Thus, the field-of-influence approach may provide a potential link to research exploring the space–time dynamics of change in regional and national economic structures.

In the next section of the chapter, we provide an overview of error and sensitivity approaches to coefficient change (under fixed price environments or those in which price changes are not considered explicitly). We describe the field-of-influence approach to coefficient change in the following section; then, we expand the concept to consider the identification of inverse important coefficients, changes in columns or rows, and the synergistic effects of changes in more than one coefficient. Finally, we offer some conclusions and suggestions for future research activity.

COEFFICIENT CHANGE IN INPUT–OUTPUT MODELS:
AN OVERVIEW

Interest in the problem of coefficient change in input–output models is not a recent phenomenon; however, what is most curious about input–output modeling is that analysts, for the most part, have not made the discussion of errors a prominent feature of the presentation of the model or the results. For the most part, attention to change in coefficients in input–output models was directed to the issue of the effect of error or changes in individual coefficients on the elements of the associated Leontief inverse matrix (Evans, 1954; Simonovits, 1975; Lahiri and Satchell, 1986). Complementing this approach was the problem of coefficient stability and the effect of coefficient change induced by technology, changing markets, structural change, and the general effects of economic growth and development.

Contributions to this literature include the seminal papers by Sevaldson (1970) and Carter (1970) and the intriguing notions of Tilanus (1966), who, using the Dutch annual input–output tables, suggested a distinction between average and marginal input–output coefficients in much the same way that a distinction is made in individual consumer theory. Lahiri (1976) approached this problem in a slightly different way, assuming that the choice of input coefficient was a function of the level of demand existing in any given industry. Clearly, Lahiri's ideas provide the entree to the development of a micro-to-macro link in input–output systems; the early developments of transaction value social accounting matrices (SAMs) (Drud et al., 1985) provide the precursors of extensions in this more general macroeconomic environment. In addition, the gradual adoption of computable general equilibrium models, in which the input–output framework is embedded, has created an even more pressing need for identification of the important parameters in the input–output part of the model.

For the most part, this work has not been generalizable to a large number of input–output systems. At the regional level, the issue of coefficient change has been more problematic because so many regional and interregional models have been assembled from nonsurvey or partial survey sources. In this regard, the regional dimension provides the possibility for a new source of error not usually associated with the national-level input–output models. The error usually arises in the transfer of input coefficients from a national model to a regional model. At the regional level, the debate has been important for focusing attention once again on the structure of input–output models and, in particular, on our ability to determine whether two structures are similar. Furthermore, derivative work emanating from this debate also focused attention on the degree to which we might be able to assign some level of "importance" to individual coefficients within an input–output model. From this work, we can identify two complementary approaches to input coefficient change, namely (1) error analysis and (2) sensitivity analysis. We will discuss the major issues raised by each approach in turn, although it will become clear that the distinction is in some sense artificial.

Error Analysis

Theil's (1957, 1972) pioneering work in entropy decomposition analysis provided a useful way of examining error or change in input structures. He suggested that change could be decomposed into a set of additive components. His approach appears not to have been examined by many others, although Hewings (1984), Hewings and Syversen (1982), Jackson and Hewings (1984), and Jackson et al. (1987) have explored the technique with the Washington state data.

West (1982), on the other hand, has approached error analysis from a relative change perspective, focusing on the effects of coefficient error on the multipliers of the associated inverse matrix. Closely allied with this approach is that of Jackson (1986), who developed the notion of probability density distributions for each coefficient and showed how this "uncertainty" could lead to serious problems in the utilization of the input–output model (Jackson and West, Chapter 15, this volume; Wibe, 1982).

Lawson (1980) has approached the problem conceptually by considering various forms of error—additive and multiplicative—and the ways in which these might be used in a "rational" approach to modeling. The notion of some "rationality" in the error or the structure of coefficient change of course underlies the widespread application of the RAS or biproportional technique in the context of updating (particularly at the national level) and estimation (using a national input–output table to estimate a regional one). Bacharach's (1970) work revealed a strong link between the RAS technique and the assumptions implicit in linear programming (LP) and nonlinear programming; the application of an LP-RAS approach may be found in Matuszewski et al. (1964). In their application, some coefficients were "blocked out" in the updating algorithm, because their true values were known or could be estimated through the provision of what Jensen and West (1980) refer to as "superior data." To this point (early 1970s), however, no attempt had been made to assess the degree to which errors in individual coefficients could be ranked or rated in terms of their importance. West (1981) provided some important directions in this regard, suggesting a relationships between coefficient size and the associated multipliers. Several of the techniques and approaches developed for error analysis were subsequently modified to perform sensitivity analysis; these are described next.

Sensitivity Analysis

Using a little-known theorem developed by Sherman and Morrison (1950), Bullard and Sebald (1977) were able to show that, in energy terms, only a very small number of the input coefficients in the U.S. model were analytically important. In applications at the regional level, Hewings (1984) referred to these as "inverse important coefficients." In a similar fashion, Jensen and West (1980) found that the removal of a large percentage of the entries in an input–output table could be accomplished with little appreciable effect on the results of using the model for impact analysis. Subsequently, West (1982) was able to show that the size and location of the coefficient within the input–output table provided the major determinants of an individual coefficient's importance. Morrison and Thumann (1980) and Hewings and Romanos (1981) extended the sensitivity notions to suggest that the "censal mentality" characterizing the developments of input–output models (namely, that all entries need to be estimated) is probably misplaced. The results of the sensitivity analyses in combination with statistical estimation techniques suggest that a more "rational" approach to coefficient change could be developed (Jackson and West, Chapter 15, this volume).

This conclusion provides the point of departure for this chapter. In addition, it is believed that these issues will also provide some important insights into the identification of FES and structure. In the next section, the new approach incorporating the concept of a field of influence will be introduced and shown to be general enough to cover a large number of types of coefficient change in input–output systems.

A NEW APPROACH TO COEFFICIENT CHANGE

In the development of this new approach, the ideas and suggestions made by Sherman and Morrison (1950), Bullard and Sebald (1977), West (1981), Crama et al. (1984), and Defourny and Thorbecke (1984) should be acknowledged. The latter analysis, in particular, sought to use structural path analysis to identify the effects of changes in one part of the system on the rest of the system, providing a concept that was not as general as the one to be presented here (Sonis and Hewings, 1988a). The new approach involves consideration of the relationship between the $n \times n$ matrix of input coefficients, $A = \|a_{ij}\|$, the matrix of incremental changes in the coefficients, $E = \|\varepsilon_{ij}\|$, the perturbed matrix, $A + E$, and the corresponding Leontief inverse matrices, $B = \|b_{ij}\| = [I - A]^{-1}$ and $B(E) = \|b_{ij}(E)\| = [I - A - E]^{-1}$. In summary, the complete relationship may be stated as follows: the coefficients $b_{ij}(E)$ can be presented as a rational function, a ratio of two polynomials, depending on the size of the increments, ε_{ij}, on the components b_{ij} of the Leontief inverse matrix $[I - A]^{-1}$, and on the cofactors of matrices derived from the matrix $C = [I - A]$ through the removal of certain rows and columns.

An Explanation

Consider the simplest case, in which the change occurs in only one input parameter, $a_{i_1 j_1}$, located in (i_1, j_1) in the direct input coefficient matrix A. Thus, the matrix E of incremental changes will include only one nonzero error ε in (i_1, j_1). In this case, we can obtain the following relationships between corresponding elements in the Leontief inverse matrices B and $B(E)$:

$$b_{ji}(\varepsilon) - b_{ji} = \frac{b_{ji} b_{j_1 i_1}}{1 - b_{j_1 i_1} \varepsilon} \, \varepsilon - \frac{I\binom{j_1 j}{i_1 i}}{1 - b_{j_1 i_1} \varepsilon} \, \varepsilon \tag{17-1}$$

where

$$I\binom{j_1 j}{i_1 i} = \begin{cases} \dfrac{1}{\Delta} \, \text{Sign}\binom{j_1 j}{i_1 i} M\binom{j_1 j}{i_1 i} & i \neq i_1, j \neq j_1 \\ 0 & i = i_1 \text{ or } j = j_1 \end{cases}$$

$$\Delta = \det(I - A)$$

$$\text{Sign}\binom{j_1 j}{i_1 i} = (-1)^{i + i_1 + j + j_1 + \sigma(i, i_1) + \sigma(j, j_1)}$$

$\sigma(i, i_1), \sigma(j, j_1) = $ the odd or even indexes of permutations (i, i_1), (j, j_1)

$M\binom{j_1 j}{i_1 i} = $ the determinant derived from Δ by removal of rows i, i_1 and columns j, j_1.

Equation (17-1) provides the structure for change in one parameter; the increment $b_{ji}(\varepsilon) - b_{ji}$ of each coefficient of the Leontief inverse includes the component

$$b_{ji} \frac{b_{j_1 i_1}}{1 - b_{j_1 i_1} \varepsilon} \, \varepsilon = b_{ji} r(i_1 j_1)$$

with the same rate of change $r(i_1, j_1)$ that is independent of (i, j). This component represents the global effect of change in the cell (i_1, j_1) on all cells (i, j). The other component

$$\frac{1}{1 - b_{j_1 i_1} \varepsilon} \, \varepsilon$$

represents the individual effect of change in the cell (i_1, j_1) on the individual cell (i, j) that is not included in the i_1th row or the j_1th column. Equation (17-1) represents a more accurate form of the Sherman and Morrison (1950) formula:

$$b_{ji}(\varepsilon) = b_{ji} + \frac{b_{ji_1} b_{j_1 i} \delta a_{i_1 j_1}}{1 - b_{j_1 i_1} \delta a_{i_1 j_1}}$$

where

$$\delta = \frac{a_{i_1 j_1} + \varepsilon}{a_{i_1 j_1}}$$

used in input–output error and sensitivity analysis by Bullard and Sebald (1977) among others. In addition, it may be regarded as a more general expression of the stochastic approach provided by West (1986), who was concerned with the relationship between the density functions for individual coefficients and their associated column multipliers. On the basis of the Sherman and Morrison (1950) formula, Hewings (1984) suggested the term "inverse-important input coefficients" might be used to describe the set of coefficients whose correct estimation [or, in the spirit of Jackson and West (Chapter 15, this volume), correct density distribution] would be deemed critical for confidence to be placed in the accuracy and integrity of the associated input–output model. An extension of this notion leads to the introduction of the concept of "fields of influence" of change in one input coefficient. It is important to underscore that Equation (17-1) provides the numerical description of the increment $B(E) - B$ for small and large changes, ε, under the condition $\varepsilon \neq 1/b_{j_1, i_1}$, which implies that det $B(E) \neq 0$.

The field of influence of the change in one input coefficient represents the linear part of this increment in the matrix form:

$$F = \| f_{ij} \|$$

where

$$f_{ji} = b_{ji} b_{j_1, i_1} - I \tag{17-2}$$

This formula can be used for the direct numerical representation of the fields of influence. Moreover, for moderately small ε, such that $|b_{j_1 i_1} \varepsilon| < 1$, the field of influence provides the "building block" for the construction of the increment $B(E) - B$. Consider ε such that $|b_{j_1 i_1} \varepsilon| < 1$, then the following decomposition holds:

$$\frac{1}{1 - b_{j_1 i_1} \varepsilon} = \sum_{s=0}^{\infty} b_{j_1 i_1}^s \varepsilon^s = 1 + b_{j_1 i_1} \varepsilon + b_{j_1 i_1}^2 \varepsilon^2 + \cdots + b_{j_1 i_1}^k \varepsilon^k + \cdots$$

Therefore, relationship (17-1) yields

$$b_{ji}(\varepsilon) = b_{ji} + \varepsilon(b_{ji} b_{j_1 i_1} - I) \sum_{s=0}^{\infty} b_{j_1 i_1}^s \varepsilon^s = b_{ji} + \sum_{s=0}^{\infty} f_{ji} b_{j_1 i_1}^s \varepsilon^{s+1}$$

$$= b_{ji} + f_{ji} \varepsilon + f_{ji} b_{j_1 i_1} \varepsilon^2 + \cdots + f_{ji} b_{j_1 i_1}^s \varepsilon^{s+1} + \cdots \tag{17-3}$$

This condition has an interesting matrix form:

$$B(\varepsilon) = B + F\varepsilon + b_{j_1 i_1} F\varepsilon^2 + \cdots + b_{j_1 i_1}^s F\varepsilon^{s+1} + \cdots \tag{17-4}$$

where the matrix $F = \| f_{ij} \| = F(_{j_1}^{i_1})$.

Therefore, the matrix F can be interpreted as a first-order field of influence of the change on the input coefficient $a_{i_1 j_1}$. The fields of influence of higher order are simply the products $b_{j_1 i_1}^{s-1} F$, that is, they are proportional to the field F with the coefficients of proportionality $b_{j_1 i_1}^{s-1}$. The first-order effect of change is given by $F\varepsilon$; the higher order effects are the products $(b_{j_1 i_1}\varepsilon)^{s-1} F\varepsilon$. The relationship (17-4) facilitates a simple computational procedure for the calculation of the field of influence of F without the use of Equation (17-2). Consider a small enough change, ε, in the input coefficient $a_{i_1 j_1}$; for such changes,

$$B(\varepsilon) = B + \varepsilon F \tag{17-5}$$

therefore, the field of influence can be derived from the approximate equality:

$$[B(\varepsilon) - B]/\varepsilon \approx F$$

Moreover, the field of influence of F can be presented graphically in such a way that the qualitative structure of influences can be ascertained. For this purpose, we could use the rank-size ordering of the elements, f_{ij}, from the largest positive to the smallest negative elements. This form of presentation should assist in the interpretation of the potential impacts of changes induced by prices, structural change, or innovation diffusion and adoption (Hewings et al., 1988b).

Thus, for the simplest case of a change in one input parameter, we have made an analytical presentation of the changes in the associated Leontief inverse through the specification of a field of influence. The general case of a change in all the direct input parameters may be ascertained with the specification of a matrix of incremental changes $E = \|\varepsilon_{ij}\|$. The coefficients, $b_{ij}(E)$ can be presented as a rational function, a ratio of two polynomials, depending on the size of the increments, ε_{ij}, on the components, b_{ij}, of the Leontief inverse matrix and on the cofactors of matrices derived from the matrix $C = (I - A)$ through the removal of certain rows and column:

$$b_{ji}(E) = \frac{b_{ji} + \dfrac{1}{\Delta} \sum_{k=1}^{n-1} (-1)^k \sum_{\substack{i_r \neq i_s i \\ j_r \neq j_s j}} \text{Sign}\begin{pmatrix} j_1, \ldots, j_k, j \\ i_1, \ldots, i_k, i \end{pmatrix} M\begin{pmatrix} j_1, \ldots, j_k, j \\ i_1, \ldots, i_k, i \end{pmatrix} \varepsilon_{i_1 j_1}, \ldots, \varepsilon_{i_k j_k}}{1 - \displaystyle\sum_{i_1 j_1}^{n} b_{j_1 i_1} \varepsilon_{i_1 j_1} + \dfrac{1}{\Delta} \sum_{k=2}^{n} (-1)^k \sum_{\substack{i_r \neq i_s \\ j_r \neq j_s}} \text{Sign}\begin{pmatrix} j_1, \ldots, j_k \\ i_1, \ldots, i_k \end{pmatrix} M\begin{pmatrix} J_1, \ldots, j_k \\ i_1, \ldots, i_k \end{pmatrix} \varepsilon_{i_1 j_1}, \ldots, \varepsilon_{i_k j_k}}$$

$$\tag{17-6}$$

where

$$\Delta = \det(I - A)$$

$$M\begin{pmatrix} j_1, \ldots, j_k \\ i_1, \ldots, i_k \end{pmatrix} = \text{the determinant derived from } \Delta \text{ by removal of rows } i_1, \ldots, i_k$$

$$\text{and columns } j_1, \ldots, j_k$$

$$\text{Sign}\begin{pmatrix} j_1, \ldots, j_k \\ i_1, \ldots, i_k \end{pmatrix} = (-1)^{i_1 + \ldots, i_k + j_1, \ldots, j_k + \sigma(i_1, \ldots, i_k) + \sigma(j_1, \ldots, j_k)}$$

and

$$\sigma(i_1, \ldots, i_k) = \text{the odd or even index of the permutation } (i_1, \ldots, i_k)$$

The reader can find the derivation of this fundamental formula in Sonis and Hewings (1988b). With this formula, we are now in a position to elaborate on general error and sensitivity analysis, drawing on the notions of inverse-important input coefficients, and developing approximate additive superposition of first-order effects, the super-position of the cross-effects and synergistic effects that arise when more than one error occurs in the A matrix.

Furthermore, the previous considerations can be transferred to the analysis of dynamic changes associated with the biproportional or RAS procedure (Bacharach, 1970). Briefly, recall the standard RAS procedure relating coefficients a_{ij} and a_{ij}^* at two different time periods (or between two regions or a region and the nation at the same time period):

$$a_{ij}^* = r_i a_{ij} s_j$$

Let $r_i = 1 + \varepsilon_i$ and $s_j = 1 + \sigma_j$, then

$$a_{ij}^* = r_i a_{ij} s_j = a_{ij}(1 + \varepsilon_i + \sigma_j + \varepsilon_i \sigma_j) = a_{ij} + \varepsilon_{ij}$$

where

$$\varepsilon_{ij} = a_{ij}(\varepsilon_i + \sigma_j + \varepsilon_i \sigma_j)$$

In this case, the coefficient change, ε_{ij}, is defined to bear some special relationship to a previous value. Clearly, the RAS technique may be seen as a special case of error analysis, which places it within a broader view of coefficient change.

Inverse-Important Input Coefficients

The notion of inverse-important input coefficients is based on the conception of the field of influence associated with the change in only one input coefficient. If this change occurs in (i_i, j_i), that is,

$$\varepsilon_{ij} = \begin{cases} \varepsilon & i = i_1, j = j_1 \\ 0 & i \neq i_1 \text{ or } j \neq j_1 \end{cases}$$

then the fundamental formula (17-6) provides

$$b_{ji}(\varepsilon) = \frac{b_{ji} - \dfrac{1}{\Delta} \operatorname{Sign}\begin{pmatrix} j_1 j \\ i_1 i \end{pmatrix} M\begin{pmatrix} j_1 j \\ i_1 i \end{pmatrix} \varepsilon}{1 - b_{j_1 i_1} \varepsilon} \qquad i \neq i_1; j \neq j_1 \tag{17-7}$$

$$b_{ji}(\varepsilon) = \frac{b_{ji}}{1 - b_{j_1 i_1} \varepsilon} \qquad i = i_1 \text{ or } j = j_1$$

or, alternatively, define

$$I = I\begin{pmatrix} j_1 j \\ i_1 i \end{pmatrix} = \begin{cases} \dfrac{1}{\Delta} \operatorname{Sign}\begin{pmatrix} j_1 j \\ i_1 i \end{pmatrix} M\begin{pmatrix} j_1 j \\ i_1 i \end{pmatrix} & i \neq i_1; j \neq j_1 \\ 0 & i = i_1 \text{ or } j = j_1 \end{cases} \tag{17-8}$$

then

$$b_{ji}(\varepsilon) = \frac{b_{ji} - I\varepsilon}{1 - b_{j_1 i_1} \varepsilon} \tag{17-9}$$

which is equivalent to formula (17-1). For each cell, the corresponding field of influence, that is, the matrix $F = F(i_1, j_1) = \|f_{ij}\| = \|b_{ij}b_{j_1,i_1} - I(^{j_1,j}_{i_1,i})\|$ can be constructed with the decomposition (17-4) to provide the effects of changes in each individual coefficient of the Leontief inverse matrix, $B(\varepsilon_{i_1,j_1})$. In addition, we can evaluate the cumulative effects of change and compare the cumulative effects of changes in individual coefficients to identify those that may be said to be inverse-important, namely, the change in these coefficients that will create the greatest impact upon the rest of the economy.

The next step is the formulation of the decision rule identifying when coefficient $a_{i_1 j_1}$ is inverse-important. This decision rule will preserve only a relatively small number of the rank-size sequence and this set will comprise the inverse-important coefficients. It is important to stress that the choice of the measure of cumulative effect in the formulation of the decision or cutting rule depends on the investigator's viewpoint.

The notion of inverse-important parameters can be connected with the fields of influence on column multipliers. The decomposition shown in (17-5) can be modified for the evaluation of change in individual coefficients on column multipliers in much the same way as that performed by West (1982). Following West's developments, let $M_j = \sum_{i=1}^n b_{ij}$ and

$$f_j \binom{i_1}{j_1} = f_j = \sum_{i=1}^n f_{ij}; \qquad I_j \binom{j_1}{i_1} = I_j = \sum_{i=1}^n I\binom{j_1 j}{i_1 i} \qquad (17\text{-}10)$$

then

$$f_j = b_{j_1 i_1} M_j - I_j$$

and

$$M_j(\varepsilon) = M_j + f_j\varepsilon + b_{j_1 i_1} f_j\varepsilon^2 + \cdots + b_{j_1 i_1}^{s-1} f_j\varepsilon^s + \cdots + \qquad (17\text{-}11)$$

For the j_1th column, $I_{i_1} = 0$ [from Equation (17-8)]; therefore,

$$f_{j_1} = b_{j_1 i_1} M_{j_1}$$

and

$$M_j(\varepsilon) = M_j(1 + b_{j_1 i_1}\varepsilon + b_{j_1 i_1}^2\varepsilon^2 + \cdots) = M_{n_1}/(1 - b_{j_1 i_1}\varepsilon) \qquad (17\text{-}12)$$

The condition (17-11) can be presented in vectorial form: let $\bar{M} = (M_1, M_2, \ldots, M_n)$ be a vector of column multipliers and $f = (f_1, f_2, \ldots, f_n)$ be a vector of first-order influences, then,

$$\bar{M}(\varepsilon) = \bar{M} + \bar{f}\varepsilon + b_{j_1 i_1}\bar{f}\varepsilon^2 + \cdots + b_{j_1 i_1}^{s-1}\bar{f}\varepsilon^s + \cdots$$

$$= \bar{M} + \sum_{s=1}^\infty b_{j_1 i_1}^{s-1}\bar{f}\varepsilon \qquad (17\text{-}13)$$

Changes in the Column (Row)

In addition to consideration of changes in individual elements, we may also consider changes in whole rows or columns (see West, 1986 for the development of a similar framework); in this fashion, we may note again that the procedure may devolve into the RAS adjustment if both row and column effects are considered. Consider the change, $\bar{\varepsilon}_{j_0}$, in the j_0th column, that is,

$$\varepsilon_{ij} = \begin{cases} \varepsilon_{ij} & j = j_0 \\ 0 & j \neq j_0 \end{cases}$$

The procedure proposed earlier can be adapted for the evaluation of the field of influence H; for ε small enough,

$$H \approx [B(\bar{\varepsilon}_{j_0}) - B]/\varepsilon \tag{17-14}$$

The same procedure holds for changes that take place in one row. Further details and proofs are provided in Sonis and Hewings (1988b).

Approximate Additive Superposition of First-Order Effects

Thus far, we have not considered the cumulative or synergistic effects of errors occurring throughout the matrix. In this and the next section, we will describe the structure of first-order effects of small changes of each input coefficient of the matrix $A = \|a_{ij}\|$. For the evaluation of first-order effects, we can choose the error matrix $E = \|\varepsilon_{ij}\|$, with small errors ε_{ij} such that the products $\varepsilon_{i_1 j_1} \varepsilon_{i_2 j_2}$ will be negligible (hence, may be ignored). Under this condition, the approximative additive superposition of first-order effects holds, namely,

$$B(E) - B \approx \sum F\binom{j_1}{i_1} \varepsilon_{i_1 j_1} = \sum_{i_1 j_1} [B(\varepsilon_{i_1 j_1}) - B] \tag{17-15}$$

This formula may be derived from the approximate formula considered in the previous section. Thus, the cumulative first-order effect of changes is the sum of all individual first-order effects associated with the changes in each individual cell (i_i, j_i). This analogous approximate superposition principle holds also for the column multipliers [see Equation (17-13)]:

$$\bar{M}(E) - \bar{M} \simeq \sum_{i_1 j_1} \bar{f}\binom{j_1}{i_1} \varepsilon_{i_1 j_1} = \sum_{i_1 j_1} [M(\varepsilon_{i_1 j_1}) - M] \tag{17-16}$$

The superposition principle can be useful for the analysis of the statistical properties of the error distributions of the elements of the Leontief inverse matrix and column multipliers (West, 1986; Jackson, 1986).

Fields of Pair-Wise Interactions

Consider the error matrix $E = \|\varepsilon_{ij}\|$ under the assumption that only first- and second-degree errors are essential (i.e., nontrivial) and that the products of errors including three or more errors are negligible. In this case, the approximative representation of the increment $B(E) - B$ takes on the following form:[1]

$$B(E) - B \simeq \sum_{i_1 j_1}{}' [B(\varepsilon_{i_1 j_1}) - B] + \sum_{i_1 i_2 j_1 j_2}{}' \left[b_{j_1 i_1} F\binom{j_2}{i_2} + b_{j_2 i_2} F\binom{j_1}{i_1} - F\binom{j_1 j_2}{i_1 i_2} \right] \varepsilon_{i_1 j_1} \varepsilon_{i_2 j_2} \tag{17-17}$$

---

1. The proof is available from the authors upon request.

where $\sum'$ means the sum not including the components corresponding to cases $i_1 = i_2$, $j_1 = j_2$; the matrices $F(^{j_1}_{i_1})$ and $F(^{j_2}_{i_2})$ are the fields of influence of the errors $\varepsilon_{i_1 j_1}$, $\varepsilon_{i_2 j_2}$, and the matrix

$$F\begin{pmatrix} j_1 \, j_2 \\ i_1 i_2 \end{pmatrix} = \left\| f_{ij}\begin{pmatrix} j_1 j_2 \\ i_1 i_2 \end{pmatrix} \right\|$$

includes the components

$$f_{ij}\begin{pmatrix} j_1 j_2 \\ i_1 i_2 \end{pmatrix} = b_{ij} I\begin{pmatrix} j_1 j_2 \\ i_1 i_2 \end{pmatrix} - I\begin{pmatrix} j_1 j_2 j \\ i_1 i_2 i \end{pmatrix}$$

where

$$I\begin{pmatrix} j_1 j_2 \\ i_1 i_2 \end{pmatrix} = \begin{cases} \dfrac{1}{\Delta} \, \text{Sign} \begin{pmatrix} j_1 j_2 \\ i_1 i_2 \end{pmatrix} M \begin{pmatrix} j_1 j_2 \\ i_1 i_2 \end{pmatrix} & \begin{array}{l} i_1 \neq i_2 \\ j_1 \neq j_2 \end{array} \\ 0 & \text{otherwise} \end{cases}$$

$$I\begin{pmatrix} j_1 j_2 j \\ i_1 i_2 i \end{pmatrix} = \begin{cases} \dfrac{1}{\Delta} \, \text{Sign} \begin{pmatrix} j_1 j_2 j \\ i_1 i_2 i \end{pmatrix} M \begin{pmatrix} j_1 j_2 j \\ i_1 i_2 i \end{pmatrix} & \begin{array}{l} i_1 \neq i_2; i_1 \neq i; i_2 \neq i \\ j_1 \neq j_2; j_1 \neq j; j_2 \neq j \end{array} \\ 0 & \text{otherwise} \end{cases}$$

This formulation provides the structure of the first-order and second-order effects of change in all input coefficients and presents the approximate superposition of first- and second-order effects. For an explanation of this superposition, consider the case of changes in only two cells (i_1, j_1) and (i_2, j_2). Let

$$\varepsilon_{ij} = \begin{cases} \varepsilon_1 = \varepsilon_{i_1 j_1} & i = i_1, j = j_1 \\ \varepsilon_2 = \varepsilon_{i_2 j_2} & i = i_2, j = j_2 \\ 0 & \text{otherwise} \end{cases} \tag{17-18}$$

For such changes, if $i_1 \neq i_2, j_1 \neq j_2$, then

$$B(\varepsilon_1, \, \varepsilon_2) - B \approx [B(\varepsilon_1) - B] + [B(\varepsilon_2) - B] + \left[b_{j_1 i_1} F\begin{pmatrix} j_2 \\ i_2 \end{pmatrix} + b_{j_2 i_2} F\begin{pmatrix} j_1 \\ i_1 \end{pmatrix} - F\begin{pmatrix} j_1 j_2 \\ i_1 i_2 \end{pmatrix} \right] \varepsilon_1 \varepsilon_2$$

$$\tag{17-19}$$

The same type of analysis holds for higher order influences of changes in all input coefficients. However, the approximate formulas assume small changes in the coefficients; in that case, the higher order effects are likely to be negligible, and thus may be ignored.

CONCLUSION

The analysis presented in this chapter provides a general approach to the problem of input coefficient change in input–output systems. In contrast to many preceding techniques, the method described here is general enough to cover changes in an individual coefficient, in two or more coefficients, and in rows or columns of coefficients. Thus, it is general enough to handle almost all cases of coefficient change. When the changes are small, the approximate formulas can be used; otherwise the complete presentation of the error structure needs to be considered. However, the major contribution of the method is the identification of a "field of influence," such that an analyst can visually inspect the "range" or extent of the effect of changes in one or more coefficients. The method should assist in the more rigorous identification of inverse-important parameters, thus contribute to the analysis of those elements of an economic system whose change is likely to be the most significant. In terms of the use of the method in analyzing the effects of structural change, it would appear to have the potential for identifying not only the main parameters of this change, but also the extent of their influence on the rest of the system.

There are a number of areas in which the field of influence might have some utility. First, in the construction of new models or in updating existing ones, resources often permit only a limited amount of information to be collected from survey instruments. Clearly, there is a strong link between importance (in an analytical sense) and the concept of a field of influence, thus creating an opportunity to select elements of the matrix for survey data collection on the basis of the strength of their field of influence. Not enough research has been undertaken to ascertain the degree to which the field for an individual coefficient remains stable as the economy in which it is located evolves.

Second, there may be characteristic fields of influence, particularly of the synergistic kind (involving subsets of coefficients) that may be associated with economies at different stages of development. The identification and classification of these fields might provide another basis for the development of a taxonomy of economies as well as contributing to enriching our understanding of the growth and development processes in economies. Finally, there is a strong potential link between this field approach and the various decompositions of social accounting systems proposed by Pyatt and Round (1979), Defourny and Thorbecke (1974), and Sonis and Hewings (1988a). Alternative decompositions might yield different "fields" within the multiplicative or additive multiplier matrix, thus contribute greater insights into our understanding of the workings of an economy. Some preliminary work with the Brazilian economy (Hewings et al., 1988a) revealed the utility of the method in uncovering some major structural changes from 1959 through 1975. The degree of stability of the "fields of influence" over time and space remains an important component for future research.

ACKNOWLEDGMENTS

M.S. wishes to thank the Fulbright Commission and the George A. Miller Committee of the University of Illinois; G.J.D.H. wishes to acknowledge support from the National Science Foundation (SES 84-05961). The comments of Rodney C. Jensen, Guy R. West, and Randall W. Jackson during the course of an informal input–output workshop at the University of Illinois in May 1986, and the assistance of the book editors are gratefully acknowledged.

REFERENCES

Bacharach, M. 1970. *Biproportional Matrices and Input–Output Change*. Cambridge: Cambridge University Press.
Bullard, C. W., and A. V. Sebald. 1977. "Effects of Parametric Uncertainty and Technological Change in Input–Output Models." *Review of Economics and Statistics*. Vol. 59, pp. 75–81.
Carter, A. P. 1970. *Structural Change in the American Economy*. Cambridge, MA: Harvard University Press.

Crama, Y., J. Defourny, and J. Gazon. 1984. "Structural Decomposition of Multipliers in Input–Output or Social Accounting Matrix Analysis." *Économie Appliquée.* Vol. 37, pp. 215–222.

Defourny, J., and E. Thorbecke. 1984. "Structural Path Analysis and Multiplier Decomposition within a Social Accounting Matrix Framework." *Economic Journal.* Vol. 94, pp. 111–136.

Drud, A., W. Grais, and G. Pyatt. 1985. "An Approach to Macroeconomic Model Building Based on Social Accounting Principles." Report No. DRDISO, World Bank, Washington, D.C.

Evans, W. D. 1954. "The Effect of Structural Matrix Errors on Interindustry Relations Estimates." *Econometrica.* Vol. 22, pp. 461–480.

Hewings, G. J. D. 1984. "The Role of Prior Information in Updating Regional Input–Output Models." *Socio-Economic Planning Sciences.* Vol. 18, pp. 319–336.

Hewings, G. J. D., and M. C. Romanos. 1981. "Simulating Less-Developed Regional Economies under Conditions of Limited Information." *Geographical Analysis.* Vol. 13, pp. 373–390.

Hewings, G. J. D., and W. M. Syversen. 1982. "A Modified Biproportional Method for Updating Regional Input–Output Matrices: Holistic Accuracy Evaluation." *Modeling and Simulation.* Vol. 13, pp. 115–120.

Hewings, G. J. D., M. Fonseca, J. Guilhoto, and M. Sonis. 1988a. "Key Sectors and Structural Change in the Brazilian Economy: A Comparison of Alternative Approaches and Their Policy Implications." *Journal of Policy Modeling* (forthcoming).

Hewings, G. J. D., M. Sonis, and R. C. Jensen. 1988b. "Fields of Influence of Technological Change in Input–Output Models." In *Information Technology: Social and Spatial Perspectives,* edited by P. Nijkamp, I. Orishimo, and G. J. D. Hewings. Berlin and New York: Springer-Verlag, pp. 163–194.

Jackson, R. W. 1986. "The 'Full Description' Approach to the Aggregate Representation in the Input–Output Modeling Framework." *Journal of Regional Science.* Vol. 26, pp. 515–530.

Jackson, R. W., and G. J. D. Hewings. 1984. "Structural Change in a Regional Economy: An Entropy Decomposition Approach." *Modeling and Simulation.* Vol. 15, pp. 241–246.

Jackson, R. W., G. J. D. Hewings, and M. Sonis. 1987. "Economic Structure and Coefficient Change: A Comparative Analysis of Alternative Decomposition Approaches." mimeo.

Jensen, R. C., and G. R. West. 1980. "The Effects of Relative Coefficient Size on Input–Output Multipliers." *Environment and Planning A.* Vol. 12, pp. 659–670.

Jensen, R. C., G. R. West, and G. J. D. Hewings. 1988a. "On the Study of Regional Economic Structure Using Input–Output Tables." *Regional Studies,* Vol. 22, pp. 209–220.

Jensen, R. C., G. J. D. Hewings, M. Sonis, and G. R. West. 1988b. "On a Taxonomy of Economies." *Australian Journal of Regional Studies.* Vol. 2, pp. 3–24.

Lahiri, S. 1976. "Input–Output Analysis with Scale-Dependent Coefficients." *Econometrica.* Vol. 44 pp. 947–962.

Lahiri, S., and S. Satchell. 1986. "Properties of the Expected Value of the Leontief Inverse: Some Further Results." *Mathematical Social Science.* Vol. 11, pp. 69–82.

Lawson, T. 1980. "A 'Rational Modeling' Procedure." *Economics of Planning.* Vol. 16, pp. 105–117.

Matuszewski, T. I., P. R. Pitts, and J. A. Sawyer. 1964. "Linear Programming Estimates of Changes in Input Coefficients." *Canadian Journal of Economics and Political Science.* Vol. 30, pp. 203–210.

Morrison, W. I., and R. G. Thumann. 1980. "A Lagrangian Multiplier Approach to the Solution of a Special Constrained Matrix Problem." *Journal of Regional Science.* Vol. 20, pp. 279–292.

Pyatt, G., and J. I. Round. 1979. "Accounting and Fixed Price Multipliers in a SAM Framework." *Economic Journal.* Vol. 89, pp. 850–873.

Sevaldson, P. 1970. "The Stability of Input–Output Coefficients." In *Applications of Input–Output Analysis,* edited by A. P. Carter and A. Brody. Amsterdam: North Holland, pp. 207–237.

Sherman, J., and W. Morrison. 1950. "Adjustment of an Inverse Matrix Corresponding to a Change in One Element of a Given Matrix." *Annals of Mathematical Statistics.* Vol. 21, pp. 124–127.

Simonovits, A. 1975. "A Note on the Underestimation and Overestimation of the Leontief Inverse." *Econometrica.* Vol. 43, pp. 493–498.

Sonis, M., and G. J. D. Hewings. 1988a. "Superposition and Decomposition Principles in Hierarchical Social Accounting and Input–Output Analysis." In *Recent Advances in Regional Economic Modeling,* edited by F. Harrigan and P. G. McGregor. London: Pion, pp. 46–65.

Sonis, M., and G. J. D. Hewings. 1988b. "A Fundamental Formula for Error/Sensitivity Analysis in Input–Output and Social Accounting Systems." mimeo.

Theil, H. 1957. "Linear Aggregation in Input–Output Analysis." *Econometrica.* Vol. 25, pp. 111–122.

Theil, H. 1972. *Statistical Decomposition Analysis.* Amsterdam: North Holland.

Tilanus, C. B. 1966. *Input–Output Analysis Experiments: The Netherlands, 1948–61.* Rotterdam: Rotterdam University Press.

West, G. R. 1981. "An Efficient Approach to the Estimation of Regional Input–Output Multipliers." *Environment and Planning A.* Vol. 13, pp. 857–867.

West, G. R. 1982. "Sensitivity and Key Sector Analysis in Input–Output Models." *Australian Economic Papers.* Vol. 21, pp. 365–378.

West, G. R. 1986 "A Stochastic Analysis of an Input–Output Model." *Econometrica.* Vol. 54, pp. 363–374.

Wibe, S. 1982. "The Distribution of Input Coefficients." *Economics of Planning.* Vol. 18, pp. 65–70.

18

On the Comparative Accuracy of RPC Estimating Techniques[1]

BENJAMIN H. STEVENS, GEORGE I. TREYZ,
and
MICHAEL L. LAHR

The problem of assessing the accuracy of nonsurvey regional input–output models, particularly in comparison with survey-based models, has been discussed at great length by Morrison and Smith (1974), Smith and Morrison (1974), Latham and Montgomery (1979), Harrigan et al. (1980), Round (1983), Sawyer and Miller (1983), Stevens et al. (1983), Richardson (1985), Willis (1987), Lahr (1987) and Robison and Miller (1988). The present authors have little to add, at this point, to the debate about how best to compare models and what conclusions can be drawn if a nonsurvey model is relatively successful (or unsuccessful) in simulating a survey-based model.

It is worth reiterating, however, that most survey-based models are based only partially on survey data, that surveys are usually incomplete and/or otherwise partly flawed, and that survey-based models are usually fairly aggregated: a high level of aggregation may generate greater errors, when the model is applied, than those caused by the use of estimated data in nonsurvey models, which are generally much more disaggregated. In any case, survey-based models are not necessarily the best standards for comparison (Stevens, 1987), in spite of the fact that most nonsurvey modelers (Stevens et al., 1983) have generally had nothing else with which to compare their results.

As an alternative to the usual survey/nonsurvey model comparisons, a more direct comparison is suggested here. There seems to be general agreement (Stevens and Trainer, 1976, 1980; Park et al., 1981), although there is some dissent (Garhart, 1985) that the accuracy of the regional purchase coefficients (RPCs) is the most crucial factor in determining the accuracy of any regional input–output model.

Recall that an RPC is commonly defined as the proportion of the regional demand for a good or service that is fulfilled by regional production as opposed to imports from other regions. Accurate estimation of RPCs is thus basic to the specialization of a set of national technological input–output coefficients to a given region. In particular, RPCs determine the extent to which indirect and induced

1. This is a substantially revised version of a paper presented at the Input–Output Sessions of the 33rd North American Meetings of the Regional Science Association on Nov. 15, 1986.

purchases become actual changes in the outputs of a region's industries. Thus, over- or underestimation of RPCs will cause over- or underestimation of secondary feedback effects on the regional economy.

This chapter will focus on a rather direct comparison of alternative methods, based on readily obtainable data, for nonsurvey model regionalization. This is done by testing each estimation method for its accuracy in reproducing a known set of RPCs.

In the next section, the methods for obtaining an observed set of RPCs are discussed. Following that, the Regional Science Research Institute (RSRI) estimation method is compared with the most common alternative methods, both for overall accuracy and for accuracy in predicting large versus small RPCs. Some comments concerning the simple methods and their potential for improvement through easy linear adjustments, plus a few concluding remarks, complete the chapter.

OBSERVED RPCs

A sample of "observed" RPCs has been estimated by the RSRI staff. The authors are confident that the sample data set is as accurate as possible, given that the estimates must be based on secondary data sources. These sources include the 1977 national input–output data, reported by the Bureau of Economic Analysis (BEA), U.S. Department of Commerce; 1977 County Business Patterns (CBP) and 1977 Census of Transportation (COT) data, reported by the Bureau of the Census; and data included in the Regional Economic Information Service (REIS) of BEA.

The first phase in constructing the "observed" RPCs by the RSRI method is to estimate total supplies and total (local) demands for each sector in each state. This consists of a multistep procedure to ensure consistency. The procedure is briefly described in an earlier form in Stevens et al. (1983) and in more recent form and greater detail in the appendix to Treyz and Stevens (1985). To recapitulate, supplies are estimated using both earnings by sector by state and BEA input–output coefficients for earnings per dollar of output. Regional earnings are estimated initially from CBP at the four-digit level, but are then adjusted so that totals of four-digit components in each two-digit industry for each state sum to the earnings reported in REIS. These latter data are consistent across states, so that national two-digit earnings are exactly the sums of state earnings.

Next, using a biproportional adjustment procedure, the estimated 1977 four-digit outputs are adjusted across states to sum to the corresponding U.S. outputs reported in the 1977 BEA table. Thus, final supplies are consistent both within and across states. Once supplies are estimated, demands are calculated using methods introduced in Stevens et al. (1983), but improved by better estimates of regional final demand by federal, state, and local governments, for capital equipment, etc.

The 1977 COT provides (some) detailed shipment data for selected commodities for some states. From these data, it is possible to calculate the proportion, PS_i^k, of all shipments of a selected commodity, i, produced in a particular state, k, that have an intrastate destination, but only for those limited number of state/commodity combinations reported in COT. After adjustments for small samples of shipments and other data anomalies, this process resulted in 1,116 observations out of a potential of 23,001 state and four-digit standard industrial classification (SIC) combinations.

The "observed" RPCs are then calculated using the basic formula

$$RPC_i^k = PS_i^k S_i^k / D_i^k \qquad (18\text{-}1)$$

where

PS_i^k = proportion of the total shipments of good i from industry i in state k with destinations within k

S_i^k = total output of i in k

D_i^k = total intrastate demand for i in k.

The initial estimates of "observed" RPCs are later adjusted to conform to observed two-digit control values, as described by Treyz and Stevens (1985). The comparisons made below, however, are based on the initial estimates.

ESTIMATION METHODS

In the RSRI approach, the RPCs are estimated by a nonlinear predicting equation, fitted as described below. For the alternatives, simpler and long-used estimating techniques are employed.

RSRI's Estimation Technique

The "observed" RPCs became the dependent variables in a regression analysis designed to fit an estimating equation. This equation is used, in turn, to predict RPCs for all sectors for all regions from the county level up. The latest RSRI estimating equation for RPCs differs substantially from that reported in Stevens et al. (1983) and is also different from, though similar in principle to, that reported in Treyz and Stevens (1985). The new equation used here is presented in the Appendix.

Alternative RPC Estimating Techniques

The alternative RPC estimating methods compared here are the traditional location quotient based on employment (LQE), the analogous location quotient based on supply (LQS), and the supply/demand ratio (SDR). These alternative methods have been used in constructing various nonsurvey models. The definition of each of these measures and its use in estimating RPCs are presented in the Appendix.

The simple LQE approach was the basic method for a number of years, starting at least before Schaffer and Chu (1969). It was used in the Regional Impact Multiplier System (RIMS) I (Drake, 1976) but recently has been somewhat less in favor. The LQS method is similar to the RIMS II method (Cartwright et al., 1981); however, the earnings location quotients used in RIMS II could not be reproduced exactly here, because some of the data used in RIMS II are not available to the public. In any case, supply and earnings are very highly correlated. The SDR method was recently used by IMPLAN (an acronym for Impact Analysis for Planning) (Alward and Palmer, 1981).

For each of these alternative methods, the same general rule is followed: if the measure being used is less than 1, the RPC estimate is set equal to the measure; otherwise, the RPC is set equal to 1. The most obvious result of this rule is that cross-hauling is assumed not to occur; a state will always supply its own needs first and will export a commodity only when its RPC = 1, implying that it will not both export and import the same commodity.

RESULTS OF COMPARISONS

Table 18-1 presents the comparisons of the RPC estimates with the observed RPCs. These include (1) the use of the estimates both raw and unadjusted, (2) linear regression of the observed on the estimated RPCs, and (3) a corresponding linear regression with logarithmic transforms of the observed and estimated RPCs (henceforth, log-linear regression). Also included are the root mean square error (RMSE) and Theil's inequality index (U) (Theil et al., 1966) along with three components of U: bias proportion (U_m), variance proportion (U_s), and covariance proportion (U_c).

Theil's U (when multiplied by 100) can be broadly interpreted as the overall percentage RMSE as indicated by the formula

$$U = \left[\sum_i (P_i - A_i)^2 \Big/ \sum_i A_i^2 \right]^{0.5} \tag{18-2}$$

where the Ps and As are the predicted and actual (observed) values, respectively. RMSE, itself, is the same as the numerator in Equation (18-2) divided by the number of observations. The RMSE and U results are also reported in Table 18-1 for large ($\geqslant 0.3$) and small (< 0.3) RPCs for reasons to be discussed below.

The main reason for presenting the linear regression results in Table 18-1 is that it was hypothesized that the three alternative methods would systematically and grossly overestimate the RPCs. This hypothesis is based both on the previous experience of two of the current authors in using these measures and on the inherent characteristics of the measures themselves (Isserman, 1977a; Stevens et al., 1979). In particular, none of the three allows for cross-hauling, which is known to be common (or endemic) and is evidenced, at least to some degree, for virtually all of the 1,116 state/SIC combinations used in this analysis.

If the three alternative methods tend to overestimate the RPCs, we would expect that linear regression equations, with slopes substantially less than 1, would enable raw measures to provide improved predictions of RPCs. This is strongly evidenced in the results presented in Table 18-1, where slopes for the linear equations (for all observations) vary between 0.349 and 0.379 for the three alternative methods (compared with a slope of 0.938 for the RSRI method).

The linear predicting equations for the alternative methods, as would be expected, also make a very substantial reduction in RMSE and U. Linear regression achieves this improvement mainly by eliminating the bias proportion, U_m, with concomitant increases in the variance and covariance proportions, U_s and U_c. The latter, as Theil notes, is usually very difficult to reduce. The variance proportion, on the other hand, can generally be reduced by the inclusion of additional explanatory variables in the predicting equation. This was not done here for two reasons. First, the highly nonlinear relationships between the observed RPCs and the LQs and SDR put severe limits on the explanatory power of any linear equation. Regression experiments indicated that added linear variables were generally nonsignificant, did not add measureably to R^2, or both.

TABLE 18-1 Comparison of Four Major Methods for Estimating Regional Purchase Coefficients

	RSRI			IQE			LQS			SDR		
	Raw	Linear	Log	Raw	Linear	Log	Raw	Linear	Log	Raw	Linear	Log
All RPCs												
R^2	—	0.450	0.391	—	0.143	0.276	—	0.144	0.276	—	0.160	0.306
Intercept	—	0.012	−0.954	—	−0.004	−1.480	—	0.008	−1.462	—	−0.019	−1.446
Slope	—	0.938	0.534	—	0.358	1.271	—	0.349	1.232	—	0.379	1.362
RMSE	0.190	0.190	0.240	0.617	0.237	0.263	0.609	0.236	0.262	0.609	0.234	0.260
Theil's U	0.485	0.484	0.612	1.575	0.604	0.671	1.554	0.604	0.669	1.555	0.598	0.663
U_m	0.001	0.000	0.196	0.774	0.000	0.177	0.761	0.000	0.175	0.777	0.000	0.171
U_s	0.147	0.197	0.563	0.001	0.451	0.512	0.001	0.450	0.501	0.000	0.429	0.502
U_c	0.852	0.803	0.241	0.225	0.549	0.311	0.238	0.550	0.324	0.223	0.571	0.327
Large RPCs (≥ 0.3)												
RMSE	0.231	0.172	0.176	0.435	0.294	0.396	0.426	0.293	0.394	0.426	0.289	0.390
Theil's U	0.389	0.289	0.296	0.733	0.496	0.668	0.718	0.494	0.664	0.718	0.486	0.656
U_m	0.321	0.000	0.023	0.760	0.609	0.786	0.752	0.615	0.788	0.785	0.613	0.787
U_s	0.020	0.444	0.547	0.011	0.212	0.141	0.007	0.208	0.138	0.017	0.223	0.143
U_c	0.659	0.556	0.430	0.229	0.179	0.073	0.240	0.177	0.075	0.198	0.164	0.070
Small RPCs (<0.3)												
RMSE	0.158	0.073	0.083	0.712	0.189	0.104	0.704	0.190	0.107	0.704	0.190	0.108
Theil's U	1.060	0.490	0.560	4.788	1.227	0.703	4.733	1.276	0.718	4.737	1.278	0.726
U_m	0.387	0.000	0.205	0.835	0.645	0.216	0.820	0.641	0.212	0.831	0.617	0.215
U_s	0.145	0.294	0.448	0.098	0.016	0.009	0.108	0.016	0.005	0.101	0.026	0.002
U_c	0.468	0.706	0.347	0.067	0.339	0.775	0.072	0.343	0.783	0.068	0.357	0.783

Note: All regression parameters are significant at the 0.01 level or better. Total observations = 1116. Large RPC observations = 444. Small RPC observations = 672.

Second, the experiments performed here were designed to test the various RPC estimating techniques currently in "vogue." The addition of other explanatory variables to the predicting equations of the alternative methods would have at least violated the spirit of this study, if not its practical purposes. The point, after all, is that the simple estimation methods, though inadequate in their basic form, can be substantially improved through simple adjustments.

With regard to the RSRI estimates, note from Table 18-1 that their use in a linear predicting equation provides no real reduction in error, at least for the total sample. This is, in part, because the bias proportion is already effectively zero in the original estimates. However, the linear equation does increase U_s relative to U_c, so that it might seem to call for further explanatory variables. The RSRI estimating equation already includes all the explanatory variables, out of a wide array of possibilities, that could be found to enter with coefficients significant at the 5 percent level. Additional variables in a "secondary" regression would raise problems of interpretation and significance not justified by the modest improvement that might be made over using the RSRI estimates in their raw form.

The log-linear regression results are included because those relationships between LQ and SDR measures and the RPCs that were found in the course of RSRI's research were generally nonlinear. RSRI's current estimating equation is, itself, highly nonlinear (see Appendix) although not so much as that reported in Treyz and Stevens (1985); thus, no improvement was expected (or found) in the attempt to predict the logs of the observed RPCs with the logs of the RSRI estimates.

The R^2s for the alternative methods are generally higher for the log-linear than for the linear predicting equation, as expected, but the error levels are also higher. This is because these RMSE and U measures are based not on logarithms, but on raw RPCs and their retransformed (unlogged) estimates.

Regression experiments indicated that the errors could be reduced and the R^2s raised by adding variables to these log-linear equations, but the improvement is only marginal. Once the full-scale regression approach is adopted, it makes more sense to move to the RSRI equation, which universally gives better results than equations containing SDR or either of the LQs.

Although some bias error might be expected to occur in retransforming from the log form, the bias proportions in the log-linear results for the alternative methods seem high relative to those resulting from the linear predicting equations. The cause for this might be that the LQ and SDR estimates of the RPCs are truncated at a maximum value of 1, thereby creating a discontinuity in the range of the estimates. A fairer test might be to see if using the LQs and SDRs in untruncated form might reduce the error levels.

Results of this second experiment appear in Table 18-2. Not surprisingly, the errors associated with the raw estimates are extremely large because many of the LQs and SDRs are substantially greater than 1, which is the logical upper limit for any RPC. Again, a linear predicting equation substantially reduces these errors, but not to levels as low as those observed in Table 18-1. Contrary to expectations, error levels for the nonlinear predicting equations are higher than those for the linear equations, although the bias proportions are not as high as those found in Table 18-1. Overall, it appears that truncating alternative measures at 1 yields better results under all conditions.

TABLE 18-2 Comparison of Nontruncated Forms of Three Alternative Methods for Estimating Regional Purchase Coefficients

	LQE			LQS			SDR		
	Raw	Linear	Log	Raw	Linear	Log	Raw	Linear	Log
R^2	—	0.008	0.194	—	0.054	0.208	—	0.052	0.222
Intercept	—	0.291	−2.000	—	0.256	−1.984	—	0.239	−1.952
Slope	—	0.002	0.608	—	0.019	0.634	—	0.034	0.745
RMSE	11.640	0.255	0.321	3.663	0.249	0.274	2.183	0.249	0.274
Theil's U	29.710	0.650	0.820	9.352	0.635	0.699	5.572	0.635	0.699
U_m	0.046	0.000	0.090	0.262	0.000	0.132	0.412	0.000	0.134
U_s	0.915	0.834	0.009	0.645	0.622	0.147	0.446	0.628	0.187
U_c	0.039	0.166	0.901	0.093	0.378	0.721	0.142	0.372	0.679

Note: All regression parameters are significant at the 0.01 level or better.

ERRORS IN RPCs BY SIZE

The rest of the results in Table 18-1 show error levels separately for large and small RPCs. Large and small RPCs are defined by the observations that are above or below a threshold of 0.3, the mean of the observations. RMSEs are larger and U values lower for large RPCs than their counterparts for small RPCs. This was expected, given the nature of these two measures, with RMSE and U being measures of absolute and relative error, respectively.

Observe here that, for the alternative measures, the RMS and U errors for small RPCs are noticeably reduced by the log-linear predicting equation in comparison with the raw and linear equation results. However, this is not true for the large RPCs, at least in comparison with linear equation results. Only in the case of the RSRI estimates do linear and log estimating equations seem to have almost neutral results for both small and large RPCs. More important, errors in the RSRI estimates of the large RPCs average only about 60 percent of the error levels found in using any version of the alternative methods.

This is important, because the larger entries in a regional input–output coefficient matrix are usually the most important determinants of model accuracy, as shown by Jensen and West (1980) and, more recently, Szyrmer (Chapter 19, this volume). However, recall that the entries in a regional matrix, r_{ij}^k, are implicitly equal to $a_{ij} \times RPC_i^k$. Thus, a large RPC does not necessarily imply a large r_{ij}^k if the corresponding a_{ij} (national technical coefficient) is small. On the other hand, it is even more unlikely that an r_{ij}^k will be large if its RPC is small; therefore, in general, we would still expect the larger RPCs to be the most important in determining model accuracy.

Unfortunately, although the RSRI equation is better than the alternatives for all sizes of RPCs, there is still more unexplained variation than most analysts would like to accept. However, to date no additional variation has been explainable by the kinds of variables that we are likely to have available to estimate RPCs, especially at the substate level.

RELATIVE CHARACTERISTICS OF
THE ALTERNATIVE METHODS

A few additional comments about the alternative methods are needed. Although the SDR method does not dominate the LQ methods by as much as might have been expected, it is certainly the second choice after RSRI's approach. All three of the alternative methods are based on the reasonable assumption that the greater the ratio of regional supply to regional demand, the more a region is likely to buy from itself; however, LQE and LQS measures are only proxies for this ratio, whereas the SDR is the ratio itself. Hence, to the extent that LQ methods fail to reflect accurately the supply/demand ratios, they should also fail to give as good results as the SDR method. Note that this conflicts with the conclusions of Sawyer and Miller (1983) and Morrison and Smith (1974) who find, in their tests, that the SDR method produces regional models whose overall accuracy when compared with survey-based models is inferior to those produced by LQ methods.[2]

There are reasons why neither type of LQ may be a satisfactory proxy for SDR. The most obvious is that either type of LQ, measured relative to the ratios for the United States, would equal the regional supply/demand ratio, only in the unlikely event that the industrial structure of the region were identical to that of the nation. For the LQE to equal the supply/demand ratio, furthermore, the labor intensity of the region's industries would also have to equal that of the nation.

Even given accurate measurement, the SDR or one of its proxies would be a good estimate of the RPC only if there were, in fact, no interregional cross-hauling (Isserman, 1977b). However, as already noted, cross-hauling is the rule rather than the exception for observed RPCs and doubtless for unobserved shipment patterns as well (Treyz and Stevens, 1981).

Current research on cross-hauling estimation (Begg and Isserman, 1986) may eventually develop a simple means for adjusting alternative measures so that they compare more closely to true RPCs. But, for the moment, we agree with Willis (1987) and Robison and Miller (1988) that LQ methods will generally give biased results, particularly if used in raw form.

CONCLUDING REMARKS

The authors feel that the superiority of the RSRI estimation method for RPCs is clearly demonstrated in comparison with alternative methods. However, in all fairness to LQ methods, a few comments should be added. First, the earnings location quotient used in RIMS II, though not available for this study, may indeed by substantially more accurate than the LQS (and LQE) used here in estimating observed RPCs. Second, of all methods, by far the easiest to use is the LQE. The required data can be derived from CBP, and the calculations are simple. Hence, for quick and dirty estimates, the LQE is probably still the best choice and deserves the popularity it has long enjoyed.

We can only hope, however, that those who use LQ methods in the future will apply the simple transformations implied by the linear regression results reported in

---

2. This may be because some of the constructors of survey-based models used LQ methods to estimate RPCs for sectors for which survey data were not available. At least one regional input–output modeler hinted to the authors that this is the case.

Table 18-1; this would markedly improve the accuracy of their RPC estimates, especially by eliminating their overestimation bias. Similar advice to users of SDR may not be necessary, because it appears that IMPLAN, the major user of this method, is now converting to an estimation method analogous to that used by RSRI in its new IMPLAN II model (Despotakis, 1985).

The reader can still reasonably question whether any of the methods, even the RSRI estimating equation, is sufficiently accurate for some of the more important decision-making applications to which regional input–output analysis is sometimes put. The only possible response to such doubts is that those who are constructing nonsurvey regional input–output models are doing their best with limited data. RSRI, for its part, will continue to refine, update, and improve its estimating procedures to the extent that the data allow. Unfortunately, such research is being hampered by the fact that the 1982–1983 Census of Transportation is almost totally inadequate for this type of analysis, and it appears that the 1987 COT will probably not be much better.

APPENDIX 18-A: DESCRIPTION OF RPC ESTIMATING METHODS

This Appendix describes the methods used to calculate the RPCs that appear in the comparisons in the body of the chapter. The first section gives a brief description of the RSRI estimating equation; the second and third sections present the traditional formulas for the alternative methods.

RSRI Equation

The current estimating equation used at RSRI is fairly nonlinear, gives predicted RPC values that are strictly between 0 and 1, and was fitted using two-stage step-wise least-squares regression. The basic equation, with commodity subscripts and region superscripts left out for clarity, is

$$RPC = e^{-1/Z} \tag{18-A1}$$

where

$$Z = a \prod_i x_i^{b_i} \tag{18-A2}$$

After repeated logarithmic transformation, Equations (18-A1) and (18-A2) reduce to

$$\ln(-1/\ln RPC) = \ln a + \sum_i b_i \ln x_i \tag{18-A3}$$

the equation to be fitted, where $\ln a$ is the intercept term, the b_is are the regression coefficients, and the x_is are the explanatory variables.

The results are given in Table 18-3. Only two continuous variables are included in the equation—the commodity's U.S. average weight/value ratio as reported in the 1977 COT and the region's share of total U.S. supply provided by the industry producing the commodity—the rest are dummy variables. Because demand does not appear in the equation, and demands are much harder to estimate than supplies, the data required to use the equation to estimate RPCs are, on average, easier to obtain than those used in the estimations reported in Stevens et al. (1983) and Treyz and Stevens (1985).

TABLE 18-3   RSRI RPC Linear Regression Results[a]
(1,116 RPC "Observations")

Variable	Regression Coefficient
Continuous and in natural log form	
Intercept (a)	1.18966
Weight/value ratio	0.18749
Region's share of U.S. sectoral supply	0.50880
Dummy variables	
South Atlantic Census Region	0.19736
West South Central Census Region	0.32299
Pacific Census Region	0.77825
North Carolina	0.35958
California	−0.41998
SIC 24 (lumber and wood products)	0.32678
SIC 27 (printing and publishing)	0.70356
SIC 30 (rubber and miscellaneous plastics)	−0.62156
SIC 36 (electric and electronic equipment)	−0.26169
SIC 38 (instruments and related products)	0.39387
SIC 2013 (sausages and other meats)	0.62169
SIC 2023 (cheese)	2.14378
SIC 2026 (fluid milk)	1.01064
SIC 2048 (prepared animal feeds NEC[b])	0.51194
SIC 2391 (curtains and draperies)	0.84184
SIC 2620 (paper mills, excluding building paper)	−0.37375
SIC 2869 (industrial organic chemicals, NEC)	−0.42265
SIC 3441 (fabricated structural metal)	0.56545
SIC 3532 (mining machinery and equipment)	1.30129
SIC 3599 (machinery, excluding electrical NEC)	1.05501

[a]1116 RPC observations. $R^2 = 0.3358$, F level $= 25.124$, and all variables are significant at the 5 percent level or better for the linear regression. After transformation back to the original form [Equation (18-A1)], $R^2 = 0.4495$ for the final nonlinear predicting equation.

[b]NEC, not elsewhere classified.

Location Quotients (LQE and LQS)

If S_i^k and S^k denote supply of sector i and total output in region k, respectively, and S_i^n and S^n denote these same measures for the nation, then the simple supply location quotient (LQS) for sector i in region k is defined as

$$LQS_i = (S_i^k/S^k)/(S_i^n/S^n) \qquad (18\text{-}A4)$$

The numerator of this measure represents the proportion of the region's supply contributed by sector i. The denominator represents the contribution by sector i to the national economy. Hence, the LQS is a measure of the regional concentration of production in sector i relative to that of the nation. Therefore, when $LQS_i < 1$, the region is less able to satisfy its own demands for i than if it had the same relative concentration of supply of i as the nation; the latter is assumed to be able to fulfill virtually all of its own needs for most commodities.

The assumption is made that the relative concentration of supply, LQS_i, is a proper surrogate for RPC_i, because supply-deficient regions will be able to fulfill relatively less of their internal demands. On the other hand, when $LQS_i > 1$, it is generally assumed that regional demands for sector i goods are totally met and that any surplus from sector i is exported. To represent this mathematically

$$RPC_i = \begin{cases} LQS_i, & \text{if } LQS_i < 1 \\ 1, & \text{if } LQS_i \geqslant 1 \end{cases} \qquad (18\text{-}A5)$$

Because annual data on output are usually not available, many researchers use the employment location quotient (LQE), which is similar in principle to LQS. The only difference is that employment is used as a proxy for supply. Studies have shown that the LQE yields results that are similar, and often superior, to those obtained using LQS (cf. the studies listed in the first paragraph of the text).

Supply–Demand Ratio (SDR)

The ratio of supply to demand would appear, in theory, to be a closer approximation to the true RPC, because it reflects, directly, the region's ability to fulfill its own needs. If $SDR_i < 1$, sector i is viewed as being unable to satisfy its regional demands. Hence,

$$RPC_i = \begin{cases} SDR_i, & \text{if } SDR_i < 1 \\ 1, & \text{if } SDR_i \geqslant 1 \end{cases} \qquad (18\text{-}A6)$$

Note that this estimation method, like the LQ methods, does not allow for cross-hauling.

REFERENCES

Alward, Gregory S., and Charles J. Palmer. 1981. *IMPLAN: An Input–Output Analysis System for Forest Service Planning*. Fort Collins, CO: U.S. Forest Service.

Begg, Robert, and Andrew Isserman. 1986. "Nonsurvey Interregional I–O Models." Paper presented at the 33rd North American Meetings of the Regional Science Association, November 15, Columbus, OH.

Cartwright, Joseph V., Richard M. Beemiller, and Richard D. Gustely. 1981. *RIMS II: Regional Input–Output Modeling System*. Washington, D.C.: U.S. Department of Congress, Bureau of Economic Analysis.

Despotakis, Konstantinus. 1985. *On the Calculation of Gross Regional Trade Flows*. Report EEA-85-01. Berkeley, California: Engineering-Economics Associates.

Drake, Ronald L. 1976. "A Short-Cut to Estimates of Regional Input–Output Multipliers: Methodology and Evaluation." *International Regional Science Review*. Vol. 1, No. 1, pp. 1–18.

Garhart, Robert, Jr. 1985. "The Role of Error Structure in Simulations on Regional Input–Output Analysis." *Journal of Regional Science*. Vol. 25, No. 3, pp. 353–366.

Harrigan, F. J., J. W. McGilvray, and I. H. McNicoll. 1980. "Simulating the Structure of a Regional Economy." *Environment and Planning A*. Vol. 12, pp. 927–936.

Isserman, Andrew M. 1977a. "A Bracketing Approach for Estimating Regional Economic Impact Multipliers and a Procedure for Assessing Their Accuracy." *Environment and Planning A*, Vol. 9, pp. 1003–1011.

Isserman, Andrew M. 1977b. "The Location Quotient Approach to Estimating Regional Economic Impacts." *Journal of the American Institute of Planners*. Vol. 43, No. 1, pp. 33–41.

Jensen, R. C., and G. R. West, 1980. "The Effect of Relative Coefficient Size on Input–Output Multipliers." *Environment and Planning A*. Vol. 12, pp. 659–670.

Lahr, Michael L. 1987. "RPC or RAS?: An Experimental Comparison of Two Nonsurvey Techniques for Estimating Regional Input–Output Relationships." Paper presented at the 25th Meeting of the Southern Regional Science Association, March 27, Atlanta.

Latham, William R., III, and M. Montgomery. 1979. "Methods for Calculating Regional Industry Impact Multipliers." *Growth and Change.* Vol. 10, pp. 2–9.

Morrison, W. I., and P. Smith. 1974. "Nonsurvey Input–Output Techniques at the Small Area Level: An Evaluation." *Journal of Regional Science.* Vol. 14, No. 1, pp. 1–14.

Park, Se-Hark, Malek Mohtadi, and Atif Kubursi. 1981. "Errors in Regional Nonsurvey Input–Output Models: Analytical and Simulation Results." *Journal of Regional Science.* Vol. 21, No. 3, pp. 321–339.

Richardson, Harry R. 1985. "Input–Output and Economic Base Multipliers: Looking Backward and Forward." *Journal of Regional Science.* Vol. 25, pp. 607–661.

Robison, M. Henry and Jon R. Miller. 1988. "Crosshauling and Nonsurvey Input–Output Models: Some Lessons from Small-area Timber Economies." *Environment and Planning A,* Vol. 20, pp. 1523–1530.

Round, Jeffery I. 1983. "Nonsurvey Techniques: A Critical Review of the Theory and the Evidence." *International Regional Science Review.* Vol. 8, pp. 189–212.

Sawyer, C. H., and R. E. Miller. 1983. "Experiments in Regionalization of a National Input–Output Table." *Environment and Planning A.* Vol. 15, pp. 1501–1520.

Schaffer, William A., and Kong Chu. 1969. "Nonsurvey Techniques for Constructing Regional Interindustry Models." *Papers of the Regional Science Association.* Vol. 23, pp. 83–101.

Smith, P., and W. I. Morrison. 1974. *Simulating the Urban Economy: Experiments with Input–Output Techniques.* London: Pion.

Stevens, Benjamin H. 1987. "Comments on 'Ready Made' Regional Input–Output Model Systems: Model Accuracy and the Value of Limited Surveys." *Review of Regional Studies.* Vol. 17, pp. 17–20.

Stevens, Benjamin H., and Glynnis A. Trainer. 1976. "The Generation of Error in Regional Input–Output Impact Models." RSRI Working Paper A1-76, Peace Dale, RI: Regional Science Research Institute.

Stevens, Benjamin H., and Glynnis A. Trainer. 1980. "Error Generation in Regional Input–Output Analysis and Its Implications for Nonsurvey Models." In *Economic Impact Analysis: Methodology and Applications,* edited by Saul Pleeter. Boston, MA: Martinus Nijhoff, pp. 68–84.

Stevens, Benjamin H., George I. Treyz, and David J. Ehrlich. 1979. "On the Estimation of Regional Purchase Coefficients, Export Employment, and Elasticities of Response for Regional Economic Models." RSRI Discussion Paper Series, No. 114, Peace Dale, RI: Regional Science Research Institute.

Stevens, Benjamin H., George I. Treyz, David J. Ehrlich, and James R. Bower. 1983. "A New Technique for the Construction of Non-survey Regional Input–Output Models." *International Regional Science Review.* Vol. 8, pp. 271–294.

Theil, Henri, with G. A. C. Beerens, C. G. DeLeeuw, and C. B. Tilanus. 1966. *Applied Economic Forecasting.* New York: American Elsevier.

Treyz, George I., and Benjamin H. Stevens. 1981. "Location Analysis for Multiregional Modeling." In *Modeling the Multiregional Economic System,* edited by F. Gerard Adams and Norman Glickman. Lexington, MA: Lexington Books, pp. 75–87.

Treyz, George I., and Benjamin H. Stevens. 1985. "The TFS Regional Modelling Methodology." *Regional Studies.* Vol. 19, pp. 547–562.

U.S. Department of Commerce. 1979. *1977 County Business Patterns.* Washington, D.C.: Bureau of the Census, Economic Surveys Division.

U.S. Department of Commerce. 1980. *1977 Census of Transportation: Commodity Transportation Survey.* Washington, D.C.: Bureau of the Census, Business Division.

U.S. Department of Commerce. 1984. *The Input–Output Structure of the U.S. Economy, 1977.* Washington, D.C.: Bureau of Economic Analysis, Interindustry Economics Division.

Willis, K. G. 1987. "Spatially Disaggregated Input–Output Tables: An Evaluation and Comparison of Survey and Nonsurvey Results." *Environment and Planning A.* Vol. 19, pp. 107–116.

19

Trade-Off between Error and Information in the RAS Procedure

JANUSZ SZYRMER

A major drawback of input–output analysis is its heavy input requirements in terms of both money and time necessary to collect the relevant information and to organize it into an input–output transactions matrix format. To describe an economic system composed of n sectors, we need at least $(n \times n) + n$ pieces of data.

For the last two decades, many input–output analysts have focused on methods and techniques for constructing complete tables, using scarce and often very incomplete data. These so-called nonsurvey (or semisurvey) procedures appeared in many cases as practically the only feasible alternative to costly and time-consuming full-survey data collection methods. A large number of nonsurvey techniques have been devised and applied to various economic systems at national, interregional, and regional levels. The availability of a number of full-survey input–output tables has allowed for intensive testing of these approaches. A typical experiment in this area consists of estimating a particular "target" input–output matrix based on the information provided by a "base" matrix and then evaluating the goodness-of-fit of the estimated matrix when compared against the "true" target matrix.[1] There are at least two serious problems in this kind of experiment: (1) lack of direct comparability among various nonsurvey techniques, and (2) lack of a commonly accepted measure of goodness-of-fit.

The lack of direct comparability is a result of the heterogeneous nature of nonsurvey techniques and their different levels of data requirements. It appears inappropriate to compare, for instance, an employment-based location quotient technique that provides estimates based on a few easily available employment figures against a regional purchase coefficient (RPC) estimate (Stevens et al., 1983) or a gravity model estimate (Leontief and Strout, 1963; Theil, 1967; Polenske, 1970), both of which draw on much larger data sets. Also, when using a particular technique, such as RPC or the iterative procedure, RAS, the performance of the technique depends

---

1. Representative examples, in alphabetical order, would include, but not be limited to Czamanski and Malizia (1969), Harrigan et al. (1980), Hewings (1977), Hewings and Janson (1980), Hewings and Syversen (1982), Hinojosa (1978), Hinojosa and Pigozzi (1986), Lynch (1979), Pigozzi and Hinojosa (1985), Sasaki and Shibata (1984), Sawyer and Miller (1983), Schaffer and Chu (1969), and Stevens et al. (1983). A thorough review is provided by Round (1983).

heavily on the quantity and also the quality of the available information on both "base" and "target" data sets.

The lack of a commonly accepted goodness-of-fit measure causes additional problems. Different authors have used different measures, which have unknown distributions and untested properties, and this tends to hamper direct comparability among results. Moreover, there is the issue of whether or not it is appropriate to view a survey-based target data set as representing the "true" values, against which to compare the estimates for their accuracy.

In this chapter, we present the results of the first stage of comprehensive and systematic study of nonsurvey estimation. The chapter is confined to only one nonsurvey technique, namely the RAS,[2] applied to the U.S. national data for four periods: 1963, 1967, 1972, and 1977; three aggregation levels: 7, 23, and 79 sectors; four categories of information: interindustry flows (Z), intermediate output sums (u), intermediate input sums (v), and total gross outputs (x); and two "kinds" of data: transactions (in dollars) and technical coefficients.

Intuitively, we expect that the more information there is available about both "base" and "target" data sets, the more accurate will be the estimation of an input–output matrix. This intuition has been tested empirically by a number of authors and challenged by some of them. Harrigan et al. (1980, p. 935), for example, found that "more complete information results in better simulation performance [for an Adjusted Cross-Industry Location Quotient regionalization technique] on all indices." However, Hewings (1977) questioned the very utility of the base matrix in RAS estimation (at the regional level), because he found that "randomly generated base coefficients could produce estimates almost the equal of those obtained with the locally observed coefficients, or those obtained from the substitution of coefficients from another state" (p. 940). Miernyk (1976, p. 48) criticized RAS both in terms of its conceptual validity—as a method that "substitutes computational tractability for economic logic"—and its operational properties. The latter has been illustrated by the "Miernyk paradox," an example in which an improvement in the available data base leads to a worsening of the estimate of the technical coefficient matrix. (See a numerical example in Miller and Blair, 1985, pp. 292–294.)

In a number of independent experiments, several authors examined the utility of information about certain kinds of data, such as the values of large technical coefficients (Jensen and West, 1980), "major" technical coefficients (Allen, 1974), row and column sums of certain blocks identified within a transactions matrix (Israilevich, 1986), and on-diagonal values of an interregional flow matrix (Szyrmer, 1984). Most of these experiments, however, were "partitive" and fragmentary. The issue is not only knowing what kinds of data are most important in improving estimates, but also knowing when to stop acquiring (at a cost) additional information (Jensen, 1980; Jensen et al., 1979; West, 1981; Phibbs and Holsman, 1982).

From the perspective of applied input–output analysis, the best way to test the various hypotheses and quantify common sense intuition is through a systematic examination of a large number of tables, at different aggregation levels, estimated by different techniques applied at different levels of knowledge (or ignorance) about the true figures. The performance of these techniques should be evaluated by different

---

2. For description of the RAS procedure and its properties see, for example, Stone (1961), Stone and Brown (1962), Bacharach (1970), and Macgill (1977).

criteria, expressed by a number of goodness-of-fit or distance measures. The experiments described herein are intended to shed light on several questions:

- How to express the goodness-of-fit of an input–output table generated by an RAS estimation? What is the behavior of a number of goodness-of-fit or distance measures when applied to the same sequence of tables?
- What is the relationship between the number of pieces of information about an input–output system and the estimation error resulting from application of the RAS procedure? What is the shape of the curve depicting that relationship? How smooth is it? Is this relationship monotonic? How robust is it? Are there any striking regularities that are preserved from simulation to simulation?
- How, if at all, is the estimation error related to the aggregation level?
- Is the accuracy of estimation significantly improved when a more recent data base is applied?
- Is the estimation error for technical coefficient tables similar to that for trans-actions tables?

We describe the preliminary stages of this experiment. The information–error relationship is simulated somewhat mechanically and exclusively in quantitative terms, whereas the results of the simulation are presented mostly in qualitative terms, without more rigorous quantitative analysis. In order to describe the information–error relationship, we count the pieces of data available for a particular run. We did not take account of various qualitative aspects, such as the difference between a matrix cell and a matrix "margin" (the sum of a number of cells), and the difficulty in obtaining a particular piece of data (some figures are more available than others). Thus, all the pieces of information remain unweighted.

DESCRIPTION OF THE EXPERIMENT

Our analysis is confined to U.S. national data for 1963, 1967, 1972, and 1977, as published in the Survey of Current Business (1969, 1974, 1979, 1984). We began by making the four input–output data sets as compatible as possible by reducing them to industry-by-industry 79-sector intermediate transactions tables, which, in turn, we aggregated to 23-sector and 7-sector levels. The corresponding total output vectors were then computed. As a result, the experimental data set was composed of 12 intermediate transactions tables, accompanied by the 12 total output vectors accounting for four benchmark years at three aggregation levels. Hence, for each aggregation level, we created six pairs of tables—1963–1967, 1963–1972, 1963–1977, 1967–1972, 1967–1977, and 1972–1977—with time intervals ranging from 4 to 14 years. The experiments were run in four variants: 1A, 1B, 2A, and 2B. The level of inaccuracy (or "badness-of-fit") of the RAS estimation technique was measured by four distance measures.

The experiments were composed of a large number of "runs." At the beginning of every run, a base transactions matrix Z^B was created from the information included in three matrices: Q, Z^0, and Z^1, where Q = a matrix of random numbers between 0 and 100 drawn from a uniform distribution; Z^0 = a year-0 transactions matrix ($0 = 1963$, 1967, or 1972), and Z^1 = a year-1 transactions matrix ($1 = 1967$, 1972, or 1977). Depending on the variant and stage of simulation Z^B was equal to Q, or to Z^0, or to Z^1, or was a combination of Q and Z^0, or was a combination of Z^0 and Z^1.

Z^B is supposed to represent a certain level of knowledge about a target matrix, Z^1; this knowledge may vary from the complete ignorance case, when $Z^B = Q$, to the perfect information case, when $Z^B = Z^1$. In addition to the base matrix, three "marginal" vectors have to be defined: x^B, u^*, and v^*. These are always based on the information contained in the year-0 and year-1 "margins"—vectors containing total intermediate outputs, u^0 and u^1, vectors containing total intermediate inputs, v^0 and v^1, and total gross output vectors, x^0 and x^1.

Given Z^B, u^*, and v^*, the RAS procedure was applied. After a number of iterations, Z^B is transformed into another transactions matrix, Z^*, such that $Z^*i = u^*$, and $i'Z^* = v^*$, where i is the summation vector (a column of ones). Finally, the estimated transactions matrix, Z^*, is normalized by the base total output vector, x^B, to compute the estimated technical coefficient matrix, A^*. The two projected matrices, Z^* and A^*, are compared with the corresponding target matrices, Z^1 and A^1, by means of several distance measures. The entire experiment is organized around four somewhat arbitrary (but necessary) rules:

Rule 1. The transactions matrix is filled with random numbers when no information about its actual values is available, or with year-0 figures, when year-0 figures are known, but year-1 figures are unknown, or with year-1 figures, when the exact target figures are known.

Rule 2. The margins are composed of year-0 figures, or year-1 figures, or a combination of year-0 figures and year-1 figures. In the case when the sum of the elements in a particular target vector is known while some or all of its elements are unknown, the proportion of an unknown element to the total is assumed to remain constant from year 0 to year 1. (Year-0 figures, in the case of the margins, are always assumed to be known.)

Rule 3. The experiments are implemented in a *ceteris paribus* format. Within a given variant, the number of pieces of information remains constant from run to run for all categories of data except one—and the category that changes is assumed to do so linearly by fixed increments. For example, when the data in the base transactions matrix, Z^B, change, all margins—u^*, v^*, and x^B—remain fixed, and when the number of pieces of information known about the u^1 vector changes, the figures in Z^B, v^*, and x^B remain fixed.

Rule 4. In every variant, the simulations proceed from the lowest to the highest level of information available, by adding consecutive pieces of information in the sequence defined by year-0 data, always from the largest to the smallest cell. For example, when the importance of information on the total output vector is being tested, the experiment starts with year-0 data, which, in n consecutive runs, are replaced with year-1 figures, beginning with the largest element of x^0 and finishing with the smallest element of x^0.

Variants of the Experiment

As noted above, the experiments were run in four different variants. In Variants 1A and 1B, the utility of information contained in the intermediate transactions tables, Z^0 and Z^1, is tested, whereas the margins are kept constant and equal to target margins: $u^* = u^1$, $v^* = v^1$, $x^B = x^1$. In contrast, the utility of the information contained in year-1 margins, given a fixed base transactions matrix, $Z^B = Z^0$, are examined in Variants 2A and 2B. In a sense, the two approaches are almost perfectly symmetric. In the former

(1A and 1B), the target margins are known, and the experiment proceeds by improving knowledge about the transactions matrix—from complete ignorance (i.e., a matrix of random numbers) to the perfect information case when Z^B becomes Z^1. In the latter approach (2A and 2B), the base transactions matrix is fixed, and the experiment proceeds, through consecutive runs, by adding piece by piece the information about target margins. At the starting point, no figures about target margins are available, whereas in the last run of each simulation, a complete set of data about year-1 margins is known.

The difference between the variants "A" and "B" lies in the sequence of execution. In Variant 1A, the information about year-0 and year-1 transactions matrices is added in the same order as that of the Z^0 figures, and in Variant 1B, in the order of the A^0 figures (always from the largest to the smallest). Variants 2A and 2B follow the same principle, but in Variant 2A, the quantity of information available increases first from largest to smallest in u, then in v, then in x, and in Variant 2B, the order is reversed to x, v, and u. In other words, Variants 1A and 1B, as well as 2A and 2B, perform identical simulations, respectively, but in a different sequence of execution. However, the starting and ending points of Variant 1A are identical to the starting and ending points of Variant 1B, and the same is true for Variants 2A and 2B. (More detailed descriptions of the four variants are provided in an earlier version of this paper, noted in the Acknowledgments , and available from the author on request.)

Distance Measures

In these simulations, four distance measures were selected, all of them having been broadly applied in the nonsurvey input–output literature. Table 19-1 contains a summary[3].

Measure 1: Standardized Total Percentage Error (STPE). STPE expresses the average deviation from an average matrix cell; therefore, it is sometimes called the Mean Normalized Deviation. This measure has been recommended by several authors (Miller and Blair, 1983; Szyrmer, 1984; Israilevich, 1986).

Measure 2: Standardized Mean Absolute Difference (SMAD). SMAD, also called Mean Relative Deviation, is a frequently used distance measure in the input–output literature. It has been criticized by many authors for its oversensitivity to the inaccuracy of small cell estimations and its inability to handle zero-valued cells.

Measure 3: Dissimilarity Index (DSI). DSI is supposed to be an improved version of SMAD. It is akin to several measures known from the input–output literature such as the index used by Schaffer and Chu (1969), the "Leontief index," and a measure proposed by Isard and Romanoff (1968), the "similarity index."

Measure 4: Mean Information Content (MIC). MIC is expressed by the Kullback–Leibler formula, which serves as the objective function to be minimized in the RAS constrained optimization problem. MIC denotes the quantity of "new information" contained in a predicted matrix, say Z^*, with respect to an observed (target) matrix Z^1, or the degree to which Z^* perturbs the true information, Z^1. As a distance measure, MIC was applied by Czamanski and Malizia (1969), Morrison and Smith (1974), and others. Like SMAD and DSI, it is not defined when either the estimated cells (z_{ij}^*) or predicted cells (z_{ij}^1) are equal to zero.

3. A recent survey of measures for input–output matrix comparison can be found in Lahr and Szyrmer (1986).

TABLE 19-1   Distance Measures

Measure		Formula[a]	Notes
Number	Title		
1	Standardized Total Percentage Error	$\left[\sum\sum \lvert p_{ij}^{*} - p_{ij}\rvert \Big/ \left(\sum\sum p_{ij}\right)\right] \times 100$	
2	Standardized Mean Absolute Difference	$1/n^{2}\left[\sum\sum \lvert p_{ij}^{*} - p_{ij}\rvert \Big/ p_{ij}\right] \times 100$	$p_{ij} \neq 0$
3	Dissimilarity Index	$1/n^{2}\left[\sum\sum \lvert p_{ij}^{*} - p_{ij}\rvert \Big/ (p_{ij}^{*} + p_{ij})\right] \times 100$	$p_{ij} \neq 0$ or $p_{ij}^{*} \neq 0$
4	Mean Information Content	$\left[\left(\sum\sum p_{ij}^{*}\lvert\ln(p_{ij}^{*}/p_{ij})\rvert \Big/ \sum\sum p_{ij}\right)\right] \times 100$	$p_{ij} \neq 0$ and $p_{ij}^{*} \neq 0$

[a] $P = n \times n$ observed data matrix, and $P^{*} = n \times n$ projected data matrix.

RESULTS

A major objective of these experiments is to evaluate the "utility" of certain categories of information in the RAS procedure. The simulations generate trade-off curves between information and error. The marginal utility of information is measured by the changes in the estimation error levels. The more useful the information, the larger the increase in the estimation accuracy, that is, the greater the decrease in the estimation error.

Representative results are presented in Figures 19-1 through 19-10. Each figure consists of a two-dimensional plot, in which the horizontal axis accounts for the number of pieces of information, whereas the magnitude of the estimation error is measured on the vertical axis. (Note that the scales and ranges of both axes vary from figure to figure.) In Variants 1A and 1B, the number of pieces of information increases gradually from 0 (when $Z^{B} = Q$), to n^{2} (when $Z^{B} = Z^{0}$), to $n^{2} + n^{2}$ (when $Z^{B} = Z^{1}$); therefore, for a 79-sector matrix, the maximum number of pieces of information is $79 \times 79 + 79 \times 79 = 12{,}482$, for which the estimation error is always zero. In Variants 2A and 2B, the number of pieces of information increases from 0 to n, $2n$, and $3n$, which reflects the sequence of year-1 margins. The maximum number on the horizontal axis ($79 \times 3 = 237$, in the case the 79-sector tables) corresponds to the situation when all three year-1 margins (u, v, and x) are known.

The figures present only a small, but illustrative, sample of these preliminary results organized into five topics: (1) distance measures, (2) coefficients versus transactions, (3) Variants "A" versus "B", (4) time intervals, and (5) aggregation levels.

Distance Measures

Figures 19-1 and 19-2 present results for the 79-sector 1972–1977 estimations, for transactions and coefficients, respectively. The four distance measures are strongly correlated and tend to change in the same direction in general, although this is not the

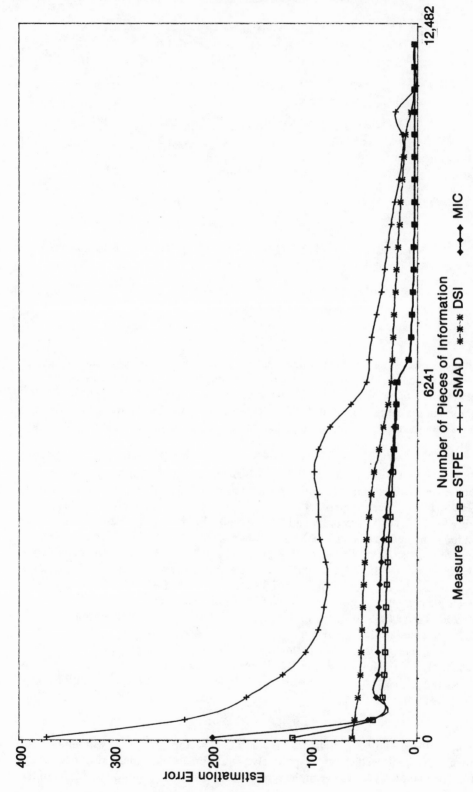

FIGURE 19-1   Estimation error measures: Variant 1A, U.S. 79-sector transactions, 1972–1977 (known: u_1, v_1).

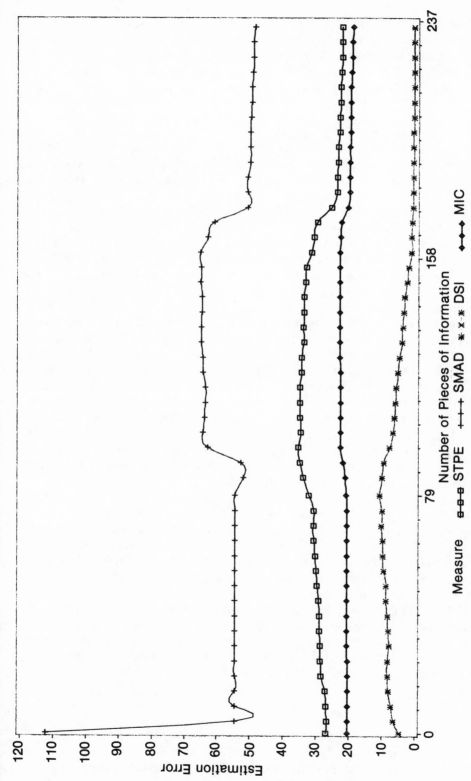

FIGURE 19-2 Estimation error measures: Variant 2B, U.S. 79-sector coefficients, 1972–1977 (known: Z_0).

case for every simulation run. There is a striking similarity between STPE and MIC; this suggests that, at least in the light of this experiment, it does not matter which of these indexes is used. As expected, SMAD is the most unstable of the four measures and sometimes appears to give unreasonably high or low values. In the remaining figures, only STPE has been used as the distance measure.

Coefficients versus Transactions

Figures 19-3 and 19-4 illustrate the differences between estimation of technical coefficients (A) and intermediate transactions (Z). The two figures show the results for the 79-sector tables for the 1963–1967 and 1972–1977 estimations. In most cases, the estimation error for transactions is lower than for coefficients. The difference is significant. The only exceptions to this rule are the 1977 transactions estimates in the upper-left corner of Figure 19-4.

In addition, the trade-off curves exhibit a relatively robust pattern, which is similar for all the time periods. In Variant 1A, there is a dramatic improvement of estimation after a few runs; then, the curves become more or less horizontal. This suggests that, in the case of year-0 data, what really matters are the first 8 percent (the largest) of the transactions cells. (This result provides some support to findings reported by Hewings, 1977, regarding a base-year matrix of random numbers.) However, in the case of a large input–output table, knowing something like 8 percent of the cells is already a sizable amount of information. Moreover, knowledge about the remaining 92 percent of the cells can also be useful, because this continues to improve the estimation precision (in the case of 1967 coefficients, the improvement is more than 50 percent). Overall, there is a great difference between knowing nothing about year-0 transactions (0 pieces of information in Figure 19-3) and knowing everything about them (6,241 pieces of information in Figure 19-3). There is again another major breakthrough as the largest cells of Z^0 are replaced by their year-1 counterparts. After replacing about one-third of the cells, the estimation becomes almost perfect, both for transactions and coefficients.

Although the results shown in Figure 19-3 are not terribly surprising, the findings illustrated by Figure 19-4 are unexpected and counterintuitive. Adding the consecutive pieces of information about target-year margins does not greatly improve the estimation. This is particularly the case with the coefficients in Variant 2A, for which the error–information trade-off curves are essentially horizontal and the A^0 matrix is almost as good as the coefficient matrix estimated by the RAS procedure, when u^1, v^1, and x^1 are known. At the point at which u^1 and v^1 are known (158 pieces of information in Figure 19-4), the estimation error is higher than at the beginning of the simulation when no data about year-1 were known. Because the estimates of technical coefficients are what analysts need for applications and because in most cases they are more stable than estimates of transactions, the analysis in the remainder of the chapter will be limited only to coefficients.

Variants "A" versus Variants "B"

Another question considered was how the results are affected by the order in which the consecutive pieces of information are added to the base matrix. As seen from Figure 19-5, it does not seem to make much difference whether the matrix cells are

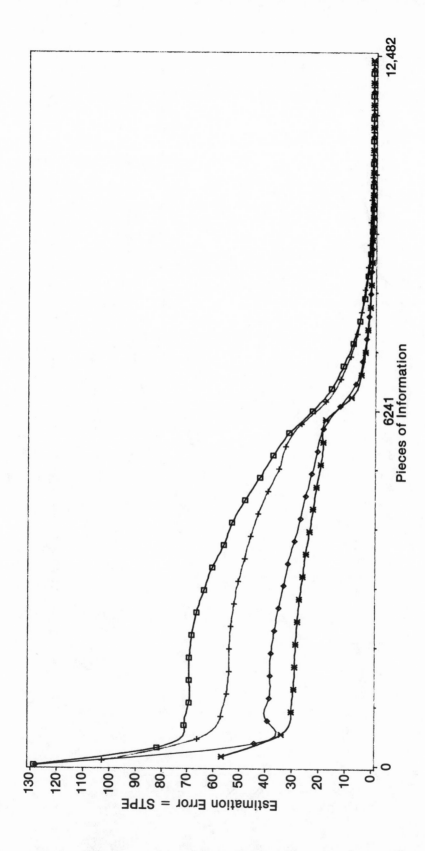

Kind   ᗷ–ᗷ COEFFS: 63-67   ◆–◆ TRANS: 63-67   +–+ COEFFS: 72-77   ✱–✱ TRANS: 72-77

FIGURE 19-3   Coefficients versus transactions: Variant 1A, U.S. 79 sectors, 1963–1967 and 1972–1977 (known: u_1, v_1, x_1).

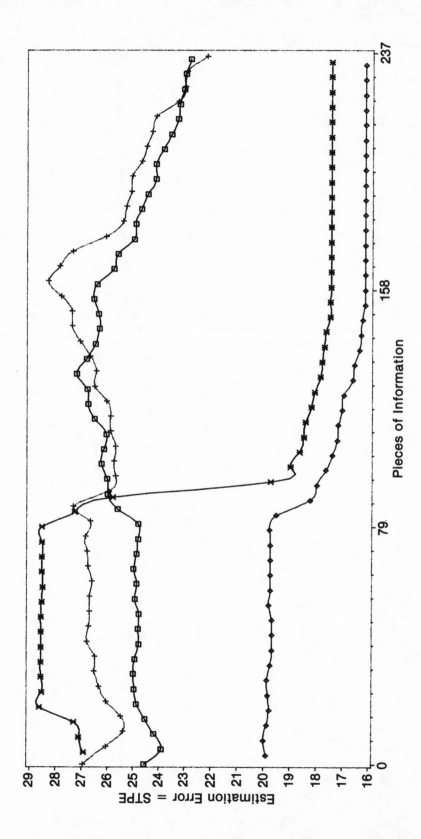

Kind ᴮ⁻ᴮ⁻ᴮ COEFFS: 63-67   ◆⁻◆⁻◆ TRANS: 63-67   +⁻+⁻+ COEFFS: 72-77   ✱⁻✱⁻✱ TRANS: 72-77

FIGURE 19-4 Coefficients versus transactions: Variant 2A, U.S. 79 sectors, 1963–1967 and 1972–1977 (known: Z_0).

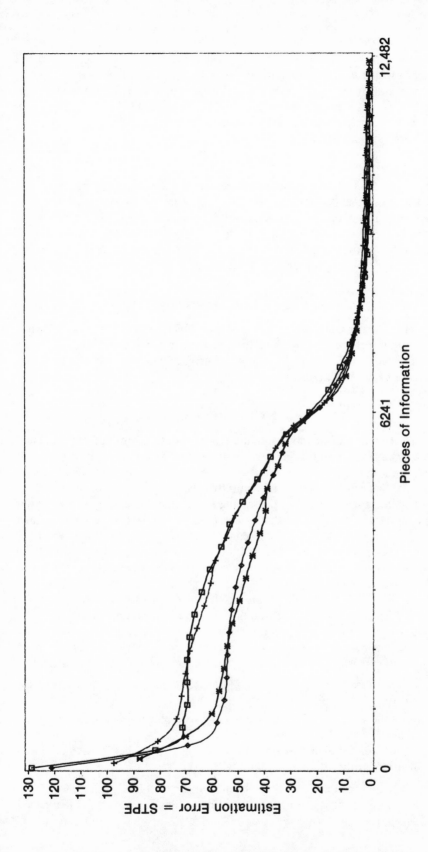

Variant □—□—□ 1A: 1963-67 ◆—◆—◆ 1A: 1972-77 +—+—+ 1B: 1963-67 *—*—* 1B: 1972-77

FIGURE 19-5 Variant 1A versus Variant 1B: U.S. 79-sector coefficients, 1963–1967 and 1972–1977.

sorted according to the values of transactions (1A) or coefficients (1B); however, it does matter in which sequence the data are organized in the case of the margins (2A and 2B). For instance (see Figure 19-6), the 2A Variant curve for 1972–1977 coefficient estimation $(u–v–x)$ is significantly different from 2B $(x–v–u)$. The remaining observations will be confined to the "B" versions of Variants 1 and 2.

Time Intervals

Figures 19-7 and 19-8 illustrate the differences obtained when using different time intervals. The 79-sector 1977 technical coefficients were estimated based on three different sets of year-0 data: 1972, 1967, and 1963. As expected, estimates using 5-year intervals are better than these spanning 10 or 14 years, although in Variant 1B the difference is not overwhelming. There is not much improvement when using 10-year-old data instead of 14-year-old data.

Aggregation Levels

The results of this experiment (Figures 19-9 and 19-10) confirm the findings of Lynch (1979) who experimented with U.K. data. In general, the error tends to decrease with a decrease in the aggregation level, although the difference here is not as dramatic as it was in the case of the U.K. tables.

CONCLUSION

The need for better up-to-date industrial interrelations data, at both the national and regional levels, has long been recognized; that it continues to be a major concern was made clear in discussions during a number of the input–output sessions at several recent Regional Science Association meetings. It is becoming apparent that agencies of federal and state governments are decreasing rather than increasing their efforts at comprehensive data collection and that attempts to reverse this trend have not met with success, nor are they likely to do so. Economic analysts will therefore have to rely increasingly on less than complete information from which to produce estimates of input–output tables. The field between full survey-based tables and those derived by completely nonsurvey methods is broad; therefore, an important question that arises is how much data, and of what kind, are needed in order to create an acceptably accurate table? For that matter, how should "acceptable accuracy" be defined?

The research described in this chapter has been motivated by these questions. The results presented above are suggestive, but by no means conclusive. A great many elaborations and extensions of these initial experiments can be made, in particular:

1. Extension of the U.S. data sets by a few additional benchmark input–output tables: 1947, 1958, 1982;
2. Repetition of the same experiment for other countries, for which a series of input–output tables is available;
3. Implementation of a similar experiment at a regional level, that is, RAS used as a "regionalization" rather than an "updating" procedure.

Moreover, experimentation with other nonsurvey methods would allow for a comparative analysis of their average and marginal estimation accuracies (expressed

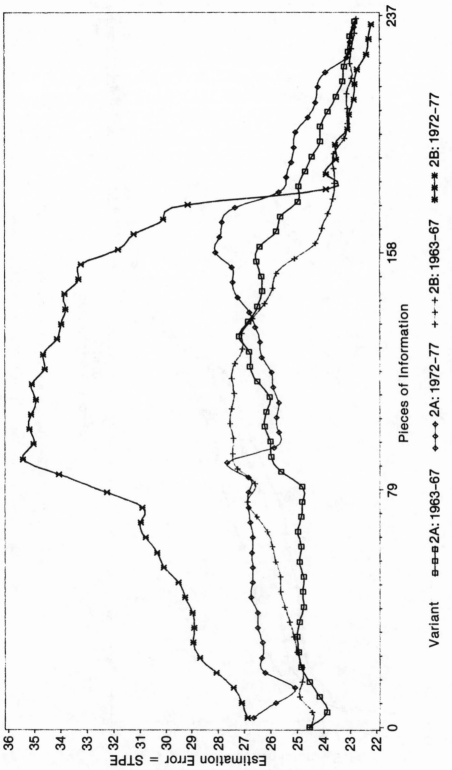

FIGURE 19-6 Variant 2A versus Variant 2B: U.S. 79-sector coefficients, 1963–1967 and 1972–1977.

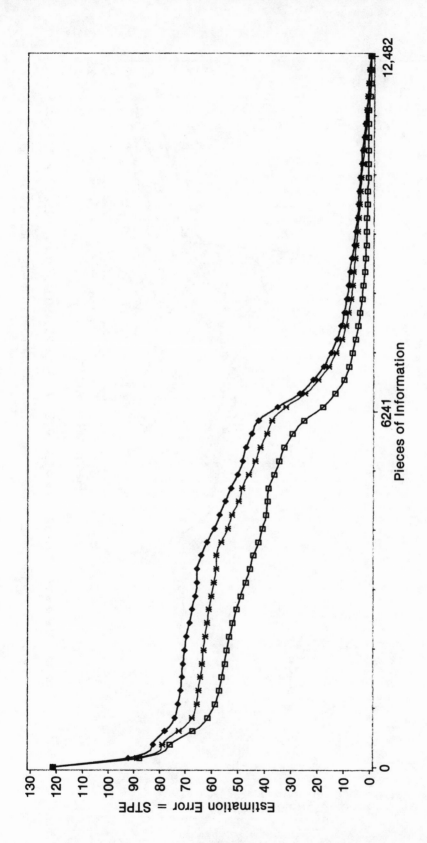

FIGURE 19-7 Time intervals: Variant 1B, U.S. 79-sector coefficients (known: u_1, v_1, x_1).

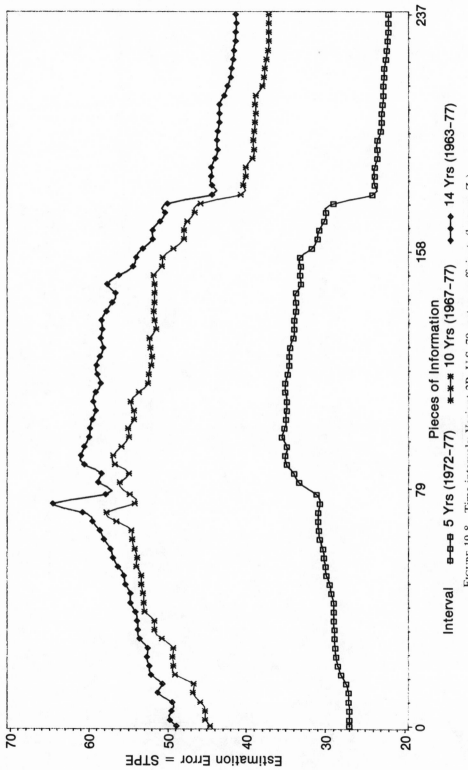

FIGURE 19-8   Time intervals: Variant 2B, U.S. 79-sector coefficients (known: Z_0).

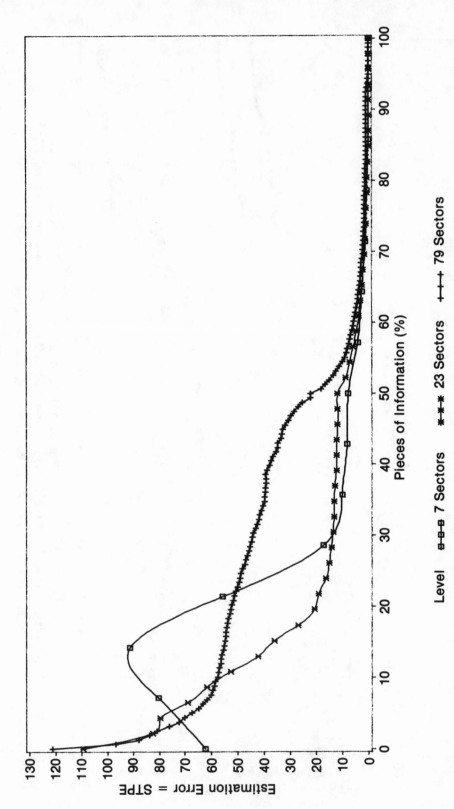

Level   ▫–▫–▫ 7 Sectors   ✻–✻ 23 Sectors   +–+ 79 Sectors

FIGURE 19-9   Aggregation levels: Variant 1B, U.S. 79-sector coefficients (known: u_1, v_1, x_1).

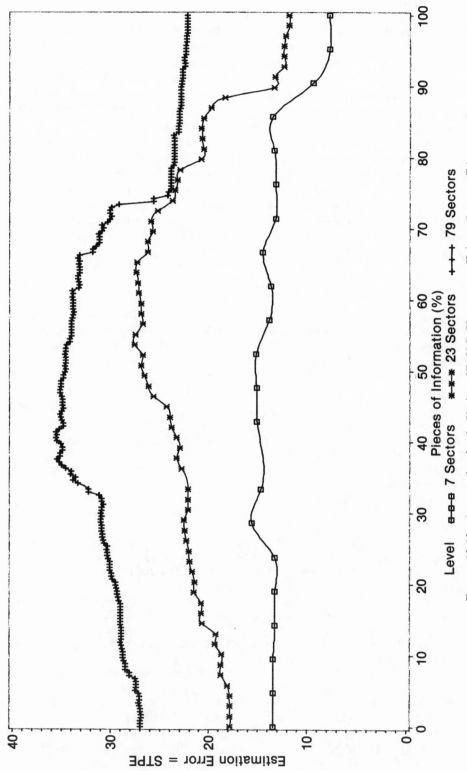

FIGURE 19-10   Aggregation levels: Variant 2B, U.S. 79-sector coefficients (known: Z_0).

per piece of information). Along with different non RAS-procedures, including location quotients techniques and coefficient extrapolation techniques, a number of variants of RAS can be reconsidered, such as Extended RAS (ERAS) (Israilevich, 1986) in which subtotals for certain blocks in the transactions matrix, rather than its individual cells, are known, or RTS (Szyrmer, 1984), in which the transactions matrix is extended by final demand columns and value added rows and only n pieces of target values (gross output vector) rather than $3n$—as in standard RAS (intermediate outputs, intermediate inputs, and gross outputs)—are known.

It is important to notice that the simulations presented in this chapter have been confined to partitive indicators, namely interindustry transactions and direct input coefficients. Experimentation with "holistic" indicators, such as the cells of the Leontief inverse or various types of input–output multipliers, would provide additional insights to the analysis. Finally, should the pieces of information be evaluated (in terms of the costs of gathering them), a cost–benefit analysis can be devised to identify the most efficient ways of gathering and using the information necessary for building large interindustry models.

ACKNOWLEDGMENTS

The author gratefully acknowledges the generous conceptual and editorial assistance of Professor Ronald E. Miller, provided at every stage of this research project. Steve Cochrane was very helpful in editing the first draft of the chapter. An earlier version of this paper was presented at the Annual Meetings of the Regional Science Association in Columbus, Ohio, November 1986.

REFERENCES

Allen, R. I. G. 1974. "Some Experiments with the RAS Method of Updating Input–Output Coefficients." *Oxford Bulletin of Economics and Statistics*. Vol. 36, pp. 215–228.

Bacharach, M. 1970. *Biproportional Matrices and Input–Output Change*. Cambridge: Cambridge University Press.

Czamanski, S., and E. E. Malizia. 1969. "Applicability and Limitations in the Use of National Input–Output Tables for Regional Studies." *Papers, Regional Science Association*. Vol. 23, pp. 65–77.

Harrigan, F. J., J. W. McGilvray, and I. H. McNicoll. 1980. "Simulating the Structure of a Regional Economy." *Environment and Planning, A*. Vol. 12, pp. 927–936.

Hewings, G. J. D. 1977. "Evaluating the Possibilities for Exchanging Regional Input–Output Coefficients." *Environment and Planning, A*. Vol. 9., pp. 927–944.

Hewings, G. J. D., and B. N. Janson. 1980. "Exchanging Regional Input–Output Coefficients: A Reply and Further Comments." *Environment and Planning, A*. Vol. 12, pp. 843–854.

Hewings, G. J. D., and W. M. Syversen. 1982. "A Modified Biproportional Method for Updating Regional Input–Output Matrices: Holistic Accuracy Evaluation." *Modeling and Simulation*. Vol. 13, pp. 115–120.

Hinojosa, R. C. 1978. "A Performance Test of the Biproportional Adjustment of Input–Output Coefficients." *Environment and Planning, A*. Vol. 10, pp. 1047–1052.

Hinojosa, R. C., and B. W. Pigozzi. 1986. "Updating Input–Output Tables Using Employment Data: A Reformulation." *Environment and Planning, A*. Vol. 18, pp. 269–276.

Isard, W., and E. Romanoff. 1968. "The Printing and Publishing Industries of Boston SMSA, 1963, and Comparison with the Corresponding Philadelphia Industries." Technical Paper No. 7. Cambridge, MA: Regional Science Research Institute.

Israilevich, P. R. 1986. Biproportional Forecasting of Input–Output Tables. Ph.D. dissertation. Philadelphia: University of Pennsylvania.

Jensen, R. C. 1980. "The Concept of Accuracy in Regional Input–Output Models." *International Regional Science Review*. Vol. 5, pp. 139–154.

Jensen, R. C., and G. R. West. 1980. "The Effect of Relative Coefficient Size on Input–Output Multipliers." *Environment and Planning, A*. Vol. 12, pp. 659–670.

Jensen, R. C., T. D. Mandeville, and N. D. Karunaratne. 1979. *Regional Economic Planning: Generation of Regional Input–Output Analysis*. London: Croom Helm.

Lahr, M., and J. Szyrmer. 1986. "On Measures for Comparing Input–Output Matrices." Paper prepared for the 33rd RSA Meetings, Columbus, OH.

Leontief, W., and A. Strout. 1963. "Multiregional Input–Output Analysis." In *Structural Interdependence and Economic Development*, edited by Tibor Barna. London: Macmillan, pp. 119–149.

Lynch, R. G. 1979. "An Assessment of the RAS Method for Updating Input–Output Tables." In *Readings in Input–Output Analysis. Theory and Applications*, edited by Ira Sohn. New York: Oxford University Press, pp. 271–284.

Macgill, S. M. 1977. "Theoretical Properties of Biproportional Matrix Adjustments." *Environment and Planning, A*. Vol. 9, pp. 687–701.

Miernyk, W. H. 1976. "Comments on Recent Development in Regional Input–Output Analysis." *International Regional Science Review*. Vol. 1, pp. 47–55.

Miller, R. E., and P. Blair. 1983. "Estimating State-Level Input–Output Relationships from U.S. Multiregional Data." *International Regional Science Review*. Vol. 8, pp. 233–254.

Miller, R. E., and P. Blair. 1985. *Input–Output Analysis: Foundations and Extensions*. Englewood Cliffs, NJ: Prentice-Hall.

Morrison, W. I., and P. Smith. 1974. "Nonsurvey Input–Output Techniques at the Small Area Level: An Evaluation." *Journal of Regional Science*. Vol. 14, pp. 1–14.

Phibbs, P. J., and A. J. Holsman. 1982. "Estimating Input–Output Multipliers—A New Hybrid Approach." *Environment and Planning, A*. Vol. 14, pp. 335–342.

Pigozzi, B. W., and R. C. Hinojosa. 1985. "Regional Input–Output Inverse Coefficients Adjusted from National Tables." *Growth and Change*. Vol. 16, pp. 8–12.

Polenske, K. R. 1970. "Empirical Implementation of a Multiregional Input–Output Gravity Trade Model." In *Contributions to Input–Output Analysis*, edited by Anne P. Carter and Andrew Brody. Amsterdam: North Holland, pp. 143–163.

Ritz, P. 1979. "The Input–Output Structure of the U.S. Economy, 1972." *Survey of Current Business*. Vol. 59, pp. 34–72.

Round, J. I. 1983. "Nonsurvey Techniques: A Critical Review of the Theory and the Evidence." *International Regional Science Review*. Vol. 8, pp. 189–212.

Sasaki K., and H. Shibata. 1984. "Nonsurvey Methods for Projecting the Input–Output System at a Small–Region Level: Two Alternative Approaches." *Journal of Regional Science*. Vol. 24, pp. 35–50.

Sawyer, C. H., and R. E. Miller. 1983. "Experiments in Regionalization of a National Input–Output Table." *Environment and Planning, A*. Vol. 15, pp. 1501–1520.

Schaffer, W. A., and K. Chu. 1969. "Nonsurvey Techniques for Constructing Regional Interindustry Models." *Papers, Regional Science Association*. Vol. 23, pp. 83–101.

Stevens, B. H., G. I. Treyz, D. J. Ehrlich, and J. R. Bower. 1983. "A New Technique for the Construction of Nonsurvey Regional Input–Output Models and Comparisons with Two Survey-Based Models." *International Regional Science Review*. Vol. 8, pp. 271–286.

Stone, R. 1961. *Input–Output and National Accounts*. Paris: Organization for Economic Cooperation and Development.

Stone, R., and A. Brown. 1962. *A Computable Model of Economic Growth (A Programme for Growth 1)*. London: Chapman and Hall.

Survey of Current Business. 1969. "The Input–Output Structure of the U.S. Economy: 1963."

Survey of Current Business. 1974. "The Input–Output Structure of the U.S. Economy: 1967."
Survey of Current Business. 1984. "The Input–Output Structure of the U.S. Economy, 1977."
Szyrmer, J. 1984. "Estimating Interregional Input–Output Tables with RAS." In Commodity
     Flow Estimation, edited by W. B. Allen et al. Prepared for the U.S. Department of
     Transportation. Unpublished.
Theil, H. 1967. *Economics and Information Theory.* New York: American Elsevier.
West, G. 1981. "An Efficient Approach to the Estimation of Regional Input–Output
     Multipliers." *Environment and Planning, A.* Vol. 13, pp. 857–867.

VI

MEASUREMENT AND IMPLICATIONS OF TECHNOLOGICAL CHANGE

20

An Input–Output Approach to Analyzing the Future Economic Implications of Technological Change[1]

FAYE DUCHIN

The determination of what gets produced and how is a complex process in any society. Yet the prospect of adopting the most modern techniques of production has virtually universal appeal, since systematic application of science and technology to production has proved uniquely effective at raising the material standard of living. In the United States, for example, the volume of output per capita has increased about seven times over the course of the past century.

Many economic historians have written about the process of industrialization and the growth of prosperity in the United States and other developed countries. They draw on a wide assortment of public and private documents and a wealth of detailed, technical studies about minor and major historical developments, the latter including the railroads, the so-called scientific management movement, and electrification. The broader analytic studies abstract from this detail, making use of economic theories about growth and development and about the adoption of new technologies, to explain the actual succession of events.

STUDYING THE FUTURE

Even the most compelling analyses of the past offer at best very general guidance, however, for formulating operational strategies to modernize traditional economies and to continue the material progress of developed economies. In addition, there is increasing concern about specific potential by-products of different technological alternatives and organizational and institutional arrangements—including pollution, large-scale displacement of workers by labor-saving technology, and the increasing relative disadvantage of the poorest, least industrialized members of the world economy—whose importance is difficult to assess in terms of general principles or simplistic extrapolations. An analytic framework within which we can carry out experiments on the basis of different scenarios about the future makes it possible to

1. This paper was presented at the Annual Meetings of the American Association for the Advancement of Science in Chicago, February 1987. An earlier version was prepared for an exchange with the National Academy of Sciences of the People's Republic of China in November 1986.

281

examine the effects of different options before they are actually implemented. One of the most far-reaching implications of automation for the economy is the prospect it offers for applying science and technology to constructing an experimental framework for the analysis of what gets produced and how.

There are some similarities, but also notable differences, of procedure when we turn our sights from the past to an analysis of the likely future structure of an economy. In principle, the mechanisms of change will be described by the same theories. The sources of information will surely be different. There is a wealth of technical information and expertise about important emerging developments including, for example, computer-based automation in its many aspects, telecommunications, and biological technologies. This raw material can be organized to play a role analogous to that played by the detailed, descriptive historical studies in the analysis of past economic changes.

The reader does not need to be convinced of the greater difficulty of analyzing the future, notably the uncertainty of many technical assumptions and, equally important, the absence of the historical record about events not directly involved in the analysis, which constrains explanations about the past from going too far astray. Fortunately, we can discipline the analysis using other methods. The modern practice of formulating economic theories as formal, mathematical models can—although it does not necessarily—ensure a clarity and concreteness of concept and a consistency of internal logic that cannot be achieved in a discursive analysis. Although these attributes are also valuable for an analysis of the past, they are indispensable to provide some structure for the systematic evaluation of alternative scenarios about the future, scenarios that are implemented using data based on the raw material described earlier.

The next section of this chapter briefly describes the past growth and modernization of the United States economy and the important class of new technologies that involves computer-based automation. The following two sections describe the way in which the input–output approach combines a formal, mathematical model of the processes of growth and of modernization in an economy of many interdependent sectors, with the realistic detail of a data base containing information about specific technological developments: although the static, open input–output model and accounting data base are now standard, these sections describe powerful extensions, including the dynamic model and engineering data base. Next, some preliminary results that have been obtained with this approach about the future prospects for the United States economy are reported. The final section discusses the nature of the task of designing scenarios and other requirements for the practical use of this approach.

STRUCTURAL CHANGE IN THE U.S. ECONOMY

The economy of the United States has undergone a massive transformation in the course of its relatively short history, both in terms of its internal structure and in relation to other nations. Americans have continuously left the farms that still employed 50 percent of the labor force 100 years ago, more than 30 percent at the turn of the century, and less than 4 percent today. Now, 6 percent as many workers produce about four times the volume of agricultural output as a century ago.[2]

2. These and the other statistics in this section can be calculated from various tables in the U.S. Bureau of the Census (1975, 1985).

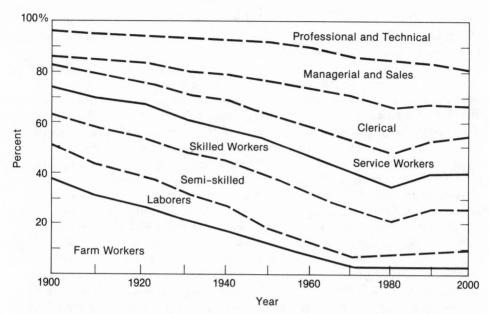

FIGURE 20-1   Occupations of American workers in the twentieth century (proportions by eight broad categories). *Sources:* U.S. Bureau of the Census (1975, series D182–232; and 1981, Table 675) and Leontief and Duchin (1986, Table 1.3). Projections for 1990 and 2000 are discussed in the text.

Although the number of factory jobs has expanded, the proportion of the labor force engaged in manufacturing, around 20 percent, has slowly fallen. In the early days, most outlays for capital goods were for structures of various kinds, including transportation infrastructure, and construction materials were a dominant component of manufactured outputs. Since the 1930s, however, outlays for machines and tools and other durable equipment have outpaced expenditures for structures—by more than 3 to 1 since the mid-1960s.

The greatest growth in the twentieth century has been in industries that produce services; they employ over two-thirds of the labor force today, including most white-collar workers. The largest relative expansion through 1980 occurred among professional and technical and particularly clerical workers (see Figure 20-1). The initial spurt in the growth of clerical work accompanied the intensive industrialization and urbanization in the decades before and just after the turn of the century and was followed by the unprecedented entry of women into the paid labor force. Since 1900, women have increased as a percentage of all workers from 18 to 43 percent, and almost one-third of all working women are employed in clerical jobs.

The composition of American exports and imports has reflected the changing structure of production in the United States relative to other countries. In the middle of the nineteenth century, the United States was still shipping raw cotton to European factories in exchange for textiles and other finished manufactured goods. With industrialization, manufactured goods steadily increased as a proportion of U.S. exports and declined as a proportion of imports throughout the first decades of the twentieth century. Subsequently, growth of imports of first semifinished and then finished products has restored to manufactured imports a relative importance (since 1970) they had not enjoyed for over a hundred years; this phenomenon mainly reflects the industrialization of the rest of the world.

The structure of the U.S. economy is now being fundamentally altered by the absorption of computer-based automation and by the changing international division of labor in which automation plays a leading role. Automation requires a systematic approach that relies on integration through standardization. Individual components (for example, hundreds of different applications that share or exchange information, or a floor of robots and the computer that controls them) can be integrated to function jointly only if physical parts that need to fit together have a compatible design and if information they share or exchange is suitably structured with common definitions, classifications, and so on. As automation proceeds, its internal logic requires the systematic analysis of the domain in which it is to be applied—partitioning it into manageably simple components and determining how they will fit together—followed by the systematic design of all the interlocking subsystems that are immediately required for its implementation or that may eventually become part of it. Significant investments are being made in the United States to standardize the interfaces between existing and potential equipment for all manufacturing and office work in a complex production environment (the manufacturing automation protocol and technical office protocol, MAP/TOP), as described by Kaminski (1986) and Farowich (1986).

A second fundamental principle ensuring the rapid spread of automation is generalization. After a system has been developed for a particular purpose and refined through successful use, it often becomes apparent that it resolves a specific instance of a more general problem. Existing special-purpose systems may be replaced by a more general one whose development costs are spread over the market. This is the case of spreadsheets and of computer-assisted design and manufacturing (CAD/CAM) systems, which are used (with different data) in the production of aircraft and of automobiles—and to make maps in urban land-use and planning offices.

These principles of rationalization also operated in earlier instances of major technological change[3]; now they are being extended by increasingly conscious design and into areas in which human efforts have been unaided by previous generations of machines. The pace of automation and of the adoption of other new technology in the United States and other countries will to a large extent be determined by economic considerations discussed in the next section.

MECHANISMS OF ECONOMIC CHANGE AND THE INPUT–OUTPUT MODEL

A major stimulus for economic change is the appearance of entirely new production possibilities for individual sectors of the economy; these are described in terms of parameters comprising the technical input–output data base. A choice must be made between continuing to use the old techniques and adopting one of the new alternatives. Each technology requires for its implementation a specific mix of raw materials, inputs produced by the various sectors, and human labor, and a new

---

3. See, for example, Rosenberg's description (1963) of the machine tool industry in the second half of the nineteenth century.

technology can be expected to change the nature or lower the price of the outputs produced using it. An input–output framework, such as the one described later, is needed for this analysis because change in one sector may be worthwhile, or may be possible, only because of changes previously or simultaneously adopted in other sectors.

The selected technology can be put to work either in a new establishment or in an existing one; this is the basis for the distinction in the model between expansion and replacement of capacity. Activities need to be undertaken in a prescribed order, such as completing construction before moving in equipment, and it may take several production periods until all the capital required for a new or substantially modified establishment can be assembled and become operational. This is represented by a several-period lag structure in a dynamic model.

The decision to allocate inputs for the growth or modernization of one sector generally means that fewer are available for other purposes, such as personal consumption or the growth or modernization of other sectors. The input–output income equation ensures that private and personal incomes and outlays are compatible with each other and with the overall levels and mix of economic activities.

In the United States where the decision-making process is decentralized to the level of individual establishments, the low-cost alternative among technically feasible options is generally selected. When prices are based on cost and the selection among technological alternatives is based on cost reduction, technological change over the long term can be expected to promote economy in production. Prices can also be based on considerations other than the cost of production, and, no matter how prices are determined, technological alternatives may be selected by criteria other than a comparison of costs, for example, by choosing the least-polluting technologies or by copying the choices made in other economies. Cost-based prices, or profits and subsidies implied by designated prices, are computed with the dynamic input–output price model.

The relative prices of labor and of other inputs to production also play another role besides guiding the choices among technological alternatives: they govern the initial distribution of income and therefore the ability of different groups to purchase varying quantities of different goods and services. These relationships are also represented in the income equation mentioned earlier.

Applications of the open, static input–output model account for most of the applied input–output work that has been carried out over the last several decades and are described in two recent handbooks, one based mainly on work about the U.S. economy (Miller and Blair, 1985) and the other, about developing countries (Bulmer-Thomas, 1982). Although many issues have been fruitfully investigated with this model, considerable elaboration is required to represent the mechanisms of economic change that have been discussed. The extended model is partly implemented and has been described in more detail in Duchin (1988).

The fundamental limitation of the standard model is that it is static, that is, it represents the economy during a single period of time within which investment in capital goods is treated as a final delivery. In a dynamic model, to which we now turn, capital goods produced by one sector in one period are represented as intermediate inputs that in part replenish and in part expand the productive capacity for subsequent periods of the sectors to which the capital is delivered.

The algebra describing the original open, dynamic input–output model is well known (Leontief, 1953, 1970):

$$x_t = A_t x_t + R_t x_t + B_{t+1}(x_{t+1} - x_t) + y_t \qquad (20\text{-}1)$$

$$e_t = L_t x_t \qquad (20\text{-}1a)$$

Two matrices of technical coefficients are required in addition to the familiar matrix (A) of requirements on current account: R_t, requirements of capital goods per unit of output to replace (or modernize) existing capacity, and B_{t+1}, requirements of capital goods per unit increase in output ($x_{t+1} - x_t$) that need to be produced during year t in order to be available for use during year $t + 1$, assuming here for simplicity of notation a uniform, 1-year lag. Changes in the A, B, and R matrices from year to year largely reflect the adoption of new technologies. Thus, the level of production of capital goods for future use is now determined simultaneously with output, and y_t includes only final deliveries for consumption and net exports. Equation (20-1a) describes corresponding labor requirements in terms of occupational as well as industrial detail. Each column of the matrix L_t contains as many entries as there are categories of workers, and each entry in the column represents person-years of labor required per unit of the sector's output.

If the model is to be computed for each year from, say, $t = 1960$ to $t = 2000$, then for each year we will need A, R, B, and L matrices and vectors y_t, plus x_{1959} to start the model. If we specify in advance plausible, or desired, vectors of final deliveries for each year through 2000, we can use the model to compute total annual output of each sector, that part of output that will need to be used to replace capacity and to expand the capital stock, and labor requirements for each sector and each category of worker.

If we replace, say, columns j of A, R, B, and L by alternative columns describing input requirements according to a different technology for sector j, all computed quantities will be different. If the alternative scenarios are plausible, so will be the results of the corresponding computations.

The greatest shortcoming of Equation (20-1) as a model of the accumulation of capital is its implicit assumption that the entire existing stock of physical capital must be fully utilized with no portion standing idle. According to this equation, when output is growing ($x_{t+1} > x_t$ for some sector), all the capital to support this growth must be produced $[B_{t+1}(x_{t+1} - x_t)]$; when output is falling, investment becomes negative [$x_{t+1} < x_t$ implies $B_{t+1}(x_{t+1} - x_t) < 0$ for any given sector], effectively transferring the contracting sector's capital stock to another sector. This principle turns out to be too efficient: the solution of the mathematical model demonstrates that it can be implemented empirically only in the case—uninteresting for the analysis of technological change—in which every sector is growing at exactly the same rate. A recent generalization of the model, which maintains the desirable properties of Equation (20-1) while allowing for idle capacity, different lag periods for different sectors, and certain other refinements, was the basis for the results reported below and is fully specified in Duchin and Szyld (1985).

Cost-based prices per unit of output can be computed according to the following dynamic price equation:

$$p_t = A_t' p_t + R_t' p_t + (1 + r_{t-1}) B_t' p_{t-1} - B_{t+1}' p_t + v_t \qquad (20\text{-}2)$$

where the prime indicates the transpose of a matrix, r is the rate of return (as a proportion of the value of its capital stock) incorporated into the unit price of each sector, and the vector v is the cost of labor (plus any mark-ups or subsidies to be included in the sectoral prices) per unit of output. If certain prices are specified, the same model can be used to determine the corresponding mark-up or subsidy.

From Equations (20-1) and (20-2), an income Equation (20-3) can be derived, which turns out to be useful, and which will need to be satisfied, no matter how prices are actually determined within a given economy (an analogous income equation can be derived for the Duchin–Szyld model):

$$v_t'x_t + r_{t-1}p_{t-1}'B_tx_t = p_t'y_t + (p_t'B_{t+1}x_{t+1} - p_{t-1}'B_tx_t) \tag{20-3}$$

This new equation states that total earnings of workers ($v_t'x_t$) plus any return on capital ($r_{t-1}p_{t-1}'B_tx_t$ where r need not be positive) must equal the total value of consumption ($p_t'y_t$) plus the cost of expansion ($p_t'B_{t+1}x_{t+1} - p_{t-1}'B_tx_t$). Equation (20-3) can be used to investigate the implications of different wage rates and other relative prices—and of changes in technology—for the distribution of income, that is, the relationship between workers' earnings and the cost of consuming a particular set of goods and services or, what amounts to the same thing, the relationship between retained earnings and the cost of expansion.

Equations (20-1)–(20-3) require that a particular technology has already been selected for use in each sector as described by the jth column in the different technical matrices, and these equations make it possible to compute the economic implications. The low-cost choices among alternative technologies within an input–output framework can be determined as a linear programming problem. See Carter (1970, chs. 10 and 12) and Leontief (1986) for the results of actual computations in the static context. Incorporating this capability into the dynamic model is discussed in Duchin (1988).

The sets of equations briefly described are intended to comprise a flexible, not a rigid, system. The basic structure of the system can be retained whereas individual equations are modified to reflect different assumptions. The linear programming approach to the choice of technology particularly needs to be used with discretion: an automatically selected, low-cost technology may be inappropriate either because it is not technically feasible or because another one that is perhaps less polluting or that ensures a higher quality output may be preferred.

TECHNOLOGICAL OPTIONS AND THE TECHNICAL DATA BASE

The community of mechanical engineers was instrumental about 80 years ago in the development and application of "scientific management" that relied on the systematic recording, transfer, and analysis of data describing all aspects of production. Some of their lasting innovations include the detailed analysis of individual tasks and standardized accounting for all elements of cost including the idle time of machines (cost accounting). After World War I, managerial concerns became largely the domain of new professional organizations, and the engineers concentrated again on the technical aspects only of engineering.

Today, the technical and more general engineering journals and the expertise and data bases of practicing engineers are our best source of detailed descriptions of the technologies presently in use and those in different stages of research and development in all branches of production; because of time lags between the discovery and application of new ideas, these are likely to include the majority of the technologies that will be entering into actual use on a significant scale in the next few decades. This literature documents the experience with prototype systems and with pioneering operational systems [see, for example, Koenig (1985) on extensively automated manufacturing operations and Gardner (1981) on new office technologies]. Technical experts examine the nature of human tasks as a basis for extending automation into previously unstructured work: for example, how white-collar workers use paper versus electronic calendars (Kincaid et al., 1985), how they organize their desks (Malone, 1983), and, more generally, how they organize and process disparate information (Donahue and Widom, 1986).

This body of information provides the raw material needed to construct input–output matrices describing future technological alternatives in terms of detailed inputs per unit of output. However, much intermediate work is necessary to piece it together and organize it into systematic, consistent projections represented in standardized classifications, definitions, units, and so on. In the United States today, engineers are demonstrating a renewed interest in technical economic decisions and will collaborate in assembling and organizing this information into the standardized, systematic structures, up-dated on a regular basis, that are required for input–output models.[4]

The familiar input–output flow tables describing transactions that took place in the past are by definition comprehensive in that they cover all sectors of the economy and consistent because of their basis in double-entry accounting. The completeness and consistency of an engineering data base, in which information about present and emerging technologies is used to project columns of coefficients for future years, require the coordination of many teams of experts. We have found it useful to begin this process by focusing first on sectors in which technological decisions are likely to have the greatest overall impact for the economy as a whole. For example, in earlier work, we concentrated on projecting coefficients describing the production and use of computer-based equipment in 1990 and 2000. These projections will be refined, based in part on alternative detailed scenarios about household automation in the United States over the next several decades.

As inputs for rational decisions about production, whether at the individual establishment or at the national level, other countries will also require the systematic collection of technical as well as economic data. The more engineers are involved in economic decisions and economists (and managers) are knowledgeable about technologies, the easier it will be to integrate these kinds of information into common data bases. Countries that intend to maintain their own institutions for scientific research and technological development and to determine their own priorities for technological choices, will need to develop their own technological data bases with greatest detail in the areas corresponding to scenarios of particular interest to them. This is true even though most of the technological alternatives considered in different countries will be the same.

Although the governments of most countries already assemble input–output matrices, quality control in the course of their production is exercised mainly from the point of view of the economist (actually, the accountant). The information is collected

4. The first phases of collaboration with the Institute for Economic Analysis are being supported by the American Society for Mechanical Engineers and by the National Science Foundation under contract No. ENG-8703347.

as flows of money values from which the coefficient tables are derived. The analysis of future technological change requires the assembling of matrices directly in coefficient form and the use of physical units of measure wherever they have a meaning. Although some countries assemble matrices of labor requirements as well as the basic current account matrices, there are today none that prepares the matrices [B and R in Equation (20-1)] required for the analysis of the accumulation and modernization of capital. These matrices must be constructed from technological information; they cannot be deduced from economic considerations alone.

IMPLICATIONS OF AUTOMATION FOR THE U.S. ECONOMY

Over the past several years, my colleagues and I at the Institute for Economic Analysis have developed and implemented a new dynamic input–output model including a data base describing the structure of the U.S. economy from 1963 to the present and alternative projected future structures through the year 2000. We have examined the implications of alternative assumptions about computer-based automation in all sectors of the economy for future employment, investment, and international trade (Leontief and Duchin, 1986; Duchin, 1989a, 1989b).

The results of this research indicate that the overall displacement of workers by automation in the United States will be steady over the next decade or two, but not unusually fast, compared with experience of earlier forms of technological change. In many sectors, the displacement of specific categories of workers will be dramatic, but this loss of jobs will be at least partly compensated by the creation of new jobs in the production of automated systems—provided that they are in fact produced in the United States. About 13 percent less human labor in the aggregate will be required in 2000 to produce a given bill of final deliveries than if the 1980 technologies remained in place over the entire period from 1980 to 2000. This amount of economy of labor, directly attributable to automation, could permit growth of real per capita consumption at an average annual rate of about 1.5 percent until 2000 without appreciable unemployment.

The effects of automation on employment in different occupations and sectors will be very different: the demand for computer professionals will continue to increase rapidly, whereas the need for human draftsmen literally disappears. Most dramatic in terms of broad categories, the proportion of the labor force accounted for by office workers—mainly clerical workers—contracts appreciably by 2000, reversing the trend of the last century. This is seen in the right-hand portion of Figure 20-1. This projection has finally been incorporated into the official government employment projections only because the relative contraction of clerical work has now begun to show up in current employment figures. The fundamental strength and usefulness of the approach reside, naturally, in the ability to anticipate such changes before they occur.

These labor savings are made possible essentially by the substitution of capital for labor: gross investment in capital goods is higher in all years than under the baseline assumption of no technological change; on average, it is about one-third greater. This increased production of capital goods provides some employment, particularly for production workers.

Sectors that experience particularly rapid growth according to the computations may turn out to be bottlenecks as it may not in fact prove possible to expand that quickly or to finance their expansion. This is the case for robotics in the 1990s and for computer software for home and on-the-job instruction: the latter will be a critically important supplement to conventional education in the preparation of a labor force with new skills. Many factors besides automation will determine whether or not this scenario is actually achieved. For example, the deteriorating position of the United States in international markets and the surplus of imports over exports compound the displacement of labor attributable to automation.

The United States regularly exchanges domestic labor for foreign capital through its international trade: we have found that over the past several decades less physical capital and more labor are required to produce an average million dollars' worth of U.S. exports than would be required for the domestic production of a million dollars' worth of competitive imports. However, our analyses have shown that the effect of computer-based automation is to diminish this difference in factor proportions.

In the past, the participation of the United States in international trade has absorbed some of the labor displaced by technological change and increased the capital available for domestic production. The latter is mainly attributed to imports of energy materials and energy-intensive goods whose extraction and production include by far the most capital-intensive economic activities in the United States. Increased reliance on domestic petroleum may ease the deficit in the balance of payments, but it can also be expected to severely restrict access to capital for many other sectors of the economy.

These results cannot be generalized to other countries, and similar analyses are now being carried out for several other countries. Production operations have been continually automated in the United States over the past 30 years, whereas office automation, based initially on the microcomputer, dates only from the early 1980s. Office workers will be disproportionately displaced in the United States over the next 15 years as the most cost-effective office operations are automated first. However, for countries in which automation is not yet significant, both sets of technologies, for the automation of the factory and the office, are now available simultaneously. Therefore, job displacement could be a lot more disruptive than in the United States although the pace of automation will be moderated by the ability to finance it. The direct displacement of production workers in the United States will be offset by their employment in the production of computers and computer-based equipment; for countries that automate by importing this equipment, job displacement could be more severe for this reason also.

ANALYZING ALTERNATIVE STRATEGIES FOR MODERNIZATION

The dynamic input–output model and engineering data base are tools for analyzing the future economic implications of technical change. This approach is now ready to move out of the research institute into an environment in which it will be used on a large scale and in a systematic way to anticipate and help resolve the practical problems of a changing economy. Building this capability, say, within a government agency or a private business, requires attention to a number of different areas. A detailed description of the model is available in the literature to facilitate the preparation of an operational computer implementation. Economists and computer scientists can customize the model for specific purposes. Both economic and technical data are needed, mainly in the form of input–output matrices and technical projections.

The design of scenarios involves the translation into the language of the formal model of alternative economic strategies. Although informed judgment is required in every phase of assembling data and using the computer model, those tasks are also extremely dependent upon standardized procedures. The design of scenarios is closer to the design of experiments in the laboratory sciences.

In most modeling work to date, scenarios have been very simple—often "high," "medium," and "low" variants differing only in the value of one or a small number of variables or parameters. As the applied literature shows, even simple scenarios have proved useful. The scenarios described in the last section are considerably more detailed, and it is for this reason that they permit a wider range of conclusions. The design of scenarios corresponding to operational strategies for an actual economy is entirely feasible but has never yet been undertaken.

Strategies expressed as very general prescriptions or as extremely detailed plans can both be analyzed with the model. For example, we are now designing a set of scenarios to explore the use of agricultural crops, wastes, and by-products for energy. Columns of coefficients corresponding to the production and use of these fuels will be introduced into the technical matrices for different sets of sectors, perhaps in one scenario only for cogeneration in food processing, in other scenarios also for use on farms and as automotive fuels. Outcomes of these scenarios will be compared as to the initial cost and subsequent effects—the cost of investment, volumes of agricultural output and petroleum imports, the level of employment, the requirements for chemicals, the new cost of production, the emissions of specific pollutants, and so on. Experience with analyzing scenarios in these ways can also be expected to improve our subsequent ability to specify the complex, intersectoral strategies that will become increasingly important for modern economies.

REFERENCES

Bulmer-Thomas, V. 1982. *Input–Output Analysis in Developing Countries: Sources, Methods, and Applications*. London and New York: John Wiley.

Carter, Anne P. 1970. *Structural Change in the American Economy*. Cambridge, MA: Harvard University Press.

Donahue, James, and Jennifer Widom. 1986. "Whiteboards: A Graphical Database Tool." *ACM Transactions on Office Information Systems*. Vol. 4, pp. 24–41.

Duchin, Faye. 1989a. "Technological Change and International Trade." Economic Systems Research (forthcoming).

Duchin, Faye. 1989b. "International Trade and the Use of Capital and Labor in the U.S. Economy." Economic Systems Research (forthcoming).

Duchin, Faye. 1988. "Analyzing the Implications of Technological Change." In *Input–Output Analysis: Current Developments*, edited by Mauricio Ciaschini. London: Chapman Hall, pp. 113–128.

Duchin, Faye, and Daniel B. Szyld. 1985. "A Dynamic Input–Output Model with Assured Positive Output." *Metromeconomica*. Vol. 37, pp. 269–282.

Farowich, Steven A. 1986. "Communicating in the Technical Office." *IEEE Spectrum* (April), pp. 63–67.

Gardner, P. C., Jr. 1981. "A System for the Automated Office Environment." *IBM Systems Journal*. Vol. 20, pp. 321–345.

Kaminski, Michael A., Jr. 1986. "Protocols for Communicating in the Factory." *IEEE Spectrum* (April), pp. 56–62.

Kincaid, Christine M., Pierre B. Dupont, and A. Roger Kaye. 1985. "Electronic Calendars in the Office: An Assessment of Human Needs and Current Technology." *ACM Transactions on Office Information Systems*. Vol. 3, pp. 89–102.

Koenig, Daniel, guest editor, 1985. "Computer-Integrated Manufacturing." Special issue of *Computers in Mechanical Engineering* (November).

Leontief, Wassily. 1953. "Dynamic Analysis." Ch. 3 in *Studies in the Structure of the American Economy*. White Plains, NY: International Arts and Sciences Press, pp. 53–90.

Leontief, Wassily. 1970. "The Dynamic Inverse." In *Contribution to Input–Output Analysis*, edited by Anne P. Carter and Andrew Brody. Amsterdam: North-Holland, pp. 17–46. Also appears as Ch. 14 in *Input–Output Economics*. New York: Oxford University Press, 1986, pp. 294–320.

Leontief, Wassily. 1986. "Technological Change, Prices, Wages, and Rates of Return on Capital in the U.S. Economy." Ch. 19 in *Input–Output Economics*. New York: Oxford University Press, pp. 392–417.

Leontief, Wassily, and Faye Duchin. 1986. *The Future Impact of Automation on Workers*. New York: Oxford University Press.

Malone, Thomas W. 1983. "How Do People Organize Their Desks?: Implications for the Design of Office Information Systems." *AMC Transactions on Office Information Systems*. Vol. 1, pp. 99–112.

Miller, Ronald E., and Peter D. Blair. 1985. *Input–Output Analysis: Foundations and Extensions*. Englewood Cliffs, NJ: Prentice Hall.

Rosenberg, Nathan. 1963. "Technological Change in the Machine Tool Industry, 1840–1910." *Journal of Economic History*. Vol. 23, pp. 414–443.

U.S. Bureau of Census. 1975. *Historical Statistics of the United States: Colonial Times to 1970*. Washington, D.C.: U.S. Department of Commerce.

U.S. Bureau of the Census. 1981 and 1985. *Statistical Abstract of the United States*, annual. Washington, D.C.: Department of Commerce.

21

The Changing Structure of the U.S. Economy: An Input–Output Analysis

PETER D. BLAIR and ANDREW W. WYCKOFF

The 1970s and the beginning of this decade were periods of considerable structural change in the U.S. economy. Foremost among these were a tripling of oil and gas prices, a dramatic increase in international trade, the ongoing penetration of office automation and computers in all sectors of the economy, and the continued rise of the service sector.

Input–output analysis is a very useful framework for examining changes in the structure of an economy over time, particularly if a series of comparable tables are available for the economy of interest. The changing structure of the U.S. economy has been the subject of numerous studies over the years including Leontief (1953), Vaccara (1970), Carter (1970, 1980), Feldman and Palmer (1985), and U.S. Department of Commerce (1986). In this chapter, we review some of the methods used in these past studies for chronicling structural change and set the framework for extending the analysis through recent input–output accounts while incorporating recent economic events such as rapid inflation and increasing intermediate imports.

We focus on the implications of the U.S. transition to a services-oriented economy in the 1970s. We define and apply a number of standard comparative measures of structural change such as changes in industry production functions, total output and value-added multipliers, and industry contribution to gross national product (GNP). We discuss the relative merits of these measures in analyzing structural change during the period of interest and discuss the nature of the data used in the analysis, that is, the Bureau of Economic Analysis (BEA) benchmark input–output tables for 1963, 1967, 1972, and 1977 along with a nonsurvey update of the 1977 table to 1980.

Among the conclusions for changes during 1972–1980 are substantial reductions in the share of GNP for natural resource intensive and manufacturing industries that pay high wages and increases in the share of GNP for services industries collectively labeled transactional: finance, insurance, business services, communications, etc. These changes have precipitated a structural realignment that includes stronger interconnections, principally backward linkages, for example, manufacturing now uses more inputs from service industries. One implication of this trend is that the static total output multipliers for services are generally about half those of manufacturing.

Much of the work presented here is aimed at providing background for a more extensive analysis recently completed at the Office of Technology Assessment (OTA).[1] The expanded analysis will contain a more comprehensive review of the sources of technical change that can be traced to major events that have affected the U.S. economy over the last several decades, such as the Vietnam war in the 1960s or the Arab oil embargoes of the 1970s. In this chapter we discuss the individual effects of changing final demand and interindustry production functions. In the expanded analysis, the interactive effects are also presented along with a much more detailed treatment of employment impacts.

U.S. INPUT–OUTPUT DATA

The analysis presented in this chapter drew primarily on the survey-based input–output data compiled by the U.S. Department of Commerce. In the following section, we discuss these data as they apply to the analysis presented in subsequent sections.

Benchmark Tables and Nonsurvey Updates

Since the late 1950s, BEA (formerly the Office of Business Economics) staff of the U.S. Department of Commerce have periodically compiled national input–output tables for the United States as a part of the national economic accounts. Benchmark survey-based tables have been compiled for 1939, 1958, 1963, 1967, 1972, and 1977. A table for 1947 prepared originally by the Bureau of Labor Statistics (BLS) staff was reworked by Vaccara et al. (1970) to conform with the economic sector classification and other conventions of subsequent tables. In addition, for some of Carter's analysis (1970), she uses the 1939 table originally developed by Leontief (1953) and a 1961 table updated through nonsurvey methods from the benchmark 1958 table. Finally, in this chapter we also include a 1980 table that is a nonsurvey update of the benchmark 1977 table prepared by BEA.

The original BEA benchmark input–output tables were developed at various levels of aggregation, the more recent ones—1963, 1967, 1972, and 1977—at approximately 85-, 365-, and 500-sector aggregations (Survey of Current Business, 1969, 1974, 1984; Ritz et al., 1979). The tables used in this preliminary analysis include the 85-sector and, for illustrative purposes, the 9-sector aggregations of these tables. All but the 1972 and 1977 benchmark tables were previously published at the 23-sector level in the *Historical Statistics of the United States* (U.S. Department of Commerce, 1975). The 1972, 1977, and 1980 tables used here are based on the conventions adopted in Ritz (1980), Ritz et al. (1979), Survey of Current Business (1984), and U.S. Department of Commerce (1985), but were reworked to conform as closely as possible with the sector classification and other conventions of the previous tables, although some significant differences remain, such as adjustments for secondary production.

Commodity-by-Industry Accounts

Since the 1972 benchmark table (released in 1977), the U.S. national input–output tables prepared by the Department of Commerce have employed the so-called

---

1. See *Technology and the American Economic Transition*, May 1988. This study includes an input–output analysis of structural change in the U.S. economy and how trends in such changes are likely to affect the economy over the next several decades.

commodity-by-industry accounting scheme. The commodity-by-industry framework was developed originally by Stone (1961) and subsequently adapted as standard system of accounts by the United Nations (Miller and Blair, 1985; United Nations, 1968). This framework was developed primarily to better account for secondary production in economic activity, that is, production of multiple commodities by a single industry sector. Although the relative level of secondary production is significant for some U.S. industries, over the entire economy, it is fairly modest, but it is somewhat sensitive to the level of sectoral aggregation. Table 21-1 shows a set of sectoral aggregations for three U.S. national input–output tables. The table shows that at high levels of aggregation, for example, 7 sectors, the secondary production ratio[2] is, with one exception, less than 4 percent. Even for the most disaggregated tables, for example, 533 sectors in 1977, the secondary production ratio is about 5 percent. However, for individual sectors, some secondary production is significant.

Based on these results, at least for the purposes of this chapter and conceivably for a much wider variety of applications, a full commodity-by-industry framework seems unnecessary. The framework is conceptually very useful in the original construction of input–output tables, particularly for ensuring consistency and providing flexibility in dealing with secondary production. In application, however, the distinctions among alternative technology assumptions may be small enough so as not to justify the added effort of developing all variations of commodity-by-industry direct and total requirements tables. In this chapter, we reduce the commodity-by-industry accounts for 1972, 1977, and 1980 to an industry-by-industry table with an industry technology assumption or, in some cases, by simply interpreting the use matrix as an industry-by-industry transactions matrix; in some sample tests the differences are very small.

TABLE 21-1   Secondary Production Ratio of U.S. Input–Output Tables at Different Levels of Sectoral Aggregation[a] (Percent)

	Aggregation Level (Number of Sectors)				
Year	7	23	38	85	533
1972	1.51	2.49	2.50	3.44	—
1977	1.56	2.77	2.78	3.64	5.47
1980	—	—	—	3.80	—

[a]These figures were computed from the U.S. national input–output tables in Ritz (1979) and *Survey of Current Business* (1984, 1986). In a system of commodity-by-industry accounts this is computed from the "make" matrix as the ratio of the sum of the off-diagonal elements to the sum of all elements in the column. The make matrix is a table of total industry output, the rows of which are the value of commodities produced by each sector in the economy, both commodities produced as primary output and commodities produced as secondary output.

2. The secondary production ratio is measured as the ratio of total secondary production (the sum of all off-diagonal elements in the input–output make matrix) to the U.S. total gross output (the sum of all elements in the make matrix).

Adjustments for Imports

To examine changes in final demand and industry production functions over the series of benchmark years, we adjusted the 85-sector tables for imports by the following:

$$A_d = (I - \hat{m})A$$

where A_d is the matrix of domestic technical coefficients, and $\hat{m}$ is a diagonal matrix with each element defined as the import share of a commodity in the domestic market, that is, the ratio of total imports of a commodity to the sum of total intermediate use of that commodity plus domestic final demand for that commodity (Young et al., 1986).

Although this adjustment introduces an assumption that the fraction of a given commodity supplied by imports is the same for each industry, it does estimate a truly domestic intermediate use table, facilitating estimates of industrial linkage, import penetration, and the employment effects of trade.

Constant-Year Prices

Because a principal purpose of this chapter is to examine structural changes in the economy, the series of U.S. input–output tables used in the analysis were adjusted to constant dollars for the benchmark year 1980. We used a set of unpublished industrial output (gross) price deflators prepared by the Office of Economic Growth of BLS. The BLS and BEA sector classification schemes are not entirely compatible, so that some reconciliation between the two was necessary, but price deflators were available for all the benchmark years used in this analysis.

Price deflators were assembled for all input–output tables at the 85-sector level of aggregation. Where the 9-sector tables are used for illustration, these tables were created by aggregating the 85-sector tables adjusted to 1980 prices. The adjustments were computed by developing price adjustment factors, defined as the ratio of commodity prices for 1980 to the corresponding prices for each of the benchmark years. These price adjustment factors were then applied to the relevant element in each row of the industry-by-industry direct requirements table and to the vectors of final demands. Because the deflators are based on domestic price series such as the Producer's Price Index, the conversion of the input–output tables into constant dollars process was undertaken after the transactions table was adjusted for imports.

SOME HISTORICAL TRENDS

Over the 13 years from 1972 through 1984, a significant realignment in the structure of the U.S. economy has occurred. Three trends appear to dominate this structural change:

1. The U.S. economy now requires considerably less in the way of raw materials, such as primary energy (oil, natural gas, and coal), iron ore, and farm products.
2. Similarly, the U.S. economy now requires considerably less output from domestic manufacturing industries characterized as high wage, such as iron and steel, glass production, and chemical processing.
3. Finally, the U.S. economy demands many more services, particularly those thought of as being transactional and distributive in nature, for example, wholesale and retail trade, communications, banking, insurance, and real estate.

These three major changes are derived from shifts not only in final demand as consumers, for example, buy more health services and fewer motor vehicles, but also from interindustry, intermediate demand reflected in businesses purchasing more business services, such as legal counsel and financial advice, and fewer manufactured products, such as steel. International trade appears to have been a relatively minor factor in this structural change between 1972 and 1980, but has taken on increasing importance since 1980—benefiting the service sectors, but hurting manufacturing.

A principal implication of this structural realignment is that the economy on the whole has become more specialized—more and more is being "contracted out" or "out-sourced." However, the service sectors that gain from this development produce products that have few connections with the rest of the economy. In other words, as manufacturing becomes more specialized and relies on out-of-house resources, such as management consultants and accounting firms, the economic output delivered by these service sectors is insular in nature, maintaining far fewer links with manufacturing than manufacturing maintains with services.

This trend may have important consequences for policy issues, particularly regarding international trade. Given the strong link between manufacturing and services, an adverse balance of merchandise trade will ripple through the economy more in the 1980s than it would have in 1972, causing both manufacturing and service industries to lose. Attempts to bolster the U.S. economy through expansion of the service sector will require much greater levels of demand for service products to generate the same level of economic activity than that derived from manufactured products because of the weak link service industries have with the rest of the economy. A major consequence of this structural change involves employment losses in manufacturing, particularly in "high-wage manufacturing," and job gains in the service sector that are typically lower paying and provide less stable jobs than those in manufacturing [U.S. Congress (1986); Bluestone and Harrison (1982); Congressional Research Service (1985)].

Total Output and Value-Added Multipliers

The trends described in the last section can be illustrated by changes in input–output multipliers and other summary measures of the input–output tables. Traditional total output multipliers, however, are not very illuminating (Table 21-2). An alternative measure that illustrates the trends just described is the value-added multiplier,

$$V = \hat{W}(I - A)^{-1}$$

where W is the row vector of total value-added coefficients (dollars' worth of value-added per dollar's worth of gross output).[3] Since $e = W(I - A)^{-1}$ (where e is a row vector of ones), these value-added multipliers are already normalized, that is, they indicate the relative contribution to value added by each sector per dollar's worth of total final demand. The value-added multipliers comparing the U.S. economy for 1972 and 1980 are shown in Table 21-3, revealing that the service sectors are rather insular whereas the manufacturing and natural resource sectors are relatively tightly linked with the economy.

In analyzing relative changes in the entire economy, we find that the effects of changing final demand are at least as important as the effects of changing interindus-

---

3. Value-added multipliers are sometimes referred to as "net flow coefficients;" see Szyrmer (1986).

TABLE 21-2   Total Output Multipliers: 1963-1980

Sector						
Number	Title	1963	1967	1972	1977	1980
1.	Natural resources	1.80	1.77	1.88	2.09	2.14
2.	Construction	2.04	2.03	2.13	2.18	2.22
3.	Low-wage manufacturing	2.58	2.45	2.53	2.47	2.46
4.	Medium-wage manufacturing	2.43	2.36	2.31	2.35	2.42
5.	High-wage manufacturing	2.36	2.30	2.34	2.56	2.61
6.	Transportation and trade	1.61	1.61	1.67	1.69	1.75
7.	Transactional activities	1.73	1.70	1.54	1.47	1.47
8.	Personal services	1.58	1.68	1.84	1.79	1.82
9.	Social services	1.26	1.26	1.30	1.38	1.43
Total weighted by total output[a]		1.97	1.94	1.94	2.00	2.01

[a]Weighted average of individual sector total output multipliers, using total gross outputs as the weights.

try structure. Multiplier analyses ignore changes in final demand, because multipliers are expressed in units per dollar of final demand. A more illustrative and indeed simpler indicator is the change in relative contributions to total value-added (GNP). Table 21-4 shows the relative sectoral contributions to value-added and total output for the U.S. economy for 1972 and 1980.

Effects of Capital Investment

Static input–output tables and models account for capital investment expenditures (including both replacement and expansion of plant and equipment) as a final demand and, therefore, exclude them from interindustry transactions. The differences in relative contributions of various industries to GNP illustrated in Table 21-4 can partially be explained by not including capital in the interindustry transactions matrix, that is, in effect ignoring the indirect impact of capital expenditures on the economy. One way to see how significant the effect of capital flows on the input–output economy might be is to "close" the static model to capital investment by adding the capital flows table to the transactions matrix (treat them as current expenditures) and removing capital investment from final demand.[4]

BEA staff assemble a set of capital flows as part of the compilation of the national input–output tables. Capital flow tables now exist for 1972 and 1977; in this chapter we use 9-sector aggregations of these tables inflated to 1980 dollars. The 9-sector interindustry transactions tables for 1972 and 1980 modified to include capital flows are included in Table 21-5.[5] A substantial portion of these capital flows is attributable to structures; the footnote to the table indicates these adjusted transactions without

4. A more comprehensive method is to use a dynamic model as in Leontief and Duchin (1984) or Miller and Blair (1985, ch. 9). We provide these tables only as illustrations. Numerous studies have shown that technical coefficients are stable over long periods, but capital coefficients may be much less stable. Capital investment includes both the replacement and expansion of durable equipment and structures.

5. For the 1980 table, the 1977 capital flows were scaled to the total capital expenditures listed as part of final demand in the BEA 1980 nonsurvey updated table.

TABLE 21-3 Value-Added Multipliers: 1972 and 1980

Value-Added Multipliers	Natural Resources		Construction		Low-Wage Manufacturing		Medium-Wage Manufacturing		High-Wage Manufacturing		Transport and Trade		Transactional Activities		Personal Services		Social Services	
	1972	1980	1972	1980	1972	1980	1972	1980	1972	1980	1972	1980	1972	1980	1972	1980	1972	1980
Natural resources	0.773	0.684	0.084	0.070	0.134	0.102	0.187	0.156	0.219	0.221	0.055	0.046	0.030	0.021	0.069	0.057	0.032	0.034
Construction	0.015	0.019	0.481	0.440	0.009	0.010	0.009	0.011	0.010	0.013	0.011	0.011	0.025	0.020	0.011	0.012	0.011	0.013
Low-wage manufacturing	0.007	0.009	0.038	0.045	0.466	0.510	0.017	0.019	0.019	0.022	0.006	0.009	0.006	0.005	0.019	0.015	0.005	0.007
Medium-wage manufacturing	0.029	0.040	0.104	0.109	0.045	0.039	0.470	0.471	0.053	0.058	0.037	0.036	0.018	0.017	0.036	0.037	0.013	0.020
High-wage manufacturing	0.058	0.067	0.098	0.067	0.136	0.110	0.128	0.102	0.532	0.454	0.047	0.040	0.025	0.014	0.081	0.047	0.020	0.023
Transportation and trade	0.038	0.065	0.096	0.114	0.098	0.105	0.082	0.109	0.074	0.109	0.711	0.690	0.029	0.027	0.055	0.074	0.020	0.031
Transactional activities	0.072	0.102	0.087	0.142	0.094	0.105	0.090	0.112	0.078	0.106	0.109	0.143	0.842	0.879	0.114	0.125	0.047	0.070
Personal services	0.006	0.008	0.008	0.010	0.012	0.011	0.011	0.012	0.009	0.010	0.016	0.018	0.013	0.010	0.610	0.624	0.006	0.007
Social services	0.004	0.006	0.004	0.005	0.008	0.008	0.007	0.008	0.005	0.006	0.008	0.007	0.012	0.009	0.006	0.008	0.848	0.794
Total	1.000	1.000	1.000	1.000	1.000	1.000	1.000	1.000	1.000	1.000	1.000	1.000	1.000	1.000	1.000	1.000	1.000	1.000

TABLE 21-4   Sector Contributions to Total Value Added (GNP) and Total Gross Output

Sector Number	Title	1963	1967	1972	1977	1980
		Contributions to Value Added[a]				
1.	Natural resources	0.143	0.133	0.115	0.091	0.088
2.	Construction	0.091	0.079	0.075	0.065	0.059
3.	Low-wage manufacturing	0.032	0.035	0.032	0.036	0.034
4.	Medium-wage manufacturing	0.086	0.095	0.097	0.100	0.098
5.	High-wage manufacturing	0.138	0.143	0.126	0.108	0.093
6.	Transportation and trade	0.157	0.156	0.174	0.190	0.195
7.	Transactional activities	0.148	0.157	0.180	0.210	0.233
8.	Personal services	0.046	0.040	0.036	0.037	0.037
9.	Social services	0.158	0.160	0.165	0.163	0.164
Total value added		1.000	1.000	1.000	1.000	1.000
		Contributions to Total Gross Output[b]				
1.	Natural resources	0.132	0.124	0.113	0.100	0.099
2.	Construction	0.091	0.081	0.084	0.075	0.071
3.	Low-wage manufacturing	0.055	0.055	0.054	0.053	0.048
4.	Medium-wage manufacturing	0.140	0.146	0.139	0.137	0.141
5.	High-wage manufacturing	0.201	0.204	0.186	0.184	0.164
6.	Transportation and trade	0.122	0.125	0.145	0.158	0.167
7.	Transactional activities	0.127	0.134	0.139	0.152	0.167
8.	Personal services	0.034	0.033	0.033	0.033	0.033
9.	Social services	0.097	0.100	0.106	0.107	0.110
Total output		1.000	1.000	1.000	1.000	1.000

[a]Each element of the product $\hat{W}X$ divided by GNP (total value added).
[b]Each element of X divided by total gross output of the entire economy.

residential structures. Finally, Table 21-6 shows the effect of capital flows on output multipliers and contributions to total value added (GNP).

Tables 21-4 and 21-6 show that although the differences in output multipliers and contributions to total value added between 1972 and 1980 are not as great as when capital is included, the implications of the trends described earlier concerning the move toward an increasing prominence of services in the U.S. economy are still evident.[6]

PRINCIPAL FACTORS AFFECTING STRUCTURAL CHANGE

We define structural change as variations in the patterns of economic output in an economy. In particular, we examine the relative changes in the contribution of a sector to gross output and value added attributable to changes in either final demand patterns or sectoral production functions. These changes seem to be more illuminating than changes in the multipliers.

6. Table 21-7 is also an extreme case, because no distinction is made between depreciation or replacement capital and new investment capital in these modified transactions tables.

Table 21-5 U.S. National Input–Output Transactions Tables Modified for Capital Flows: 1972 and 1980 (Millions of 1980 Dollars)

Transactions[a]	1	2	3	4	5	6	7	8	9	Final Demand	Total Output
1972											
1. Natural resources	128690	4173	14157	84919	145287	18191	8612	4093	11290	93225	488937
2. Construction	39188	1765	3036	6775	10306	24227	161591	12629	21007	87107	363940
3. Low-wage manufacturing	2094	25015	71450	11639	19684	5883	4005	6227	3229	101693	234099
4. Medium-wage manufacturing	27033	72160	10534	107205	62605	39364	21315	8455	10359	371604	598336
5. High-wage manufacturing	40323	59602	40494	108580	219325	55861	23005	19798	10301	272261	800160
6. Transportation and trade	14242	35640	16798	40448	44648	47433	17406	8017	9152	633803	624663
7. Transactional activities	23382	18961	10277	29175	27707	63480	100468[1]	14444	20132	559479[2]	601212
8. Personal services	1658	1313	1693	5022	4065	13087	9382	6650	2946	123099	143577
9. Social services	930	264	888	2180	1477	3846	6373	499	3845	547564	455852
Total intermediate input	277539	218894	169328	395944	535103	271373	352156[3]	80811	92260	1917369[5]	
Total value added	211398	145046	64772	202392	265057	353290	249056[4]	62766	363592		
Total gross output	488937	363940	234099	598336	800160	624663	601212	143577	455852		4310778
1980											
1. Natural resources	140775	4561	11073	92108	173731	20771	10334	5738	14798	38748	512636
2. Construction	54328	1017	2881	8735	11668	26134	157141	4934	20218	80574	367630
3. Low-wage manufacturing	2284	27245	68751	14768	19587	11329	4407	5007	4858	92684	250920
4. Medium-wage manufacturing	39278	77726	10429	147157	69046	57574	36718	11139	21568	260000	730635
5. High-wage manufacturing	54340	37019	42010	115890	254014	72629	15918	14339	18902	224491	849551
6. Transportation and trade	29246	43074	20003	65718	69273	83645	24436	13971	16820	501401	867587
7. Transactional activities	28983	36374	11464	38269	31817	109057	152553[1]	17031	33442	408514[2]	867505
8. Personal services	2488	1708	1455	5380	3868	19292	9514	8084	4754	112375	168916
9. Social services	1428	278	976	3075	1682	4435	7455	1077	6984	540477	567867
Total intermediate input	353149	229001	169043	491100	634686	404864	418476[3]	81320	142343	2259264[5]	
Total value added	159488	138629	81877	239535	214865	462723	449029[4]	87596	425524		
Total gross output	512636	367630	250920	730635	849551	867587	867505	168916	567867		5183246

[a]For transactions without residential construction replace the footnoted transactions with the following:

	1972	1980
1.	99280	140119
2.	560667	420948
3.	350968	406042
4.	250244	461463
5.	1918577	2271698

TABLE 21-6   Effect of Capital Flows on Total Output Multipliers and Value-Added Contributions: 1972 and 1980

	1972			1980		
	Static	With Capital (w/o R)[a]	With Capital	Static	With Capital (w/o R)[a]	With Capital
Value-added fractions						
1. Natural resources	0.115	0.103	0.110	0.088	0.067	0.071
2. Construction	0.075	0.071	0.076	0.059	0.058	0.061
3. Low-wage manufacturing	0.032	0.032	0.034	0.034	0.034	0.036
4. Medium-wage manufacturing	0.097	0.099	0.106	0.098	0.100	0.106
5. High-wage manufacturing	0.126	0.129	0.138	0.093	0.090	0.095
6. Transportation and trade	0.174	0.172	0.184	0.195	0.193	0.205
7. Transactional activities	0.180	0.186	0.130	0.233	0.243	0.199
8. Personal services	0.036	0.031	0.033	0.037	0.037	0.039
9. Social services	0.165	0.177	0.190	0.164	0.178	0.188
Total	1.000	1.000	1.000	1.000	1.000	1.000
Total output multipliers						
1. Natural resources	1.878	2.343	2.417	2.138	2.835	2.914
2. Construction	2.125	2.481	2.564	2.220	2.578	2.667
3. Low-wage manufacturing	2.533	2.865	2.952	2.463	2.823	2.892
4. Medium-wage manufacturing	2.306	2.608	2.692	2.417	2.797	2.870
5. High-wage manufacturing	2.337	2.643	2.716	2.610	3.075	3.148
6. Transportation and trade	1.665	1.980	2.079	1.752	2.098	2.187
7. Transactional activities	1.538	1.770	2.470	1.475	1.702	2.199
8. Personal services	1.839	2.329	2.438	1.816	2.159	2.239
9. Social services	1.302	1.457	1.501	1.430	1.598	1.643

[a]Excluding capital expenditures on residential construction.

Effect of Changing Final Demand

The changing nature of final demand is of considerable importance in analyzing economic structure. For example, as the demand for finished goods, such as cigars, declines, so will the output from the tobacco sector. This shift in demand, however, affects not only the tobacco sector, the cigar producers, but also the whole network of sectors that collectively satisfies the demand for cigars—the agricultural service sector, which supplies the seeds for tobacco, the chemical and fertilizer mining sector, which makes pesticide, the farm and garden machinery sector, which produces the tractor, the business services sector, which creates the advertising plan, and the wholesale and retail trade sector, which sells the cigar.

To examine the influence of demand using input–output analysis, we can hold the technology of production in its 1980 form and force this economy to satisfy the demand for products as it appeared in 1972, 1977, 1980, and 1984.[7] Doing this, we can observe how significantly final demand for finished products influences structural change, independent of changes brought about by changes in production functions. In particular, this illustrates how sector output would change if only the demand for products, not the process that makes them, is allowed to follow the changes that happened between 1972 and 1984. This is a trend that is very difficult to gauge by examining only the multipliers.

This experiment for the 9-sector aggregations of the U.S. models described earlier caused a total change of over 5 percent of the GNP with four sectors gaining share, four losing, and one staying at a constant level. Table 21-7 shows the changes in output share that occur if only demand is allowed to change. Over the 12 years, the sectors that lost output share as a result of demand are the natural resource intensive,

TABLE 21-7   U.S. Structural Changes Resulting from Changes in Final Demand[a]

Production Sectors	1972	1977	1980	1984[b]
Natural resources	10.7	9.4	8.8	9.3
Construction	6.9	6.4	5.9	6.2
Low-wage manufacturing	3.6	4.2	3.4	3.3
Medium-wage manufacturing	9.5	10.0	9.8	10.0
High-wage manufacturing	9.9	9.9	9.3	9.0
Transportation and trade	18.2	18.9	19.5	19.4
Transactional activities	20.7	23.1	23.3	23.6
Personal services	3.8	4.0	3.7	3.7
Social services	16.5	17.3	16.4	16.3
Other[c]	0.2	−3.2	0.0	−0.9
Total	100.0	100.0	100.0	100.0

Source: Office of Technology Assessment.

[a]Constant dollar output share for selected years of final demand; output shown by production sector and calculated using the 1980 input–output data (percent).
[b]Output derived from demand estimated from the NIPA Accounts.
[c]Other includes scrap, rest of world, noncomparable imports, and inventory valuation adjustment.

7. The 1984 demand vector is based on National Income and Product Account data converted to input–output categories, using bridges supplied by BEA and trade estimated by the BLS and rebased into 1980 dollars.

construction, low-wage manufacturing, and high-wage manufacturing sectors. Transactional activities, medium-wage manufacturing, and transportation and trade registered a gain in their share of output. This turnover attributable to final demand alone was responsible for a little less than half of all of the output share exchanged when both demand and recipe (columns of the technical coefficients matrix) were allowed to vary. Domestic demand, particularly that originating from consumers, was the primary factor behind the change. In comparison, the effect of international trade on output share was relatively small until after 1980.

Effect of Changing Production Functions

Although the effect of final demand on output share is significant, it accounts for the demand for goods and services only at the point of final sale. For example, the consumer's purchase of a new car would be counted as final demand. Input–output analysis is more traditionally used to study changes in intermediate demand, which measures the demand for goods and services used as ingredients in the process of creating a product for final consumption. As prices, technology, and a myriad of other factors change, so will the "recipe" used for production. For example, the desire to boost fuel efficiency and the advent of high-strength plastics have allowed the auto industry to change the recipe it uses for producing a car, substituting plastic for steel. Over the past 10 years, the portion of iron and steel in the average U.S. made automobile has fallen from 81 to 69 percent; the percentage of aluminum and plastic has risen from 6 to 11 percent (Larson et al., 1986).

To produce a 1980 dollar's worth of natural resource intensive output in 1972 required 4.8 cents of input from the transactional activities sector. By 1980, the recipe of production changed to the point where 5.7 cents of input from the transactional activities sector was required. Generally, however, the process of changing this recipe historically has been very slow and gradual; even a large shock such as the quadrupling of oil prices between 1972 and 1980 had a long lag period before an adjustment was incorporated into industry production processes (Carter, 1980).

In addition to examining the production functions themselves, we can illustrate the effects of changes in the production processes by seeing how the output from different industries changes as we attempt to satisfy a fixed set of final demands (in this case 1984) with the varying technical coefficients matrices for 1972, 1977, and 1980. For example, what would the GNP look like if we used the production recipe of 1972 to satisfy the demand for a car compared to the recipe used in 1980?

This experiment of holding demand fixed but varying the technical coefficients between 1972 and 1980 reveals that the impact of recipe on structural change overall was roughly the same as that of final demand. As exhibited in Table 21-8, from 1972 to 1980, more than 5 percent of the GNP shifted from losing to gaining sectors as a result of changes in recipe. Those sectors that increased their output share were typically the same sectors that benefited from changes in demand: transactional activities, transportation and trade, and medium-wage manufacturing, although the individual industries that benefited differed widely. The exceptions were low-wage manufacturing and personal services; both of these sectors experienced a gain in share as a result of recipe, but lost share as a result of demand. The sectors that lost output share because of changes in both recipe and demand were high-wage manufacturing, natural resource intensive, construction, and social services.

TABLE 21-8   U.S. Structural Changes Resulting from Changes in
Production Recipe[a]

Production Sectors	1972	1977	1980
Natural resources	10.1	9.7	9.3
Construction	6.8	6.6	6.2
Low-wage manufacturing	2.9	3.3	3.3
Medium-wage manufacturing	9.7	10.0	10.0
High-wage manufacturing	11.3	9.7	9.0
Transportation and trade	18.8	19.4	19.4
Transactional activities	21.0	22.0	23.6
Personal services	3.5	3.6	3.7
Social services	16.8	16.5	16.3
Other[b]	−0.9	−0.9	−0.9
Total	100.0	100.0	100.0

Source: Office of Technology Assessment.

[a]Constant dollar output share derived from 1984 total final demand; output share shown by production sectors, using 1972, 1977, and 1980 input–output data adjusted to 1980$.
[b]Other includes scrap, rest of world, noncomparable imports, and inventory valuation adjustment.

The sector that lost the most because of changes in recipe was high-wage manufacturing. Approximately 70 percent of the decline in this sector's output share as a result of changes in recipe happened between 1972 and 1977 and was located in three industries: petroleum refining, chemicals, and primary iron and steel manufacturing. These industries account for over four-fifths of the 1972 to 1980 drop in high-wage manufacturing's output share because of recipe changes. Unlike the situation when demand was changed, the motor vehicle industry experienced only a small reduction in output share because of changing recipe. The causes behind these changes seem to be primarily threefold: (1) the influx of foreign intermediate inputs as ingredients in the production recipe, (2) the sharp increase in crude oil prices in the early 1970s that pushed up the price of chemicals and refined petroleum products, forcing a recipe change, and (3) the availability of new materials, such as plastics, that can act as substitutes for steel.

The loss of output share by high-wage manufacturing as a result of recipe changes between 1972 and 1980 was balanced by a gain in the share of GNP held by the transactional activities sector, which picked up nearly two-thirds of the shift in share that occurred between 1972 and 1980 as a result of recipe changes. Growth was strong between 1972 and 1977, but even stronger between 1977 and 1980, and, presumably, if we had a 1984 recipe, this sector would have gained even more. The recipient of nearly three-fourths of this increase was the business services industry, which includes activities such as advertising, legal services, and computer and data processing services (Feldman and Palmer, 1985). Finance and insurance came in a distant second. After the transactional activities sector, the sector that gained the most in terms of output share was transportation and trade. The wholesale and retail trade industry was responsible for most of the 1972–1980 increase gained by this sector. This is not surprising considering the increasing role marketing plays in the delivery of a product and the fact that interindustry activity and thus wholesaling and transportation increased over the period.

More complex business networks seem to require larger numbers of transactions, contracts, and "middle people" resulting in more intermediate demand for services such as those provided by bankers, lawyers, truckers, and wholesalers. Decisions to contract out work that was previously done "in-house," increasing geographic dispersion of production, including the increasing tendency to "out-source" components from other countries also result in an increase in transactional activities and transportation and trade. For example, many manufacturing firms now contract out for janitorial services that had previously been performed internally. Although the actual amount of work has not necessarily increased, it appears to grow because it is now counted as an "arms-length" market transaction.

The change in the recipes of production that occurred between 1972 and 1980 had a significant impact on the structural composition of the economy, but one that was substantively different from that caused by shifting demand. Industries traditionally thought of as suppliers of raw or semifinished materials to heavy industry, such as refined petroleum, chemicals, and steel, declined in importance. The production structure calls for a greater contribution from the transactional activities sector, particularly the business services industry, than that required by the 1972 recipe.

CONCLUSION

The U.S. economy has undergone a number of significant structural changes over the past decade. These changes are not readily apparent from traditional input–output measures such as the total output multiplier, but are clear from trends in contribution to total value added (GNP), perhaps the most important of which is the increasing prominence of services in the U.S. economy relative to manufacturing and natural resource-intensive industries.

ACKNOWLEDGMENTS

This chapter draws on past and on-going work at the Office of Technology Assessment (OTA). The opinions expressed in this chapter, however, are the authors' and not those of OTA or the Technology Assessment Board. The authors gratefully acknowledge considerable insight and conceptual contribution of Henry Kelly in the course of this research. In addition, the thoughtful and incisive comments of Ronald Miller, Adam Rose, and Janusz Szyrmer are greatly appreciated.

REFERENCES

Bluestone, B., and B. Harrison. 1982. *The Deindustrialization of America*. Boston, MA: Basic Books.

Carter, A. P. 1970. *Structural Change in the American Economy*. Cambridge, MA: Harvard University Press.

Carter, A. P. 1980. "Changes in Input–Output Structure Since 1972." *Interindustry Review*. Data Resources Inc. (Summer).

Feldman, S. F., and K. Palmer. 1985. "Structural Change in the United States: Changing Input–Output Coefficients." *Business Economics* (January), pp. 46–47.

Larson, E. D., M. H. Ross, and R. Williams. 1986. "Beyond the Era of Raw Materials." *Scientific American*. Vol. 254 (June), pp. 34–41.

Leontief, W. 1953. *Studies in the Structure of the American Economy.* New York: Oxford University Press.

Leontief, W., and F. Duchin. 1984. *The Impact of Automation on Employment, 1963–2000.* A final report to the National Science Foundation, Contract No. PRA-8012844. (April), pp. 4.16–4.25.

Miller, R., and P. Blair. 1985. *Input–Output Analysis: Foundations and Extensions.* Englewood Cliffs, NJ: Prentice Hall.

Ritz, P. 1980. "Definitions and Conventions of the 1972 Input–Output Study." Washington, D.C.: U.S. Department of Commerce, Bureau of Economic Analysis.

Ritz, P., et al. 1979. "The Input–Output Structure of the U.S. Economy: 1972." *Survey of Current Business.* Vol. 59, No. 2 (February), pp. 34–72.

Stone, R. 1961. *Input–Output and National Accounts.* Paris: Organization for European Economic Cooperation.

Survey of Current Business. 1969. "The Input–Output Structure of the U.S. Economy: 1963." Vol. 49, No. 11 (November), pp. 16–47.

Survey of Current Business. 1974. "The Input–Output Structure of the U.S. Economy: 1967." Vol. 54, No. 2 (February), pp. 24–56.

Survey of Current Business. 1984. "The Input–Output Structure of the U.S. Economy: 1977." Vol. 64, No. 5 (May), pp. 42–84.

Survey of Current Business. 1986. "National Income and Product Accounts." Table 6.4B (March).

Szyrmer, J. 1986. "Measuring Connectedness of Input–Output Models: Part II Total Flow Concept." *Environment and Planning A.* Vol. 18, pp. 107–121.

United Nations. 1968. *A System of National Accounts.* Series F, No. 2, Revision 3. New York: Department of Economic and Social Affairs.

U.S. Congress, Congressional Budget Office. 1986. *Has Trade Protection Revitalized Domestic Industries?* Washington, D.C.: U.S. Congress, Government Printing Office (November).

U.S. Congress, Congressional Research Service. 1985. *The Service Sector: Employment and Earnings in the 1980s.* Washington, D.C.: U.S. Congress, Report No. 85-167 E (April).

U.S. Congress, Office of Technology Assessment (OTA). 1988. *Technology and the American Economic Transition.* Washington, D.C.: U.S. Congress, Government Printing Office (May).

U.S. Department of Commerce. 1975. *Historical Statistics of the United States.* Washington, D.C.: U.S. Government Printing Office.

U.S. Department of Commerce. 1985. "The Input–Output Structure of the U.S. Economy: 1980." Unpublished.

U.S. Department of Commerce. 1986. "Changes in the Structure of the U.S. Economy since 1960: A Primer." Working paper of the Office of Economic Affairs (January), pp. 8–11.

Vaccara, B. 1970. "Changes over Time in Input–Output Coefficients for the United States." In *Applications of Input–Output Analysis,* edited by A. P. Carter and A. Brody, Vol. 2, Amsterdam: North-Holland, pp. 230–260.

Vaccara, B., A. Shapiro, and N. Simon. 1970. "The Input–Output Structure of the U.S. Economy: 1947" (unpublished mimiograph). Washington, D.C.: U.S. Department of Commerce, Office of Business Economics (March).

Young, K., A. Lawson, and J. Duncan, 1988. "Trade Ripples across U.S. Industries." Washington, D.C.: U.S. Department of Commerce, Office of Business Analysis (January 14).

22

An Input–Output Analysis of Technological Changes in the Japanese Economy: 1970–1980

HIDEO KANEMITSU and HIROSHI OHNISHI

The main purpose of this research is to investigate some aspects of technological change in the Japanese economy in the period from 1970 to 1980, with an emphasis on the economic impact of technological change in the production system of Japanese manufacturing. To do this, we examine the nature and characteristics of the structural change in the input–output system of the Japanese economy, making use of three input–output tables for the years 1970, 1975, and 1980 [Government of Japan, n.d. (a), n.d. (b); Ministry of International Trade and Industry, n.d.].[1]

Specifically, we are concerned with the assessment of technological change in individual sectors and the total production system of the economy as a whole. Typically, in a competitive market economy, firms choose an alternative new technology if and only if the technology is more cost effective than conventional technology. The reduced costs brought by the new technology will eventually lead to a fall in product prices through competition.

Influences of improved technologies to other parts of the economy flow along two paths. One is cost reduction in the intermediate inputs of the other sectors of the economy that purchase products of improved sectors at lowered prices. In addition, if the economy has alternative technologies that are more cost efficient under given price vectors, the amount of actual cost reduction would be larger than that calculated from the Leontief technology because of "substitution effects." The second is a resource-saving path, which represents a chain of resource savings initiated from a reduction on

---

1. The 1965–1970–1975 Link Input–Output Table (Government of Japan, n.d.) and 1980 Input–Output Table (Government of Japan, n.d.) were used. Special 35 sector input–output tables were compiled for this study. The reasons standard classification tables were not used are as follows: (1) from a preliminary test study (Kanemitsu and Ohnishi, 1985), we found that the accuracy of some real input coefficients is sensitive to the classification of sectors when the commodity groups contain products that have high rates of price change, for example, most of machinery products and crude petroleum, and (2) for testing and developing the methods in this chapter, a tractable table size was preferred.

Implicit deflators (based on 1975 prices) of output, imports, exports, and domestic demand for the 35 sectors were calculated from the 1965–1970–1975 Link Input–Output Table (Government of Japan, n.d.) in the case of 1970 and from the 1980 Input–Output Table (Ministry of International Trade and Industry, n.d.) in the case of 1980.

some intermediate inputs used by the sector that introduced new technology. This resource-saving path is particularly important in analyzing the resource efficiency of the Japanese economy in which raw materials are heavily dependent on imports.

In this chapter, we present a series of estimation methods concerning the measurement of technological change. First, we attempt to measure technological change in an individual industry by how much the intermediate costs of production will be reduced when an existing technology is replaced by a new technology with the value-added terms being fixed. This is called the "cost effect" of technological change. Second, we attempt to measure technological change in an individual industry by how much the amount of intermediate demand of various industrial outputs will be diminished in order to satisfy a constant level of final demand. This is called the "resource effect" of technological change. Finally, we attempt to evaluate individual technological change by a change in nominal value of final demand on the one hand and by a change in nominal value of products on the other. In the input–output model, the cost evaluation of technological change in final demand coincides with the resource evaluation of the same technological change, which is shown as a sum of changes in nominal value added and in value of imports.

This type of a quantitative measurement of technological change has been examined by Carter (1970) in connection with structural change in the U.S. economy and more recently in its extended form has come to be known as "Structural Decomposition Analysis" (see Skolka, 1989; Rose and Chen, 1989). However, we have developed our estimation method of technological change independently (Kanemitsu and Ohnishi, 1985). Carter's analysis emphasized the economic impact of technological change on factor requirements (especially, labor), whereas we have formulated our method of technological assessment in order to integrate the dual aspects of technological change, that is, cost efficiency and resource requirements in an intermediate structure of production.

COMPARATIVE STATIC ANALYSIS OF TECHNOLOGICAL CHANGE

To introduce a formal production system of Leontief technology with competitive imports, we use the following notation:

X_i = output of product i, $i = 1, 2, \ldots, n$;

$X = (X_i)$: gross domestic output vector (n-column vector);

$D_{Iij} = j$th industry's intermediate demand for product i, $i, j = 1, 2, \ldots, n$;

$D_{Ii} = D_{Ii1} + \cdots + D_{Iin}$: intermediate demand for product i, $i = 1, \ldots, n$;

$D_I = (D_{Ii})$: intermediate demand vector (n-column vector);

F_{Di} = domestic final demand for product i, $i = 1, 2, \ldots, n$;

$F_D = (F_{Di})$: domestic final demand vector (n-column vector);

F_{Ei} = export demand for product i;

$F_E = (F_{Ei})$: export vector (n-column vector);

M_i = import of product i, $i = 1, 2, \ldots, n$;

$m_i = M_i/(D_{Ii} + F_{Di})$: import coefficient of product i;

$\hat{M} = (m_i)$: import coefficient matrix ($n \times n$ diagonal matrix);

$a_{ij} = D_{Iij}/X_j$: input coefficient of industry j with respect to product i, $i, j = 1, 2, \ldots, n$;

$a_j = (a_{ij})$: technology vector of industry j (n-column vector), $j = 1, 2, \ldots, n$;

$A = (a_j)$: input coefficient matrix ($n \times n$ matrix);
$I = (n \times n)$ identity matrix;
P_j = domestic price of product j, $j = 1, 2, \ldots, n$;
$P = (P_j)$: domestic price vector (n-row vector);
P_{mj} = import price of product j, $j = 1, 2, \ldots, n$;
$P_m = (P_{mj})$: import price vector (n-row vector);
V_j = nominal value added per unit of output of industry j, $j = 1, 2, \ldots, n$;
$V = (V_j)$: (n-row) vector of nominal value added per unit of output.

Basic Input–Output Model with Competitive Imports

The balance condition between supply and demand of the total output is described in vector form as

$$X + M = D_I + F_D + F_E$$

We introduce two fundamental assumptions, one for input coefficients and the other for import coefficients. We assume that

$$D_I = AX \qquad \text{(Leontief's assumption of constant input coefficients)}$$

and

$$M = \hat{M}(D_I + F_D) \qquad \text{(an assumption of constant import coefficients)}.$$

We therefore have

$$X = (I - \hat{M})(AX + F_D) + F_E \tag{22-1}$$

Similarly, the balance condition between price and cost under the above two assumptions can be described as

$$P = P(I - \hat{M})A + P_m\hat{M}A + V \tag{22-2}$$

where the intermediate cost of each industry j is decomposed into expenditures on domestic products and import products.

We assume that the matrix $[I - (I - \hat{M})A]$ is nonsingular. Solving (22-1) and (22-2), respectively, we obtain

$$X = [I - (I - \hat{M})A]^{-1}[(I - \hat{M})F_D + F_E] \tag{22-3}$$

$$P = (P_m\hat{M}A + V)[I - (I - \hat{M})A]^{-1} \tag{22-4}$$

Furthermore, since $M = \hat{M}(D_I + F_D) = \hat{M}AX + \hat{M}F_D$, we have

$$M = \hat{M}A[I - (I - \hat{M})A]^{-1}[(I - \hat{M})F_D + F_E] + \hat{M}F_D \tag{22-5}$$

Comparative Static Analysis of Technological Change

In a simple input–output model with Leontief technology, equilibrium levels of output, prices and imports will be uniquely determined at each time period, t, given the technology parameter, $A(t)$, import structure, $\hat{M}(t)$, domestic final demand, $F_D(t)$, export demand, $F_E(t)$, import prices, $P_m(t)$, and value added per unit of output, $V(t)$. We may express the equilibrium levels of output, prices, and imports as

$$X = X[A(t), \hat{M}(t), F_D(t), F_E(t)] \tag{22-3'}$$

$$P = P[A(t), \hat{M}(t), P_m(t), V(t)] \qquad (22\text{-}4')$$

$$M = M[A(t), \hat{M}(t), F_D(t), F_E(t)] \qquad (22\text{-}5')$$

We are principally interested in examining the effect of parametric change in technology A on these three key sets of variables under the condition that the other parameters, such as $\hat{M}$, F_D, F_E, P_m, and V, are held constant.

Cost Effect of Technological Change

We first attempt to examine the degree of technological change in terms of cost efficiency. For this purpose, we estimate the price level computed on the basis of the previous (old) technology, $A(s)$, at time s, $(s < t)$, when the new structural parameters of an economy, $\hat{M}(t)$, $P_m(t)$, and $V(t)$, prevail. That is,

$$P[A(s)] = [P_m(t)\hat{M}(t)A(s) + V(t)]\{I - [I - \hat{M}(t)]A(s)\}^{-1}$$

where a hypothetical price, $P[A(s)]$, is obtained from the equilibrium price in which the newly developed technology $A(t)$ is replaced by the previous technology, $A(s)$, other parameters, $\hat{M}(t)$, $P_m(t)$, and $V(t)$, being fixed.

Let us define an (n-row) vector of the price difference

$$dP(dA) = P[A(t)] - P[A(s)] \qquad (22\text{-}6)$$

where the jth element, $dP_j(dA)$, denotes the change in intermediate costs of industry j as a result of the joint technological change of the economy from the old technology $A(s)$ to the new technology $A(t)$. Thus, we call the price difference (22-6) the "cost effect of joint technological change." A negative jth element of the cost–effect vector would indicate a cost reduction in industry j, which measures the technological change in terms of "cost efficiency" in the production of industry j. Observe that industry j realizes its cost reduction effect only when the technological structure of the whole economy changes entirely from the old structure $A(s)$ to the new $A(t)$.

In order to measure the degree of individual technological change in a specific industry, we define a technology matrix

$$A(t, k:s) = [a_1(t), \ldots, a_{k-1}(t), a_k(s), a_{k+1}(t), \ldots, a_n(t)]$$

that is, the technology matrix $A(t)$ whose kth column vector, $a_k(t)$, is replaced by the kth column vector, $a_k(s)$, of the old technology matrix $A(s)$. The shift from a hypothetical technology set, $A(t, k:s)$, to the new technology $A(t)$ is to be interpreted as individual technological change with other industries maintaining the same structure of the technology at time t.

A hypothetical price

$$P[A(t, k:s)] = [P_m(t)\hat{M}(t)A(t, k:s) + V(t)]\{I - [I - \hat{M}(t)]A(t, k:s)\}^{-1}$$

will be compared with the current price, $P[A(t)]$. Let us define the difference

$$dP(da_k) = P[A(t)] - P[A(t, k:s)] \qquad k = 1, 2, \ldots, n \qquad (22\text{-}7)$$

We call the difference, $dP(da_k)$, the "cost effect of individual technological change" in industry k. Notice that this cost effect indicates how much the individual technological change in industry k contributes to a decrease in the cost of production in industry k [represented by the kth component $dP_k(da_k)$ of $dP(da_k)$] and in the cost of production in other parts of the economy that will be represented by the remaining components, $dP_j(da_k) j \neq k$. Because the relationship between dPs and A is nonlinear, the sum of the cost effect of individual technological change, $dP(da_k)$ $k = 1, 2, \ldots, n$, is not exactly equal to the cost effect of the joint technological change, $dP(dA)$.

We are interested in evaluating the cost effect vectors, $dP(da_k)$s, in terms of the cost efficiency of the national economy. An improvement of the cost efficiency in production has a welfare significance in so far as it reduces a cost of realizing final demand. We, therefore, adopt the real final demand vector, $(I - \hat{M})F_D + F_E$, at time t as a weight. Let us define a scalar value

$$dP(da_k)\{[I - \hat{M}(t)]F_D(t) + F_E(t)\} \qquad k = 1, 2, \ldots, n \qquad (22\text{-}8)$$

that indicates the degree of individual technological change in terms of change in nominal final demand. Because the components of real final demand are assumed to be fixed, the scalar value obtained from (22-8) represents the degree of efficiency in terms of a general price fall induced by individual technological change in industry k.

Domestic Resource Effect of Technological Change

In order to examine the impact of technological change on the intermediate use of resources, we attempt to compute the level of total output required for production of the current level of final demand on the basis of the previous technology, that is, we compute the following hypothetical output vector:

$$X[A(s)] = \{I - [I - \hat{M}(t)]A(s)\}^{-1}\{[I - \hat{M}(t)]F_D(t) + F_E(t)\}$$

Let us define the difference

$$dX(dA) = X[A(t)] - X[A(s)] \qquad (22\text{-}9)$$

that will serve as a measure of resource efficiency of the current technology, $A(t)$, as compared with the previous technology, $A(s)$, in delivering a given final demand for domestic products. That is, as long as the ith component of (22-9) is negative, the intermediate consumption of product i is diminished in the process of producing the current level of final demand. We call the difference, $dX(dA)$, the "domestic resource effect of joint technological change." Observe that the amount of ith (domestic) resource is reduced by $dX_i(dA)$ only when the technology of the whole economy changes jointly from the old technology, $A(s)$, to the newly developed technology, $A(t)$.

In order to estimate the resource effect arising from individual technological change in one specific industry, we compute

$$X[A(t, k:s)] = \{I - [I - \hat{M}(t)]A(t, k:s)\}^{-1}\{[I - \hat{M}(t)]F_D(t) + F_E(t)\}$$

Define the difference

$$dX(da_k) = X[A(t)] - X[A(t, k:s)] \qquad k = 1, 2, \ldots, n \qquad (22\text{-}10)$$

that indicates how much the amount of intermediate use of product i $(i = 1, 2, \ldots, n)$ would be diminished when industry k succeeds in replacing the old technology $a_k(s)$ by the new technology $a_k(t)$, with all other industries maintaining the same structure of the current technology at time t. We call the difference, $dX(da_k)$, the "domestic resource effect of individual technological change" in industry k.

We are also interested in evaluating the resource effect vector $dX(da_k)$ in terms of a resource efficiency of the national economy. For this purpose, we introduce the unit value added vector, $V(t)$, as a weight. Let us define

$$V(t)dX(da_k) \qquad k = 1, 2, \ldots, n \tag{22-11}$$

that indicates a change in nominal value added arising from individual technological change. The value of reduction in terms of primary factor inputs is partly measured by the reduction of value added (domestic production income) induced by efficient use of intermediate commodities. Equation (22-11) also indicates a net value of domestic products, which is reduced by individual technological change in industry k.

Import Resource Effect of Technological Change

The impact of technological change on imports will be easily estimated by applying the following two formulas. First, we define the "import resource effect of joint technological change" as

$$dM(dA) = M[A(t)] - M[A(s)] \tag{22-12}$$

where

$$M[A(s)] = \hat{M}(t)A(s)\{I - [I - \hat{M}(t)]A(s)\}^{-1}\{[I - \hat{M}(t)]F_D(t) + F_E(t)\} + \hat{M}(t)F_D(t)$$

Furthermore, we define the "import resource effect of individual technological change"

$$dM(da_k) = M[A(t)] - M[A(t, k:s)] \qquad k = 1, 2, \ldots, n \tag{22-13}$$

where a hypothetical import vector $M[A(t, k:s)]$ will be obtained from the import vector $M[A(t)]$ by replacing the technology matrix $A(t)$ by the technology matrix $A(t, k:s)$.

The total amount of reduction in import resources may be evaluated by using import price vector as a weight. Define a scalar value

$$P_m(t)dM(da_k) \qquad k = 1, 2, \ldots, n \tag{22-14}$$

that indicates the value of import resources reduced by individual technological change in industry k.

Dual Relationship between Cost Effect and Resource Effect

We have from (22-6) and (22-9)

$$dX(dA) = \{[I - (I - \hat{M})A(t)]^{-1} - [I - (I - \hat{M})A(s)]^{-1}\}[(I - \hat{M})F_D + F_E]$$

and

$$dP(dA) = [P_m\hat{M}A(t) + V][I - (I - \hat{M})A(t)]^{-1} - [P_m\hat{M}A(t) + V][I - (I - \hat{M})A(s)]^{-1}$$

where a suffix of time period t is omitted from $\hat{M}(t)$, $F_D(t)$, $F_E(t)$, $P_m(t)$, and $V(t)$. Hence we have

$$dP(dA)[(I - \hat{M})F_D + F_E] = [P_m\hat{M}A(t) + V]X[A(t)] - [P_m\hat{M}A(s) + V]X[A(s)]$$

$$= P_m dM(dA) + VdX(dA) \tag{22-15}$$

or

$$dP(dA)(I - \hat{M})F_D + dP(dA)F_E = VdX(dA) + P_m dM(dA) \tag{22-16}$$

We note that the left-hand-side of Equation (22-15) shows a numerical evaluation of technological change in terms of cost efficiency and the right-hand-side shows a numerical evaluation of technological change in terms of domestic and import resource efficiency. The first term of the left-hand-side of (22-16) indicates the diminished value of domestic final demand and the second term indicates the diminished value of foreign demand. On the other hand, the first term of the right-hand-side of Equation (22-16) indicates the reduced level of value added and the second term indicates the reduced value of imports.

From (22-7) and (22-10), we obtain a similar relationship on individual technological change, that is

$$dP(da_k)[(I - \hat{M})F_D + F_E] = P_m dM(da_k) + VdX(da_k) \qquad (22\text{-}17)$$

or

$$dP(da_k)(I - \hat{M})F_D + dP(da_k)F_E = P_m dM(da_k) + VdX(da_k) \qquad (22\text{-}18)$$

COST EFFECT OF TECHNOLOGICAL CHANGE

In this section, we examine several aspects of the influence of technological change on production costs.

Joint Technological Change

We have computed the cost effect of joint technological change in Equation (22-6) for two cases: first for $s = 1970$ and $t = 1980$ and second for $s = 1975$ and $t = 1980$. In order to clarify the magnitude of the cost effect, we have computed its percentage change with respect to 1980 price level $P(1980)$, that is, $dP_i(dA)/P_i(t) \; i = 1, 2, \ldots, 35$ (see Figure 22-1). In Figure 22-1, technological change from the old technology $A(1970)$ to the new technology $A(1980)$ gives a distinct picture of a general tendency toward reduced costs of production in most industries.

First, machinery on the whole has achieved a remarkable cost reduction from 1970 to 1980. This is observed for most of the machinery industries, for example, office machinery (-186 percent) and computer (-84 percent). Second, most material industries have also achieved cost reductions, for example, medicine (-36 percent) and iron and steel (-24 percent), with some exceptions, such as ceramics (10 percent). Third, primary commodities show an opposite effect, namely a tendency toward an overall cost–price increase in sectors such as domestic crude petroleum (30 percent). Fourth, most of the service industries also show cost increases, for example, transport (32 percent) and gas supply (31 percent), although wholesale and retail (-6 percent) and construction (-2 percent) show cost decreases.

The cost effect of joint technological change from 1975 to 1980 is also depicted in the results presented in parentheses. In Figure 22-1, the cost effect of joint technological change from 1970 to 1975 can be obtained as the difference between the cost effect of 1970–1980 and that of 1975–1980.

Actual Price Change and Explanatory Power of the Cost Effect

We notice that in our estimation procedure of cost–price structure, price change has been explained exclusively by change in the intermediate costs of production. The other determinants of prices (value added, import coefficients, and import prices) are

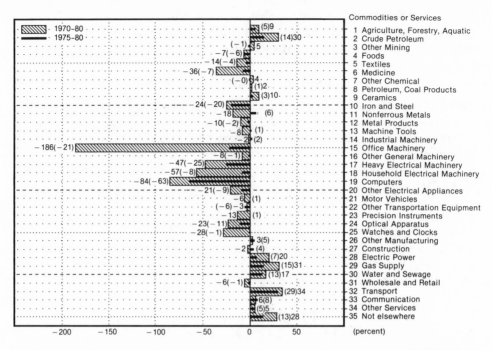

FIGURE 22-1   Cost effect of joint technological change on prices (percentage of 1980 price).

held constant in measuring the net effects of technological change. Therefore, a question naturally arises as to whether actual price change would be explained appropriately by the change in intermediate costs. In order to examine the relationship between the cost effect and actual price change, we estimated a regression equation of actual price change on the cost effect of joint technological change for the period from 1970 to 1980. The result is as follows (with standard errors given in parentheses):

$$[\text{Actual price change}] = 51.567 + 0.806\,[\text{cost effect of joint technological change}]$$

$$(1.776)\qquad(0.044)$$

$$r^2 = 0.9101,\; s = 10.08\;(\text{percent})$$

The intercept term of the regression equation, 51.6 percent, corresponds approximately to the change in general price level that is not contained in the measurement of cost effect. The actual change in general price level calculated from the change in output deflators for all industries is 56 percent from 1970 to 1980. The marginal coefficient of the cost effect, 0.806, represents an average price adjustment rate with respect to intermediate cost change during the decade.

The coefficient of determination, 0.9101, indicates that 91 percent of the variation in actual price change is explained by the variation resulting from intermediate cost change. In other words, the rest of actual price change, that is, the independent variation resulting from other determinants of prices, makes a smaller contribution, 9 percent, to total price change. This small contribution of other factors is confirmed by the regression of actual price change on the price change resulting from other factors (difference between actual price change and the cost effect).[2] The coefficient of determination of the latter regression is 0.1168, that is, approximately 12 percent of actual price change is explained by the variation caused by other factors.[3]

Individual Technological Change

The cost effect of individual technological change in a given industry is computed by its own rate of price change $dP_k(da_k)/P_k(1980)$. According to our computation, most of the machinery industries have achieved a remarkably large own rate of price change generated by their own technological change, for example, office machinery (-156 percent) and computers (-83 percent). Furthermore, some of the material industries, particularly medicine (-42 percent) and iron and steel (-30 percent), have also achieved a substantial price fall.

In sharp contrast, public utility industries show, on the whole, a radically opposite effect of price increase, for example, transport (34 percent) and gas supply (29 percent). Perhaps these results indicate a deterioration of marginal productivity in these industries caused by an overconcentration of population and economic activities in relatively small geographic areas.[4]

DOMESTIC RESOURCE EFFECT OF TECHNOLOGICAL CHANGE

In this section, we examine several aspects of the influence of technological change on resource use in production.

Joint Technological Change

We have computed the domestic resource effect of joint technological change in Equation (22-9), first for $s = 1970$ and $t = 1980$ and second for $s = 1975$ and 1980. The change in use of each resource, $dX_i(dA)$, is evaluated at the 1975 price level (see Figure 22-2). In Figure 22-2, we observe that the joint technological change has reduced intermediate use of resources for the primary commodities and materials. The largest resource-saving effect of joint technological change is observed in the case of the iron and steel products (a 6265 billion yen decrease of the intermediate use of iron and steel, 28 percent of the 1980 output of iron and steel).

In contrast with these negative resource effects, the resource effect for the products of the medicine and machinery industries turns out to be a positive value. That is to say, the intermediate use for these products has increased as a result of the joint technological change in the economy in this period. For example, medicine has a large positive resource effect (a 1892 billion yen increase of intermediate use of medicine, 53 percent of the 1980 output of medicine).

2. Because Equation (22-4) is nonlinear, the difference between actual price change and the cost effect contains the cross terms of the cost effect and the change in other factors.

3. The difference between the two percentages, 12 and 9 percent, is the result of the common variation contained in the intermediate cost change and the change in other factors.

4. There are two other possible causes for the deterioration in the primary commodity industry and the service industries (except for wholesale and retail trade): (1) the change in the quality of products, which is not sufficiently accounted for in price deflators, and (2) the existence of regulations and protections in these industries.

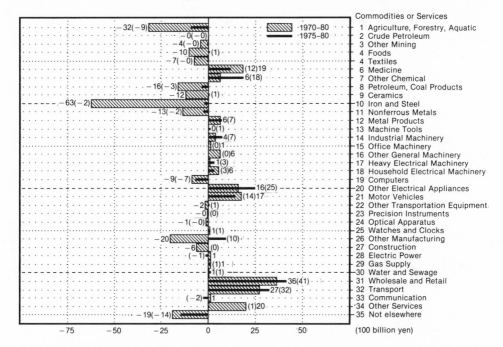

FIGURE 22-2. Domestic resource effect of joint technological change on output (100 billions of yen).

Resource Effect and Substitution Effect

The reason for the resource-using effect, that is, a positive value of the resource effect, observed as products of the machinery industries and medicine can be interpreted as the "substitution effect," which arises primarily from a substantial price fall of the products caused by cost-reducing technological change in these industries. If the substitution effect is dominant in an economy, the ith component of the resource effect of the joint technological change, $dX_i(dA)$, would have an inverse relationship with the ith component of the cost effect of joint technological change, $dP_i(dA)$.

In Figure 22-3, the cost effect in product i, $dP_i(dA)$, is measured horizontally, and the domestic resource effect in product i, $dX_i(dA)$, is measured vertically. Most of the machinery industries and medicine are found in Quadrant II, in which a cost reduction ($dP_i < 0$) is accompanied by a positive resource effect ($dX_i > 0$). On the other hand, most of the primary commodity and material industries are found in Quadrant IV, in which a positive cost effect ($dP_i > 0$) is accompanied by a negative resource effect ($dX_i < 0$).

Some of the material industries, such as iron and steel and nonferrous metals, are found in Quadrant III, in which cost reduction ($dP_i < 0$) is accompanied by a negative resource effect ($dX_i < 0$). The consumption of iron and steel or nonferrous metals has diminished because they have been replaced by other materials as a result of metal-saving technological changes by other industries. This is also true for computers, which have been replaced to a large extent by other electronic devices, such as various kinds of integrated circuits or LSIs.

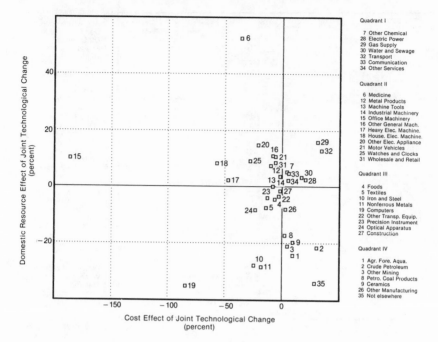

FIGURE 22-3   Relationship between cost and domestic resource effects of joint technological change, 1970–1980 (percentages of 1980 price and output).

Public utilities and most of the service industries are found in Quadrant I, in which a positive cost effect ($dP_i > 0$) is accompanied by a positive resource effect ($dX_i > 0$). The reason for this is found in the tendency toward extensive urbanization, which has necessitated a larger amount of communication, transportation, public utilities, and other kinds of services.

Overall, the substitution change (caused by price change) found in Quadrants II and IV had a strong tendency in the Japanese economy during the period from 1970 to 1980. Nevertheless, the tendencies of joint technological change found in Quadrants I and III are "complementary," rather than substitutionary, in the sense that it is generally hard to develop a new technology that is cost efficient in every resource use.

Individual Technological Change

We have also computed the domestic resource effect of individual technological change in Equation (22-10), first for $s = 1970$ and $t = 1980$ and second for $s = 1975$ and 1980. For summarizing the resulting 35×35 tables of individual technological change, we use the base year price vector $P(1975)$, whose components are all unity, as a weight in evaluating the resource–effect vectors (22-9). Furthermore, we use the 1980 real gross domestic output (scalar) as a base level for the percentage evaluation of the total domestic resource effect.

From 1970 to 1980, the technological change in the iron and steel industry produced the largest domestic resource effect (a 5328 billion yen saving of the domestic resource consumption, 1.3 percent of the 1980 real gross domestic output).

The technological change in household electrical machinery (a 4329 billion yen saving of the domestic resource consumption, 1.0 percent) and wholesale and retail trade (a 4053 billion yen saving, 1.0 percent) also achieved a large amount of resource savings in this period.[5]

The value of the domestic resource effect of individual technological change depends largely on the three factors that are related to the characteristics of each industry: (1) the degree of technological change in terms of reduced costs, (2) the amount of final demand for the product, and (3) the intermediate input structure of the economy. In our view, the input structure of the economy is the primary factor that marked the (total) resource effect of the individual technological change of the iron and steel industry at the top of the industry ranking. The amount of final demand is important for wholesale and retail trade (the third in ranking), whereas both of the first two characteristics are important for household electrical machinery (the second in ranking).

IMPORT RESOURCE EFFECT OF TECHNOLOGICAL CHANGE

In this section, we examine several aspects of the influence of technological change on the use of imports in production.

Joint Technological Change

The import resource effect of the joint technological change with respect to product i, $i = 1, 2, \ldots, 35$, is summarized in Figure 22-4. During the period from 1970 to 1980, joint technological change has achieved a substantial reduction in import resource consumption of the primary commodities, for example, crude petroleum (a 1282 billion yen decrease of crude petroleum imports, 22 percent of the 1980 imports of crude petroleum). Furthermore, the decreases in import resource consumption have also been achieved in the products of the material industries, for example, nonferrous metal products, and petroleum-coal products.

Individual Technological Change

We summarize the import resource effect of individual technological change by using the same procedure used in the evaluation of the domestic resource effect of individual technological change. The import resource effect vectors are evaluated by using the base year price vector, $P_m(1975)$, as a weight. From 1970 to 1980, technological change in the iron and steel industry has the largest import saving effect (a 1289 billion yen decrease of import resource consumption, 5.0 percent of 1980 aggregate imports). Technological change in the wholesale and retail trade industry has the second largest

5. The deterioration effect produced by the technological change in the transport sector from 1975 to 1980 is very large (a 9660 billion yen increase of the domestic resource consumption, 2.3 percent of 1980 real gross domestic output). This large effect is primarily the result of increases in three input coefficients in the transport sector. They are input coefficients with respect to petroleum and coal products, motor vehicles, and wholesale and retail trade. From these changes in specific input coefficients of the transport sector, a trend of motorization naturally looms. However, the degree of deterioration is still questionable. We, therefore, point out the problem of industry classification and the accuracy of price deflators. Because more appropriate official data, 1970–1975–1980 Link Input–Output Tables, were announced after we finished this study, the question would be clarified from the new data.

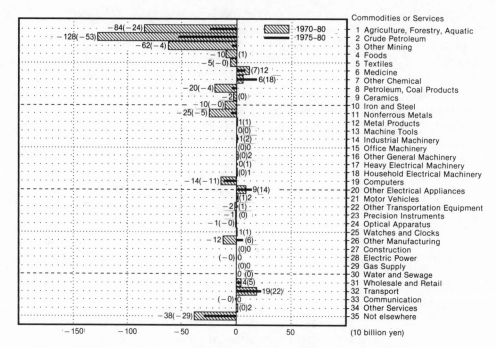

FIGURE 22-4   Import resource effect of joint technological change (10 billions of yen).

import-saving effect (a 873 billion yen decrease, 3.4 percent of 1980 aggregate imports), which mainly consists of a reduction of crude petroleum imports (a 633 billion yen decrease) indirectly realized by saving intermediate use of petroleum and coal products and motor vehicles.

UNIFIED VIEW OF COST AND RESOURCE EFFECTS OF TECHNOLOGICAL CHANGE

We estimate performance of each technological change in three vectorial measures: (1) the cost effect of technological change, given by Equations (22-6) and (22-7); (2) the domestic resource effect of technological change, given by Equations (22-9) and (22-10); and (3) the import resource effect of technological change, given by Equations (22-12) and (22-13).

Furthermore, we have suggested evaluating these vectorial measures by three scalar values: (4) change in nominal final demand, given by Equation (22-8); (5) change in nominal value added, given by Equation (22-11); and (6) change in nominal imports, given by Equation (22-14).

From the dual relationship between the cost effect and the resource effect of technological change, these scalar values are interrelated within the input–output structure of the economy. Decomposing the change in nominal final demand into domestic final demand and foreign demand, we can analyze the effect of each technological change from the four different aspects of the economy shown in Table 22-1 [see Equations (22-16) and (22-17)].

The results of our computation are summarized in Table 22-2. We observe that joint technological change generated by the entire industry during the period from

TABLE 22-1   Change in Value of Net Products and Costs of Final Demand, 1970–1980

Source of Technological Change	Change in Value of Net Products			Change in Costs of Final Demand		
	Domestic	Imports	Total	Domestic	Exports	Total
Industry k	$VdX(da_k)$	$P_m dM(da_k)$		$dP(da_k)(I - \hat{M})F_D$	$dP(da_k)F_E$	
Joint	$VdX(dA)$	$P_m dM(dA)$		$dP(dA)(I - \hat{M})F_D$	$dP(dA)F_E$	

1970 to 1980 achieved a total contribution (a 3696 billion yen reduction, 1.5 percent of 1980 nominal GDP), which consists of the increased value of net domestic products (a 2052 billion yen increase, 0.8 percent of 1980 nominal GDP) compensated by the reduced value of imports (a 5748 billion yen reduction, 15.1 percent of 1980 nominal imports), reduced value of domestic final demand (a 333 billion yen reduction, 0.1 percent of 1980 nominal GDP), and reduced value of exports (a 3364 billion yen reduction, 9.7 percent of 1980 nominal exports). Thus, on the one hand, technological change in the Japanese economy from 1970 to 1980 made a significant contribution to foreign consumers in reducing the costs of Japanese products by approximately 10 percent of Japan's total exports.[6] On the other hand, Japan's technological change has made a remarkable contribution to world resource use in saving imports for domestic production by 15 percent of Japan's total imports.

CONCLUSION

The numerical results we obtained in this study are summarized as follows:

1. In the Japanese economy from 1970 to 1980, a distinct feature of technological change is observed in the machinery industries and the material industries, which have succeeded in substantially reducing production costs and lowering prices. In contrast with this technological improvement, the primary commodity industries and particularly the service industries have suffered a considerable degree of technological deterioration, which is reflected in the increased unit cost of production.
2. Cost-reducing technological change in the material industries (notably iron and steel), machinery industries, construction, and wholesale and retail trade has generated a substantial degree of resource economy by diminishing domestic output and imports to satisfy the required level of final demand.
3. As a result of technological change in the whole economy, the remarkable price fall observed in the machinery industries and medicine has brought a significant increase in intermediate demand for these products, whereas a price increase observed in the primary commodity industries has been accompanied by decreasing demand for these products in domestic production. Thus, we have observed an inverse relationship between the cost effect and the resource effect of technological change that demonstrates a strong tendency of "substitution effect," a fundamental trend of technological change derived from economic rationality in a competitive market economy.

6. From the viewpoint of comparative advantage, innovative products are exported because of their low relative prices.

TABLE 22-2   Effects of Technological Change in Material, Machinery, and Other Industries, 1970–1975–1980 (Billions of Yen)[a,b,c]

Source of Technological Change	Change in Value of Net Products		Change in Costs of Final Demand		
	Domestic	Imports	Domestic	Exports	Total
1970–1975					
Material industries (sectors 4 to 12)	−2,807	−1,905	−3,633	−1,079	−4,712
Machinery industries (sectors 13 to 25)	−4,544	−1,485	−3,760	−2,268	−6,028
All other industries	721	−1,340	−1,103	484	−619
Joint technological change	−5,776	−4,669	−7,451	−2,995	−10,445
1975–1980					
Material industries (sectors 4 to 12)	−3,130	−3,226	−4,788	−1,567	−6,355
Machinery industries (sectors 13 to 25)	−1,906	−903	−1,988	−822	−2,809
All other industries	12,983	3,355	14,310	2,028	16,338
Joint technological change	7,828	−1,079	7,118	−369	6,749
1970–1980					
Material industries (sectors 4 to 12)	−5,937	−5,130	−8,421	−2,646	−11,067
Machinery industries (sectors 13 to 25)	−6,450	−2,388	−5,749	−3,089	−8,838
All other industries	13,704	2,015	13,207	2,512	15,719
Joint technological change	2,052	−5,748	−333	−3,364	−3,696

[a]Effects in 1970–1975 are defined as the differences between the effects in 1970–1980 and the effects in 1975–1980.
[b]The sum of effects for three groups of industries is not exactly equal to the effect of joint technological change because of the nonlinearity.
[c]1980 gross domestic product = 250,128 billion yen, 1980 imports = 38,372 billion yen, and 1980 exports = 34,543 billion yen.

4. A high correlation ($r^2 = 0.91$) is observed between actual price change and intermediate cost change computed as the cost effect of joint technological change. This supports significantly the validity of our approach in which the analysis of technological change is exclusively based on the change in intermediate input structures.

5. Joint technological change from 1970 to 1975 is remarkable, on the one hand, in reducing the value of net domestic products (a 5776 billion yen reduction, 2.3 percent of 1980 GDP) and the value of imports (a 4669 billion yen reduction, 12.2 percent of 1980 imports) and, on the other hand, it has reduced the value of domestic final demand (a 7451 billion yen reduction, 3.0 percent of 1980 GDP) and the value of exports (a 2995 billion yen reduction, 8.6 percent of 1980 exports). This total amounts to a reduction of 10,445 billion yen (4.2 percent of 1980 GDP) (see Table 22-2).

6. In sharp contrast, joint technological change from 1975 to 1980 has essentially resulted in a deterioration effect on the domestic resource efficiency by increasing the value of net domestic products (a 7828 billion yen increase, 3.1 percent of 1980 GDP) and also increasing the value of domestic final demand (a 7118 billion yen

increase, 2.8 percent of 1980 GDP). On the other hand, the reduction in the value of imports (a 1079 billion yen reduction, 2.8 percent of 1980 imports) and the reduction in the value of foreign demand (a 369 billion yen reduction, 1.1 percent of 1980 exports) are made possible. Hence the total deterioration effect amounts to 6749 billion yen (2.3 percent of 1980 GDP) from 1975 to 1980 (see Table 22-2).

ACKNOWLEDGMENTS

The authors wish to acknowledge helpful comments from R. Downey, K. Imai, C. Moriguchi, and A. Rose. The financial support of the Kikawada Foundation for our research is gratefully acknowledged.

REFERENCES

Carter, A. P. 1970. *Structural Change in the American Economy.* Cambridge, MA: Harvard University Press.

Government of Japan. n.d. (a). *Shōwa 40-45-50nen Setsuzoku Sangyō Renkan Hyō(1965–1970–1975 Link Input—Output Tables).* Tokyo: Government of Japan.

Government of Japan. n.d. (b). *Shōwa 55nen Sangyō Renkan Hyō (1980 Input–Output Tables).* Tokyo: Government of Japan.

Kanemitsu, H., and H. Ohnishi. 1985. "Technological Innovations and Structural Changes in the Japanese Economy: 1970–1980." Paper presented at the Conference of the High Technology Research Project, Honolulu, Hawaii.

Ministry of International Trade and Industry of Japan. n.d. *Shōwa 55nen Sangyō Renkan Hyō: Enchō Hyō (1980 Input–Output Tables: Extended Version).* Tokyo: Government of Japan.

Rose, A., and C. Y. Chen. 1989. "Sources of Change in Energy Use in the U.S. Economy," *Resources and Energy,* forthcoming.

Skolka, J. 1977. "Input–Output Anatomy of Import Elasticities," *Empirical Economics,* Vol. 2, pp. 123–126.

Skolka, J. 1989. "Input–Output Structural Decomposition Analysis." *Journal of Policy Modeling,* forthcoming.

Index